A WORLD OF THEIR
OWN MAKING

Also by the author:

For Better, For Worse: British Marriages, 1600 to the Present
Youth and History: Tradition and Change in European Age Relations
Commemorations: Politics of National Identity (ed.)

A
WORLD
OF
THEIR OWN
MAKING

MYTH, RITUAL, AND THE
QUEST FOR FAMILY VALUES

John R. Gillis

BasicBooks
A Division of HarperCollins*Publishers*

FIRST EDITION

Library of Congress Cataloging-in-Publication Data
Gillis, John R.
    A world of their own making : myth, ritual, and the quest for
family values / John R. Gillis.—1st ed.
      p. cm.
    Includes bibliographical references and index.
    ISBN 0-465-05414-5
    1. Family—Folklore. 2. Family festivals—History.
3. Family—North America—History. 4. Family—Europe—
History. I. Title.
GR465.G55 1996
306.85—dc20   96-3843

96 97 98 99 00 / 10 9 8 7 6 5 4 3 2 1

This book is dedicated to Ben, whose death shattered one world, and to Tina, Chris, and Kathy, whose love is building another.

CONTENTS

LIST OF ILLUSTRATIONS

PROLOGUE

I NEVER THOUGHT I would write a book about myth and ritual. I did not seek out the subject; it was something that found me. Like most men of my generation, the images and symbols that sustained my family life were something I simply took for granted. As an only son born in 1939, who married and became a father of two sons in the early 1960s, the family worlds created by my mother and wife presented themselves to me as perfectly natural, requiring little or nothing on my part except for the occasional gesture of appreciation. And even that was not always forthcoming because, like most men busy with their careers, I resented both the time spent on family occasions and the female control they represented.

I might never have realized the role that myth and ritual played in my life had not the comfortable family world I inhabited been abruptly and utterly shattered by the events of Christmas 1991. We had decided to gather that year in California. I was spending a sabbatical in Berkeley, where my wife Tina was then employed. My mother and one of our sons, Chris, joined us. Our other son, Ben, was unable to be with us because, after searching in vain for employment as a pilot in the United States, he had returned to Kenya to fly with a small charter company. The high point of the day was his call from Mombasa. It came before we sat down to dinner, though it was already evening on the other side of the world. Ben described a Christmas spent on the edge of the Indian Ocean with his friend Michelle and their new Labrador pup, Beja. Late that night another phone call came from Africa. It was Michelle, who told us that Ben's plane had gone down on the morning flight to the Masai Mara. No one had survived.

In that instant, all predictability, order, and meaning went out of our world. The future ceased to matter, and the past became a void. Time ceased to flow in the way it had just hours before, and family life suddenly seemed empty, though we continued to go through the motions. In the weeks that followed, we had hundreds of letters and messages from Ben's immense circle of friends. Michelle brought back his ashes from Nairobi, and we made plans for a January memorial service in Princeton, New Jersey, our original home. Having no religious affiliation, we found ourselves confronted for the first time with the task of creating and performing a ritual entirely of our own making, a remembrance of Ben that would recall all the dimensions of his life and spirit.

Later, in July, Chris, Tina, and I carried his ashes to our summer place off the Maine coast. There the three of us created a second ceremony. In the presence of friends and neighbors who had known Ben from infancy, we buried the ashes in the island cemetery among the graves of earlier generations, many of whose fate it had also been to die before their time. Though there were moments on both occasions when we did not know whether we would be able to carry out our own wishes, in doing it our way, we discovered a love for one another that we had rarely had occasion to express before and could never doubt again.

Although we found strength through creating our own ways of remembering Ben, our tendency was to hold even tighter to the old family times and places. These failed to ease the pain. It seemed as if my small world were collapsing inward, crushing me under the weight of dreams never to be realized and memories, once pleasurable, that were now unbearable. In the months that followed, I found little meaning in anything that had mattered to me before, including my work. Even worse, it seemed that our grief was dividing Tina and me. Nothing had prepared me for the difference between her memories of Ben, so crisp and ready, and mine, so vague and elusive. Her ability to recall the minutest details of his early life were meant to comfort, but they reminded me of just what a stranger I had been, that I had found so little time for the boys during the first decade of their lives, and in fact had chosen to teach on the very day Ben was born. My memories of their later years were proportional to my growing involvement with them in their teens, but the recognition of what had been forfeited was a source of intense guilt that made it increasingly difficult even to talk about Ben.

The very rituals that were meant to draw us together were now threatening to tear us apart. As Christmas 1992, and the anniversary of Ben's death, approached, we all felt a sense of dread, though none of us dared express it. Finally, Tina declared that she wanted nothing to do with the usual festivities, and I had to admit that I felt that going through with it might be worse than having no Christmas at all. It was Chris who saved the day by declaring that he would cook the dinner, substituting his favorite recipe of vegetarian chile for the traditional roast. Bringing something new to the old had the most marvelous effect. The spell was broken, and we were able to talk about Ben for the first time. The stories we told had a profoundly healing effect. Instead of feeling his absence, we sensed his presence. Time began to flow again, and since then the vegetarian dinner has become a tradition.

We felt Ben's presence again in the summer of 1995 when Chris married Kathy Armstrong on the lawn of the summer house within sight of the cemetery. The wedding, the joint effort of two families, took place on a day that began with the threat of squalls and ended with a brilliant sunset. It endowed the summer place with yet another layer of meaning, connecting us with a past that we do not wish to forget while allowing us to dream of yet another generation extending our world into an indefinite future.

New rituals have replaced the old and are all the more powerful because this time they are the product of a conscious, collaborative effort on everyone's part. While I still feel less adequate than Tina when it comes to creating the times and places we live by, I find the effort very satisfying. I remain a rationalist, but I no longer think it rational to be dismissive of that which so evidently gives meaning to our lives. The challenge, as I have come to see it, is to examine the appropriateness of our current myths and rituals, altering them if necessary to serve our current circumstances. Writing this history of family cultures is my way of contributing to a process of cultural reconstruction that I regard as vital to our future as families and to the creation of more caring communities. If, in reading this book, others, especially men, come to a deeper understanding of the rituals and myths they have lived by but taken little responsibility for, I will consider my efforts successful. For the recognition that what once seemed so natural is in fact historical will surely move them, as it has moved me, to see the importance of taking a hand in creating new family cultures that acknowledge the changes in the world we inhabit and make that world more habitable for everyone.

ACKNOWLEDGMENTS

THERE HAVE BEEN many times when this book seemed to me to be beyond my capacities. Although I owe much to many scholars, my first debt is to the members of my immediate family world, to Tina, Chris, Kathy, and my mother Ruth, and to those who are family to me, Lance and Marjorie Farrar, and Susanna and Alexandra Barrows, who have helped write this book in ways that even I am not aware of.

Gratitude of another kind goes to those institutions that have supported my research and writing: the Woodrow Wilson International Center for Scholars, Clare Hall of Cambridge University, the Rutgers Center for Historical Analysis, the Center for the Critical Analysis of Contemporary Culture (Rutgers), the Institute for the Humanities at Aarhus University, and the Center for Advanced Studies in the Behavioral Sciences at Stanford, where my stay was funded by a grant from the Andrew Mellon Foundation.

It would be impossible to thank all those who have commented on one or another parts of this work at various stages and in different venues, but particular thanks go to Bob Nye, Mary Joe Nye, Dorothy Thompson, Edward Thompson, George Chauncey, Philip Greven, Bonnie Smith, Uffe Ostergaard, Hans Fink, Peter Laslett, Lawrence Stone, Rod Phillips, James Gilbert, Joe Kett, Ellen Ross, Gerry Bruns, Frank Furstenberg, Judith Stacey, Arthur Kleinman, Joan Kleinman, Buck Schliffren, Alida Gersie, Bob Scally, Jonas Frykman, Orvar Löfgren, Jackson Lears, Mary Hartman, Thomas Laqueur, Jim Reed, Prosser Gifford, Roger Schofield, Louise Tilly, David Levine, Lisa Cody, Marcia Ian, Victoria de Grazia, Leonardo Paggi,

Jack Talbott, Stuart Hauser, Barbara Hauser, Bob Scott, Emmanuel Sivan, Martine Segalen, Wally Seccombe, David Thelen, Stanley Brandes, Jay Winter, Jan Lewis, Mary Blanchard, Harvey Kaye, Lee Davidoff, Erika Rappaport, David Lowenthal, Alon Confino, Arlene Skolnick, Nikki Gullachi, Gerald Handel, Ted Koditschek, Susan Groag Bell, Phyllis Mack, Lynn Mahoney, Ginger Frost, Elizabeth Roberts, Carolyn Williams, Elizabeth McLachlan, Jim McLachlan, Lige Gould, Cynthia Daniels, Candace Falk, Matt Matsuda, and Eric Leed.

I am also much indebted to Steve Fraser, who saw this project through the first phases, and to Gail Winston, who ensured its completion.

INTRODUCTION

Our understanding of families in contemporary American society can be only as rich as our understanding of what The Family represents symbolically to Americans.

Jane Collier, Michelle Rosaldo, Sylvia Yanagisako,
Rethinking the Family[1]

W E NOT ONLY LIVE with families but depend on them to do the symbolic work that was once assigned to religious and communal institutions: representing ourselves to ourselves as we would like to think we are. To put it another way, we all have two families, one that we live *with* and another we live *by*. We would like the two to be the same, but they are not. Too often the families we live with exhibit the kind of self-interested, competitive, divisive behavior that we have come to associate with the market economy and the public sphere. Often fragmented and impermanent, they are much less reliable than the imagined families we live by. The latter are never allowed to let us down. Constituted through myth, ritual, and image, they must be forever nurturing and protective, and we will go to any lengths to ensure that they are so, even if it means mystifying the realities of family life.

Today every family has its cherished myths and legends; each has its storyteller, together with a designated archivist and a keeper of family rituals and memories. One family I know has constructed a dictionary of pet names and sayings peculiar to itself. They did so just before their eldest daughter married a young man of very different background so that he could enter more easily into their family culture. The same family produces a Christmas letter, which, like the millions of others posted each December, is not so much a chronicle of all that has happened over the year as a carefully crafted chapter in a much longer story that this family is fashioning for itself.

Such newsletters are now so common that we take them for granted. Somewhat out of the ordinary, however, is the monthly missive produced by a New Jersey woman, who provides a running account of her family life, including the doings of her former husband, his new wife, and their children. *The Ludwig Chronicle* is read not only by the family itself but by over one hundred friends and acquaintances who subscribe to it. At the end of the twentieth century, it is not enough just to *live* a family life.

With an energy and earnestness unique to this age, we research, document, photograph, videotape, and narrate family in public ways that earlier generations would have found quite embarrassing and totally unnecessary. But then, they did not have to furnish themselves with families to live by. We do.

Our efforts to construct and maintain the families we live by take a multitude of forms, many of them astonishingly elaborate. Our desire to represent ourselves has turned our living rooms into family portrait galleries and our attics into archives. Our residences are mini-museums, filled with heirlooms, mementos, and souvenirs of family. Millions of Americans and Europeans now go to great expense to maintain a second home, which they regard as the "homeplace." Even if it sits empty for most of the year, knowing it is there is a comfort even to those family members who rarely, if ever, get a chance to visit it.

These imagined families and mythic homes are no less real than those found in the census return or the survey result. Indeed, it is through our imaginings—our images, myths, and rituals—that family takes on meaning. The way we live by our families is just as important as the way we live with them, even more so today than at any time in the past. Never before has family taken on a greater cultural significance in mediating the tensions and contradictions built into a political and economic system based on the values of competition, instant gratification, and amoral calculations about persons as well as things.[2] Finding no other location for such values as cooperation, enduring loyalty, and moral consideration, modern Western culture has mapped these exclusively onto the families we live with, a cultural burden that members of these domestic groups find difficult, if not impossible, to sustain on an everyday basis.

This is not the first time families have found themselves unable to represent the values attributed to them. Today when there is so much talk of the decline of family and the eclipse of family values, we are being encouraged to see the good family life as a "world we have lost."[3] However, this notion is also central to the myth of family we live by. The fact is that there has always been tension between the families people live with and the families they live by. What sets our age apart from all others is that each family is now the creator and custodian of its own myths, rituals, and images. In earlier centuries, people could find families to live by in the cosmos or in the community, relieving them of the burden of providing myths and rituals on their own. They also found their homeplaces elsewhere than their own dwellings and felt much more at home in the world than we ever can. What sets the culture of contemporary family life apart and accounts for our obsession with family myths, rituals, and images is the fact that we no longer have access to other locations onto which we might map our deepest moral values.

What follows is an effort to tell a part of the history of Western family life that has not been told before. We are quite well informed about the families Europeans and North Americans lived with over the centuries, but we know little about the families they lived by. Family has usually been thought of as belonging to nature, not to culture, and therefore as accessible only through observable behavior. As a result, family has been the domain of demographers, sociologists, and psychologists, who have busily studied its measurable dimensions by means of the facts revealed by census and survey. Of late, historians have joined in this endeavor, applying similar methods to the past, so that we now know a vast amount about households past as well as present.

The same cannot be said of the families we live by, however, for there exists no comprehensive cultural history of Western family life. The idea of family has gotten some attention, but the history of ideas is not the same as the history of the myths, rituals, and other cultural practices of the families people live by. The myths and rituals we take very seriously when we encounter them in other cultures have been treated as ephemeral when discovered closer to home. They are so embedded in our everyday lives that they either remain virtually invisible or, when detected, are put in the category of folklore, primordial and timeless. Yet these cultural practices also have origins that need to be taken into account if we are to understand family life as we now experience it.

Family cultures have altered radically over the past two centuries as the symbolic systems through which we interpret the world have undergone tremendous change. With the eclipse of religious and communal cultures capable of providing models of the good family life, both the opportunity and the burden of producing family myths, rituals, and images have passed to the domestic group itself. Today each family is its own symbolic universe, its own cosmos, its own community.[4] Its ritual experts are more likely to be women than men, for the production and consumption of modern family cultures is a highly gendered affair and part of the complicated relationship between women and men in contemporary Western society.

It seems time, then, to explore the origins and significance of the imagined families we live by. Doing so requires departing from the usual biological and sociological approaches to family and turning instead to an anthropological perspective that pays attention to meaning as well as behavior. A cultural history of family life involves examining the "silent languages" of space and the "hidden dimensions" of time that escape our notice when we approach family too literally, ignoring its symbolic dimensions.[5] Convinced that the demographers' numbers and the social historians' structures tell only part of the story of change over the centuries, I have set out here to reconstruct the history of the Western family imaginary from its beginnings in the late Middle Ages to the present.

Humans have been imagining and reimagining family throughout recorded history. The families we are born and marry into have always been too fragile to satisfy fully the existential need for a sense of continuity, belonging, and rootedness. The unique configuration of Western family life, with its emphasis on single-family households, may or may not exacerbate this fundamental tension between the way families are and the way we would like them to be, but the Western family imaginary has varied not only from that of other cultures but over time itself. From the late Middle Ages through the late eighteenth century, Europeans populated the cosmos and the community with images and icons of the good family life. Religious and communal myths and rituals provided them with a sense of family and home that was not dependent on their actual domestic arrangements. It was not until the Victorian era—and, initially, mainly among the Protestant middle classes of northwestern Europe and North America—that families began to provide their own family myths, rituals, and images. The Victorian creation of a distinctive set of family times and homeplaces marked an epochal turning point in Western family life. Today our mental maps are filled with homeplaces and our mental clocks set to family times that did not even exist before the nineteenth century. As the burden of representing the good family life shifted, the meaning of motherhood, fatherhood, and childhood underwent an equally radical transformation. Never before had every father, mother, and child been expected to be a role model. And it is not only the living but the dead who, in the absence of cosmic and communal icons, are pressed into service as families to live by.

Today, despite all the differences in detail, and regardless of class, ethnicity, or region, there is striking similarity in the way family cultures are practiced. The similarities between northwestern Europe and North America are striking. Cultural practices that had their origins among the Protestant middle classes are now almost universal at all class levels and among Catholics and Jews.[6] Each group has its own myths and rituals, but these function in quite similar ways. The significance of the Jewish Mother is indistinguishable from the meaning of the Italian Mama or the English Mum. Furthermore, it would be hard to find a great deal of difference between the way home is currently represented in northwestern Europe and North America. Everywhere people have become attached to their homeplaces. The fact that every nationality and ethnic group sees its particular family and home culture as unique should not mislead us into thinking that these are fundamentally different. The quest for roots, leading to an emphasis on disparate origins, has become a universal feature of life in modern societies, but, as in so many other things, when it comes to family, we are united by our differences.

PART I

Different Times, Different Places

Meanings of Family and Home before the Modern Age

CHAPTER 1

Myths of Family Past

This acute awareness of tradition is a modern phenomenon that reflects a desire for custom and routine in a world characterized by constant change and innovation. Reverence for the past has become so strong that when traditions do not exist, they are frequently invented.

Witold Rybczynski, *Home*[1]

M UCH ABOUT MODERN family life is changing, but one thing that never seems to change is the notion that family is not what it used to be. Families past are presented to us not only as more stable but as more authentic than families present. We imagine their times to have been the days when fathers were really fathers, mothers true mothers, and children still children. Families past are invariably portrayed as simpler, less problematic. We imagine them not only as large but as better integrated, untroubled by generational divisions, close to kin, respectful of the old, honoring the dead. Families past are imagined as rooted and centered, identified with particular places and loyal to their own pasts. We think of them as "traditional," not only because they belong to the past but because they were supposedly more attached to it. And because we imagine previous generations to have been such dedicated keepers of custom, we regard all our own family occasions in the same light in which we regard the old furniture passed down from generation to generation—as having seen better days.

But like antiques, family traditions have actually acquired their value by the passage of time and are far more treasured today than when they were new. It comes as a considerable surprise to most people that our cherished family traditions are of relatively recent origins, few older than the mid-nineteenth century. It was the European and American Protestant middle classes, the Victorians, who were the first to value the old as such. They invented the modern notion of antiques and were also the first to assign the past that quality of authenticity we so readily accept.[2] The more things change, the more we desire to keep them the same. Never has the old silver shown brighter or custom been kept in such mint condition. No period in human history has been so devoted to preservation, restoration, and reenactment as our own. In earlier times, the past belonged only to elites, who kept heritage just as they kept offices and land—for themselves. Today the past has been democratized and we all must have our own history. What was once a luxury has become a necessity. What was once a privilege is now a right.

It is the present that endows antiques with their current value, and it is the present that has given family past its huge significance. The unity, continuity, rootedness, and traditionalism ascribed to families past, first by the Victorians and then by each succeeding modern generation, parallels the way in which community is seen as being in a perpetual state of disintegration. On both sides of the Atlantic there has been a tendency to pick a particular time and place as the epitome of community—for Americans the New England town, for Swedes the villages of the Darlana region, for Germans the small walled city, for the English the villages of the so-called Home Counties—and to designate it the epitome of the traditional community, causing everything that followed to be seen in terms of destruction and loss.[3]

When we talk about family in terms of tradition, the result is the same. In projecting a static image of family onto a particular past time and place, we immediately begin to describe change in terms of "decline" or "loss." Ironically, we are also in the habit of updating the traditional community and family periodically so that the location of the golden age is constantly changing. For the Victorians, the traditional family, imagined to be rooted and extended, was located sometime before industrialization and urbanization, but for those who came of age during the First World War, tradition was associated with the Victorians themselves; today we think of the 1950s and early 1960s as the location of the family and community life we imagine we have lost.

Summoning images from the past is one of the ways we generate the hope and energy necessary to strive for better communities and families in the future. But when the remembered past becomes an end in itself, becoming "mere nostalgia, it degenerates into a terminal bubble of the past that closes one off from the living spontaneity of the present and denies the possibility of a future."[4] Either way, the notion of the traditional family is a myth many families live by.

Looking back from the 1990s, and preoccupied with rising divorce and illegitimacy rates, we perceive the 1950s as a rock of stability. But that was a decade gripped by anxiety about family life, and especially about the threat posed by the new youth cultures. The 1950s version of the traditional family was an idealized image of the Depression family, which was imagined as holding on by holding tight to one another.[5] But those who lived through the 1920s and 1930s would not have recognized themselves in the myths that later generations made of them, for these were the same people who saw themselves to be in the midst of a sexual revolution.[6] The so-called Lost Generation felt wholly cut off from a past they imagined to have been as stable as their present was chaotic. For them, the Victorian family was tradition. But as we have seen, the Victorians were by no means sure of themselves when it came to family matters. They were deeply anxious about the loss of community resulting from rapid urbanization and no more secure in their family life than we are. In 1851 the American Horace Bushnell looked back with regret on the passing of the days when families were "harnessed, all together, into the producing process, young and old, male and female, from the boy who rode the plough-horse to the grandmother knitting under her spectacles."[7]

The European middle classes were also believers in progress, but like their American counterparts, they saw the good family life as behind rather than in front of them. Nostalgia was not unknown before this time, but it had always been focused more on place than on the past as such. It was not until the Victorian age that Western cultures began to associate paradise with origins rather than with destinations and to transform the past, particularly childhoods past, into an ideal.[8] "God has given us each our own Paradise, our own old childhood, over which the old glories linger—to which our own hearts cling, as all we have ever known of Heaven upon earth," wrote James Anthony Froude in 1849, establishing a precedent for the yearning for times past that has been particularly pronounced in Western middle-class cultures, especially among middle-class males, ever since.[9]

The Victorians—or more specifically, the Protestant middle classes—were the first to experience the pastness of the past. Feeling themselves ravaged by time, they exempted earlier generations from history, calling them "traditional" and imputing to them a static and naturalized status. They imagined earlier families to have been large and cohesive, inclusive of kin as well as multiple generations, rooted in place and tradition, and more deeply religious than themselves.[10] From those sturdy foundations all else descended, or more accurately, degenerated, because for the Victorians, as for us, the past offered the authentic original of family life, so perfect that they could do no better than build on it. As in all subsequent versions of the traditional family, the Victorian version included fathers and mothers who were always larger than life, and children who were always devoted and obedient.

Middle-class Victorians were not necessarily the first to invent a usable family past. For centuries, those pretending to aristocratic or patrician status had been creating pedigrees for themselves. But prior to the nineteenth century, genealogy had been a very exclusive enterprise; very few families were conscious of their own origins, much less interested in the history of family generally.[11] The working classes were anything but nostalgic about their pasts. Until very recently, their family stories were about hard times, and their memories of childhood often bitter.[12] Middle-class Victorians started by inventing traditions for their own families, but they quickly became advocates of tradition in general. By 1900 they had founded hundreds of genealogical and historical societies in Europe and North America. Enthusiasm for family traditions was slower to arrive at other social levels, but by the 1970s the search for roots had become a mass preoccupation, and today everyone is a family historian. Children learn to value family history in school, magazines tell us how to refurbish our family traditions, and software programs make it ever easier to construct the family tree. Today every family wants its own history and its own traditions. Arising alongside the new familism is a new ethnicity, which stresses the uniqueness of every group's identity based on the uniqueness of its particular history.

Yet despite all the diversity, there is a certain uniformity: the "traditional family" imagined by WASPS is strikingly like that conjured up by Jews, Germans, and Mexican Americans. All these visions of family past emphasize stability and unity, rootedness and continuity. When they remember earlier generations as more cooperative and caring, African Americans are no different than Asian or Irish Americans. Cross-national comparisons show a similar uniformity. The images of the old homestead held by Swedes and Poles are not all that different from those held by Californians and Australians. It turns out that we are all seeking essentially the same thing, namely, a reassuring myth of family past that can serve our present needs and future aspirations.

We must be careful not to confuse the family past we live by with the families that previous generations actually lived with. Until quite recently, historians also failed to make this distinction, but in the last two decades demographic and social history research has revealed a very different picture of families past, one that suggests much more continuity between families past and present in actual behavior than anyone would have imagined. It seems that the fragmentation, instability, and discontinuity that we feel so keenly today has been part of the European experience of family life since at least the late Middle Ages. Europeans who came to the Americas carried a dream of caring and cooperation with them but were unable to realize it in the new land. Throughout the seventeenth and eighteenth centuries, family unity and continuity remained elusive on both sides of the Atlantic, and, in the great industrial and political upheavals of the nineteenth century, it became even more so.

Human reproduction has never been straightforward, and no society has found a way to eliminate its contradictions. Different peoples have found a bewildering variety of ways of coping; over time it is not the problems that have changed but the answers. The questions that Western civilization has had to face over the centuries are to some degree the same as those that every preindustrial society has to confront, namely, how to manage the fragmenting effects of high levels of mortality and fertility along with low levels of very unevenly distributed resources. Until our own century, no part of the world was able to control death or birth rates or produce the levels of affluence that would have given hope that all families might share in roughly the same resources.

We know that Europe, and particularly northwestern Europe, departed from the preexisting domestic practices of both the classical Mediterranean world and Germanic peoples beginning in the Middle Ages, setting it on a course of development different from most parts of the world.[13] At the core of the unique European family system, and distinguishing it from the family systems of Africa, Asia, and the pre-Columbian Americas, was the single-family household established by monogamous marriage. The first "rule" was that marriage should not take place without the couple first having established a basis of economic independence. "When thou art married, if it may be, live of thyself with thy wife, in a family of thine own," was the advice offered to English young people by William Whateley in 1624.[14] Colonial settlers also heeded his maxim that "the mixing of governours in a household, or subordinating or uniting of two Masters, or two Dames under one roof, doth fall out most times, to be a matter of unquietness to all parties."[15]

Multiple-family households continued to predominate in southern and eastern Europe, but in northwestern Europe and those parts of the world its peoples settled, the single-family household contributed to a second unique characteristic: a relatively high age of marriage. From at least the fourteenth century onward, the marriage age of men averaged about twenty-six years, and women generally married at twenty-three. In contrast to other world regions, these ages were both remarkably high and relatively evenly matched. European marriage age did not fall significantly until the late eighteenth century, but even then it remained high by world standards. And today it seems to be returning to its old levels once again, confirming a pattern that has lasted for almost six centuries.

The linkage between late age of marriage and household formation led to two more unique features of the Western family system. The late age of marriage gave rise to a very large pool of unmarried young people. Most of them hoped to gain a household and marry eventually, but given the straitened circumstances of the medieval and early modern economies, not all would have this opportunity. Rates of lifetime celibacy therefore never fell below 10 percent and sometimes went as high as 20 percent, in sharp contrast to other world regions where some form of marriage was virtually universal. Wedlock did not become universal in the West until the twentieth century; now, as we approach a new millennium, the old pattern of late marriage and low marriage rates seems to be reasserting itself.[16]

Only the wealthy and powerful were ever guaranteed access to marriage, but even they could not escape the effects of the high mortality rates that prevailed right up to the present century.[17] Mortality before the twentieth century was catastrophic by any standard. The average life expectancy was the midforties for both sexes, mortality was distributed across the age spectrum, and rates of infant mortality ranged from 15 to 30 percent for the first year of life. By the age of twenty, a half or more of the birth cohort was deceased, and life remained very uncertain throughout middle age as well. It was not until the twentieth century that mortality declined significantly: two-thirds of the longevity gains in the entire history of the human race have been attained in the last one hundred years.[18]

High rates of mortality have always been associated with high rates of fertility. Simply to replace the children who died, women in the past had to devote their entire married life to childbearing. From the fourteenth through the nineteenth centuries, married women had an average of four to six children. They might have had more had not the age of marriage been so high and so many women either died or reached the limits of their physical capacity to have children. In any case, population growth in Europe and North America remained moderate by the standards of today's Third World, where early marriage combines with lengthening life expectancies to produce very high birth rates.

Despite the relatively moderate nature of European population growth, families in the past had difficulty rearing all their children, partly owing to parental mortality: in England prior to the midnineteenth century, 17 percent of children were fatherless by age ten, and 27 percent by age fifteen. Peter Laslett has estimated that one-half to two-thirds of all young women had lost their fathers by the time they married in their midtwenties.[19] Given this very high level of orphanage, it is not surprising that children lived elsewhere than in their natal homes. What is astonishing is that even children with two parents moved out of the natal house at a very young age in large numbers. Some did so as mere children, but the greatest exodus happened in the midteens, when virtually all young people lived and worked in another dwelling for shorter or longer periods of time. David Herlihy has estimated that in late medieval and early modern Europe, two-thirds to three-quarters of the entire population spent some part of their childhood and youth living away from their families of birth.[20] In England, one-fifth of all rural people in the early modern period were living in households other than their own.[21]

Extrafamilial residents included not only orphaned children but large numbers of unmarried servants and apprentices, plus a fair number of married adults who were forced by poverty or other circumstances to work away from home. On the death of a marriage partner, it was common for the surviving spouse to remarry immediately so as to maintain the household, but when he or she was unable to remarry, the household was likely to disperse, with widows and widowers constituting a large part of the adults living apart from their families of birth and marriage.

Thus, contrary to myth, the three-generation household was relatively rare. Throughout the late medieval and early modern periods, the two groups least likely to be living with their own kin were children in their teens and old persons. The young were accommodated by the institutions of apprenticeship and servanthood, which had been fixtures in the West since at least the fourteenth century. The elderly were taken care of by a combination of poor relief and arrangements worked out when they were no longer able to sustain their own households. While some old folks made out "retirement" contracts with their own families, a surprising number lived in the households of nonrelatives. Most, especially those whose children had predeceased them, had little choice, but others chose such a living arrangement because it sustained some small part of their independence.

Today we are so used to thinking of the poor as having the greatest numbers of children that it comes as a shock to learn that, before the nineteenth century, the largest households were those of the wealthy. Not only were the wealthy better able to afford to keep more of their own children, but they actively recruited the largest numbers of servants and live-in workers. In the household economy that prevailed from the fourteenth to the nineteenth centuries, the "big houses" benefited from the surplus labor of their less fortunate neighbors, whose own residences were not ordinarily dignified with the word *house*, much less the word *home*. The upward circulation of young people in their teens and twenties also benefited poorer families by relieving them of feeding and housing costs, and thus there functioned a unique system of exchange of children that sustained the economic, social, and political order of Europe and North America until the nineteenth century.

Even moderately well off families regularly ceded their rights over their children through apprenticeship contracts that ensured good treatment of youngsters in return for their loyalty to their masters and mistresses.[22] Parental rights were socially and legally rather than naturally defined. The social order was understood to depend on a hierarchy of households, with each head of house, starting with the monarchy, exercising parental (usually patriarchal but sometimes matriarchal) authority over all the inhabitants, related or not. In this multitiered system, only a minority of families could rely solely on their own reproduction to form and sustain a household. All families, rich and poor, were dependent on one another to some degree. And this central fact of economic, social, and political life was contingent on the ability of everyone to imagine family as something other than that constituted by birth or marriage. For most of its history, therefore, the Western family system has functioned with an imaginary that has enabled individuals to form familial relations with strangers and to feel at home away from home.

Our myths of family past tell us that people used to be more monogamous and that sex was always contained within marriage, but here again the historical reality proves to be quite different. It took a very long time for the church to assert its control over marriage and divorce, and, even as late as the nineteenth century, common-law nuptials and folk customs of divorce were common in both Europe and North America. Until then, the line between married and unmarried persons was often somewhat indistinct. While illegitimacy rates remained moderate in most places throughout the centuries, premarital pregnancy rates were somewhat higher, never falling below 10 percent and sometimes rising to 30 percent.[23]

In the agrarian and rural manufacturing economies that prevailed until the nineteenth century, there were never enough resources to afford everyone access to a farm or a trade and thus to marry and have a family of their own. But this fact did not prevent people from establishing intimate relationships outside the single-family household system. The distinction between the big house and the little house had its parallel in the distinction between big weddings, solemnized by the church and recognized in law, and the little marriages that people conducted to sustain ties that did not receive the same official or even social recognition. Prior to the church's regulation of marriage in the twelfth century, Europeans had legitimated their sexual unions and the resulting children in all kinds of rituals of their own making. Wells, bridges, and prominent natural features served as altars where vows were exchanged. Rings and other love tokens predated church marriage, which ultimately, but somewhat reluctantly, incorporated these pagan symbols into its ceremonies.[24] For a very long time the church itself accepted the consent of the parties as sufficient validation of a marriage. Its own rites did not triumph completely until the nineteenth century.

We may like to think of the big church wedding as traditional, but it too is of very recent origins. Before the nineteenth century, no great fuss was made about premarital pregnancy or even illegitimate birth as long as the community was assured that it would not be unduly burdened by the child.[25] Merely having a child did not change a person's social status. In eighteenth-century Maine, Martha Ballard's son Jonathan continued living with his mother as her son even though he was the father of Sally Pierce's child. And Sally remained with her own family until, some four months after the birth, she married the reluctant Jonathan. Yet the couple lived with both the Ballards and the Pierces for another month before they "went to housekeeping." Only when they had their own household did Jonathan take his place among the town fathers of Hallowell. His rite of passage was quite public and formal. He became a man of the town when, along with six other recently married men, he was initiated into the mock office of "hog reeve."[26]

The rites of female passage were typically less public, but we can be fairly sure that having her own house changed Sally's status from girl to woman. It surprises us that giving birth to a child was not the transformative event then that it is today, but prior to the nineteenth century, motherhood, fatherhood, and childhood were all socially rather than biologically defined statuses. Mothers were those women, including many who had not given birth, who were engaged in the tasks of mothering; fathers were those men, including bachelors, who headed households. The various tasks of mothering were shareable and separable from childbearing. Wet-nursing was common on both sides of the Atlantic, and infants were often removed from the birth family for long periods. In households where mothers were either busy or absent, older daughters frequently acted as "little mothers" to their younger siblings.

Indeed, child-rearing was by no means exclusively the domain of women: prior to the midnineteenth century, fathers were expected to be at least as involved as mothers with the raising of children. Fatherhood, like motherhood, was defined socially rather than biologically. Fathering meant much more than inseminating: it was understood as a well-defined set of domestic skills—provisioning, hospitality, and child-rearing—that male heads of households were expected to acquire and share with other men. Many a bachelor head of house had "his own family" in the eighteenth century, and over a lifetime the German *Hausvater* would be father to many children not his own, while his children were being fathered elsewhere.[27]

Today we think of motherhood, fatherhood, and childhood as natural conditions inherent in the biological relationship itself, a conception quite the opposite of these earlier understandings of mothering and fathering as skills to be acquired, used, and then set aside. Even children were expected to learn to be children, for until the midnineteenth century, domestic advice manuals were directed as much to them as to their parents. Treated as a social role rather than as a biologically defined age category, both childhood and youth were something to adjust to. In fact, all family relationships were achieved rather than natural. Social definitions of family invariably prevailed over biological definitions. The social father, the *pater*, took precedence over the natural father, the *genitor*, just as natural mothers gave pride of place to social mothers in a world where a child's survival often depended on having a variety of nurturers, male as well as female.

The economic necessity that compelled young people to postpone and even forgo marriage and forced parents to give up their children was made palatable by a contemporary understanding of family flexible and capacious enough to provide everyone with surrogate family relations of one kind or another. Origins did not matter much to the very large part of the population who, because of mortality or mobility, were cut off from their pasts.

Prior to the nineteenth century, families on both sides of the Atlantic had little of the stability and continuity we now want to attribute to them. In the

Old Country as well as in the New World, families rarely dwelled in one place (much less the same house) for even two generations. Farms and townhouses had an identity of their own independent of the succession of families who inhabited them. Places gave their names to people, not vice versa. Elite families were sometimes referred to as "houses" only because the house defined the family. The term "family" still meant all the members of the house—servants, boarders, live-in employees, as well as resident blood relations. In those days, even visitors were regarded as part of the family.[28]

This constant changeover was built into a hierarchical social order in which everyone knew his or her place, even if they knew little of their pasts. The rich could claim not only the productive and reproductive capacity of the poor but their very identities. This prerogative was most evident in slave-holding regions, where the big house claimed rights superior to those of the natural families under its purview by forbidding slave marriages and refusing to legitimate slave offspring. Such patriarchy was not confined to plantations, however, for all masters claimed the right to the loyalty of those who lived under their roofs, including the right to forbid the marriages of servants and apprentices. What millions of African Americans were forced to do by enslavement, the European poor were compelled to do by the terms of their bonded labor.[29]

Only a small number of families could claim a past and a future. The relative lack of surnames prior to the seventeenth and eighteenth centuries testifies to how little family name meant to any but those at the highest levels of European and American society. It was not uncommon for slaves and poor people to adopt their masters' names and family identities. In eighteenth-century Virginia, "blacks and whites were in one family, by blood and by adoption," according to Mechal Sobel.[30] There the big houses initially housed both slaves and masters. The latter talked about the former as family, calling them "uncle," "aunt," and "mammy." In return, slaves took the master's name and adopted his family history as their own, often using this fictive kinship as a defense against the inhumanity of slavery.[31] In Europe, live-in servants and journeymen were also "family" and became equally adept at manipulating the patriarchal ideology to serve their own purposes.[32]

In effect, most people lived for much of their lives according to the rhythms and the spaces of families other than their own by birth or marriage. In Virginia, slaves celebrated births and mourned the deaths of the members of their masters' families.[33] Nobody prior to the nineteenth century would have entertained our notion that every natural family deserves its own rituals and myths, its own history, its own roots. Medieval Catholicism placed the family of origin furthest from its divine archetype, and the Protestant emphasis on life being a journey that leads to union with God further limited the importance of family and place of origin. Until the early nineteenth century, Western culture was far more concerned with endings than beginnings, with destinations rather than starting points.[34]

Until the midnineteenth century, most Americans and Europeans still located themselves spatially in the Great Chain of Being rather than temporally in the Great Line of Progress. It was through place rather than history that they made themselves at home in the world. We who have lost that sense of place depend much more on time for our bearings, and specifically on origins, which we believe give meaning and value to both things and people.[35] A person, a family, a nation—nothing without a past can have meaning or substance.[36] But apart from the genealogies of the aristocratic elites, premodern knowledge of ancestors did not extend back more than two generations. Most would neither have known nor cared where their forefathers were buried. Except for the elites, nobody tended family graves or organized formal anniversaries. Ralph Josselin, a seventeenth-century English clergyman, showed little interest in his forebears; he thought of himself and his wife as the trunk of a tree and his children as its branches. What is striking is that Josselin's family tree had no roots.[37]

Such an attitude does not fit with our cherished myths of family past, through which we project our obsession with ancestors onto earlier generations. Partly because of communication difficulties and partly because of employment conditions, family reunions were rare before the nineteenth century, though family members were usually dispersed over only a ten- or twenty-mile distance. But there is also little evidence that anyone cared to come together in a regular, ritualized way.[38] Baptisms, weddings, and funerals, which we imagine to have been bigger family events in the past than they are now, were rarely attended by kin and often not even by the immediate family. Baptisms were often hurried affairs that took place while mothers were still confined to the house by the prescribed lying-in period. Betrothal largely ended the family role in marriage, and the bride was escorted to the church by a raucous crowd, not by her father. Parents played a very minor role in premodern weddings. Gifts came from the community rather than from family and kin, and it was also the community that gave the dead their final send-off. Only in the nineteenth century did funerals become family occasions.

In the language of preindustrial Europe and colonial America, the distinctions between kin, and between kin and nonkin, were much more ambiguous than they are today. Before the nineteenth century, no one made a sharp distinction between friendship, by implication a matter of choice, and kinship, with its sense of obligation. Families past were not especially familiar with their relatives, especially those who lived at a distance, and they did not distinguish clearly between their various in-laws. The terms "mother-in-law" and "stepmother" were often used interchangeably, and grandmothers and grandfathers could be any older female or male relative, or sometimes a familiar older person. The more intimate language of "grandma" and "grandpa" did not emerge until the middle of the eighteenth century and was not popularly adopted until much later.[39] The term "friend" was used for relatives, neighbors, and members of the same religious faith. In turn, the familial idiom was extended to guilds, confraternities, monasteries, and the military—groups that today we would not call families.[40]

The language of family was kept open and fluid for good reason. Parents taught their children not to be too reliant on blood ties alone, and New England Puritans reminded themselves constantly not to love their spouses and children too much, for doing so might detract from their love of God. "Look not for Perfection in your relations. God reserves that for another state where marriage is not needed," they told themselves.[41] Parenthood, childhood, and marriage were all terminated at death. Thomas Hooker wrote that there would be "no marrying in heaven," for, as he and his contemporaries imagined Paradise, everyone would be "as dear to another, as if all relations of husbands, and wives, of parents, and children, and friends, were in every one of them."[42] Until well into the nineteenth century, heaven was represented not as a community of families but as one large community of friends.[43]

Prior to the nineteenth century, when it was place, not past, that gave people their sense of identity, almost everyone lived in a household. In parts of New England, it was illegal to live on one's own, while in Europe long-standing household and hostel systems kept the number of those living alone to a minimum. Home was the place that sheltered you at the moment, not the one special place associated with childhood or family of origin.[44]

Contrary to what we have come to believe, our ancestors were not more sessile. Nor were they attached to particular houses; the moves we find traumatic, they took in stride. The Maine midwife Martha Ballard made a record in her diary, on April 21, 1791, of leaving a place where she had been resident for twelve years: "We removed from the mills to the house which was Old Leut Howards, and Peter went to the mills with his family." The notation for the next day read: "At home. Began my gardin." As Laurel

Thatcher Ulrich notes, "Her story of the transition from one house to another is told almost inadvertently, in the course of a quiet chronicle of daily work."[45] For Martha Ballard, home was simply the here and now, a work site like any other, with no sentiment attached to it. Her diary entry also suggests that home was a destination rather than a place of return, another difference that separates her world from ours.

We assume that homemaking skills have degenerated over time, but once again a common belief turns out to be an illusion. In fact, the old households were very difficult to domesticate, for they were busy places of work and heavy traffic that resisted the strenuous efforts of even the most dedicated housekeeper. Houses in the eighteenth century seemed to have a will of their own, defying their owners to bring peace and order to their interiors. Houses sheltered people but did not comfort them. Martha Ballard sometimes found her household so much "up in arms" that even her strong will was defeated, and she had little good to say about her domestic space, as opposed to her garden.[46]

No doubt, Martha Ballard was using the image of the unruly house to express her own sense of declining powers, but it was typical of eighteenth-century people to think of the space around them as alive, as something they had to make peace with. They had a personal relationship to the places where they lived, but they attached their sentiments to land- and town-scapes rather than to particular houses.[47] Old houses meant much less to them than they do to us. Their dwellings were on the whole less permanent than ours, and they had no compunctions about tearing them down or moving them when circumstances required.[48]

Our ancestors were anything but homebodies. They had a stronger sense of place and felt more at home in the world at large than we do. They moved easily in and out of one another's households, for the ancient traditions of hospitality were by no means dead; the presence of strangers in the household was still perceived as an enhancement to status.[49] In the eighteenth century, comfort had not yet triumphed over generosity; for instance, William Byrd II, the head of one of Virginia's great families, was either visited or visited others on more than three-quarters of the days of the year. At a humbler level, it seems that visiting enhanced vital bonds of community, creating interdependencies that were invaluable in times of illness or hardship. Some visits were brief, but others, especially those of young people, could be quite extended. In big as well as little houses, the constant traffic of people precluded the cozy home life we imagine to have existed in the past.[50]

In eighteenth-century North America, women may well have done more moving about than men. They referred to this as "gadding"; it had little of the formal, ritualistic character that the Victorians associated with female visiting.[51] People entered without knocking, even without acknowledgment, and seated themselves at the hearth or the table with an air of familiarity that we would find quite astonishing and disturbing. Even the middle classes moved between households so frequently that it was often difficult to tell which family belonged where.[52] The house had yet to become a strictly private space associated exclusively with the nuclear family. It was still the primary place of work and the meeting place of different classes, genders, and ages. Little about it conforms to the myth of the old homestead as a peaceful refuge, the original home sweet home.

We must also dispense with the notion that families past were more concerned with maintaining custom and tradition, and that they maintained the "quality time" we see as so threatened in our own day and age. By and large, premodern Europeans and Americans were less concerned with the economy of time than with the economy of space. Households took their time together pretty much for granted, allowing it to be governed by the rhythms of work and leisure and not setting apart any strictly family times. As we shall see, they lived by an entirely different culture of time than we do. The past had not yet taken on that quality of irrecoverable pastness that causes us so much anguish. Even the dead were within reach in the village graveyard, and people were more likely to be haunted by them, troubled by their presence [53] It is we, rather than they, who are ancestor worshipers.

The eighteenth century did not think of generations as we do. The term itself simply meant the offspring of a common parent and implied sameness rather than difference.[54] By this definition, all generations occupied the same capacious present. The young were not necessarily identified with the future, nor the old with the past. In the premodern economy of time all ages were conceived of as equidistant from death, and the age differences we make so much of today mattered much less.

People then may have been less obsessed with temporal differences than we are now, and less aware of age than we are, but when it came to sharing space, trouble could erupt. This was precisely what happened when Martha Ballard was forced to share her house with her son Jonathan and his wife Sally. It was common under such circumstances for the parties to draw up an agreement about the rationing of space and resources so as to avoid strife. The Ballards made such an agreement, but it was not sufficient to prevent tensions between Martha and her daughter-in-law.[55]

Contrary to another of our favorite images of families past, the desire for closeness for closeness' sake was notably absent. Families usually gathered to work or to pursue communally organized leisure, not to have family occasions as such. Most such gatherings were returns to community rather than to family as such, and the nostalgia we associate with family occasions was entirely missing. No graves were visited or ancestors remembered. In the premodern economy of time, no rupture between past and present was visible, and there was no compelling need to connect with other generations or to memorialize the dead.

Given the separation and loss that resulted from the demographic and economic realities of the preindustrial era, it is no wonder that our ancestors regarded forgetfulness as a kind of blessing. We like to think of our ancestors as having better memories, but like so many of our ideas about the past, this belief is more a projection of our fears of forgetting than a true reflection of what was important to them. Montaigne was convinced that "an excellent memory is often conjoined with the weakest intellects."[56] In premodern Europe and North America, people were under no religious obligation to remember earthly things, not even their own families. "The things and relationships of this life are like prints in the Sand, there is not the least appearance of remembrance of them," declared Thomas Hooker. "The King remembers not his Crown, the Husband the Wife, the Father the child."[57] It was God, not man, who remembered.

We want to believe that families past were less fragmented, discontinuous, and divided than families now, but historical reality is anything but reassuring on this point. Lawrence Stone has calculated that the proportion of marriages broken up by death in earlier centuries is just about the same as the proportion broken up by divorce today.[58] Of course, one kind of separation is involuntary and the other is a choice, but it is hard to argue that fragmentation and loss of family ties are anything new, or that we are facing today a situation unprecedented in the history of Western civilization.[59] What has changed are the cultural resources that different periods have had at their disposal to cope with the perpetual challenge of creating a sense of continuity and permanence. Propagating the myth of families past as more stable and united than families present is contemporary culture's way of achieving this result.

It is imperative that we disabuse ourselves of our misconceptions of family past, but we must not stop there. Those who would simply debunk the myths of family past seem to think that we can transcend myth entirely. Marina Warner is right to warn us that "pleas for a return to reason, for simply stripping away illusion, ignore the necessity and the vitality of mythical material in the consciousness as well as unconsciousness."[60] We are no more able to live without our imagined families than were our ancestors. The only difference lies in the fact that their myths, rituals, and icons were pro-vided by religion and community, while ours are self-generated. We will not understand our own engagement with myth and ritual until we understand how earlier generations engaged with theirs. In this way, we can use the past to throw light on the present.

CHAPTER 2

At Home with Families of Strangers

The family is not an institution, but an ideological, symbolic construct that has a history and a politics.
Judith Stacey, "Good Riddance to the Family"[1]

T HERE IS MUCH TALK today of lost family values and the eclipse of home life. Social scientists have joined moralists in suggesting that we are now rapidly approaching the end of the family as we have known it. "Over thousands of years the institution of the family has stripped down to its bare nucleus, and now that nucleus appears to be splitting apart," declares David Popenoe, a sociologist and a leading proponent of the family decline thesis.[2] Separating the nuclear family from its extended kin was bad enough, but now something more fundamental is at stake. What triggers the current apprehension is the notion that a natural law is about to be violated. "Family history comes to an end in this elemental essential unit of human procreation," Popenoe declares.[3]

According to the sociobiological premises that stand behind his gloomy pronouncements and those of others, the nuclear family reproduces us not only physically but culturally. In the past, family values were strong because the nuclear family was strong, but today both are in danger of extinction because the nuclear unit is fragmenting and single parents cannot pass on their values to their children. As a result, says Popenoe, "familism as a cultural value has diminished."[4]

Yet when asked what they value most in life, Americans and Europeans consistently place home and family ahead of everything else, including religion and community. Despite all the talk of the decline of family and the collapse of marriage, surveys show that over the last thirty years Americans' personal desire for marriage has held at a remarkably high 96 percent. Over the same period, however, the actual proportion married over the course of their lifetime has rarely reached 90 percent. In a similar way, the desire for children exceeds actual fertility.[5] Although it has become increasingly difficult during the past two decades to purchase a house, the desire for home ownership is at a historical high point. Never have so many Europeans as well as Americans owned their own residences, and millions now have second homes.[6] As a value—something people believe in even when they cannot always realize it in practice—family and home cannot be said to be in decline. The extraordinarily high rate at which divorced people remarry, the obvious anguish of childless couples, and a pervasive fear of homelessness all testify to just how much we value home and family.

The same surveys find that family values and family behavior are rarely consistent. One poll found that "the emotional quality of family relationships is felt to be more important than the formal status of those relationships. . . . Having a happy marriage is more highly valued than being married. Respecting one's children ranks higher than having children. The inner qualities of relationships are valued more than is the simple existence of those relationships."[7] It appears that family has been added to the long list of things more honored in the breach than in practice. There is also a large gap between what people say about the sanctity of the home and the violence and abuse that occurs there.

The prophets of family decline bemoan the gap between the ideal and reality, cynics take it as proof of the hypocrisy of contemporary society, and both assume that sometime in the near or distant past things were different, that there was a time when home and family were all they were meant to be. But just when was this golden age? You will search in vain for a time when people found it possible to realize in the families they lived with all the values they wished to live by, when people felt wholly at home in their places of residence.

This is not the first time Europeans and Americans have lived their family and home lives vicariously, attracted to images of the good family life even when they have found it difficult to realize their ideals in their own day-to-day existence. Taking the longer view, it is possible to see that matching ideal and reality has never been easy. However, before the nineteenth century there were not only a variety of cosmic and communal families—families of strangers—to live by but a plethora of homes away from home to turn to. We will better understand our problems in coping with the families we ourselves live with if we begin by looking at the imagined families and mythic homes that earlier generations had available to them when they faced the problems of living with the families they were born and married into.

We easily assume that family has always been the location of people's highest values, but in the ancient world there was no concept of family as a source of moral values. "The ancients . . . lacked a clear sense of the primary descent group as a distinct moral unity," writes David Herlihy.[8] The Roman *familia* encompassed all that belonged to the *paterfamilias*, including slaves and servants as well as relatives by blood or marriage. The members of this heterogeneous group had no common culture or moral standing. In late antiquity, little value was placed on marriage or procreation. Formal matrimony was common only among the patrician classes. Slaves and common people did not expect to marry or to raise the children born to them. Celibacy was widespread, and infanticide and abandonment of infants were widely practiced, among Christians as well as pagans, throughout the Mediterranean basin.[9]

The ancients distinguished between life and the good life, family life and the good family life, placing their cherished values safely out of the reach of the ravages of time and place. Both Judaism and early Christianity accepted and institutionalized the distinction between natural families, subject to the depredations of time and distance, and eternal families, resistant to all forms of disorder and degeneration. "Go from your country and your kindred and your father's house to the land I will show you," Yahweh commanded Abraham. God tested his chosen people by demanding that they love him more than their own families. Ultimately, Judaism would come to value the patriarchal family, but the followers of Yahweh have always remained vigilant against putting the love of family before the love of God.[10]

A similar tension has been manifest in Christianity from its very beginnings. Christ's own family situation was highly ambiguous. His human mother and father were not married at the time of his conception, and he had no blood relations in the strict sense of that term.[11] In his preaching, he clearly subordinated the family of man to the family of God, giving priority to the claims of the spirit over those of blood: "If any man come to me and hate not his father, and mother, and wife, and children, and brethren, and sisters, yea, and his own life also, he cannot be my disciple" (Luke 14:26). His was a family of the spirit rather than of birth or marriage: "Whoever does the will of God is my brother, and sister, and mother" (Mark 3:34–35).[12] For the first century after the death of Christ, the faithful suspended worldly commitments in anticipation of the Second Coming. "To the unmarried and the widows I say that it is well for them to remain unmarried as I am," advised Saint Paul (1 Corinthians 7:8).[13] Early Christianity was accused of breaking up homes and families (a charge leveled against religious cults today). The sanctity of celibacy would remain a powerful theme in Christianity even after its adherents began, reluctantly, to renew their ties of marriage and kinship in the second century. When, about A.D. 200, Christians living in Pontus finally became convinced that the kingdom of God was not going to arrive momentarily, "the young girls got married; the men went back to the fields."[14]

Were Christ and his disciples living today, they would undoubtedly be deemed antifamily by many Christians. Even as the glorification of nuclear family ties reaches new heights among both fundamentalist Christians and Orthodox Jews, other voices, more consistent with the spiritual traditions of both religions, can be heard warning believers that "there is an orphaned state required for the sake of the kingdom of heaven."[15] Both Judaism and Christianity have traditionally rejected the worship of nature and the biological family. They are what the anthropologist Carol Delaney has called "monogenetic" religions. Their God is the Creator, the original and perpetual source of all life. Other religions admit the creative powers of nature itself, but the Christian church especially has long remained ambivalent toward nature's claims.[16] For the first thousand years, it treated marriage and procreation as inferior to chastity and celibacy. Saint Jerome had a numerical ranking system, a scale of holiness, by which he scored virginity as 100, widowhood as 60, and marriage as 30. "I praise weddings," he said, "but only because they generate virgins."[17] Until the twelfth century, monastic families were more valued than ordinary families. The early Middle Ages, a period in which spirituality appeared to be incompatible with biological maternity and paternity, produced no married saints.[18]

Early Christianity produced the notion of the Trinity, but no concept of the Holy Family. The figure of God the Father so overshadowed the human parents of Jesus that during the early Middle Ages Joseph was only dimly perceived as a shadowy stepfather, and Mary was viewed more as Jesus' consort than as his mother. While Christ was represented as the King of Heaven, Mary was imagined as its Queen. It was not her maternity but her virginity that was emphasized. A model for nuns but not for ordinary women, the early medieval Mary was not yet the object of popular worship she was later to become. To find models of motherhood they could draw strength and comfort from, ordinary women resorted to local saints, half-disguised pagan fertility goddesses.[19] We do not know how early medieval fathers represented themselves to themselves, but we can be certain that the celibate holy fathers of the church offered little in the way of role models for ordinary fathers.

The ancient world had shown no great attachment to home, and early Christians were scarcely homebodies either: they were under a spiritual injunction to journey in search of holiness, a quest that would shape Western notions of time and space until the nineteenth century. As Yi-Fu Tuan has pointed out, cultures that emphasize journeys tend to devalue physical places.[20] Christianity inherited the Judaic tradition of placing great value on a spiritual destination as the true home, thereby denigrating all other places, including places of origin. Early Christians projected home beyond history and nature. It was said that they lived "in their own countries, but only as aliens. . . . Every foreign land is their fatherland, and yet for them every fatherland is a foreign land. . . . They busy themselves on earth, but their citizenship is in heaven."[21]

In the most transcendent versions of Christianity, the domicile is just a camping spot, a point of departure but never of return. As the church became more involved in the world, it would ultimately elevate some places to the level of the sacred, though only as way stations on the journey to God, never as ultimate destinations. Medieval Christianity came to recognize the value of worldly journeys, but only in the highly ritualized form of the pilgrimage. Notes Gwen Neville:

> The village or town resident who wished to "see the world" was provided with a socially acceptable format for temporary exploration in the institution of the pilgrimage; he or she could enter into the *communitas* of the pilgrim journey and visit the shrine as a way of escaping for a time from the pressing obligations of the structure within which all of the routine daily life was necessarily enacted.[22]

Holy travel served the purpose of removing the individual from the bonds and snares of his or her household—liberating the soul from its imprisonment in the flesh and blood of the nuclear family—to seek a spiritual home where, for a moment at least, it was possible to work toward individual salvation in the company of the real or imagined family of God, "some visible, some invisible, some natural, some supernatural: God; Mary, mother of God; the angels; the saints," all of whom were assumed to be present at the pilgrimage site.[23]

For ordinary Christians, pilgrimage brought them temporarily into the company of the holy. Catholicism provided a few with a lifelong pilgrimage in the form of the nunnery or the monastery, but prior to the sixteenth century most Christians had only a few moments when they were ritually separated from their flesh and blood and could enter into communion with a spiritual kindred capable of facilitating salvation. One such moment was the Catholic rite of baptism, a symbolic second birth that represented the ritual separation of the infant from its natural parents, its delivery into the hands of the holy father at the font, and its reception by the godparents, its spiritual kindred.[24] Similarly, the medieval rites of death involved a ritual separation of the deceased from the family of origin and a symbolic incorporation into the company of the dead. The corpse was buried without regard to family of origin, for the world beyond was imagined as reunion with God and the heavenly hosts, where all would live as one, without regard to birth or marriage.[25]

All the pilgrimages between birth and death followed the same pattern of separation from the nuclear family and incorporation into the visible and invisible spiritual kindred. These were often undertaken by local confraternities, who were an even more perfect representation of spiritual kinship than godparents.[26] The fact that pilgrimage sites were often presided over by holy families of monks and nuns endowed them with a sacramental value, and the relics and souvenirs brought back by pilgrims served the purpose of connecting the faithful, wherever they might be, to these meccas of spiritual comfort.[27]

In late antiquity and even the early Middle Ages, Christians were little different from their pagan neighbors in their low estimation of home and the nuclear family. The Germanic and Celtic peoples of northern Europe valued childbearing more than the Romans did, but they did not honor monogamous marriage. Among them, the claims of bilateral kinship remained strong, and they did not recognize the primary descent group as a moral unit. It was not until the twelfth century that Europeans began to imagine the nuclear family as having a value of its own, although they were far from granting the biological family the sanctity it has acquired in modern times.[28]

Mother and father saints did not appear on the scene until the late Mid-

dle Ages. Even then the Catholic church found it difficult to reconcile biological with spiritual parenthood. It imagined the cosmos as a great hierarchy of family types, with the family of God at the top and the family of man
at the bottom, scarcely above the animals. The highest forms of family life
were not achievable in the here and now but existed only beyond time and
space in union with God. It was the otherworld, the supernatural and trans-
historical world, that was permanent and predictable. We organize our
sense of time and space anthropocentrically; they organized theirs theo-
centrically.[29] Our fixed points are terrestrial; theirs were celestial. We measure our days from the date of our birth; they measured theirs from the day
of their death. Life for us is an eternity, but for them it was the "small
parenthesis" between the eternity that exists before and after the individual's brief existence on this orb.[30] While on earth, the Christian was in a
state of orphanage as well as exile, waiting to return home to his or her true
family, the family of God.[31]

The next best thing to the family in heaven were the various spiritual
families established by the church from the fourth century onward.
Supreme among these were the celibate holy orders, affiliation with which
required another kind of orphanage and exile. The church provided elaborate rites of passage for those who wished to leave behind their natural families and enter into the holy orders as the brides or brothers of Christ. But
the majority of believers were destined to live a lower life associated with
the natural family, effectively depriving them of the good life in this world,
if not in the next.

If their own families could not represent sacred values, medieval Christians had a set of imagined families that did. Godparenthood had certain
practical benefits, but more important, it symbolized the values that real
families were not always able to produce on their own.[32] The institution
kept alive familial ideals of love, trust, and caring at a time when high rates
of both child and adult mortality, extremes of poverty, and political disorder
made the good family life difficult if not impossible for many Europeans to
achieve.

In addition to godparenthood, Catholicism offered other spiritual families—confraternities, village guilds, and pilgrimage groups—through which
laypeople could represent themselves to themselves in the most positive
light, if only momentarily. By the fourteenth and fifteenth centuries, these
spiritual families were a ubiquitous feature of the European social landscape, assisting at births, celebrating marriages, burying the dead, providing homes away from home on a long- or short-term basis—in other words,
offering the kind of services we expect today only from immediate family
and close kin.[33]

A pilgrimage to a site associated with a saint brought a sense of well-being, perhaps even physical cure, to troubled or ailing family members. Through the ritual of pilgrimage, men and women could achieve, if only for a moment and in a place other than their own overcrowded houses, a sense of family feeling as well as assurance of being at home in the world. In effect, medieval Catholicism offered a rich mix of imagined homes and families in which people could allay their fears in a world plagued by violence and death.

Medieval people were more likely to find the good family life outside than inside the home. Just as God had given his only begotten son to save mankind, so Christians believed it no shame to give up one's own children if doing so served a higher purpose. As John Boswell has pointed out, "No Christian writer articulated the position that engendering a child necessarily created an obligation to support him." Continuing a practice rooted in the ancient and Germanic worlds of giving up children to the "kindness of strangers," medieval parents made gifts of their children to monasteries, convinced that this act, known as oblation, would guarantee them a spiritual and material well-being they could not provide for themselves.[34]

It was not just children who benefited from the kindness of strangers. Before the modern era older persons also found refuge in families other than their own.[35] Even those in the prime of their lives often found families of strangers a desirable alternative. Trade guilds and journeymen's associations, which constituted themselves as "a family and a fraternity," flourished throughout the medieval and early modern periods. Their initiations, modeled directly on Christian baptism, established yet another kind of familial relationship that offered both practical benefits and safe storage for values that were hard to keep at home.[36] From the Middle Ages onward, families relied on the assistance of strangers, a Christian tradition of neighborly aid that was codified during the early modern period in laws obligating parishes to assist those in trouble.[37]

The distinction between higher and lower forms of family life, assigning higher value to spiritual families and families of strangers than to families of birth and affiliation, proved vital to the expansion of economic and political institutions during the Middle Ages and well into the early modern period. Fictive kinship was a primary means by which early medieval Europe emerged from a state of virtual anarchy; the feudal bonds of trust thus created stretched over time and space, transcending blood ties and allowing the creation of a new political, religious, and economic order.[38] Of course, keeping the nuclear family at the lowest rung of the hierarchy of imagined families made it easier for institutions like the church, the guilds, and various "big houses" to recruit members and maintain loyalties. Contrary to what contemporary prophets of family decline imagine to be the nuclear family's heritage, Western civilization, in a very real sense, was constructed at the expense of the nuclear family.

The elaboration of the Western single-family household system coincided with the emergence of a hierarchy of imagined families and mythic homes, with the Holy Family at its pinnacle. It was not until the twelfth century that Mary ceased to be seen as the queen and consort of her son and became a fully embodied mother figure. It was then that she "gradually took the place of the old, familiar, and beloved local saints and acquired some of their characteristics—intimacy, immediacy, and parental concern for the affairs of her children." Promoted by a church now bent on shaping the lives not just of monks and nuns but of the laity, the cult of Mary swept aside the old pagan goddesses and the newer virgin saints to become a central feature in the lives of those who were seeking reassurance in a world of high rates of infant and maternal death. Places like Chartres, which became associated with the Holy Mother, quickly became major pilgrimage sites. "The insecurity and real dangers of medieval childhood created powerful, persistent fantasies of protection and rescue by an omnipotent, loving mother," notes Clarissa Atkinson.[39]

Still, until the late Middle Ages, high holiness and family life had seemed incompatible. Only then did married persons begin to be canonized. It was also then that mother saints and father saints became imaginable for the first time and the Holy Family, "presented for example and edification," became a central feature of Christian worship. "Christians were encouraged to emulate and even seek holiness through roles and relationships modelled on Jesus and his mother, foster father, and grandmother."[40]

At first the Holy Family was imagined as an extended kin group, consisting of infant and mother, the maternal grandmother, Saint Anne, and various cousins. The matrifocality of this imagined family seems to have reflected the realities of early medieval family life, which still revolved around women.[41] The high valuation placed on extended kin ties was consistent with the feudalistic effort to forge a political and economic order that would transcend the interests of the nuclear family, but by the twelfth century this need seemed less imperative.[42] With the restoration of peace, the revival of trade, and the rise of a modest merchant class, the stage was set for a reevaluation, by both the church and the state, of the primary descent group. Over the next two centuries, the image of the Holy Family would change radically, becoming both more nuclear and more patriarchal.

For most of the early Middle Ages, Joseph remained a marginal figure whose paternity was overshadowed by that of God. Just as the early Mary took a distinctly unmaternal form, Joseph appeared as a foolish old man, a jealous husband, whose claims on paternity were the subject of scholarly skepticism and popular jokes. By the fourteenth and fifteenth centuries, however, Saint Joseph was coming to have a place in the Holy Family, eventually displacing Saint Anne. Images of the Nativity were becoming more common, foregrounding the nuclear family of procreation and pushing kin forever into the background. Mary's maternity became fully developed, and Joseph acquired not only a saintly character but a more youthful image, making his paternity plausible for the first time. Equally significant, the Holy Family acquired its first "home," a house that had been mysteriously transported from Nazareth to the tiny Italian village of Loreto, where it became a major pilgrimage site in the late fifteenth century.[43]

"Here was indeed a novel conception of the Holy Family," notes John Bossy. "Invented from scratch in the fifteenth century, and promoted by the Post-Reformation Church, it made a great deal of difference to the history of the human Christ and probably to the history of the European family as well."[44] It makes equal sense that the history of the European family made a huge difference to the reconfiguration of the Holy Family, for this was precisely the time when the single-family household became dominant, especially among the emerging middle strata of the towns. The one change is clearly inseparable from the other. Archetypes are always reflections of existing social relations, but at the same time they shape those relations. The reimagining of the Holy Family as a distinctly nuclear, patriarchal unit was clearly bound up with the rise of a new urban middle class, a class that would give an altogether new function and meaning to the godly household from the fifteenth century onward.[45]

The teachings of the Renaissance humanists prefigured this shift, but it was during the Protestant Reformation, centered in northwestern Europe, that the old hierarchies of spiritual families were first overthrown and the patriarchal household displaced the pilgrimage site as the moral center of the Christian universe.[46] Reformers like Martin Luther and John Calvin returned to Old Testament family values, insisting that the good family life could take place only in godly households. As John Bossy points out, the reformers retained the notion of the Holy Family, "though this was for them rather less an essential link in the chain of salvation, rather more a model for human imitation."[47] The reformers not only did away with the healing powers of the mother and father saints who populated the late medieval Catholic imagination but deposed godparenthood and all the holy fathers and mothers of the religious orders. They also made a clean sweep of the old families of strangers, including the village guilds, confraternities, and pilgrimage groups, leaving only the godly household in place.

The Reformation spiritualized the household but refused to sanctify the nuclear family as such.[48] Protestants believed even more insistently than Catholics that life was an exile, and death the only sure means of return to the heavenly home. The New England Puritans were extremely ambivalent about their family commitments, viewing marriage and procreation as duties but not as ends in themselves.[49] John Cotton cautioned his congregations that they should marry and procreate only as a means "to be better suited to God's service, and bring them nearer to God." He warned that "where we exceedingly delight in Husbands, Wives, Children, [this] much benumbs and dims the light of the Spirit."[50] The view that prevailed among Protestants until the early nineteenth century was that the family of man is a preparation for, but no substitute for, the family of God. Death was reimagined in a wholly theocentric way as the final rite of passage that frees believers from all earthly bonds, thus allowing them to return to the Father in heaven.[51]

Protestantism's idealization of the patriarchal single-family household was not only a logical extension of the Western family system but a timely complement to the emergent absolute monarchies and commercial capitalism, both of which began to shape the Western world in the sixteenth and seventeenth centuries. Absolute monarchy legitimated itself as a hierarchy of patriarchal households, with the monarch at the top, ruling through the loyal heads of households constituting his kingdom.[52] Capitalism in its commercial proto-industrial phase was equally dependent on the godly household as its central place of production. In Protestant lands, all the alternatives—holy orders, confraternities, pilgrimage groups—were forced to give way to the godly household. Although guilds and journeymen's associations continued to imagine themselves in familial and fraternal terms, serving as homes away from home until the nineteenth century, the Western family imaginary was sharply contracting.

While a number of families of strangers for men continued to exist—colleges and the military in addition to the trade guilds and journeymen's associations—women henceforth had really only one option. In sixteenth-century Augsburg, for example, single women were required by law to lodge with a godly household.[53] The status of married women was thus enhanced, but at a price. "In Protestant Europe, motherhood became a sign, even a precondition, of a woman's moral and physical health," writes Clarissa Atkinson. "Obedience replaced virginity and poverty as the essential female virtue and road to holiness," making it virtually impossible for a woman to become a good Christian "except through marriage and motherhood."

Even in Catholic lands, where the celibate life was still an option for women, the convent was placed under the strict control of "fatherly" bishops.[54] It was simply no longer possible to imagine a family consisting entirely of women.

Thus, the godly household became not only the crucial locus of political control but the engine of a remarkable period of economic and demographic growth. Replacing the otherworldly asceticism of the monastic family with the innerworldly asceticism of the household and plantation produced a massive increase in material production and political power throughout Protestant Europe and North America.[55] Protestants no longer felt the need to travel to find the sacred. They rejected the Catholic focus on pilgrimage, replacing it with the equally sacred notion of the "journey of life," which demanded spiritual rather than physical movement to achieve the ultimate union with God.

The radical reformers of the sixteenth century initially devalued all worldly places. They not only rejected the concept of the holy pilgrimage site but the *communitas* of pilgrimage itself, substituting for it the actual community of believers and obviating the necessity of physical journey.[56] According to Gwen Neville, "the individual's entire life becomes a pilgrimage process, a journey from birth to death walking with the laws of God."[57] This journey could be accomplished without ever departing from home, though in practice children and old people would continue to circulate at very high levels until the nineteenth century. Protestant families remained dependent on the community, but the community was more likely to be defined as the community of coreligionists rather than immediate neighbors. Quaker networks of mutual aid would stretch over vast territories, even across the Atlantic, creating perhaps the most far-flung family of strangers the Western world had ever known.[58]

From the sixteenth through the early nineteenth centuries, Protestantism remained a religion of destinations rather than origins, conceding no sanctity to place of origin. True to the Old Testament, the religion of Luther and Calvin held that the only true home was with God in heaven.[59] Those closest to the end of life were sometimes considered homeward bound, but everyone else was to think of themselves as orphans and exiles. There was only one homecoming, and that was with the Almighty.[60]

The rites of separation and incorporation through which Catholics had enacted their dramas of salvation were suspended by Protestants. Among them, life no longer began and ended with rites of passage. Infant baptism and the last rites were dispensed with. Salvation was no longer available through sacraments but depended entirely on the grace of God. Godparenthood was abandoned, and families ceased to give up their dead to the collectivity, burying them instead next to predeceased family members whenever possible.[61] Graves remained unadorned and generally untended, however, for the world beyond was not yet imagined to consist of families. The reformers invested neither in houses nor in tombs, for the ultimate destination could be reached only by following the straight and narrow path through this world and making no attachments to particular places. Wherever the Reformation prevailed, the old Catholic pilgrimage spots were stripped of their religious significance, though they continued to be visited for their healing powers well into the eighteenth century.[62]

Protestants were not supposed to feel entirely at home in this world, and before the nineteenth century there was nothing very homey about most houses. As places of production as well as consumption, they were very busy, noisy, and cluttered; characterized by a frenzy of coming and going, houses had no set times or set places for the family itself. If one distinction between the home and the house is the control of space over time in the former, then there was little that was homelike about these households, especially the "big houses," which contained the largest numbers of people.[63]

Those seeking temporal and spatial regularity were more likely to find it outside the house; indeed, our ancestors spent much of their lives in public places, where they found comforts unavailable in their busy households.[64] Shakespeare wrote that "men are merriest when they are from home" (*King Henry the Fifth*, I.ii.271), while Milton was convinced that "it is for homely features to keep home" (*Il Penseroso*, l. 745). In the seventeenth and eighteenth centuries, the journeyman on his *Wanderjahr* was joined by the young gentleman on the grand tour, but it was not just men who traveled. For the poor of both sexes, mobility was a necessity, but even the well-to-do liked to get their children out of the house, preferably into another godly household. The resulting movement of young people in their late teens and early twenties makes the adolescents of today look quite sedentary by comparison.

Of course, there was no intention of allowing the young to be completely on their own. Their movements across Europe were carefully supervised by a number of patriarchal trade and collegiate institutions. These did not develop in the New World, but there too the rule (and sometimes the law) directed all single persons, men as well as women, to reside in a household.[65] However, it was not just the young who had homes away from home in the seventeenth and eighteenth centuries. Many adults, especially the poor, lived in someone else's household. The old tended to be boarded out in other people's houses as well. And even wealthy householders looked elsewhere for the peace and comfort of home. We find the seventeenth-century Massachusetts governor Thomas Dudley complaining that he had "yet no table, nor other room to write in than by the fireside upon my knee." He found it particularly difficult in winter, when everyone crowded indoors. Family togetherness irritated him, for "they break good manners and make me many times forget what I would say and what I would not say."[66]

This desire for a home away from home lasted well into the nineteenth century. Until the 1840s and 1850s, all classes frequented pubs, cafés, and lodging houses. In London, everyone had their clubs, while in Birmingham, "almost every man had his tavern, where he regularly spent a portion of each day. . . . He looked upon his publican's house as his second home." Mrs. George was the proprietor of the Woolpack, a "sanctum, a bar parlour . . . in which she prescribed and reinforced the most rigid etiquette and decorum, [that] was the evening resort of some remarkable men" who presumably could not find the same tranquillity in their own houses. But it was not just the gentlemen who frequented such places. Evidence from both North America and Europe indicates that middle-class women were away from home just as often as men until the midnineteenth century.[67] As for the lower classes, the street, the tavern, and the pub remained their second home much longer. Even today what Raymond Oldenburg has called the "great good places"—the café, the beauty salon, and the corner tap—are still home to their "regulars, although such places are much reduced in number and only a pale version of their predecessors."[68]

The most important home away from home remained, however, the godly household, incorporating not only natural parents and children but apprentices, servants, lodgers, and anyone assigned to live under its roof. From the sixteenth through the nineteenth centuries, households were large, complex institutions that constituted themselves by recruiting the offspring of other families, usually but not always from less fortunate families. Households were expected to treat their apprentices, servants, and/or slaves in the same way they treated their own children. Everyone in the household was equally subject to the absolute control of the master and mistress and was legally and culturally a "child" of the household for the duration of their residence. Servants, apprentices, and slaves were expected to give their obedience and labor in return for shelter and nurture. For their part, the *Hausvater* and *Hausmutter* were expected to represent the highest standards of parenting, superior to those expected of natural parents, whose attachments to their children were regarded with a certain suspicion.[69]

The Reformation brought exalted status to the patriarch but did not sanctify paternity as such. In a similar way, Protestantism devalued virginity and made it possible for married women and mothers to gain access to spirituality but also made them wholly dependent on the household for this moral status.[70] Fertility alone did not guarantee a woman moral value. Until the midnineteenth century, motherhood was largely subsumed under wifehood, which took on a new aura in the sixteenth century. The treatment of unwed mothers became increasingly harsh during the early modern period as bastardy itself was stigmatized for the first time. While never the equal of her husband, the Protestant wife now stood in relationship to his authority as the priest had once stood in relationship to God—taking an active role in the household, society's moral unit, but often taking a less active role in the public world.

The household was vested with a practical and symbolic importance in the early modern period that it had never had before and has not had since. In the absence of celestial and terrestrial competitors, it became the center of the Protestant universe, providing not only shelter and physical nurture but symbolic comfort through images of a new sainthood, composed of pious patriarchs, "goodwives," and obedient children. This refiguring dispensed with the need for medieval notions of the Holy Family, the cult of Mary, and a host of lesser representational practices that retained currency in Catholic countries and continued to enjoy considerable popular support even in places where religious reform had taken root.

At this stage of economic and political development, the godly household was truly the "little commonwealth," serving not only important economic and political functions but also the vital cultural purpose of holding up to society an ideal vision of itself. In the view of the seventeenth-century English preacher William Gouge: "A family is a little church, and a little commonwealth, at least a *lively representation* thereof, whereby trial may be made of such as are fit for any place of authority, or of subjection, in church or commonwealth."[71]

Before the coming of factory forms of production and the nation-state, the community of godly households was the foundation of both the material and the moral order. Protestants found their models of saintly behavior closer to home than did Catholics. Their imagination no longer dwelt on the heavenly hosts but came down to earth. Eulogies for godly individuals became a standard part of the Protestant funeral service in the sixteenth and seventeenth centuries, and epitaphs to faithful husbands, obedient children, and dutiful wives abounded in American as well as European churchyards. When she died in 1643, Dorothy Dudley was eulogized on her gravestone as a woman "Eminent for Holiness, Prayerfulness, Watchfulness, Zeal, Prudence, Sincerity, Humility, Meekness, Patience, Weanedness from ye World, Self-denial, Publick-Spiritedness, Diligence, Faithfulness & Charity."[72] As Laurel Thatcher Ulrich observes, "It is difficult for us to approach a world in which neither innovation nor individuality was celebrated, in which the rich particulars of daily life were willfully reduced to formulaic abstraction. Yet, the purpose of an epitaph was not to commemorate, but to transcend, personality. A good wife earned the dignity of anonymity."[73]

The image of the goodwife effectively obliterated Dorothy Dudley's actual biography, and the history of her family life goes unrecorded as well, not because it was unavailable to those who grieved her passing but because it was regarded as irrelevant. In the seventeenth century, the epitaph was not meant to remember the person but to remind everyone of a certain type of person. In Dorothy Dudley's world, it was still considered unseemly to commemorate the living. Lives were usually summed up at the end rather than narrated throughout life, as we have become accustomed to doing. Few people wrote their autobiographies, and those who did paid much less attention to their early years than to their later years, presenting their "journey of life" in spiritual rather than social terms. Posthumous eulogies and biographies followed the same pattern, presenting what seems to us oddly impersonal, static portraits of their subjects. But such portraits were typical of the culture and the time, when all literature and art was designed not "to show us a person, but a kind of person," in effect sustaining an image of the good family life rather than representing its reality.[74] The particularities of a life were less important than the generalities that could be drawn from it. Until the late eighteenth century, "lives were conceived not as diachronic continuities but as instances of constant, universal principles."[75] No doubt, Dorothy Dudley lived a life far richer and more complex than her epitaph reveals, but it was not important to ensure that all her contemporaries remember its details so long as God remembered it. Until the nineteenth century, that was what really counted.[76]

Of course, we will never know whether Dorothy and the other domesticated saints of the reformed movement were the perfect fathers, mothers, and children they were made out to be. We can be reasonably sure that the new saints did not regard themselves in this light, for the sin of pride was something good Protestants avoided at all cost. What we can be certain of is that, unlike Catholics, they no longer had to renounce the world in order to find models to imitate.

In Protestant lands, but also in much of Catholic Europe, the concentration of production in the household, as well as its political and religious responsibilities, left little time or space exclusively for the nuclear family or for those occasions that today are exclusively home-centered. Christmas was more a public than a domestic celebration until the late nineteenth century, and neither birth nor death were completely domesticated until the industrial era. Contrary to myths about the universality of both home birth and home death, the preindustrial household made no formal provision for either the beginning or the ending of life.

But it was not just the household's busy schedule and crowded spaces that drove people to find comfort elsewhere. Equally important in earlier centuries was the nature of public space, which afforded a sense of place the ordinary house could not. Ancient and medieval cities and towns functioned effectively as memory sites, as did the precapitalist countryside, whose man-made as well as natural features were sufficiently enduring to be used to construct individual and collective memory.[77] Before the nineteenth century, a particular house was more likely to disappear than a tree or a market cross. Individual houses were neither numbered nor named, but people found their way by other signs, invisible to us but constituting the visual vocabulary of place that allowed them to feel at home in the world beyond their own residences.

Eighteenth-century people had the same intimate and even personal relationships with town- and landscapes that we do with houses. Homesickness, a term that did not come into the English language until the late eighteenth century, referred more to territories than to houses. Reportedly, the first sufferers were late seventeenth–century Swiss mercenaries who were diagnosed as troubled by the "continuous vibration of animal spirits through the fibres of the middle brain in which the impressed traces of ideas of the Fatherland still cling."[78] It is not at all surprising that people feared the loss of place more than the loss of dwellings, for only a minority had a house they could call their own, while many more had rights in the parishes where they dwelled. Europeans who had migrated to North America were more likely to be home owners than those who stayed behind, but our myth of the frontier homestead grossly exaggerates the number of Americans who had a home of their own until this century.

Before the nineteenth century, only a minority of adult propertied males were householders in the full legal and economic sense of that term. The rest of the population—including all young people through their midtwenties, most females (with the exception of propertied widows), and all propertyless men—lived either under someone else's roof or in temporary shelters of one kind or another. Yet they were not defined as homeless, for as long as people "knew their place" and were part of someone else's household, they were at home in the world and no threat to the patriarchal order. Our idea that good order rests on everyone having a home and family was to them a formula for chaos; when this idea was first raised during the English Revolution of the seventeenth century, it was quickly put down by every means possible.[79]

Even though the householding elite remained longer in one place than their constantly changing housefuls of servants, apprentices, elderly boarders, and visiting kinfolk, they were not particularly home-centered. Their "home" was also the fields and marketplaces, and women as well as men were as "at home" outside the house as within it. The house was measured by its utility, valued for its warmth in winter, spoken of in the same terms as a bird's nest or an animal's burrow, but readily left behind in the summer months when the barns or yards provided more commodious and comfortable places for eating and sleeping.[80] In short, the house did not occupy the same place in the temporal or spatial imagination that the modern home does. It was a place of the moment, neither anticipating the future nor recalling the past. Before the nineteenth century, people could have cared less about old things. They stored their memories elsewhere, and when they dreamed, it was not of houses. Prior to the nineteenth century, ghosts tended to haunt bridges and marketplaces rather than dwellings.[81] Life flowed through the house, but it was not yet the special place of beginnings and endings that it would later be imagined to be.

As long as they were in familiar territory, people felt at home not just in their own place of residence but in all local households. In both Europe and North America, visitors arrived at any time of the day or night. Everyone would be accommodated in the big room around the hearth. If there were not enough beds, the people would double up. Such practices existed in rural North Carolina until this century: "Why we didn't never get lonesome. . . . Boys them days be courting; lots of them lived far off. They'd spend the night, and eat supper and breakfast."[82]

In a society where the boundary between locals and strangers always lay just beyond the horizon, the domestic threshold had very little meaning. People came and went unceremoniously, as they still did in rural Ireland up to a couple of decades ago. As in Balleymenone, "the door, open on good days, unlocked at night, offers no resistance, swinging often to let people out and in. Visitors do not pause at the threshold, so the community extends smoothly from the grassy fields to every fire, incorporating all kitchens within its territory. The community is precisely the space linking the hearths."[83] Visitors passed directly into the core of the house, a single large room, often called "the house," where the fire burned continuously.[84] Entry halls were absent in all but the largest dwellings, and everyone had immediate access to the hearth, where all the household activities—work and leisure, sleeping as well as eating—took place.

There are few accounts of what it was like to enter an eighteenth-century house, simply because the threshold was not marked and the process of entry was unremarkable. This remained the case in many rural places up to just a few decades ago. When Henry Glassie visited Balley-menone in the 1960s, he found that Irish folk felt at home at one another's hearths. He describes their kitchens as

> gracefully vulnerable, open and occupied. People from without pierce quickly to its center, where a fire burns, ready to boil for tea. People within must pass through the kitchen as they move from space to space, and as they do, they orient themselves by the hearth, gauging every movement as carrying them up or down. When the motion stops, people are usually in the kitchen, at the hearth. There they sit, ready to give talk and aid, ready for encounter to eventuate in union.[85]

Before the modern era, most interiors were essentially the same. Domestic space was functional rather than decorative, and the furniture was designed to be moved around according to circumstances.[86] Houses' rhythms were dictated by the seasons, by the communal calendar, and by patterns of production, which overrode the cycles of individuals and families. We think a family requires a house, but in those days it was the house that required a family. Like a modern office or factory, the house was an institution with a set of well-defined roles that required a certain complement of persons. When the nuclear family was not sufficient to fill these, strangers were readily recruited. Depending on its function, the size of the household could vary from a nuclear core to dozens of persons, but it did not change much over time. When a couple was young, servants and apprentices filled in, leaving when children were old enough to take over.[87]

In the eighteenth century, changing places was more a practical than a symbolic matter. A new child was expected to fit into the existing space; new couples replaced old without changing anything about the house. Being able to marry depended on one's ability to establish and maintain a household, and when a couple could make no such guarantee, the community was either ready to deny them access to nuptials or, if more favorably disposed, willing to assist them, as the Welsh put it, in "starting their world." This sometimes took the form of a house-raising, but more often a community collected subscriptions of money, food, and other necessary household items, which were as much a gift to the house as to its occupants.[88] Our ideal of starting a home from scratch, buying all new furniture, was not only unaffordable but unthinkable.

Those who assisted in establishing a household subsequently made sure that it lived up to communal standards. People had no hesitation about intervening in the lives of others when they feared that domestic disputes threatened their collective well-being. Religious congregations took similar responsibilities upon themselves, insisting on approving all marriages, interceding in domestic disputes, and supporting broken families. It was difficult to keep anything from neighbors, and behavior norms as well as householding standards were clearly defined and strictly observed throughout the late eighteenth and early nineteenth centuries.[89]

Over the course of a lifetime, the ordinary early modern American or European would have lived in many houses, regarding none of them as special. The nostalgia for the childhood home that is endemic in our time did not exist; when in 1762 James Woodford's cousin Bob announced he was "going home," he was speaking not, as we would assume, of returning to his family or place of origin but simply of the place where he was employed.[90] As long as each person knew his or her place, rich and poor, related and unrelated, could occupy the same space without threatening anyone's personal or collective identity. In the late eighteenth and early nineteenth centuries, the sense of place was strong enough to serve everyone as long as all accepted the inequalities and hierarchies involved. Housing was very unevenly distributed, but even the houseless were not homeless in the contemporary understanding of the term.

Protestantism "broke the continuity, cut the umbilical cord between heaven and earth, and thereby threw man back upon himself in a historically unprecedented manner."[91] Even with the cosmos and its archetypes brought down to earth, however, religion and community, not the biological family, continued to provide the safest storage for all that previous generations held dear. The death of the cosmic archetype and its replacement by the communal exemplar coincided with the abandonment of the traditional calendar of holiness and the pilgrimage sites that still sustained the Catholic faithful. But if Protestants were finding their icons closer to home, they did not necessarily expect to find them within their own families of origin or marriage. Their saints were part of their communities, but nobody expected every family to live up to the highest standards. Not every woman who bore a child needed to be a model of motherhood; not every man who fathered a child was considered a father figure. And prior to the nineteenth century, whose child you were depended more on circumstance than on biology.

The distinction between family and the good family life held firm right through the eighteenth century.[92] As long as it prevailed, images of godly

households and holy families were fully compatible with comic, even profane representations of ordinary family life. In the eighteenth century, it
was possible for artists like William Hogarth to ridicule mothers and fathers
and lampoon children with impunity. Popular theatrical and graphic depictions of ordinary families presented them in all their messy, violent reality,
something our modern media feel uncomfortable in doing. As long as a few
godly households sustained the ideal, the foibles of families were fair game
for writers and artists.[93]

   In the past, images of the good family life were relatively invulnerable.
Today we panic at even the smallest dose of family reality. The case of middle-class unwed motherhood presented in the television series *Murphy
Brown* was taken as proof by many Americans of the death of family values.
Although Vice President Dan Quayle's denunciations of Murphy Brown did
not swing the popular vote in the Republican Party's favor in 1992, its symbolism has become even more potent over time. Today both Democrats
and Republicans deploy equally apocalyptic visions of family decline and
social disorder. And although most Americans do not believe their own
family life to be in immediate danger, they are quick to perceive their
neighbors as being in total disrepair. Lacking those cosmic and communal
archetypes that reassured our ancestors, we have become ever more vulnerable to the modern prophets of family decline.

CHAPTER 3

Life and Death
in a Small Parenthesis

> Time is not given but . . . fabricated. Chronotypes are themselves temporal and plural, constantly being made and remade at multiple individual, social, and cultural levels. . . . They change over time and therefore have a history or histories.
> John Bender and David Wellbery, *Chronotypes*[1]

W E LIVE WITH our allotted time, but also by our images of time, our chronotypes, which allow us to live meaningfully with temporal constraints and with the overwhelming fact of human existence: finitude.[2] The imagined times of our lives function in the same way as do our imagined families, and are just as historically mutable. The modern notion of the lifetime—a vector of time divided into a series of distinct ages that occur at standardized intervals and in the same sequence in the life of every person—is just one of several chronotypes that have been invented by mankind to give meaning to human temporality.[3] We like to think that we have discovered the secret of aging, but in fact it too is one of our inventions. As with so much else that constitutes our so-called facts of life, childhood, youth, middle age, and old age are cultural creations. They are the modern Western solution to the universal human quest for what Barbara Adam has called "time-transcendence": "having a relationship to our own finitude, accommodating a temporal world to the principles of permanence."[4] In every known society, people have invented and reinvented the ages they live by, representing these to themselves as given and unalterable. The age-graded lifetime is our modern answer to an eternal question, but it is only one answer among many.

To be sure, the real time that people in the past had at their disposal was very different from the time we have today. Before the middle of the nineteenth century, Europeans and Americans lived on average only two-thirds the number of years we do. Significantly, however, they never knew when to expect the Grim Reaper, for mortality came to every age group and not preponderantly to the elderly, as it does today. While their lives were shorter and more uncertain, they did not necessarily long for the longevity we have come to crave, for their chronotypes allowed them to live with their allotted time and gave meaning to lives that seem to us to have been nasty, brutish, and short. They imagined that the end was near, yet death did not hang over them as it does over us; they accepted mortality and could imagine an immortality beyond time itself, while we, unable to accept mortality, have substituted longevity for eternity. "The price of exchanging immortality for health," Zygmunt Bauman has pointed out, "is life lived in the shadow of death; to postpone death, one needs to surrender life to fighting it." Modernity, he notes, "deconstructed mortality one cannot overcome into a series of afflictions one can."[5]

Able to imagine something beyond time, something eternal, our ancestors were able to disconnect aging and death from biology as such. Aging meant to them something very different from what it means for us.[6] It was understood that one could age spiritually at a rate quite different from that by which one aged biologically. "Just as we speak of bodily age, whereby we proceed from infancy to boyhood . . . and so forth . . . so spiritual age is a progress from virtue to virtue, from grace and grace, from good to better, from perfection to greater perfection," wrote Thomas, Bishop of Brinton, in 1380.[7] We have great difficulty imagining aging apart from the physical body, but they had no difficulty accepting the miracle of the *infantia spiritualis*, the holy or wise child, or the child prodigy. For the same reasons, they were prepared to believe stories of persons who lived hundreds of years.[8]

By contrast, we live, literally as well as symbolically, by the numbers. While most people in the past were quite unsure of their exact chronological ages, we mark each passing year. This is not to say that earlier generations were unaware of deterioration of the mind and body or the finitude of life. The facts of life caused them no less anxiety than we feel and, in the absence of modern medicine's capacity to relieve pain and suffering, probably more. However, they had images, rituals, and symbols to assuage their fears and make sense of life as worth living. The differences between us and them, then, lie not only in the actual amount of time allotted us by historical circumstances but in our images of time. Their images of time were cosmic and communal; ours are much more personal and individualized.[9] Their models of aging, of the good life and the good death, were provided either by supernatural beings or by certain exemplary persons. We find our images much closer to home, in our own bodies or the bodies of those we are closest to, usually family members on whom we have become dependent for our images of the good death as well as the good life.

We are in the unique position of being able to represent age and aging to ourselves, but doing so places us under an enormous obligation that earlier generations did not have to face. Just as they were able to store their ideals of the good family life at a cosmic or communal level, beyond the reach of time and their own grim domestic realities, so they were also able to find comfort in transcendent ideals of the good birth and the good death without fearing that, if they did not live by the same standards, they would automatically be called failures. We, who have placed ourselves under the obligation to age successfully and to live long and healthy lives, find ourselves tortured by our inability to live up to our numerical norms. This is not to say that people in the past aged better or worse than we do. "The past does not have 'answers' for the present," cautions Thomas R. Cole. "It does, however, contain the fundamental human stock of ideas, images, beliefs, wishes, superstitions, feelings, dreams, hopes, and fears about aging."[10]

All peoples attempt to form what David Cheal has called temporal convoys, individuals who share a common sense of time, sustaining one another through the difficulties of life's journey.[11] The convoy metaphor summons up an image of safety from the dangers lurking just below the surface, and indeed, temporal convoys offer us reassurance against the ravages of time and the fact of human finitude. In the past, temporal convoys were provided largely by church and community. The models of aging that people lived by were not their relatives or even their friends, but religious archetypes and communal exemplars. Church and community also provided the rites of passage between one phase of life and another, as well as the models of the good life and the good death. They launched the temporal convoys that allowed earlier generations to pilot through the rough seas of time to the safe harbor with God in an eternity beyond time itself.

Because we form our temporal convoys largely with family, family members' aging and death have a much greater impact on us. It is not that people in the past were less caring, but that they found themselves in convoy with a larger circle.[12] The Catholic church provided a huge repertoire of saintly aging and dying, while Protestantism tended to locate its exemplars closer to home, though still at some distance from the nuclear family. By the seventeenth and eighteenth centuries, the masters and mistresses of godly households were providing most of the images of the good life and the good death for northwestern Europe and North America. This role put a great burden on a relatively few persons, but as long as they were willing to act out the great public passages of life—birth, marriage, and death—the rest of the population had reassuring images to live by.

It was God's, not man's, time that Europeans and Americans lived by before the nineteenth century. The God of the Judeo-Christian tradition was a temporal god whose first act had been to divide day into night, thereby creating a sense of time for his chosen people to live by. By laying down a seven-day cycle, Yahweh created a calendar that set the Jews apart from all other peoples.[13] Even when they no longer had a place to call their own, they had a time, the Sabbath, that was strictly theirs, an important resource for Jewish identity over the centuries.[14] The God of the Christians was also a temporal deity, operating in history, shaping it to his will, and demanding that believers suspend all other time in obedience to his. In expectation of the Second Coming, the early Christians abandoned ordinary time and lived in expectation of that moment. The waiting became unbearable by the second century, when they established their own religious routines, but the theocentric notion of time would remain a part of Christian theology, giving believers their own version of the Sabbath, which also maintained their unique collective identity no matter where they found themselves.

Living by God's time alone proved very difficult for most Christians, however. For most of the Middle Ages, only monks and nuns were privileged to live strictly by a divine clock and calendar. They were subjected to an otherworldly asceticism from which the laity and most of the regular clergy were exempted. Ordinary people crafted their own sense of time out of materials closer to hand: the harvest, the seasons, the biological rhythms of the body. Like the earliest measures of space—the foot and the hand—time was measured in terms of bodily functions. They talked in terms not of minutes or hours but of the time it took to milk a cow, or a "pissing while."[15] The temporal discipline of the holy orders had no place in lay life during the Middle Ages. Rabelais was reflecting the popular attitude of his time when he wrote, "Never will I subject myself to the hours, hours are made for men and no man for hours. . . . I treat time like stirrups, which I shorten or lengthen as I please."[16]

The medieval church was very accommodating when it came to the times that ordinary rural people had traditionally lived by. It took into account that most believers would continue to live close to the rhythms of agriculture and, as it went about converting the indigenous population of Europe, it allowed its own calendar of holy days to be coordinated with the ancient pagan chronotypes that had honored the movements of the sun and the moon, the changes of season, and human as well as animal rhythms. The church transformed preexisting pagan occasions into saints' and other holy days. The midsummer solstice became Saint John's Day, and the Christmas season took its shape from pagan winter festivals. By the late Middle Ages, Christian time had acquired an astonishing nuance and complexity. The year was punctuated not only by 180 official holy days but also by many local festival times that filled each year, month, week, and day with meaning. Christian and pagan times became so completely commingled that it was no longer possible to distinguish one from other.

The medieval image of both time and history was a wheel, endlessly turning. Life was also seen as a cycle from womb to tomb, not as a linear development through a fixed set of ages ending with death, as we conceive it. Imagined as a wheel of fortune, life was perceived as unpredictable, as "nothing so endless, nothing sooner broke."[17] People of all ages were equidistant from death, that unpredictable event that broke the cycle to open the way to eternal life.[18] Birth and death simply happened. In an era before anyone had the power to control birth or postpone death, these events could be awaited but not anticipated. Time was not man's to give, and any attempt to do so was a challenge to the divine will. And while our ancestors were obsessed with divining the right moment to give birth, to marry, even to die—and attempted to do so using a variety of rituals and symbols that brought some sense of order into their very uncertain lives— this concern was complementary to their belief that events were ultimately beyond human control, that there was no way to stretch the amount of time allotted to each life.

The understanding of time that the Renaissance inherited from the Middle Ages was equally self-contained; it did not stretch infinitely into past or future but was, as Donald Gifford has described it, a "closed medium in which events in succession were dominated by the specter of human mortality." He cites Sir Thomas Browne, whose own life spanned almost seventy years in the seventeenth century and whose understanding of time was typical of his day: "Think not thy time short in this world, since the world itself is not long. The created world is but a small parenthesis in eternity: and a short imposition, for a time, between such a state of duration as was before it and may be after it."[19]

Sir Thomas's chronotype, a legacy of the Middle Ages, was already under challenge by some of his contemporaries, but it is utterly different from our own understanding of a lifetime. When we think of eternity, we think of infinity, but Browne did not. Eternity existed on a plane transcendent over both human time and human history. It bracketed life at each end with birth and death, making it impossible for Browne and his contemporaries to imagine neither prelife nor afterlife in temporal terms. A newborn had no prenatal history, and the deceased also existed beyond time.[20] Before the nineteenth century, neither heaven nor hell were imagined to have a temporal dimension.[21] Souls flew off to heaven or to hell, where they existed without further development for time eternal.

Browne and his contemporaries had no desire to fight mortality, to make life last beyond its appointed time. They evinced no desire to save or preserve time, to restore old things. Nor did they want to see beyond the present into the future, for they had little curiosity about times other than their own. Eternity seemed as real to them as it seems unreal to us. For them, it was the past and the future that lacked substance; this perception underlay their lack of any desire to extend life. It was eternity rather than longevity that medieval people desired and that motivated them to keep the boundaries around their small parenthesis firm: they ritually welcomed the infant into the world from its previous state of nonexistence by the ritual of baptism, and the church's last rites speeded the souls of the dead on their way to eternity. The beginnings and endings of life were no less mysterious to them than they are to us, but they managed to reduce their fear of their own finitude by imagining an eternity that existed beyond time and was immune to its ravages.

The collective history of mankind was also seen as a closed system with an abrupt beginning and an equally abrupt ending. There was no concept of prehistory—that other kind of history, natural or otherwise, that we think of as preceding our own. The idea of the prehistoric was inconceivable, but so too was the posthistoric time we imagine through science fiction and futurology.[22] Because time extended neither very far back nor very far forward, the present seemed reasonably capacious, even when average longevity was not much more than forty years for both men and women. Of course, those like Browne who survived the early years of life had a good chance of living much longer than forty years. Nevertheless, because the death rate for every age group was higher than it is today, people were faced with the fact that their lives could end at any time.

The perpetual possibility of premature death may well have contributed to the unwillingness of Browne's contemporaries to think beyond the small parenthesis, yet the relative insecurity of life only partly answers the question of why they were so much less obsessed with longevity than we are. More fundamental is the fact that the time they lived by and attached the greatest meaning to was not their own but God's. They had no great desire to establish a right relation to their own time, to their own aging bodies, for their primary duty was to establish a right relationship with the Creator.

With eternity occupying the space we would assign to the past and the future, people of the Middle Ages and the Renaissance were protected against feeling overwhelmed by the weight of the former or the uncertainty of the latter. For ordinary people, history began only one or two generations back. Their sense of the past did not extend much beyond the "living memory" of the village elders, and their futures were similarly foreshortened, so that they felt the present to be more capacious than we could ever imagine.[23] The educated elites were aware of the longer sweeps of time, but their horizons were also remarkably limited by modern standards. It was not until the seventeenth century that anyone cared to fix a date for the divine events recounted in the Book of Genesis, but when Archbishop James Ussher did so in 1650, he reckoned the Creation to have happened only a few thousand years earlier: at 9:00 A.M. on October 26, 4004 B.C.[24] The archbishop's precise dating was consistent with the old view that history, like life, was a closed system bounded by very clear beginnings and endings.

To us, Sir Thomas's idea of the small parenthesis seems intolerably confining. We like pasts that run deep and futures that remain open. We have developed an aversion to both clear beginnings and abrupt endings. However, prior to the nineteenth century, Western culture seems to have been quite comfortable with the fact that women and men lived close to their beginnings and their endings. This fact colored not only their sense of history but their understanding of their own age and the ages of other family members, to which they paid less attention than they did to the birth and death dates of their favorite saints. By and large, they were content to live in what Saint Augustine called the "present of things present" (*Confessions*, XI.20.26).[25]

This conception of life as lived in a capacious present survived in parts of rural Europe and North America until quite recently. Henry Glassie found it alive and well in 1960s Balleymenone, a townland in Northern Ireland. There people were much more concerned with middles than with beginnings or endings. "They craft centers with care, leave edges ragged, letting the whole take care of itself," Glassie observed. In Balleymenone, people put little effort into remembering their own birth dates or those of family and friends. The times of their lives, which they called the "Great Days," were moments when "time spreads both ways, backward and forward, to form seasons; seasons become years, years lost in time."[26]

Numerical age had similarly little meaning for most people before the nineteenth century. Time, measured out in quantitative units of years, months, weeks, and days, mattered less to both the individual and the community.[27] There were no standard systems of timekeeping as we know them today. Each locality kept its own kind of time, and the number of time zones was virtually infinite. As late as 1870, the United States had two hundred.[28] Each village had its own peculiar calendar; each household counted time according to its own requirements. Time had not yet separated itself from place. "When" was largely determined by "where," for few told time by means of a clock, relying instead on the much less precise but no less certain sense of what was happening around them. Evening began when the cows came home; night came when everyone went to bed; morning announced itself by the crowing of the cock or the smell of the cooking fire.[29]

Age was equally dependent on place. Most rural people could not tell their numerical age with any great precision, but they could make rough calculations of how young or old a person was by his or her relationship to certain remembered events—a saint's day, a flood, a harvest. When a manor court in England acted to determine the exact age of William Fish in 1602, it called a number of witnesses, including Thomas Storr, who testified that he knew William had been born in August because he remembered Fish's father, John, coming to him "when he was mawing [mowing] berlie [barley], to request him to be a wyntness [witness] at the baptisme of the said William." Storr's way of measuring the years that had elapsed was simple. He counted them by "the cropps of corne sowne since that tyme." The midwife, Johanna Craven, confirmed his recollection: "She was the keper [nurse] of his mother when she lay in childebedd of the said William and that was upon Bartholomewe day which letter her going to Stockwith fare [fair]."[30] Time was still measured this way in rural England as late as the First World War, when children, asked to give their birthdays, replied: "Our Charlie's birthday is when they cuts the corn, and Alice's is when they ears the corn."[31]

Until the nineteenth century, most individuals were at the beck and call of households, guilds, the church, and the community, whose imperatives largely determined the movement and sequencing of their lives. Life was more situational and more spontaneous. It was lived day to day, year to year, within that small parenthesis in which there was little planning for the future. Absolute age was less important than relative age, for it was not how old you were but whether you were a younger son or eldest daughter that determined your educational or marriage chances. How young or old you were depended less on numerical age than on your place in the hierarchical system of single-family households, a condition that held true among the working classes even into this century. Winifred Foley, who was born into a poor English miner's family at the turn of the twentieth century, remembered that "in families like ours, there were only three important birthdays in your youth; the one marking your arrival into the world; the fifth, which meant you could go to school and leave a bit of room under mother's feet; and the fourteenth. This birthday meant, for a daughter, that she was old enough to get her feet under someone else's table [earning her own room and board in service]; in the case of a son, that he could follow his father down the pit." The final birthday was not a happy moment for Winifred, who found herself under pressure to accept a change she was not prepared for. When her mother told her that once in service she would have to give up her childhood, including the name she had always gone by, she felt that she did not want to be "a young 'oman, a Winifred, just Polly."[32]

As in some contemporary African societies, the assignment of age was also more a matter of social negotiation than of automatic assignment by numbers of years.[33] Well into the nineteenth century, working people were still compelled to underreport their age if they were to get work and stay out of the dreaded workhouse. When Frederick Bettesworth died in late nineteenth-century Surrey, his relations did not know what age to mark on the coffin. George Bourne, who knew the old man well, wrote that "Bettesworth wished me to think him younger than he was. But it is quite possible that he was not himself certain of his own age."[34] For most of human history prior to the twentieth century, only elites were entitled to celebrate and mark birthdays and anniversaries. All other men and women had their ages defined for them.

The place someone occupied in the household was the best indicator of whether he or she was perceived as young or old. As in Winifred Foley's family, the needs of the household economy determined when a girl became a woman. A laborer like Fred Bettesworth had little chance of ever being considered a man in the full sense of the term, for his menial position defined him as one of the "lads" regardless of age, just as in America a black man was always a "boy" regardless of his years. Old people were very reluctant to retire from being the active head of a farm or small business because doing so deprived them of the status of an elder in the community. They therefore entered into negotiations with their heirs to establish both written and implicit understandings about the honor and respect they would be accorded in retirement.[35]

Acquiring the status of an elder was not just a function of being elderly, and not every child was guaranteed a childhood. These chronotypes seem to have worked reasonably well, though they often led to people of the same age being on very different schedules. Ages of entry into work and school varied enormously. Even the lives of children of the same family could follow very different paths.[36] The middle years followed no set pattern either, and the age of retirement varied hugely, ranging from the thirties through the eighties.[37]

Numerical age also had very little effect on the decision to marry. Before the nineteenth century, marriage was distributed across a spectrum of ages, with access to an economically viable household the prime determinant of the event. "Do not marry till you find that you can stand on your own legs," a seventeenth-century father told his son.[38] People simply did not talk about age as a reason to marry. There was some sense of when it was too early, but it was rarely deemed too late. And the same attitude prevailed toward other life transitions: schooling, leaving home, parenthood, none were determined by numerical age norms or followed in the regular temporal sequences we regard as normal. At schools and universities, young boys shared benches with mature youths. At Oxford University, student ages varied from the early teens to the late twenties until well into the nineteenth century.[39] Nor did it bother anyone that many of these young men repeatedly interrupted their schooling for employment, thus ignoring the sequence of learning and working that we have come to take for granted. No one seemed nervous about precocity before the nineteenth century: although access to power and wealth was generally regulated by rules of seniority, nobody objected when a prodigy stepped out of a line of succession.[40] The youthful appearance of an old person would be remarked on, but it was the spirit rather than the body that mattered most. Many people we would consider too old to hold responsible positions did so. "In a culture that valued eternal life rather than eternal youth, this preference is not surprising," remarks Thomas Cole. "Transcending one's age allowed a person to triumph over secular time, to enter into the timeless world of eternity."[41]

The notion of a continuous lifetime proceeding in a timely and sequenced manner from birth to death was simply unavailable to those who imagined themselves living in the small parenthesis. Their image of life as a wheel of fortune was well suited to contemporary levels of mortality and

mobility. Imagining life in this way made sense to people who had very little control over their own fates. Except for the very rich and powerful, any
effort to plan life would only have been a source of frustration for most people. There was for them no such thing as a life in which one stage led to the
next, in which there was a logical connection between what one did with
one's youth and what one became as an adult. Thus, it is not surprising that
in the Middle Ages life was conceived of as a "series of distinct transits from
one distinct phase to another, rather than a process of continuous development."[42]

Medieval people differed as to just how many phases or "ages of man"
they recognized. Some were satisfied with dividing life into two ages, but
others insisted on three, four, even seven ages. Obviously, there was little
agreement as to the duration of life stages; nor was there much agreement
until the nineteenth century on the images of childhood, youth, maturity,
and old age. Some would have confined youth to the teen years; others saw
it as stretching into the late twenties; still others thought youth ended at
marriage.[43] The various descriptions of middle and old age reflected the
lack of aging norms. It did not really matter if certain ages were skipped
over, repeated, or even omitted entirely. For instance, the man or woman
who did not marry was not violating a norm, for there was still a place for
older single persons in the household. They simply remained "boys" or
"girls" for their entire lives. Most people lived vicariously by the icons of the
ages of man, living them out in their own lives only partially.[44]

Under the conditions of high mortality that prevailed throughout the
Middle Ages, young and old alike had to be prepared for any eventuality.
People "aged" as suddenly as they changed places in the social order. A
young man or woman automatically became an adult upon marriage,
regardless of years, just as the retirement of the head of a household
brought a sense of loss that had nothing to do with physical capacity. Children were taught to prepare for their deaths at very early ages, but they also
learned to be ready for other contingencies as well. Junior members of a
family often found themselves instantly transformed into elders upon the
death or retirement of their parents, and they learned not to be too shocked
by these sudden, apparently premature, reversals.

Today children, especially teenagers, complain that time passes slowly
and that they are ready for life long before it is ready for them. Modern life
suffers from a condition that might be described as postmaturity: life is
lived in slow motion because everything can be anticipated and planned for.
When we are sure of everything, including death, the future always seems
to hang over us. Not only do the young show impatience, but even the old
feel they are ready to die before their time.[45] Our ancestors were more

exposed to death throughout their lives but, because they accepted their own mortality, lived less in its shadow. They had difficulty anticipating or planning for anything, but they also did not have to act their biological age, as we feel compelled to do.

Most Europeans, especially those involved in agricultural and pastoral pursuits, lived by the image of life as a wheel of fortune until the nineteenth century. Beginning in the sixteenth century, however, there emerged among the Protestant urban middle classes of northwestern Europe a new concept of the lifetime as a continuous, spiritual development, what came to be known as the Journey of Life.[46] Catholics still had to leave home, even retreat from the world, in order to pursue spirituality, but Protestants could now attain a measure of holiness through the daily life of their own godly households. The good life came to consist of an orderly movement through childhood and youth to marriage and family, leading ultimately to a reunion with God.

Pilgrimage had been one of the good works by which Catholics had earned admission into heaven, but now Protestants relied entirely on the grace of God, which relieved them of the duty of physical pilgrimage and committed them to a personal asceticism in which every stage of life, every moment, counted equally. The reformers did not wait until the day of death to put things right with God but devoted their entire lifetime to the project. As John Donne put it in a funeral sermon he preached in 1628: "Our critical day is not the very day of our death but the whole course of our life."[47] Access to heaven no longer lay, as it did for Catholics, in the last rites, the funeral masses, and the penances paid by grieving family and friends. Purgatory, a place the late Middle Ages had created as a kind of holding pen for the souls whose fate was still to be determined, was banished from Protestant imaginings of the afterlife.[48] There was no longer any way that the living could assist the dead.

The conception of a lifetime as a continuous spiritual journey was consistent with the worldly orientation of the emergent merchant classes.[49] It complemented the rise of the patriarchal household as a spiritual as well as economic center. Initially, the images of the spiritual pilgrims were entirely male, but by the seventeenth century women were included in images of the good lifetime, though their spiritual journeys were invariably portrayed as subordinate to those of men and were played out in the domestic roles of goodwives and mothers. In a similar manner, images of youth were domesticated. An age group that had previously been imagined as brave knights and bonny lasses, venturing far from home, was reconfigured to fit the needs of household production. Henceforth, the ideal was the industrious apprentice and the dutiful daughter.[50]

These new images were no more descriptive of the real life of all young people than the old, but they gave meaning to a new social and economic order based on commercial capitalism, which demanded greater intergenerational continuity and more long-term family planning. Whether the new understandings were causes or effects of commercial capitalism is a question that cannot be answered here. It should be sufficient to point out that Protestantism's innerworldly asceticism, with its emphasis on deferred gratification, would have been impossible to put into practice without the support of images of a continuously developing life in which each age led to the next in an orderly, if not precisely timed, fashion.[51] In the Middle Ages there were too many conflicting lateral obligations to kin, the church, and the community to permit this kind of assured development. We have already seen why multigenerational succession was nearly impossible for all but the very wealthy. Contrary to the way we like to imagine families in the past, sons found it difficult to follow in the footsteps of their fathers, and daughters were just as often unable to model themselves on their mothers.

When legal and social obligations to kin and community began to relax in the fifteenth and sixteenth centuries, it became possible, even necessary, for some families to concentrate their resources on the development of their children. The emerging merchant classes became increasingly reliant on family and kin to accumulate skills and capital.[52] Among this group, parents began to invest both greater time and money in the education of their children while demanding a greater degree of obedience in return.[53] Seeing the child as the guarantee of the family future was something quite new to Western civilization, and an expectation peculiar to the rising Protestant middle classes.[54] They were the first to imagine childhood in terms of development: the young person ceased to be seen as a miniature adult whose nature was fixed from birth. It became the task of parents to be concerned with the child's growth into adulthood.[55] Nevertheless, until the nineteenth century these godly households could not depend exclusively on their own offspring to build their family futures. They remained dependent on the circulation of children to perpetuate themselves, and their definition of the parent-child relationship continued to be suitably flexible.

In spite of these changes, life was still not conceived of as a predictable sequence of numerically defined ages. Protestants were in some ways even more ambivalent about the clock and the calendar than Catholics. To make way for the spiritual pilgrim's progress, the reformers had cleared away the clutter of Catholic holidays and festivals, giving believers direct access to the time of the Almighty and allowing them to form with him, as the most significant other, a personal convoy through the dangerous waters of time.

A God who made and remade time by his own inscrutable will could not be worshiped on schedule; some early Protestant sects rejected both the notion of the Lord's Day and sacred places of worship because they believed that the believer must be ready to worship God at any time and in any place. More conservative Protestantism would ultimately restore regular places and times of worship, but all true Protestant believers would continue to be painfully aware that the time they were living on was God's, not their own, and that they had to be prepared to meet their maker on his schedule, not theirs. In the sixteenth and seventeenth centuries, they prayed by the roadside, confessed to their diaries, and fasted whenever they sensed the approach of divine disapproval.[56]

Protestantism did not strive for personal longevity any more than Catholicism did, but the new notion of the journey of life gave credence to the idea that those who lived a long life were blessed by God. Even as age drained them physically, the elderly were assumed to be closer to salvation. Although older people were not always treated well, their contemporaries looked beyond their degenerated bodies for signs of spiritual vitality. Protestants tended to pay more attention to the later years than the early ones because the end of life was regarded as the most portentous time of life: it was then that God's will could be most clearly perceived. In recollections of the lives of model men and women of the community and in seventeenth- and eighteenth-century autobiographies, it was not their childhoods but their later years that were given most attention.[57] A long life was supposed to be providential, and pious elders were treated as "visible monuments of sovereign grace."[58]

A long life, perceived as a precious gift from God, was something to be prized, even venerated, but until the nineteenth century no one thought they had any right to, or much control over, their own longevity.[59] As long as they saw time as a gift of God, Protestants were no more tempted than Catholics to make much of birthdays and anniversaries. Their gaze remained firmly fixed on destinations rather than origins, and it was only in old age that they began to number their days with any regularity.[60] And even then, they used the numerical markers by which we get our temporal bearings to disconnect from time, to seek the eternal. Birth dates called for no celebration. They were moments for the individual to make himself or herself right with God's timetable. If people noted their birth dates at all, they did so, as William Gladstone did, to contemplate not beginnings but endings. He regarded his diary as "an account book of the all precious gift of Time," and he used it on his twenty-eighth birthday to record his view of that day: "May the day of my birth bring to my mind the consideration of the day of my death."[61]

Earlier generations may have had only hazy notions about the beginnings of life, but they had a very clear vision of the end, for which they were well prepared.[62] The portents that today we attach to the beginnings of life, earlier generations found in endings. The signs of the future we search for in our newborns they looked for in those about to die. When life was lived as a spiritual journey, it was not how long you lived but how well you met your end that really counted. There was then no aura of shame or guilt, no wall of silence, surrounding death. On the other hand, people were expected to put on an appropriate performance, to die well, and any deviation from this norm could produce disappointment in one's contemporaries. When Lord Kames passed away in 1782, James Boswell complained: "I regretted that he did not say one word as a dying man. Nothing edifying, nothing pious."[63]

We would like to think that people in the past died at home surrounded by family, but as we have already seen, mobility and the dispersion of kin made this impossible in most cases. What were called hospitals in the Middle Ages served as hospices for the dying, but medical doctors were almost never at the deathbed. When they had done all they could, the dying person was turned over to the priest or parson, the real specialists in death. When the medical profession took over the hospices in the eighteenth century and began to turn them into something resembling the modern hospital, they made them off-limits to the dying, for medicine still had no answers for the mysteries of death. In the nineteenth century, only the poor died in the hospital, and it was not until much nearer to our own time that death returned there. Until the nineteenth century, death was in the hands of the church or the community, with family playing a secondary role. If they were informed in time, close kin tried their best to reach the dying, but the absence of family was not nearly as disturbing as we might imagine it to have been, because people were accustomed to seeing others die in the presence of strangers and were themselves attracted to the deaths of strangers. The more prominent the person, the more public the death. The death of the head of a royal house was a great spectacle, but even quite ordinary patriarchs and goodwives were expected to die in the prescribed style of the time, offering themselves as exemplars of the good death. Their last moments were carefully recorded and recounted, and it was "death-days" rather than birthdays that were annually remembered.[64]

There is no reason to idealize this way of dying. As in all cultures, people died as they had lived. The poor died alone and in obscurity.[65] Their graves were rarely marked, nor were their lives remembered. Men's deaths attracted more attention than women's, but well into the nineteenth century status was perhaps the most important predictor of the significance of a person's death. Just as there was as yet no universal right to a childhood, to marriage, or to family life as such, so there was no right to die with dignity or to receive a decent burial. The poor were haunted by the prospect of being buried in a pauper's grave, something they did everything they could to avoid.[66]

Death was an event for all ages, and special care was taken to expose children to the dying for the sake of their own education in death. Death was a powerful moment for everyone involved, for it was not only the time when the dying person made last requests of the living—requests that often carried very heavy obligations—but the time when pent-up envy and hostility was released, even in the presence of the dying. As Norbert Elias has observed, premodern life was less restrained and people behaved no differently at death than they did at any other time. The deathbed was the site of great tenderness but also of astonishing cruelty. As with other moments of life, premodern people made little distinction between public and private modes of behavior.[67]

While attracted to the dying, earlier generations were repelled by the dead. For those still living in the small parenthesis, it was very important to maintain the boundary between the living and the dead, for the benefit of both. There is no culture that does not put distance between itself and the dead body, but in the seventeenth and eighteenth centuries the corpse was often disposed of with a haste that seems to us quite indecent. Burial occurred just as soon as it was certain that the spirit of the person had made its safe escape from this world into the next. The bodies of the poor were carted off to common graves and unkempt cemeteries, and even the bodies of the well-to-do were treated in ways that would cause scandal in our society. Below the very highest echelons of society, little time or money was spent on funerals, and the period of formal mourning was extremely brief even by today's standards.

It must be remembered that Christians had never been very respectful of the body or the nature it symbolized, and so it is not surprising that the burial practices of the seventeenth and eighteenth centuries involved quick disposal. Christianity offered the greatest denial of the body of all, namely, the idea of the immortality of the soul, an idea that also explains the ways in which the aging body and the corpse were treated before the midnineteenth century.

For us, our own bodies and those of family members have become the sole means of representing aging and death. Today, decay and dying can never cause anything but a sense of dread, a reminder of our impermanence and the finitude we are all too aware of. Having lost the ability to distinguish between physical and spiritual aging, we have become obsessed with our aging bodies, desperately trying to shape and transform them to ward off the terrors of time. But, as we shall see, we will also do almost anything to keep the dead alive, haunting them in a way that our ancestors would have found distasteful, even blasphemous. The distinction earlier generations made between physical and spiritual aging, between time and eternity, allowed them to see something more than wrinkles when they encountered old people and to perceive something more than a failing body when they gathered to witness the dying. We would not for a minute wish to experience the levels of morbidity and mortality they endured, but we cannot but be intrigued by the chronotypes that allowed them to grapple with the inevitabilities wrought by time. In the same way that they could feel at home away from home in the families of strangers, they found a relationship to their own finitude in the lives and deaths of cosmic and communal figures no longer available to us as we struggle with the same problem.

PART II

Enchanting Families
The Victorian Origins
of Modern Family Cultures

CHAPTER 4

A World of Their Own Making

The members of a family—parents and their young children—
inhabit a world of their own making, a community of feeling and
fantasy, action and precept.
Gerald Handel and Robert Hess, *Family Worlds*[1]

BIOLOGY BY ITSELF is incapable of providing us with a habitable world.
Unlike animals, humans must be born twice, once physically and a second
time culturally, for only culture can provide us with the sense of security
and direction that to animals is instinctual. The symbolic universes we
inhabit are populated with our significant others, with meaningful objects,
and with the times and places we hold sacred. Constituting our mental
maps and calendars, they provide us in a magical way with a sense of order
and predictability that allows us to cope with the chaos of daily life.[2] Symbolic universes vary from culture to culture, and over time as well as space.
What sets the modern era apart is its dependence on the smallest of all possible symbolic universes—the communities of feeling and fantasy we call

our family worlds, worlds of our own making that, as such, are subject to all the foibles and finitudes of human existence.[3]

For centuries, Europeans and Americans relied on symbolic universes much larger and in many ways more stable and enduring than those we now inhabit. Before Christianity banished the pagan gods and goddesses, the natural world had been alive with meaning. And so too was the household, haunted by the spirits of the dead and inhabited by a complement of domestic deities. Once the church stripped the flesh-and-blood world of its sacred power, Catholics came to depend for their sense of continuity and security on heavenly hosts. Protestants brought religion back down to earth in what Peter Berger rightly calls an "audacious attempt to conceive of the entire universe as being humanly significant," but their effort to live solely on God's time, oriented toward a home in heaven, disenchanted the world still further.[4] In the seventeenth and eighteenth centuries, the household gods and goddesses seemed to be gone forever. Magic was by then in full retreat, and if the spirits still haunted the dark margins of civilization, they dared not enter godly households.

When Thomas Clarkson visited American and English Quakers in the early 1800s, he found a wholly disenchanted domesticity, simple and unadorned; one domestic space was indistinguishable from any other. Not only was there no sign of the icons and religious pictures found in Catholic homes, but the Quakers, and most other Protestants, felt no need to display images or reminders of loved ones. There were no "portraits either of themselves, or any of their families, or ancestors, except in the latter case, they had been taken before they became Quakers," because, he reported, "they had but a mean idea of their images. They were of the opinion, also, that pride and self-conceit would be likely to arise to men from the new and ostentatious parade of their own persons."[5]

Clarkson found no mirrors either, for Quakers did not like to reflect on themselves, either literally or figuratively. Reliant on the memory of God alone, they were repelled by all physical monuments. Their graves were simply marked, and their mourning was "worn in the mind." Memory was to be "perpetuated rather in loving hearts, and kept alive in the edifying conversation of their descendants, [not] in the perishing tablets of canvas fixed upon the walls of their habitations."[6] They cherished no objects and kept nothing except for its use value. Believing their legacy to lie in the next world, they kept in the household nothing that was not useful. The very idea of the antique was unknown at this time, and those family portraits and heirlooms that did exist belonged almost exclusively to the nobility.

The disenchanted household of the eighteenth- and early nineteenth-century Protestant middle classes had a spirit all its own, one that was much more open and informal than we might imagine. By all accounts, life in those households was "injected with spontaneity, amusement, and copious gestures of affection." In the Protestant culture of the Word, the oral mattered much more than the visual. Conversations were as intense as they were animated. Husbands listened to wives, and children were heard as well as seen, their opinions solicited and valued. In a setting where everyone knew his or her place, exchanges between the sexes and across generations posed no threat to the standing order.[7] The formality that we have been led to believe dominated all premodern sociability had no place in the house itself. Conduct books applied only to the public realm; the first domestic etiquette books did not appear until the 1830s.[8]

Protestants had done everything possible to erase the boundary between the sacred and the secular. Distinctions between public and private behavior had no meaning for them, and they did not set aside separate times for family. They treated all the days of the week the same, reserving Sunday as a day of rest on the wholly utilitarian grounds that everyone needed some respite from constant labor. There were no family days in the Protestant annual calendar. Unless Christmas fell on a Sunday, it was treated like any other day, with no special meaning for the family. Baptisms, marriages, and funerals were all treated with a minimum of ceremony, for just as there were no family images, there were no family scenes.[9]

Protestants abhorred all theatricality, associating it with Catholicism and personal inauthenticity. "A true Church keeps simplicity of ceremonies. . . . Outward glory and splendor . . . drawes away the minds of the people," wrote a seventeenth-century Scottish preacher. The most extreme among them, the Quakers, refused even the simplest rituals, including greetings and farewells. They took no stock in names or titles, which they believed to be superficial. They insisted on calling everyone "friend," strangers as well as family members.[10] The equanimity with which Protestants treated their own family members was a product of both their theocentric religious convictions, which made God the sole center of their affections, and their involvement with a world of godly households in which the commandment to honor thy parents applied to all fathers and mothers, not just to one's own. Spouses were warned not to love one another too much, and parents prepared themselves and their children for separation through their daily meditations on death and the ultimate union with the Almighty. The family's image of itself was thin and insubstantial, and the home in heaven presented itself much more vividly than did any earthly dwelling.

Family life was simply part of everyday life, immediate, transparent, and unreflexive, unmediated by any representations of itself, lived on a day-to-day basis, without reference to custom or tradition. The very direct, matter-of-fact way in which parents and children treated one another posed no threat to a society in which the social order was still firmly in place. Parents would never wish to set themselves up as household gods, for there was in the Protestant universe only one divine original; all else was an imperfect copy. The idea of worshiping the child was equally alien. Protestants distrusted all worldly bonds, flesh and blood included, and as late as the 1840s the leading American expert on child care, the Reverend Horace Bushnell, was advocating the "putting out" of children on the grounds that the nuclear family circle was too narrow for Christian nurture.[11]

In the late eighteenth and early nineteenth centuries, the importance of families of strangers and kin increased for the early phases of the Industrial Revolution strained the resources of the nuclear family to its limits. Success in business and farming now demanded an even greater degree of cooperation among households, a strategy the new middle classes capitalized on to build an unprecedented position of wealth and power in a relatively short period of time. At a time when both child and adult mortality remained high, the recruitment of replacements was a vital necessity to any successful farm or small business. Among the new middle classes, the circulation of children actually accelerated, with aunts and uncles acting as surrogate parents and older siblings bringing up younger ones.[12] Instead of contracting, middle-class households expanded to include large numbers of kin as well as the usual complement of servants and live-in laborers.[13]

Probably at no other time in Western family history have kin ties had a greater practical value. Because banks and stock markets were still poorly developed, inheritances, loans from kin, and marriage portions constituted a leading source of the capital that financed the world's first industrial revolutions.[14] Networks of kin also enhanced the marriage prospects of sons and daughters who were not otherwise able to wed on the resources of their family of origin. Cousin/cousin marriages were probably more common during this period than before or after, and in many places community and kin became almost indistinguishable.[15] A young man brought into an uncle's business would end up marrying the daughter of the house; women were encouraged to join their property to that of their brothers' or fathers' business partners.[16] A young Rochdale salesman clearly saw no contradiction between interest and emotion, business and marriage, when he sent his fiancée this poem in 1811:

If the stock of our bliss is in stranger's hands rested
The fund ill-secured oft in bankruptcy ends

But the heart is given bills, which are never protested
When drawn on the firm of Wife, Children and Friends.[17]

The growing strength of the middle classes lay as much in their spiritual as their blood ties, however. Bonds of kinship were often reinforced by kinlike relations with persons of similar religious persuasion, allowing the Protestant bourgeoisie to transcend the limits of locality and to operate on a national and even international basis. The Quakers are the most notable example of this phenomenon, but everywhere in Protestant Europe and North America spiritual families overlapped with kin to a considerable extent, often becoming indistinguishable where there was a strong tendency toward intermarriage among members of the same faith.[18] On such bonds was built the class consciousness that encouraged the bourgeoisie to challenge the aristocratic monopoly of wealth and power.

Those who experienced the first phase of the Industrial Revolution together with the political revolutions of the late eighteenth and early nineteenth centuries saw themselves on the frontier of the unknown, caught between a past that seemed to be receding too rapidly and a future only dimly perceived. It was this sense of limbo that Thackeray was expressing when he wrote in 1860:

> It is only yesterday, but what a gulf between now and then! *Then* was the old world. Stage-coaches, more or less swift, riding-horses, pack-horses, highway-men, knights in armour, Norman invaders, Roman legions, Druids, Ancient Britons painted blue, and so forth—all these belong to the old period. . . . But your railroad starts a new era, and we of a certain age belong to the new time and the old one.[19]

John Stuart Mill called his the "age of transition," a moment when "mankind have outgrown old institutions and old doctrines and have not yet acquired new ones."[20] He and his contemporaries looked back not to recapture a lost past but to orient themselves toward an uncertain future. They thought of themselves as living in a period of "fusion and transition. . . . Old formula, old options, hoary systems are being thrown into the smelting-pot; they are fusing—they must be cast anew: who can tell under what new shapes . . . they will come forth from the moulds?"[21] James Anthony Froude remembered the 1840s as a time when "all around us, the intellectual light-ships had broken from their moorings, and it was then a new and trying experience. The present generation which has grown up in a new open spiritual ocean, which it has got used to and has learned to swim for itself, will never know what it was to find the lights all drifting, the compasses all awry, and nothing left to steer with but the stars."[22]

Indeed, when we take the time to listen to what these early Victorians were actually saying, we discover anguished expressions of "depression and *ennui*," which Matthew Arnold said was the "disease of the most modern societies, the most advanced civilizations!"[23] Walter Pater's evocation of his generation's "inexhaustible discontent, langour, and home-sickness" sounds oddly familiar, a premonition of our own age of angst.[24] Writing in his diary in 1854, John Stuart Mill observed:

> Scarcely any one, in the more educated classes, seems to have any opinions, or to place any real faith in those which he professes to have. ... Those who should be guides to the rest, see too many sides to every question. They hear so much said, or find that so much can be said, about everything, that they feel no assurance in the truth of anything.[25]

The sense of transition applied to family life as much as everything else. In fact, the early nineteenth century saw the most sustained period of experimenting with family and marriage prior to the 1960s and 1970s. Before they settled on what we now think of as the Victorian family, Americans and Europeans tried out a wide range of communal and spiritual options. The early nineteenth century saw the most startling proliferation of families of strangers and homes away from home since the Middle Ages. New father and mother figures rose to meet the need for security and continuity, and people broke with their flesh and blood, not in opposition to religion but in its name, to find shelter in the spiritual families created by the religious revivals that coursed across North America and Europe in the late eighteenth and early nineteenth centuries. Such families were both the product of and the solution to the massive changes associated with the Industrial Revolution, for religious enthusiasms legitimated not only the breakup of old household forms but the creation of new ones. Like the early Christians, those moved by the spirit of revival felt "compelled to forsake father and mother, brother and sister, and in the face of a sneering world, were enabled to take up the cross."[26]

Significantly, women and young people were the first to be "born again" into religious sects that not only described themselves in the egalitarian terms of brotherly and sisterly love but constituted themselves as nonpatriarchal families. Men, especially heads of traditional households, felt threatened by the revivals and the alternative family forms they inspired, but economic change was gradually undermining their base of authority; eventually many would follow their wives and children into the new spiritual families spawned by the revivals.[27]

Evangelical religion was not the only provider of these new families of strangers, however. The rich associational life evident on both sides of the Atlantic in the 1820s and 1830s produced yet another set of options for those seeking the security no longer available through the traditional household. Hard-pressed to raise children properly on the resources of the nuclear family, women joined together in mutual aid societies called maternal associations. These not only assisted mothers in practical ways but provided a whole new vision of motherhood that promised to transform the position of women, especially in relationship to children. Careful not to "derogate from the prerogative of the father, or deprecate the influence which he is capable of exerting upon the character of the family," the maternal associations and mothers' unions nevertheless proclaimed that "the mother's appropriate sphere and pursuits give her a decided advantage in the great work of laying the foundation of future character; inculcating those principles and sentiments [that] are to control the destiny of her children in all future time."[28]

The new vision of motherhood was very difficult to realize under the straitened conditions of a single family and therefore depended on the cooperation of women across households. At this time concepts of home and community expanded again, and innumerable new families of strangers sprang up to serve the needs of young people who could no longer rely on their families of origin. Many of the thousands of friendly societies and mutual aid organizations founded in the early nineteenth century adopted the idiom of brotherhood and sisterhood. For young men with no inheritance to claim, new organizations like the Young Men's Christian Association provided a nurturing culture of thrift, sobriety, and mutual aid, as well as the practical benefits of shelter, food, and companionship. Above all else, they created a new image of youth as a separate stage of life, with its own rights and prerogatives independent of the old patriarchal household.[29] Trade unions and journeymen's associations also used the idiom of brotherhood, and sisterly feelings found expression in a parallel series of female organizations, which also defined a new role for women outside the nuclear family.[30]

Moreover, the patriarchs themselves were being lured into a variety of new organizations—the Masons, Odd Fellows, and a host of temperance fellowships—that provided an alternative definition of manhood: men were encouraged to be more sober, more industrious, and considerably more self-reliant than ever before. Among these fraternal orders, the measure of manliness was no longer the amount of liquor a man could hold, or the degree of patriarchal authority he wielded, but his ability to provide for himself and his family.[31] In this respect, the new men's organizations served to reform fatherhood in the same ways that the maternal associations and mothers' unions reformed motherhood. A new notion of father as provider was being created, not inside the family but outside it. However, until the middle of the century, this new vision, like the new vision of motherhood, remained difficult to realize in the context of the nuclear household. The dependency on cooperation across households drew men to new family-like arrangements, which seemed for the moment to be supplanting the bonds of flesh and blood as what it meant to be family.

The Christian tradition provided many precedents for the redefinitions of family that were taking place in the early nineteenth century. Some attempted to follow the model of the early Christian sects, turning from marriage and procreation entirely and finding their father and mother figures elsewhere. The Englishwoman Ann Lee, an abused wife and frustrated mother who had seen all four of her children die in infancy, took those deaths as a message from God. She claimed that he had revealed to her that "marriage of the flesh is a covenant with death and an agreement with Hell," and she declared that henceforth she was "married to the Lord Jesus Christ. He is my head and my husband, and I have no other." Taking the name "Mother Ann," she became a visionary leader to a following composed mainly of those, including many widowed and deserted women, who were finding that the household economy could no longer support them. Calling themselves Shakers, Mother Ann and her followers emigrated to America in the 1770s. There they founded a series of communities that practiced strict celibacy, renewing themselves solely by recruitment of outsiders—families of strangers in the strictest sense.[32]

The early nineteenth century saw a significant revival of the traditions of celibacy and spiritual marriage, but there were also those who took up another strand of the Judeo-Christian tradition: the practice of polygamy and complex marriage as a valid alternative to the single-family household. Evangelical religion was the source of Joseph Smith's patriarchal vision, which led to the founding of Mormonism and experiments with godly polygamy. The Latter-Day Saints' promise of a better family life converted thousands in both North America and Britain in the 1830s and 1840s.[33] Similar beliefs led John Humphrey Noyes, known to his followers as "Father Noyes," to experiment with equally unconventional forms of reproduction.[34] It is no accident that many of those who turned to these powerful father figures came from broken homes and marriages. Everywhere visions of spiritual regeneration, some of them bordering on the apocalyptic, produced the greatest questioning of conventional marriage and family since the millenarian sects of the Reformation era.

Religion was not the only transport for the new visions of family that were crisscrossing the Atlantic in the early nineteenth century. Robert Owen, the English social reformer who rejected Christianity as the basis for domestic happiness, thought of conventional marriage as "an artificial union of sexes, as devised by the priesthood, requiring single-family arrangements and generating single-family interests." He and his followers gave his ideas concrete form in several settlements they established in England and North America in the 1820s and 1830s. They believed that in cooperative housing, feeding, and educational arrangements "the instinct of the family would, for the first time in human history, become productive of individual felicity and public benefit."[35]

The Owenites conceived of their communities as extended families organized on the basis of egalitarian brotherhood and sisterhood rather than on patriarchal principles. Marriage choices were to be free of all property considerations, and divorce was allowed when love was absent, providing that the offspring of the union were taken care of—in their own case, by the community. To achieve what Owen called the "enlargement of the home," his followers abolished private property and inheritance. All children were to have access to a common heritage. In Owen's extended family, there would be no bastards or orphans. Nor would there be involuntary spinsters or bachelors, deserted mothers or absent fathers, for all young people would have enough to marry on, and men and women would share equally in work and family life to the degree that was humanly possible. As William Thompson wrote enthusiastically to Anna Wheeler in 1825, here was

a better state of society, where the principle of benevolence shall supercede that of fear; where restless and anxious individual competition shall give place to mutual cooperation and joint possession; where individuals, in large numbers male and female, forming voluntary associations, shall become the mutual guarantee to each other for the supply of all useful wants.[36]

Few of these visionary projects survived the 1850s. The era of experimentation came abruptly to an end when the Industrial Revolution reached another of its turning points: production was severed from the household, thereby making family connections increasingly irrelevant to employment and marriage chances. Among the working classes of Europe and North America, kin ties and access to families of strangers continued to be useful to those seeking places in the new industrial world, but for middle-class people, access to a viable career became a matter of education rather than direct inheritance of the means of production.[37] Family was supposed to provide a good upbringing—for males, a chance for further education and for females a respectable marriage—but it was now up to the individual to make his or her way in the world.

In the second half of the nineteenth century, banks and the stock market replaced family and kin as sources of capital. No longer centers of production, households could dispense with the labor of their own offspring and the children of neighbors and kin. At this time children became a cost rather than a benefit, and the middle classes on both sides of the Atlantic began systematically to limit fertility. Households remained large, owing to the presence of domestic servants, but by 1900 the family in residence was shrinking to the nuclear core.[38] This was also the time when wives ceased to be involved in their husband's business and marriage was no longer a practical matter of finding the person with the right skills or capital to perpetuate the family farm or business.[39] While the financial worth of a prospective husband or wife never became wholly irrelevant, no respectable middle-class couple could henceforth admit to marrying for anything but love. In the second half of the nineteenth century, the networks of community and kin, which had previously been crucial to middle-class family formation, became largely irrelevant. Marriage, like career, had become a matter of individual choice, involving only the two families of origin.

The triumph of individualism affected both men and women, though to different degrees and in different ways. The upwardly mobile young man put home behind him as early as possible. It became extremely rare for young men to circulate among kin. They were much more likely to be at school or living on their own before marriage. Middle-class girls were much less likely to leave home, however. Their working-class counterparts continued to go out to work, but this practice ceased to be respectable among the upper classes. Even the circulation of young women among families of kin virtually ceased, throwing them back entirely on their families of origin for their sense both of the world at large and of themselves.

In the past, one acquired an adult identity by emulating one of the innumerable role models available in the community. As long as childhood and youth were at least partially spent in families of strangers, women as well as men knew what to expect. Parenthood was no mystery to young adults who had been involved in the upbringing of their younger brothers and sisters. The various families of strangers they belonged to allowed them to practice adult roles, while communal rites of passage guided them in crucial moments of transition. As long as the community continued to enforce its expectations on the household, people were left in little doubt about either their roles or their identities.[40]

But now that the family had cut itself off from the wider world, the range of role models was drastically restricted; young people were much more on their own when it came to finding appropriate roles and identities. What had once been bestowed had now to be discovered. The transition from youth to adulthood became a complex, tenuous process, no longer guided or enforced by the community. As the symbolic universe shrank to the limits of the nuclear family, young people were reduced to looking for their models in a shrinking circle. Even as the physical distance between children and parents increased, their symbolic interaction intensified. Off-spring projected onto their parents highly idealized images of fatherhood and motherhood, and in turn, parents began to see in their children an innocence and perfection that was never there and could never be.[41]

Middle-class Victorians turned the family into an object of worshipful contemplation. As a result of the crisis of faith that had caused so many to have serious doubts about the existence of God and his transcendent order, the family became proof of the existence of the divine.[42] In what would have appeared to earlier generations as a pagan if not papist inversion of the divine order, Victorians on both sides of the Atlantic began to worship God through their families. Family life became a kind of sacrament for those, like Charles Kingsley, who declared that "fully to understand the meaning of 'Father in Heaven' we must be fathers ourselves; to know how Christ loved the Church, we must have wives to love, and love them." Fatherhood was thus sanctified, but the image of motherhood was even more exalted, for to men like Kingsley women were "most divine because they are most human." Henceforth, they would be assigned a role in the family analogous to the role of the clergy in the church—becoming its guide and most per-fect incarnation.[43]

The archetypes had been brought down to earth, but in turning away from the cosmos and the community for families to live by, the Victorians had taken on the cultural project of creating and sustaining their own symbolic universe. Their imagined families could no longer be taken for granted but needed constant attention. This fundamental transformation opened up vast new possibilities for individuals to construct identities, marriages, and family worlds to their own specifications, but it also placed huge burdens on marriage and family to produce those models of behavior—the saintly mother, the good family man, the perfect child—that had previously been found only in a divine original or communal exemplar, never in the family itself.[44]

Cut off from the old cosmic and communal archetypes by the combined forces of secularism and individualism, the Victorian middle classes would turn those they lived with into their significant others, attributing to them qualities that previously had been associated with divine or communal archetypes. What religious and communal rituals, images, and symbols had previously provided, these household gods and goddesses would now be responsible for. To the challenge of sustaining the material basis of family life was now added the awesome task of providing for its spiritual requirements. A revolution in family life occurred: in a few short decades during the second half of the nineteenth century, the household ceased to be like any other place and became an enchanted world populated by mythic figures.

Had Thomas Clarkson revisited Quaker homes only a half-century later, he would have found them replete with family portraits, mementos, and mirrors, and their calendars filled with rounds of newly invented family occasions. Previously unadorned domestic space had become representational. Mirrors invited reflection; portraits and photographs guaranteed the presence of family even in its absence. More and more of what people came to think of as family life was not so much the lives that family members actually lived but the representations of that life they produced for one another. Alain Corbin has noted that, in the nineteenth century, "visual contact became more important than physical contact."[45] In a shift that presaged in some ways the "virtual reality" being talked about today, the simulacra of family became the measure of family. The copy took on a reality that had previously belonged to the thing itself.[46]

The image of family, which had been blurred and indistinguishable from the larger collectivities of friends and neighbors, now took on a new sharpness.[47] Family had put itself on display. Mothers and children, rarely the focus of family portraits in earlier periods, were henceforth the icons of family life, present on all its important occasions and in all its representations. Previously valued for their labor and earning capacity, children took on symbolic value to the point that by the end of the nineteenth century they were seen as priceless possessions whose loss could never be compensated for.[48] While children had always played a minor role in religious and communal rituals, they were now central to all those occasions on which the family represented itself to itself. Christian baptism, previously a communal event, became home-centered for the first time. And not accidentally, the Jewish rite of circumcision, the *bris*, was shifted from the synagogue to the house in the same period.[49] Children's birthdays, of no significance previously, became a centerpiece of the family calendar, and by 1900 Christian confirmation and the Jewish bar mitzvah were such major family occasions that religious authorities began to worry that they were losing their religious meaning.[50]

By the twentieth century, middle-class families could no longer imagine themselves without children. Offspring were kept at home longer, and even when they left, they remained a powerful symbolic presence. Their pictures were kept in family albums, and their toys and school things carefully stored away in attics and basements. Children were never allowed to leave the mental worlds that families now inhabited. Even their rooms were kept as they were, an object of nostalgia for young adults, but equally important insurance against the loss of parental identity for those whose time of parenting was over.[51] By the twentieth century, a couple without children no longer qualified as a family. It even became common to say of those whose children had grown up that their family had left them.[52]

Motherhood assumed a similar iconic function. In Victorian images of the good family life, mothers occupied an increasingly central position, displacing the father figure to a very large extent. By the end of the century, men were more likely to be behind the family camera than in front of it. They became the missing presence, literally and figuratively, in a family world that was increasingly organized around the symbolic interaction between women and children.

As mothers became the central symbols of generational continuity, the image of the grandmother underwent a remarkable transformation. In previous centuries, grandparents had rarely appeared in the family imaginary, and when they did, it was usually the male ancestor who figured most prominently. Grandmothers had once been viewed as meddling, even threatening figures, but now they were seen in a much more favorable light. By the end of the nineteenth century, the older woman had lost her image as a willful, sexual being and become the epitome of a loving presence.[53] The grandfather image also softened to the point that, despite continued high mortality, which often prevented grandparents from playing much of a role in their grandchildren's lives, the symbolic importance of elders was enormously enhanced, even as the generations grew further apart in every other respect.

With the rise of these new icons, the patriarchal figure was largely displaced. Just as the nation-state was now represented by the female form, the house was more likely to be identified with the wife than the husband.[54] Yet men were keener than ever to see themselves as a part of the family circle, even though much more of their lives were now spent outside the home. "The child and its mother are no longer relegated to the woman's apartments as in the past," noted a French observer. "The child is shown while still an infant. Parents proudly present the child's nurse. It's as if they were on stage, making a great show of their production. In short, a man is father today as he would have been a citizen a little less than a century ago—with a great deal of show."[55] The fact that fathers were more of an absence than a presence in the everyday life of the household only made the display of fatherhood that much more urgent. As with everything else connected with family life, the representation of fatherhood became as important, if not more so, than fathering itself.

Families not only saw but spoke of themselves in an entirely new manner. By the midnineteenth century, the definition of the word *family* distinguished it from *household* or any other residential unit.[56] The idiom of parenthood and siblingship was reserved to flesh and blood alone, and children ceased to address their parents as "Sir" and "Madame"; the terms they had once used in speaking to all adults now seemed inappropriate for those special persons they were calling "Daddy" and "Mommy" for the first time.[57] Such terms of endearment, together with the pet names Victorians became so fond of using, swathed each family with a language of its own making, as transparent to them as it was opaque to those who spoke another family tongue. Language defined the boundaries of particular families just as it defined the borders of nations. Caught up in their own rhetorics, in the stories they told themselves and nobody else, imagined families took on a life no less real than the imagined communities that had come to underlie the national consciousness.[58]

Names too were endowed with a magic they had not had previously. In the eighteenth century, naming had ordinarily not taken place until there was assurance that the newborn would survive, and the names given were symbolic of ties other than those of family.[59] Catholics chose from a limited stock of saints' names, while Protestants preferred names that were emblematic of virtue—Patience, Preserved, Chastity—rather than family connections. Frequently, the same name was used more than once, transferred from a dead to a living sibling. But from the midnineteenth century onward, names took on unprecedented significance, and the christening ceremony, previously a relatively minor part of Christian baptism, became its most meaningful moment, an important family occasion, a rite of passage not into an extended spiritual community but into the family world itself. Thus, a rite that had once symbolized the inadequacy of the flesh and blood became one of its principal celebrations.[60]

Only the nobility had been able to lay sure claim to a family name in earlier centuries. As late as the eighteenth century, the connection between the individuals and surnames was tenuous, even for males. Names were more likely to be attached to land than to family, one of the reasons it was customary in some places for the man to take the surname of his bride when marrying into a landed family.[61] Many men would never have this good fortune, and many among the poor were called solely by their first name or nickname for their entire lives. However, by the end of the nineteenth century, the possession of a surname divided people by gender rather than by class. It would be some time before women would gain (or regain) the right to retain their own name in marriage, but already the family name was the first thing a child learned, the first sign of its intelligence, and its initiation into the mysteries of its own special family world.[62]

Names became the family's symbolic link with its past and the promise of its future. They were carefully recorded in family Bibles and entered into the family trees that in the Victorian era became a sure sign of membership in the middle class.[63] While the aristocracy had always invested itself in its pedigrees, the middle-class passion for genealogy was entirely new. In the second half of the century, dozens of genealogical societies were founded on both sides of the Atlantic.[64] What had been considered a vanity and an affectation earlier became an indispensable emblem of connection for family members who found themselves increasingly isolated from one another. A mass search for roots would not occur until a century later, but already Americans' obsessive quest for ancestry had reached the point where Mark Twain could satirize it in *Huckleberry Finn* by having "the rightful duke of Bridgwater" and "the pore disappeared Dauphin, Looey the Seventeenth," join Huck and Jim on the raft.[65]

What earlier generations had kept alive in "loving hearts" and "edifying conversations" now found concrete expression in myriad household objects and in the house itself. There was a long tradition of aristocratic attachment to particular houses, but the middle class had never before felt the need to represent itself through its dwellings.[66] Now they too found comfort in bricks and mortar. The house became a status symbol and, more important, a memory palace, the repository of all that united families mentally even when they were physically apart.

Furniture, silver, and other household objects that had been assigned only economic significance earlier were magically transformed into priceless possessions. Known in prior centuries as "lucks" by the aristocracy, who had jealously guarded them as legal proof of their rights of inheritance, heirlooms entered into middle-class life only in the middle of the nineteenth century.[67] By the nineteenth century, even though they had lost their legal standing, household objects handed down over the generations had increased immensely in their symbolic capacity to link past and present. By the 1880s antiques had become "narcissistic equivalents of self" for the upper middle classes, and even quite ordinary objects came to carry great symbolic weight as the passion to collect and preserve spread rapidly during the next few decades.[68] And when the genuine article did not exist, it could always be invented. In Marcel Pagnol's story *My Father's Glory*, an old rifle bought in a secondhand shop becomes for the boy his grandfather's gun, creating a bond across generations that no longer had much contact with one another.[69]

Objects served as mnemonic devices capable of recalling family even in its absence. By the end of the century, animals were serving a similar purpose. They had become the "sovereign masters of domestic space," symbolizing those qualities that families often found wanting in themselves.[70] Dog had become man's best friend, and cats were idealized for their supposedly familial qualities. The middle classes were the first to thoroughly domesticate their pets, to transform them into the equivalents of human significant others. The image of loyal Fido refusing to leave his master's grave could be found in parlors and bedrooms on both sides of the Atlantic. Families mourned their pets as they mourned their own relations, consoled by the thought that the family dog or cat would be waiting for them in heaven. By the 1870s there were pet cemeteries in France and elsewhere, constituting yet another family plot where the symbols of family remained forever safe in stone even if family itself seemed perpetually endangered.[71]

It now seemed that family was perpetually on display. The spontaneity and directness of manners and speech that earlier generations had so valued were banished, and family became a kind of performance, demanding just the right language, dress, and etiquette.[72] The middle classes developed family life to the level of an art, but an art that was heavily dependent on a gendered division of labor: men were the producers, and women were the directors of the family drama. In earlier centuries, it was the head of the household who served as master of ceremonies, but men now readily ceded that role to their wives.

Women's work, previously inseparable from that of men, was given new names—"housework" and "homemaking"—and a new meaning. No longer associated with toil, it came to be seen as "an emanation of Woman's nature," something that women should find revitalizing.[73] Among the better off, the real toil of housework was being assumed by domestic servants, but where the woman of the house did most of the domestic tasks, convention demanded that she represent it as a labor of love. To the beneficiaries of female domestic labor, ironed shirts and elaborate dinners appeared as if by magic. "Like a mechanic at the opera, she controls everything that happens, yet no one sees her do it," was the way one contemporary characterized it.[74]

It became increasingly difficult for women as well as men to discern the reality behind the illusion. A man who was a good provider was automatically a "family man," but for women the demands made by the family tableau involved a good deal more. Ever on call, they were expected to be the selfless sex, a notion that some, like Florence Nightingale, found intolerable:

> The family uses people, *not* for what they are, nor for what they are intended to be, but for what it wants them for—its own uses. It thinks of them not as God has made them for, but as something which has been arranged that they shall be. It wants someone to sit in the drawing room, *that* someone is supplied by the family, though that member may be destined for science, or for education, or for active superintendence by God, i.e. by the gifts within.[75]

Strong-willed women like Nightingale could achieve a measure of autonomy, but only outside marriage and family. Many chose this option during the second half of the nineteenth century, supported by a variety of religious and secular institutions—women's colleges, clubs, and sisterhoods—that validated female celibacy, which continued at a relatively high level until the turn of the century. At that point, the traditional supports for spinsterhood weakened significantly, and it became increasingly difficult for women to find a place for themselves outside marriage and family.[76]

By then an increasing amount of women's work was devoted to the creation of the rituals, myths, and images on which the newly enchanted world of family had come to depend. Women were the ones who facilitated the symbolic communication among family members. They were the ones who told the family stories, remembered the birthdays and anniversaries of distant relatives, organized family holidays, and were most involved in mourning and commemoration.[77] Women became the keepers of the family's schedule and its calendar. While men's diaries constituted a record of their own personal accomplishments, women's diaries, devoted to family events, constituted a running chronicle of marriages, births, and deaths. As such, women's diaries, like women's letters, were not protected by the same rights of privacy as a man's. They were assumed to be open to the inspection of a father or husband, who considered it to be as much his as hers.[78]

In the eighteenth century, family correspondence had been the husband's responsibility, and personal messages shared the page with news and business matters. By the midnineteenth century, the family letter had come into its own and fell increasingly within the feminine domain. It was then that family letters took on the novel symbolic dimension they have retained ever since, less valued "for what they said as [for] the regularity of their exchange."[79] The ritual of writing became far more significant than what was written. The quality of the paper, the care of composition, all contributed to the symbolic weight of the family letter. Meant to be kept and reread, it constituted a presence in the absence of a lover or family member.[80] Over the course of the Victorian era, family correspondence became both more frequent and more formal. Facilitated by the newly created national and international postal systems, the family letter facilitated the kind of intimacy at a distance that since then has become so characteristic of modern family life that we are scarcely aware of how its forms have changed over time.

The first holiday and greeting cards that circulated among kin were handmade. By the end of the century, however, bought cards accounted for an increasingly greater share of family correspondence as people took advantage of this relatively cheap form of symbolic interaction to extend their family worlds still further. In the early twentieth century, telephonic technology added still more possibilities for symbolic communication. The ritual of calling replaced to some extent the exchange of cards and letters. The desire for tangible signs of connection persisted, however, and conversation, by itself, never regained the place it had once had in the life of families.[81]

Cards and letters found their way into the albums that were the conversation pieces of every Victorian parlor. Babies' locks, dried flowers from wedding bouquets, the souvenirs of family vacations—all became sacred objects, relics too precious to part with.[82] When photography became more accessible after the 1850s, family pictures took on a similar magical power, capable of bringing the past into the present. Family photos were then, as now, less a statement of what the family actually was than what it imagined itself to be. They assured the Victorians, as they continue to assure us, of family solidarity and endurance. As Susan Sontag has put it:

> Photography becomes a rite of family life just when, in the industrializing countries of Europe and America, the very institution of the family starts undergoing radical surgery. As that claustrophobic unit, the nuclear family, was being carved out of a much larger family aggregate, photography came along to memorialize, to restate symbolically, the imperiled continuity and vanishing extendedness of family life. Those ghostly traces, photographs, supply the token presence of the dispersed relatives. A family's photograph album is generally about the extended family—and, often, is all that remains of it.[83]

Among the middle classes, which so highly valued individualism, it became incumbent on family members to disguise their dependency from one another. It was unacceptable for adults to acknowledge or reciprocate the material aid of other family members, a major reason why exchanges of cards and photos and brief, highly ritualized visits came to be the favored medium of family communication.[84] Working-class people, whose relations with kin continued to function on a much more practical basis, had little use as yet for the symbolic exchanges that by 1900 had already become so central to middle-class culture. Their occasions remained relatively low-key and informal.[85]

Family members only rarely exchanged gifts in premodern society. Its gift economy had operated largely between rather than within households, among neighbors rather than kin, with gifts flowing from the rich to the poor at regular times determined by religious and communal calendars. Family members sometimes aided one another in material ways, but gifts were reserved mainly for strangers. But by the end of the nineteenth century, the old gift economy had virtually disappeared. Charity still passed from the rich to the poor, but now through public institutions. In the modern era, gifts circulate mainly among family, their timing and volume determined by its calendar.

Middle-class gift exchange began on a modest scale, with mostly handmade items given on birthdays and anniversaries, at Christmas, New Year's, and Easter, and on other calendar occasions. But by the beginning of this century, gifts were primarily bought rather than made. To disguise their commercial origins and monetary value, price tags were removed and gifts were elaborately wrapped and ritually presented. The value of the gift now lay entirely in what it symbolized. The less useful the offering, the better it served this purpose. By 1900 people were looking back to a time when

> Christmas was not the burden that it is now. . . . That Yuletide has come to be anticipated—with trepidation—is no secret. Each year this becomes more obvious. With midwinter comes the nerve-wracking realization that before many days all good "Christians" must be prepared somehow to spend money that they cannot afford, to purchase "things" the recipients do not want.[86]

Despite shrinking size and physical isolation, middle-class families managed to create a sense of kinship reaching further in time and space than anything imaginable to earlier generations. By 1900 the family year was marked by calendar occasions such as Christmas and the American Thanksgiving, when ritual acknowledgment of distant relations was obligatory. The newly invented practice of family reunions served a similar symbolic purpose.[87] Even as relatives had less and less to do with one another in everyday life, their presence at moments in the life course—funerals as well as weddings—when discontinuity was greatest and the isolation of the nuclear family was most keenly felt became ever more important. Over time, and with access to better communications and transportation, these highly ritu-alized gatherings have only grown in size and frequency, until today they constitute such a normal part of the modern social scene that we take them wholly for granted.[88]

As Alexander Shoumatoff discovered when he examined the current Euro-American obsession with roots, our longing for kinship has grown in direct proportion to the decline in everyday contact with relatives. His find-ings confirm Octavio Paz's observation that "as a counterbalance to their immoderate cult of the future, Americans continually search for their roots and origins."[89] Family reunions, gift and card exchange, weddings and funerals, all serve to create the desired community of feeling and fantasy without endangering our precious sense of personal autonomy. "For most of the time and in most places, the extended family is an imagined family, present in photos and videos, remembered or anticipated, but no less real in the minds of those who carry it with them as part of their symbolic estate," observes the French anthropologist Martine Segalen. "It enables the individual who is unhappy with his job or the place he lives in to situ-ate himself in space and time and to stand in relationship to a family history which gives him an identity and identification which his work and place of residence cannot provide. The imaginative landscape of the family also offers comfort and assurance."[90] That this community of fantasy and feeling is rarely of a *man's* own making should not escape our notice, however. As with so much that sustains modern individualism, our symbolic estate is most often the work of women.

CHAPTER 5

Making Time(s) for Family

The cyclical depends on the linear as much as the linear depends on the cyclical.

Michael Young, *The Metronomic Society*[1]

SINCE THE MIDDLE of the nineteenth century, Western societies have been living with not one but two kinds of time, one quantifiable and linear, the other qualitative and cyclical. Objectified and externalized in the ticking of the clock and the pages of our calendars, linear time is divided into standard units, each with its own distinct beginning and end. Cyclical time also has its distinct moments, but they cannot be standardized. While linear time is irreversible and forever lost to us, cyclical time can be slowed, stopped, and even reversed.[2] Linear time is the product of the imperatives of the modern economy and the nation-state; nothing is beyond its reach, including families. But families have learned to live with linear time by creating their own kinds of cyclical time to compensate for the ephemerality and fragmentation that have resulted from what David Harvey calls modernity's "time-space compression": the acceleration in the pace of life that has left everyone wishing they had more time for family.[3]

Modern European and American families work very hard at bringing linear and cyclical time into some kind of tolerable relationship. Family birthdays and anniversaries number our days, providing us with very precise beginnings and endings that get us through our tightly scheduled lifetimes. But even as these occasions remind us of the inevitability of the aging process and the ultimate finitude of our lives, they are also rituals that connect us to family and friends, providing us with what David Cheal has aptly called convoys of persons with whom we share the times of our lives, both the good times and the bad.[4] Even as they help us acknowledge the finitude of time, these special family times shield us against its terrors by convincing us, despite the evidence of clock and calendar, of a certain permanence and continuity in all things human. The same is true of other family occasions—confirmations, bar and bas mitzvahs, graduations, and retirement parties—that mark the passing of linear time but also connect past, present, and future, slowing, stopping, even reversing time, if only for a moment.

Modern families actually teach the linear notions of age and generation that cause them so much discomfort. Other modern institutions manage to survive the aging and death of their members by treating them as replaceable, but families do not operate according to the same principles.[5] The aging and passing of its members represent losses for which families have developed compensatory rituals—birthdays, anniversaries, memorial occasions—that illustrate T. S. Eliot's observation in *Burnt Norton* that "only through time, time is conquered." In the nineteenth and twentieth centuries, family has displaced religion and community as Western culture's chief creator of times out of time, giving us a set of hidden rhythms that we can live by even as we live with a time that is perpetually threatening. So accustomed have we become to thinking of these times as a natural part of our cultural landscape that we are not even aware of their functions or their origins. We think of them as old when in fact they are relatively new. To put the record straight and to understand our own complex relationship with time, we need to think of family time(s) not as an immutable part of nature but as the product of history.

The Victorians initiated the idea that there is a time as well as a place for everything; between 1870 and 1970 Western societies underwent a process of temporal standardization that Martin Kohli has called chronologization.[6] The imposition of numerically standardized linear times and ages was partly the result of capitalist industrialization, with its emphasis on mechanization and synchronization, but no less important an influence was the emergence of the modern nation-state, which constituted its identity by creating a uniform timescape as well as a uniform territory.[7] Its laws, setting minimum and maximum ages for everything from working to drinking, have made everyone age-conscious to the point that today a person without a birth certificate is quite literally a person without a country. Immigrants from parts of the world where age is not a defining attribute often encounter great difficulty when they cannot present acceptable proof of age.[8]

In the nineteenth century, numerical age became the gateway to work, schooling, even leisure. France pioneered in setting standard ages of consent to marry, to inherit, to vote, and to be drafted, but it was not long before every European country had minimum ages in place.[9] Laws protecting children from labor exploitation introduced age standards into the workplace, while universal schooling, institutionalized in most parts of Europe and North America by the last third of the nineteenth century, established both minimum and maximum school ages, making of childhood and adolescence the most standardized of all the life phases.

Infants are taught their age almost as soon as they are able to speak. Knowing one's age is the earliest sign of comprehension, while forgetting it is deemed a sure sign of dementia. Young people became modern society's most age-conscious group when civil and social privileges (not to mention duties), which had previously been assigned on the basis of competence, were linked to numerical age for the first time. The setting of drinking and entertainment ages around the time of the First World War, together with later limits on driving and other adult entitlements, made the young hypersensitive to age.[10]

Age-consciousness was also imposed on the other end of the life course when national norms for retirement were established, beginning with Germany in the late nineteenth century and spreading everywhere by the middle of the twentieth century. At first the age of retirement affected only a minority of the population, namely, men in regular employment. There was no retirement for women who worked within the home, and, if they were able, most working-class men and women continued to labor beyond the standard age just to make ends meet. It was not until after the Second World War that everyone could afford to retire, and by the 1970s older people were protesting against compulsory age limits.[11]

It is not surprising that people are now more acutely conscious of numerical age than at any time in human history. The counterpart to doing everything on schedule and on time is acting your numerical age, something earlier generations had no notion of. Demographers have been able to show that the ages of going to school, entering work, getting married, and establishing families became ever more standardized in the period 1870–1970.[12] Variations in the retirement ages of men have also tended to narrow as people internalize certain ages as the standard for their own behavior.

Not only were the ages at which people accomplished major life events becoming more standardized, but so too were the sequences in which they did them. In earlier periods, young people thought nothing of moving back and forth between school and work, but by 1900 the flow was going all in one direction. Returning to school after beginning a career violated not only social norms but a person's sense of self. The result was that by 1970 everything and everyone seemed temporally coordinated; never had there been so little variation not only across but between Western societies. Science and medicine had taught Western society to think of aging as part of nature's laws. So as not to appear unnatural, everyone did their utmost to act their age from birth to death.[13]

Chronologization coincided with an unprecedented extension of the lifetime. In the past one hundred years, some thirty years have been added to the average life span in the West.[14] The decline of mortality rates at every age stage has also made life much more predictable. Today death is firmly linked to old age in an unprecedented way. But no less significant has been the cultural redefinition of the lifetime that has accompanied its biological extension: during this same period the Protestant ideal of living a long, productive life ceased to be a vehicle for the spiritual journey and became an end in itself. In the second half of the nineteenth century, longevity replaced eternity as the primary goal of life, and acting one's age took precedence over the spiritual quest. Previously, old age had been a sign of sanctification; now longevity itself was sanctified.[15]

By the beginning of our century, Western civilization was no longer running on God's time but on man's. Production was no longer located in the household under the watchful eye of a conscientious master or mistress; the external monitors of clock and calendar were substituted for the internal monitors of the Protestant work ethic. Punctuality, something earlier generations of Protestants had cared little about, became central to worship as well.[16] Strict Sabbatarianism arose only in the Victorian era, and certain dates in the Christian calendar, like Christmas, took on a whole new meaning as a sign of faithfulness. Henceforth, bourgeois civilization would rely on the authority of science, which claimed to have discovered the natural laws of time and aging. It had accepted the Reverend William Paley's 1802 metaphorical understanding of the universe as a clock made by God but left to tick on by itself until the end of time.[17]

Age, like time, was no longer seen as a gift from God over which the individual had little control. Now both time and age were seen as a kind of private property, capital that, when used well and invested correctly, would produce more time and better aging, but when used badly could bring failure and humiliation. In the second half of the nineteenth century, the meaning of old age changed abruptly. A long life was no longer a sign of God's grace but an accomplishment attributable to the virtues of the individual. Hard work and the right habits of consumption were now the source of longevity, just as illness and death were sure signs of moral failing.[18] By 1900 science and medicine were called in to assist individuals in this new quest for longevity. Although it can be shown that high mortality rates had been vanquished by a combination of better nutrition, improved sanitation, and medical improvements available to the entire population, individual Americans and Europeans had been convinced that proper aging leading to a long life was a matter of moral choice.[19]

Not just individuals but whole nations became obsessed with aging. Americans, determined to keep their republic young and virile, chose a spry old man, Uncle Sam, to symbolize their nation's longevity.[20] Other nations, such as France, that were afflicted with low birth rates began to fear their "younger" rivals. By the end of the nineteenth century, the old were seen as degenerate and old age was classified as a disease. The world seemed to belong to the young, who were imagined to be the most progressive and healthiest part of the population despite evidence that neither progress nor health yet belonged to any particular generation.[21]

The Protestant quest for salvation beyond time had become a quest for salvation through time, and because the young seemed to have more of it, they were now presented as symbols of regeneration.[22] From the midnineteenth century onward, the old, and especially debilitated men, were seen as alien, even dangerous. Defined as useless to the workforce and hopeless in public affairs, older males were increasingly forced into retirement, usually within the domestic sphere, where they were considered capable of filling only one role: to be, like the women and children also confined there, a quiet model of genteel behavior.[23]

For the first time, old age was a separate age group, with its own special times and places. The poorhouse, which had once housed all ages together, gave way to the "old age home," as it came to be called. And within the household, where most elderly people were still to be found in the nineteenth and twentieth centuries, segregation was also the order of the day. The old codger confined to his favorite chair and the widow with her nose in her sewing rather than other people's business became stock images of the "old folks at home."[24] As Ann Douglas has described it, the grandfather became "the ancestor comfortably stowed away in the rocking chair, the male softened by the kindly touch of time."[25] Grandmothers did not need such softening, for women were deemed passive throughout their whole lifetimes, but for the very same reasons, old women who stepped out of their domestic roles were likely to be regarded as even more deviant and dangerous than the unretiring older man. In the iconography of the nineteenth century, the vicious "old witch" joined the "dirty old man" as images of aging gone wrong.[26]

Age is a social construct not unlike gender and race, a categorization of people without regard to their actual character and abilities. And it is significant that, from the late nineteenth century until quite recently, the old were seen in almost exactly the same terms as women and racial minorities, allegedly sharing with them "skill in handling children, a liking for menial work, religiosity," even in the face of overwhelming evidence of individual variation.[27]

The images of a linear sequence of precisely enumerated ages were complementary to a political, economic, and social order that concentrated power in the hands of middle-aged, middle-class men, whose lives conformed to the new vector of time known as the "career." A projection of the middle-class male's experience of aging, the male life course was represented in literature and science alike as invariably progressive and linear. Women's life course was represented at the time as just the opposite: static, dominated by natural cycles that prevented them, as well as children and old folks, from being able to compete with middle-aged men for economic and political power.[28]

Of course, people did not always behave according to the new age stereotypes. The young, whose lives were the first to be tightly scheduled by schooltime and legally imposed age minimums, expressed their resistance through truancy and other forms of juvenile delinquency that began in the late nineteenth century and have persisted ever since.[29] Working people had far more trouble marrying and giving birth on time than did the middle classes, a fact partly reflected in their higher rates of recorded illegitimacy; such statistics, however, never account for the many couples who did not make it to the church on time but later married.[30] For most working people, there would be no fixed retirement age until the advent of universal pensions in the midtwentieth century. Nor did most women have the luxury of conforming to the grandmotherly roles assigned to them. The leisured grandparenthood that middle-class Victorians imagined did not become a reality until our own day, when a majority of old people have finally gained access to the resources, including the longevity, it requires.[31]

It was the middle-class, middle-aged male who had the best chance of meeting the new age norms, which had been laid down for the most part by men of similar background. Everyone else had no option but to age the best they could. Whether they did so well or badly according to the increasingly strict rules of behavior dictated by the emerging science of gerontology had less to do with virtue than with economics. But even if they could not act their age in everyday life, they learned to do so on those civic holidays and family occasions when the young and the old were called upon to represent the ideal ages to one another.[32]

In earlier eras, the idea of everyone having a childhood, an adolescence, a prime of life, and an old age was unthinkable. A person's age was in large part determined by his or her place in the social hierarchy. After the midnineteenth century, however, age became a social force of its own, and aging became the universal problem it remains today.

Abstract notions of time were first introduced in the public sphere and reinforced by the factory clock and the calendars set by state schooling. But from the midnineteenth century onward, family life also became clocked and calendared. "That house only is well conducted where there is a strict attention paid to order and regularity," counseled the Englishwoman Mrs. Ann Martin Taylor, adding that "to do everything in its proper time, to keep everything in its right place, and to use everything for its proper use, is the *very essense* of good management."[33] Dr. Kitchener advised Americans in the 1830s that there should be clocks in every room of the house and that, "in a well-regulated family, all clocks and watches should agree."[34]

Yet the new mechanical time divided rather than united. Mrs. Sarah Ellis was already worrying in 1838 that men's rigorous work schedules made them strangers to their own families. Fathers worked such long hours that they saw their children only on Sunday, and their wives for only five minutes a day, "until we almost fail to recognize the man, in the machine."[35] In the nineteenth century, schooltime would also remove children from the household for a large part of the day. Women's time was less regulated by linear time, and they were becoming the only family members who were thought to have time for family. As a result, women became not only the principal managers of family time but its main symbol. Beginning among the Protestant middle classes, people learned to associate family time(s) almost exclusively with women, especially mothers.

The less time families had together, the more certain times came to matter to them—that is, as real time grew scarce, symbolic time loomed ever larger. Victorian families were the first to feel the need for what we now call "quality time." The daily, weekly, and annual occasions they bequeathed to us provide, according to David Harvey, "a sense of security in a world where the general thrust of progress appears to be ever onwards and upwards into the firmament of the unknown."[36] It was in the 1850s and 1860s, exactly when work and school time were first imposing their relentless regime on middle-class families, that families began to organize the day into an endless cycle of meals and bedtimes that has changed remarkably little ever since.

Earlier, no one had thought of setting aside a special time for the family to eat together on a daily basis. Eating had always had its ritual features, but these had been more connected with religious and civic occasions. Apart from the households of the very rich, people had attached little formality to meals. The poor ate out of the same pot around the hearth, but they did not dine as such. As late as the 1830s, there were few dining rooms even in most middle-class homes, and the "eating room," as it was then called, belonged more to men than to women, who remained largely excluded from the formal dinners that took place in the house. Chairs were scarce and, as symbols of authority rather than ordinary furniture, were reserved for the heads of households. When they were not serving, women and children often ate standing up.[37]

British women were apparently somewhat more accustomed to dining with their husbands, for the English traveler Mrs. Trollope was troubled by the lack of conjugal companionship she found among Americans in the 1820s: "Women are just looked upon as housekeepers in this country, and as such are allowed to preside at the head of their own table, that they might see that all goes right."[38] But women everywhere had always been outsiders to dining, with its male rituals of drinking and profane toasting; even though European women were sometimes included, it was still the custom for them to retreat from the table to the "withdrawing room" at the later stages of a meal, thus allowing men to carry on their old customs, a practice that Americans found strange once they had more fully integrated their tables in the nineteenth century.[39]

Dining, as opposed to eating, was domesticated late. Until the early nineteenth century, etiquette books had little to say about domestic as opposed to public manners.[40] It was not until the midnineteenth century that domestic eating was formalized and acquired a fixed time even in middle-class households. As one early nineteenth-century observer noted, for American men, eating was "only a disagreeable interruption of business, an interruption to which he yields himself because it cannot be avoided, but which he abridges as much as possible."[41] On one of his American tours, Charles Dickens noted how "nobody says anything, at any meal, to anybody."[42] But Dickens himself was generally silent on the eating habits of women and children, who, according to British and American accounts of the early nineteenth century, had no special time or place for eating, inside the house or out. Even more than men, they were likely to eat on the run, gulping down their food and drink in silence before rushing back to work or play.

The poor ate whatever and whenever they could, but even the middle classes, which could afford an adequate diet, had no notion of the "meal" as we have come to know it. They ate frequently and irregularly in a manner not unlike modern snacking. After all, Johnson's great eighteenth-century dictionary had defined lunch in just those terms: "As much food as one's hand can hold."[43] And adults as well as children often ate with their hands, in the absence of cheap utensils and plates, well into the early nineteenth century.

If there was anything remotely resembling a family meal in the late eighteenth and early nineteenth centuries, it was "tea," taken in the evening. But the drink for which the meal was named was expensive, and only the wealthy had the settings and services that later came to be known as the "family silver" or the "family china."[44] When the architect Calvert Vaux offered plans for rural houses in 1857, he had to admit that many Americans had not yet become proper diners: "It is the custom with some farmers to make a constant practice of taking all meals in the kitchen; but this habit marks a low state of civilization."[45]

Yet that same decade, the 1850s, marked an epochal turning point in the ritualization of family meals. The dining room, a term first used in the eighteenth century, was finally separated from the kitchen, lost its masculine connotations, and became, for the first time, the archetypal family room. Middle-class house plans on both sides of the Atlantic now invariably represented it as a separate space where the family ate while servants took their food in the kitchen, from which it was set off by doors to keep out the sounds and smells of food preparation. The furniture of dining had previously consisted of boards set on trestles, which could be removed at will. Chairs were borrowed from other rooms, for until the middle of the nineteenth century, no distinctions were made between the furnishings in the various public rooms of the house. Now, however, the middle-class home distinguished itself from a mere place of "room and board" by its solid dining room table, which still "represents, as no piece of furniture can, the family as a whole."[46] It was accompanied by a matching set of dining chairs, one for each member of the family, occupied only by them and left vacant in their absence, even after their death.[47]

The representative functions of the dining room not only underlined the gender and age hierarchies of the family—with the father occupying the high end of the table, the mother the lower, and the children arranged according to age and sex on the sides—but ritually constructed a sense of togetherness. Earlier, it had been common to sit on just one side of a table, all facing in the same direction. The newly created dining room table was smaller, either rectangular or circular in shape, and allowed families to turn in on themselves. More than any other piece of furniture, its heavy dark woods suggested solidity and continuity, and this quality was reflected in the preference for antique tables that emerged as early as the 1870s.

The dining room's sober decor and elaborately carved sideboards, "their Gothic style exuding a quasi-religious aura over the dining ritual," gave it a feel different from that of any other part of the house.[48] The bright light of gas had made its entry into the home through the kitchen, but dining rooms were still lit by candles or paraffin lamps, for the flame, now removed from the hearth to the table, not only shed a warmer, more intimate light but was the symbol of life itself; such lighting came to be regarded on domestic occasions, especially birthdays and Christmas, as indispensable.[49] The flame suggested duration; like the rest of the decor, it seemed to extend the scarce resource of time, putting all the clocks, literally as well as figuratively, in the shadows.

Special places evoke special times and vice versa. Even as conflicting school and work schedules made it more difficult for family members to spend time with one another, the family dinner took on its modern form and fixity. By the middle of the nineteenth century, eating had become a carefully arranged sequence of breakfast, lunch, and dinner, an ascending order of significance and copiousness that marked off the middle class from the big lunch eaters lower down the social scale. Ladies were known to send away much of their lunch as a show of their respectability, but it was not so much the size as the timing and duration of the meal that came to demarcate social status and bring families togetherness.[50] Breakfast was the least ritualized occasion. Families rarely ate lunch together because men's, women's, and children's lunch hours had become quite separate; the weekday "luncheon" became an entirely female occasion. Dinner in the early evening thus took on its modern association with family, becoming ever more important in the twentieth century even as family breakfasts and lunches became even less feasible.[51]

In the eighteenth century, dinner had occurred around 3:00 P.M., but to accommodate the longer, uninterrupted working and school days, it was steadily moved back to the early evening, where, since the 1860s, it has remained to this day, becoming gradually the preferred time in most Western societies.[52] Titus Salt, the English Victorian businessman and philanthropist, is said to have stood every evening, watch in hand, ready to ring the bell for family dinner with the same punctuality he used to summon the workers to his factories.[53] Until the 1860s, American cookbooks never mentioned specific meal times, urging instead that they be "conformed to family convenience, but [kept] quite independent of the caprices of fashion."[54] Thereafter, however, the dinner hour became so common that nobody needed a watch to know what time it was in the typical middle-class suburb. It was the one time of the day when the streets were empty and quiet. In the nineteenth century, you could tell people's class not only by where but by when they ate.

In Protestant Europe and America, family meals were deliberately kept simple and separate from more elaborate dining occasions. The "average" middle-class Englishman of the 1880s declared: "'My living is plain, always toast or boiled'—words which but too clearly indicate a dreary monotony, not to say unwholesomeness, of his daily food, while they furthermore express his satisfaction, such as it is, that he is no luxurious feeder."[55] But the "average" American was no less committed to the ordinariness and repetitiveness of family meals, for it was precisely these qualities that gave them their meaning and effectiveness in creating a sense of family togetherness. As Margaret Visser has pointed out, the fact that a meal is ordinary by no means deprives it of significance, for the root of *ordinary* is *order*, and that was the essential element that the newly invented Victorian family dinner provided. In earlier centuries, "ordinary" was the name of a tavern or inn where a certain allowance of food could be had at a fixed price.[56] At one time an ordinary meal could be acquired only outside the home. The Victorians so thoroughly domesticated it that by the 1920s American restaurants like Schraft's were using the lure of "home-cooked" meals to bring in customers, anticipating the advertising patterns of the self-styled family restaurants that have become so popular in recent decades.[57]

The Victorians were the first to make time for dinner, but dinner also made time for family. The new family dinner hour was dictated by the clock, but not ruled by it. The family dinner was the one meal of the day that could not be hurried. Its distinctive feature was its ritualized duration, a time out of time, which made it an object of both special anticipation and vivid memory. It was the only meal of the day that had a ritual beginning and ending: the saying of grace. Prayers had previously given church and school time their special shape, but now they did the same for family time. Praying at the table was not new, but having children offer grace was a distinctive Victorian innovation. Grace might not be said when strangers were present, but the ritual was always present when relatives joined the family.[58] It gave those times their special character, connecting family members and distinguishing family from not-family. Saying grace gave dinnertime a sacred quality, but even when the practice subsided in this century, sitting down to eat as a family retained a ritual pattern. Like all repetitive behavior, dinner rituals have their communicative and didactic functions, lending to family an identity that time has threatened to take from it.[59]

It was at the table that children learned not just manners but the shape of the world they were to inherit. Food and learning had long been associated in public settings, but the Victorians were the first to domesticate the process, using food both as an incentive and a punishment and attaching to certain foods meanings of goodness and badness or intimacy and strangeness. The dinner hour became like school.[60] It taught not just punctuality but the basic temporal order in which food, like life itself, had a certain fixed sequence. In the eighteenth century, everything was brought to the table at once, and what you got to eat was dictated by your position in the household. While children were permitted to consume foods and drinks, including alcohol, that we now reserve only to adults, the needs of the latter always took precedence. Adult males had first claim to any meat, a practice that continued among British working-class families well into the twentieth century.[61] The break came when the Victorian middle classes insisted that everyone eat essentially the same dinner in larger or smaller portions. Men still got the larger share of the meat, but women and children now had their servings. Children were forbidden wine and beer, snuff and tobacco, and taught to control their appetites, but they could anticipate that in due time they too would enjoy these forbidden fruits of adulthood. Family meals, like family life, now proceeded in a set sequence from soup to dessert, presenting yet another lesson in the progressive order of things.[62]

Children too young to learn were excluded from the table. It was a time for parents to speak and the young to listen, and often the only time of day when the middle-class father was present. "We can hardly imagine an object of greater envy than is presented by a respected, portly paterfamilias carving . . . his own fat turkey, and carving it well," noted Mrs. Beeton.[63] Carving was one of the few occasions when fathers could demonstrate their authority and remove the aura of strangeness that normally attached to them. In this ritualized moment, men's time was fused with that of women and children, making this the one and only truly family time of the day.

Protestantism had been a religion of the word and the ear but was rapidly becoming one of taste, smell, and sight. This change was reflected in the popularity of ritualism in both American and European churches from the 1860s onward—and at the table, where food had become the kind of icon that earlier generations would never have tolerated.[64] Children learned to associate certain foods with family. "Taste and smell alone, more fragile but more enduring, more unsubstantial, more persistent, more faithful, remain poised a long time, like souls, remembering, waiting, hoping, amid the ruins of all the rest," Marcel Proust would write.[65] Food not only connected one family member to another, but each to his or her own past. In virtually every Victorian memoir, it is the encounter with a particular taste or smell that summons family past. By the early twentieth century, food had become sacred to Catholics and Jews as well. Among the latter, keeping a kosher kitchen, a practice previously associated only with certain high holy days, became an everyday routine.[66]

Over the past 150 years, family food tastes have remained almost as constant as the dinner hour. People prefer the foods they ate as children, but if continuity were merely a natural process, food ways would never change at all. In fact, the stability of family food ways is relatively recent: the fetishistic preference for the "home-cooked" and the "home-baked" began only in the second half of the nineteenth century.[67] A sense of nostalgia about certain foods is the product of culture, not nature, and seems to have been particularly strong among men, who distanced themselves from food preparation in the middle of the nineteenth century and came to have a different, more symbolic, relationship to food than did women, who did virtually all the cooking. In our own century, wives must still contend with men's attachment to certain foods, which they seem unable or unwilling to cook for themselves. "I know a cousin of mine eats nothing but chips," reported one Welsh woman. "In fact, his mother-in-law had to cook him chips for his Christmas dinner and she went berserk."[68]

It is still the women who spend their increasingly scarce time making the food associated with a proper family dinner. Patty Winters, who works full-time but rushes home to feed her family, is typical of the women who continue to perform this double shift. "Some nights," she says, "it is not so easy. But I come home and cook dinner because everything these days is at such a fast pace."[69] In the past two decades, leisure time has declined for everyone, but more for women than for men.[70] Ironically, a good part of this loss is due to the time women feel they must put into domestic work, particularly cooking. It is women who spend the most time providing the family time that other family members take for granted.

Meal times permit those around the table to imagine themselves to be sharing more than food. The ritual quality of a meal allows them to think of themselves as having more in common with this set of people than with any other. Like all rituals, it concentrates time in space, allowing family present to connect with family past. "Ritual inevitably carries a basic message of order, continuity, and predictability," Barbara Myerhoff has written.

New events are connected to preceding ones, incorporated into a stream of precedents so that they are recognized as growing out of tradition and experience. By stating enduring and underlying patterns, ritual connects past, present, and future, abrogating history and time. Ritual always links participants one to another and often beyond, to wider collectivities that may be absent, even to ancestors and those yet unborn.[71]

The very ordinariness of family foods serves as their link with the past. Even as it came into being in the midnineteenth century, the big Sunday dinner was already being spoken of as "traditional," thereby obscuring its recent origin and collapsing time and space in such a way that the Victorians could see family meals as the pivot of their hectic lives, a fixed point undisturbed by the passage of time and generations. In the same way that the ordinariness of family meals symbolizes family togetherness, so the sameness of Christmas and Thanksgiving dinners across whole nations has contributed to the notion of "the British Family," or "the American Family." The idea of all families sitting down to eat the same food on the same day, even at the same hour, was also one of the means by which peoples divided by race, age, and gender could imagine themselves as having a common national identity.[72]

Today we tend both to exaggerate the frequency with which families ate together in the past and to underestimate the commitment to the family dinner in the present.[73] The dinner hour has become a sign of family togetherness, though it is also known to be the time when family arguments and fissures are most likely to occur. As Michael Lewis explains it: "The family dinner table has to carry a great deal of the burden of family togetherness. It is often a more tension filled arena than one would anticipate." There is nothing contradictory here, for we should expect that at the very moment when people are supposed to act like family, the contradictions built into modern domesticity are most likely to surface.[74] It is the only time of the day when we come face to face with what we are supposed to share— family—and it is then that we are also confronted with our real differences.

In the nineteenth century, family became more nocturnal. What it lost to the centrifugal forces of daytime, it made up for in the centripetal moments of the evening homecoming, dinner hour, and bedtime. Victorian depictions of the family circle are invariably interior, usually illuminated either by the soft glow of the fireplace or by a table lamp. The radio dial and television screen would later illuminate similar family scenes, for we continue to prefer to see ourselves in these softer lights. Even when gas and electricity offered much brighter illumination, the living room and dining room lamps were shaded and the windows draped to keep out the harsh light of day.[75] Even now, families feel closer when gathered around the open flame of the hearth or candle, symbols of life whose meaning is heightened by the surrounding darkness. Daylight disperses the family, while nighttime brings it together and, with the exception of Saturday, forbids anyone to leave. Of course, Victorians, especially men, were very much creatures of the night, the inventors of "night life" as we know it. But women and children, or the family as a group, were supposed to stay at home during the evenings.

Evening became the time of homecoming, and the bourgeois threshold became the site of this new ritual. In the iconography of Victorian genre painting, the figure in the home-leaving or homecoming always seems to be a father or son. When a female crosses the symbolic threshold, she is invariably a fallen woman, about to be cast out of home or family.[76] These images faithfully reproduced the way Victorians represented themselves to themselves every day. The movement of women and children in and out of the house went unmarked, in part because the culture denied them access to the world outside the home and made their comings and goings invisible, but also because, being purely domestic beings, there was no need to treat them as strangers. Men, on the other hand, belonged to the world and required a ritual reincorporation at the end of each day.

The anticipation of this event structured the time of Victorian women and children on both sides of the Atlantic, anchoring them to the home. Men were supposed to leave their worries as well as their work at the threshold; in many Victorian homes, the evening hours were a time when fathers showed a very different face to their children, entering joyfully into their games and pranks, even at the risk of upsetting the domestic order so carefully constructed by their wives. In the bosom of the family, fathers were more likely than mothers to be uninhibited, playful, even childish, as if they had not only returned to their children but to childhood itself.[77] Women's work of child-rearing, cooking, and cleaning made these playful occasions possible, but women were not permitted to enter into them. A huge quantity of women's time went into enabling men to have "quality time" with their children.[78]

Bedtime also took on a special meaning it had never had before. In earlier generations, the household rose and retired together, but with separate schedules for adults and children, bedtime took on increasing importance, especially for fathers' relationships to their offspring. Mothers (or female servants) bathed and prepared the children for bed, but it was the father's kiss or prayer that sent them off to sleep. Two sociologists who looked at American family rituals immediately after the Second World War commented that if a father "is to spend much time being fatherly he must almost of necessity catch his children out of their own routines and activities and make appointments with them. This has led to father-child ritual schedules from the infant level up through adolescence."[79] Today bedtime retains its special meaning for mothers as well as fathers, though it has been moved to a progressively later hour, especially in families where both parents work and do not return home until the early evening. Adults who remember their own bedtime as being earlier may take this change as a sign of disorder, but in fact, the more child and adult time have diverged, the more bedtime has gained in significance, not just for fathers but for working mothers.[80]

Fathers' domestic time has been typically more ritualized than that of mothers. "The suburban husband and father is almost entirely a Sunday institution," noted one American commentator in 1900.[81] By contrast, motherhood has been perceived as having a timeless quality, with no daily or weekly schedule and virtually no ritual recognition apart from Mother's Day, which began in America in 1911 and spread quickly to Europe. But setting aside one day of the year has only underlined the identity of women's time with that of the family. Having one day when mothers can expect to be served breakfast in bed and taken out to dinner is a ritual inversion of the usual domestic division of labor, but, like all such occasions, it serves to confirm the social order being inverted. It is no accident that the popularity of Mother's Day has increased in direct proportion to the burdens of motherhood.[82]

In the same way that evenings compensated symbolically for time lost to the work and school day, the Victorian Sunday and weekend made up for what was taken away by the increasingly hectic workweek. "The mere word 'Sunday' is apt to give a mental shiver to people with long memories. The outer world shut down," wrote Vivien Hughes, who grew up in London in the 1870s.[83] The prohibition on Sabbath work goes back to the twelfth century, but it was the Victorians who completed what even the Puritans could not accomplish, namely, the prohibition of all public trading and leisure activities, even to the point of closing museums and galleries.[84]

The Protestant Sabbath's reputation for gloomy boredom is wholly undeserved in one respect, however. The mood of the inner world was by no means identical to that of the outer, but in fact just the opposite. Life at home became ever more animated. Vivien Hughes's father was particularly relaxed on Sunday, a day that always began with the only big breakfast of the week, followed by church at St. Paul's and then the family dinner in the middle of the day, a moment that glowed in memory years later, thanks to the efforts of Mrs. Hughes, who "put all the cheerfulness she could into the food, against which there seemed to be no Biblical taboo."[85]

In America as well Sunday took on new meaning after the 1850s. It had previously been a public day and, as such, more a man's day than a family day. Children had been expected to worship with their parents, and women had been largely excluded from leadership roles in public worship. As Protestantism "moved from being the religion of the converted adult to being the education of the innocent children," Sunday schools were provided for children and mothers assumed ever greater responsibility for religious instruction, which moved from the church pew to the dinner table.[86] By the end of the nineteenth century, public activities had again become respectable, but Sunday remained a day for family dinners followed by long walks that were ultimately replaced in America by a ride in the family car at a leisurely pace that gave us the image of the "Sunday driver."

In time, the newspaper, then radio, and finally television would invade the privacy of the family Sunday, but not necessarily to its detriment. In Vivien Hughes's childhood, newspaper reading was forbidden on Sundays, but only a generation later it had become a focus of family activity. In a similar way, radio and movies were first abhorred and then embraced by the family. When television was introduced in the 1950s, it was seen as the medium that would bring families home again from the cinema, and in its earliest years much of the Sunday programming was geared to family, with *The Ed Sullivan Show* providing a fitting end to the perfect family day.[87]

Sunday was the only day the family had to itself, but it was not just the absence of work and school that made it special. Sundays provided not only more time for family but a different kind of time: slow time, unclocked time, time that, to fidgety children, seemed endless but that to adults, and particularly to men, was a time out of time. By ritually positioning the big family meal at the center of the day, Sunday time flowed backward and forward in a manner different from weekdays, when everything led up to the evening meal. Long family walks and parlor songs and games gave the day a sense of wholeness that all others lacked.

But above all it was the ritualized predictability of Sunday that gave it a special quality. On this one day, families could feel themselves in the presence of their pasts and futures. Not only did the clocks seem to tick less relentlessly, but history itself was suspended. Sunday was the one day of the week when people did not read the papers for news.[88] It was imagined that on Sunday the world stopped. Yet its elaboration brought even more work for women; what was a day of rest for everyone else in the family was no respite for them. In imagining themselves as freed from the cares of the world, families completely ignored the labors of wives and female servants that made the weekly ritual possible. Their time was family time in a way that men's time was not.

Sunday dinner with family became the pivot of the family week. Its roast would be served again cold on Monday and become hash on Tuesday, creating a descending order of meals that everyone knew would be renewed the next Sunday.[89] The only other day the family sometime called its own was Monday, known as "Saint Monday" to the working people who took it as a day off in the early nineteenth century.[90] Ultimately, however, the time demands of the new factory system would turn Monday into a day of labor like any other, and the working classes would trade in Saint Monday for a half-day of rest on Saturday.

This change shifted sporting and other leisure events, including family occasions, from the beginning of the week to the end and gave birth by the 1870s to the first truncated notion of the "weekend," the first time that word was used. It was not until the 1930s that almost everyone (except store clerks and service personnel) had Saturday off, but already Friday had replaced Saturday as the traditional cleaning day, and the Saturday night bath had become a universal ritual.[91] In our era the weekend has expanded still further, starting on Friday, or even on Thursday, and ending on Sunday. But even as Sunday lost its special character and blended into the long weekend, it remained the ultimate family day, if not in reality then in popular imagination.

The rapid pace of urban industrial change emptied not only the day and the week but also the year of its earlier meanings. The seasons, which had meant so much to rural people, no longer gave structure to the lives of urban people. Midsummer games and harvest festivals became memories, objects of nostalgia, floating somewhere in a timeless time known as the "good old days" but no longer fixed points in the bourgeois calendar. To take their place, the middle classes invented an annual calendar all their own, complete with its own seasons and wholly different from anything that had existed before. The Victorian's year was more domestic than communal, initially revolving around family gatherings at Christmas and ultimately adding another season of summer holidays. By 1900 the family year had been firmly anchored around these two magic times, each greatly anticipated and fondly remembered. Nature's seasons were abandoned, only to be replaced by new seasons that relied heavily on natural symbols.

The Victorians invented the modern Christmas, giving it a special association with family it lacked when it had been more community-centered, an extended period of doling, wassailing, mumming, and guising during which households turned themselves inside out to accommodate those who came to its door. W. Carew Hazlitt described English mumming as "a Christmas sport, which consists in changing clothes between men and women who, when dressed in each other's habits, go from one neighbour's house to another, partaking of Christmas cheer, and making merry with them in disguise."[92] Mummers acted like today's Halloween visitors, threatening dire consequences if they were not offered hospitality in the form of food and drink. It was the season for gifts to flow from the rich to the poor, through either the "boxes" given by masters and tradesmen or the dinners and drinks provided to the endless stream of visitors, old and young, male and female, that began early in December with Saint Thomas Day and did not end until Twelfth Night on January fifth.[93] Christmas was not so much a day as a season, focused on relations between households rather than within them and having more to do with adults than with children. It was a time of communal renewal, one of several times during the year when neighbors otherwise divided by wealth, age, and gender utilized obligatory forms of gift exchange to symbolize their solidarity.[94]

Christmas mumming was common in the American colonies too, and it survives still in Philadelphia's New Year's celebrations. But already in the 1830s men and women in wild attire, singing rude songs and making mocking gestures, were being refused admittance to the houses of respectable people.[95] Dissenters and evangelical Protestants had never been particularly hospitable to the old Christmas, regarding it as pagan and papist. When Christmas did not fall on a Sunday, they did not even attend church but worked right through the day, insisting that their employees do the same.

In the early nineteenth century, it seemed that the season might well die out in Protestant Europe and North America, not just in Scotland, where Presbyterian opposition was particularly strong, but everywhere the evangelical revival was under way.[96] In Devon and Cornwall, landowners organized their benevolence on a different basis: "The school fete, the ploughing match, the horticultural show, have driven out May-poles and Christmas misrule."[97] In the new industrial towns like Manchester, employers were also reorienting the yuletide revels in an obvious effort at class reconciliation. There the mechanics' institute organized an annual Christmas party to which both owners and workers were invited. Its meeting room was decorated to reproduce the feel of a baronial hall; a young man dressed as a Christmas prince and a girl costumed as Maid Marion entertained the throngs by dancing around a maypole, all for the purpose of "promoting a more kindly sympathy, and warmer concord amongst the various classes of the community."[98] However, some workers refused their employers' self-interested charity and created their own holidays that were meant to symbolize class rather than community solidarity. This was the purpose of the Christmas rites invented by the Owenites in the 1830s and the Chartists in the 1840s, manifestations of class division that the middle classes found very threatening.[99]

"There seems a magic in the very name of Christmas. Petty jealousies and discords are forgotten. . . . Would that Christmas lasted the whole year through (as it ought)," wrote Charles Dickens.[100] But Christmas was turning inward, the result of the failure of the religious and social movements that in the 1830s and 1840s had tried to make cooperation and harmony a year-round endeavor but were in retreat by the 1850s. Despairing of the possibility of transforming society, idealists like Dickens turned to family myths and rituals to achieve what could not be created by other means.[101] Dickens put his own vaguely Christian socialist convictions wholly at the service of the domesticated Christmas. He did more than any other individual to privatize the holiday, but he was not alone in this effort. Much of the idealism that had flowed into public life in the first half of the century was redirected to the private sphere thereafter.

The first printed Christmas card, showing three generations (including children) lifting what are clearly wine glasses to toast absent family, was produced in England in 1843. The early cards were strikingly secular, variously illustrated with birds, animals, and children, including girls scantily dressed. The themes were initially quite contemporary and unseasonable, and it was not until the end of the century that pictures of the seaside and summer flowers were replaced by the old rural homestead blanketed in snow and populated by children in old-fashioned costumes. Ironically, it was only toward the end of the century, when the middle classes ceased to be regular churchgoers, that cards came to bear more religious messages.[102]

As time went on, the time and effort devoted to Christmas expanded enormously. Looking back to her childhood in the 1870s, Vivien Hughes noted that "nowadays it is difficult to realize that no Christmas preparations were made until a week before the day itself." The holiday was then still a do-it-yourself affair, for the commercialization of Christmas was only beginning. The children painted their own cards, and on Christmas Eve, when father returned home, they put on a play and opened presents. "We never fussed with a Christmas tree or stockings or make believe about Santa Claus," Hughes remembered. Christmas Day was much like a Sunday, except for the excitement of the arrival of the mail, which would contain special cards from friends and relatives, and the big Christmas dinner, which had already become "traditional," meaning, in the Hughes household, turkey and plum pudding.[103]

The figure of Santa Claus, which originated in America in the first part of the century, arrived in England in the 1860s.[104] He was a secular substitute for the religious figure Saint Nicholas. At first this fact bothered some people, but, in time, Santa himself became almost sacred. The Christian calendar provided the occasion but not the meaning of modern Christmas. It was not the Christian churches that created the modern Christmas, for Protestantism had always been a little uneasy about it and Catholics were openly hostile. As late as 1951 the Catholic clergy of Dijon, France, burned Father Christmas in effigy, as a symbol of paganism, before several hundred children. Protestantism was more receptive, but it was not until this century that its churches accommodated themselves fully, rescheduling services on Christmas Eve so as not to interfere with family celebrations.[105]

It was middle-class families, not the church, that invented Christmas as we know it. By the 1850s Christmas had become a very private affair, and in London it was said that "Christmas meetings among the middle ranks in the metropolis are now chiefly confined to family parties, which may be characterized as *happy*, though not *jovial*, as they were want to be; but in *country* places, and among the working classes *in town and country*, much more of the older merriment may be recognized."[106] Goodwill to all men continued to be a major theme of yuletide celebrations, but the bourgeois Christmas closed its doors to all but the nuclear family and close kin. "Perhaps the greatest characteristic of Christmas Day at present is the very general custom of regarding it as a domestic and family festival," wrote William Rusk at the end of the 1860s. "The thoughts of men seem to turn on that day more especially towards home and kindred, and members of families who have during the rest of the year been scattered assemble to join at the table of the head of the family."[107]

The old mummers and wassailers were turned away from the door. Caroling enjoyed a revival in the 1870s, but it was detached from begging and turned over to schoolchildren, whose pious versions of the old songs were judged to be innocent enough to be reincorporated into the church service, from which they had been excluded since the seventeenth century.[108] On the other hand, mistletoe, which had previously decorated churches as a symbol of communal affection, was "now restricted to the social circle, upon the sound and sober principle that *there is a place for every thing*."[109] The Christmas tree, which had been imported from Germany by British royalty earlier in the century, was a part of virtually every middle-class home by the 1880s. These symbols of nature, previously regarded by Protestants as pagan, were now domesticated to the extent that the family no longer had to go outdoors or to the countryside. Nature now came to it, reinforcing the image of family as the most natural and enduring of all the institutions of frantic urban life. Christmas thus shrank space, symbolically bridging the gap between town and country, while at the same time expanding time, bringing the past into the present as no other modern holiday could do.

Modern Christmas is a time not only for returning home but for looking back. The ritualized nature of the day, with its emphasis on doing things just as they always have been done, gives it the unique feel of being time out of time, the opposite of linear time in the sense that it is recoverable time, what Mircea Eliade would call a "succession of eternities."[110] Christmases past are always symbolized as bigger and better regardless of all evidence to the contrary.[111] Nostalgia was present from the very beginning. Charles Dickens lamented the holiday's better days: "People will always tell you that Christmas is not to them what it used to be."[112] But no Victorian really ever intended to go back to the old Christmas; doing so would have reopened the door to the lords of misrule. Ironically, both sides of the Atlantic broke with the past in the name of tradition. Today lamenting the decay of Christmas is as much a part of the holiday as the tree and the plum pudding.

The railway allowed families to come together, but in the iconography of Victorian yuletides, it is invariably the old-fashioned horse-drawn coach that brings the schoolboys home to the glowing hearth around which mothers and sisters have prepared the archetypal homecoming. From the beginning, the modern Christmas has been offered as a refuge from the very things that have made it possible. Even as it was being established, there were those who thought it incompatible with modern urban life: "Gladly at the present time may we fly—from the sad realities of Railroads, British Banks, etc, Indian Mutiny, Money-Panic, and impossible Leviathan (our modern Babel) to Ye Christmas of ye Olden Time."[113] There is a similar sense of loss in the *Morning Chronicle*'s description of Christmas 1860:

> On Christmas Day, England gathers around the hearthstone and assembles in the family. The son separated by the cares of the world in the battle for life is reunited with his father, his mother, and his sisters. But this grand opportunity of uniting the love of families is in some danger of being lost to us. Our intense commercial life has brought with it something of a peripatetic existence to us all.[114]

Like the Victorians, we find it impossible to imagine a future Christmas in any other terms but those of the past. Like an heirloom, its value increases over time. Writing just before the First World War, Clement A. Miles lamented: "In Modern England we have almost lost the festival habit, but if there is one feast that survives among us as a universal tradition it is

Christmas." For Miles, the value of Christmas was that it gives us access to our past and thus to our true selves, individually and collectively. Its rituals are performed "with a deliberate attempt to throw ourselves back into the past, or to reenter for a moment the mental childhood of the race." He rightly remarked that the modern Christmas

> is above all things a children's feast, and the elders who join in it put themselves upon their children's level. . . . At no time in the world's history has so much been made of children as today, and because Christmas is their feast its lustre continues unabated in an age upon which dogmatic Christianity has largely lost its hold, which laughs at the pagan superstitions of its forefathers. Christmas is the feast of beginnings, of instinctive, happy childhood.[115]

Miles was correct. There was nothing in the old Christmas for or about children in general. The old yule season was more about aging and death, with its major symbol old Father Christmas, a figure bearing a close resemblance to grim Father Time. Children had their own saint, Nicholas, and their own day, but it came early in December. Christmas did not become a day special to them until Saint Nick underwent a fictional makeover in Clement Clarke Moore's *The Night before Christmas* (written in America in 1822 but not published in Britain until 1891) and was given his present costume and image as Santa Claus by Thomas Nast, the American illustrator, during the 1860s.[116]

Once he became Santa Claus, Father Christmas lost his association with death and became the eternal grandfather figure, no longer so judgmental as the old Nicholas figure—who used to visit children with warnings as well as gifts—but now jolly and bountiful, a provider symbol that every middle-class father hoped to be in the eyes of his children. Soon adult men were acting out Moore's fiction, dressing up as Santas to the delight of their children. Christmas was a day that allowed them to enter fully into the world of their children. As David Roberts has observed, Victorian fathers "preferred to be remembered for presiding over festive occasions."[117] What appeared to be a children's festival was therefore really a ritual for adults, and especially men, a "succession of eternities" capable of restoring to them what they felt they had lost through the relentless passage of linear time. Before the nineteenth century, they sought eternity at the end of time, but having lost faith in the redeeming powers of death, they turned back to time—ritualized family time—to recover what was lost. "Even of the very things which we most search for in the business of life, we must go back home to find the healthiest types, . . ." wrote James Anthony Froude in

1850. "The wildest pleasures of after-life are nothing so sweet as the old game, the old dance, old Christmas."[118]

Women were less likely to enter figuratively into the rituals of the new yuletide, though without them the new Christmas would have been literally impossible. They shopped for the gifts, decorated the house, and, of course, prepared the big dinner, but Christmas was made by rather than for them. Mothers symbolized the origins men dreamed of returning to; women were supposed to satisfy the imaginings of others, to be more wifely and more motherly on this day than on any other.[119] For men, on the other hand, Christmas was a time of considerable license. They were permitted to dress up as Santa, to join the children in their play, even to dress as women.[120] Christmas had always been a topsy-turvy time, a time of masks and cross-dressing, but in their domesticated forms Christmas rituals were now directed mainly to the needs of males. Women had only one role to play: the wife and mother.

Christmas established a successful precedent for the creation of a new kind of family time. You did not even have to be Christian to practice it: in the 1950s a sample of American Jews showed that 40 percent had Christmas trees. By this time Hanukkah, a holiday that had been on the decline, was also undergoing a revival. "It all goes to show," noted one rabbi, "that if you work away at it you can revive a holiday."[121] The family Thanksgiving followed a similar pattern of development. A communal holiday, it had been honored only intermittently before the nineteenth century and was not given a fixed date on the American calendar until the Civil War, when President Lincoln declared it a national holiday as part of the war effort. It was also in the 1860s that Thanksgiving first became a time for family reunions.[122]

In subsequent decades, the family calendar was extended still further with the advent of family vacations. Elites had always had villas in the countryside, but it was not until the late nineteenth century that middle-class people were buying up country cottages and populating the mountains and seasides of Europe and North America. Initially, men and women took separate summer holidays, but by the end of the century whole families were being transported, making more work for women. The pleasure of going away "consists largely in talking about it beforehand," wrote Phyllis Bourne in the 1870s, expressing the ambivalence that women still feel toward the family holiday.[123]

By 1900 the family vacation had taken on all the qualities of the ancient pilgrimage, except that those who set out were no longer trying to distance themselves from home and family but endeavoring to find the mythic family that eluded them at home. The tendency of vacationers to turn to the same spots year after year reflected a desire not just to find time for family but to connect the present with the past and the future. The ideal family vacation was one that slowed the clocks, one with no surprises, just ordinary food and uneventful days. The seaside and mountains offered the best chance of achieving these goals; by the 1870s the British had come to value the country cottage as the place where time stood still, and during the same decade Americans began to build their Chautauquas—summer communities that beckoned as places of eternal return for hundreds of thousands of middle-class families by the early twentieth century.[124]

The family vacation, like the family weekend, was much slower to be adopted by the working classes. Very few nineteenth-century workers could even think about taking a week off without wages, though as early as the 1860s the better-off factory hands in the textile towns of Lancashire had begun to take a few days off in seaside Blackpool. By the 1880s this practice had become a mass exodus, facilitated by the annual shutdown of whole factories. It was not until after the First World War that most workers had a summer week off, though the introduction of the August Bank Holiday in the 1880s gave families a day in addition to Christmas to get away from it all.[125] In America the advent of the summer family vacation also restructured the family year around two seasons. Previously, ordinary people had been induced to save for the only thing regarded as certain: death. But by the end of the nineteenth century, holiday and Christmas clubs were competing with burial societies for the scant resources of working people. As soon as Christmas was over, families began saving for their summer holidays; once those were ended, it was time to begin to anticipate the Christmas season.[126]

The first study of British working-class vacationers, done at Blackpool in the 1930s, showed that saving and planning for the family occasion involved every member, but each for very different reasons. Men looked forward to it as respite from work: "I want to forget the clock, the newspaper, and the public." They looked forward to playing with the children on the beach or boardwalk. For wives, a Blackpool vacation meant "quietness and rest from duty," especially the duties having to do with cooking, cleaning, and child care. In effect, they saw it as a holiday from family. Blackpool offered a fantasy of family life, but more to men than to women. There "father has a special function of guide and friend to the holiday child, while mother— who has this job all the weekdays of the rest of the year—takes a little comparative rest, and leaves games almost entirely to fathers."[127]

As generation followed generation to Blackpool, the symbolic meanings became even more powerful. As one father put it, he just wanted to "play with the youngster in the sand, and be a kiddie myself once again just for the holidays." By the mid–1930s, the resort's advertising was explicitly appealing to this kind of magic: "And not only do the kiddies enjoy themselves, but the grownups return to their second childhood and romp and play completely irresponsible of everyday worries at home." But women could never leave such worries behind. "After a week away from home, always glad to get back home," said one mother. "Still home to me, thankful to get back and begin saving again."[128]

Holiday resorts and summer places have become the modern family's pilgrimage site. Going back to the same place year after year appeals because, as one Lancashire woman remarked, "It revives past memories, love affairs."[129] After the Second World War, as the automobile became more generally available, the appeal of the Chautauquas and Blackpools began to dim. More people were able to buy their own places, although at a cost—not just the burden of paying a second mortgage but the extra cooking and cleaning work, invariably women's work.[130]

Yet the desire for the family vacation remains undiminished. Even though resented by young children and much complained of by adolescents, this ritual serves adults, particularly men but now also working women, for whom it has become a fixed point in otherwise frenzied lives. Some American summer places have now been in the same family for three or four generations. No matter how many times they change their regular residence, the summer house is always a fixed point of return, a common pivot on which all lives can turn. "This became a rooted place for our children," notes a middle-aged New Jersey minister who has been going to Lake Placid since the 1930s. "This was their home.". He takes delight in watching his grandchildren do the same things that he and his children did before them, noting that the lake "became a kind of shared childhood." His house, Camp Tapawingo, meaning "House of Joy" in the local Native American dialect, is only a few hundred yards from Red Wing, his own father's place. Everything is kept as it was when he bought Tapawingo in 1957, for, as he says, "it is the only place in the world where I don't have to tell people, 'This is the way it was,' because it still is that way."[131]

The family vacation is invariably better in retrospect. "Sometimes family vacations become better the more distance you have from them," notes one American psychologist, who has both studied and lived them.[132] Few families can afford to bring family past so fully into the present as our New Jersey minister, and even when they do, they find the experience less than satisfying. But however tense and disappointing the actual experience of the time spent with family, these times provide an abundance of myth and ritual for families to live by. Holidays are always represented positively and remembered fondly. Postcards going back to the late nineteenth century bear a remarkably consistent message: "Having a great time." Looking at the earlier vacation photos, we find the poses to be strikingly familiar: everyone looks relaxed, everyone is smiling.[133] As Susan Sontag has observed, photography is the way we combat "the imperiled continuity and vanishing extendedness of family life."[134] Today, when our everyday lives seem so overwhelmed by the pressures of work and school, the weekend or summer house has become our favorite pilgrimage site—or, when we cannot be there, the mental place to which our thoughts tend to wander. "Once there, the whole family slips into its past and its patterns," writes Amy Cross. "Those patterns are reassuring, in some ways; the family may not be attached, but like ghost pains of amputees, the feeling is remembered." These are increasingly the chosen places for family weddings and burials, more likely to be photographed and videoed than the family's regular residence.[135]

As we have seen, making time(s) for family began when families had to cope with relentless linear time, separating generations and tearing apart the nuclear family. Ironically, parents work very hard at inculcating those numerical norms of aging that will ultimately separate them from their children. The Victorian middle classes were the first to organize children's birthday parties and to number the years of every family member. But by chronologizing family life, they ensured that childhood, adolescence, and family itself would be left behind and "lost," becoming ultimately objects of intense nostalgia.

In the eighteenth century, houses lived on even when their inhabitants aged and died. Before the Victorian middle classes abandoned the practice, families supplemented their own lineal natural reproduction with lateral social recruitment. Families were made, not born, and because they were defined by place, not by time, they felt no need to celebrate either birthdays or anniversaries. Today we think of families as temporal, beginning when the first child is born and ending when the last child leaves home.[136] Having committed ourselves to reproducing lineally rather than laterally, we are keenly aware of the passage of time and the threat it poses.

The ritualized family occasions that fill our days, weeks, and years represent an effort to recover what has become obsolete about family life. Even as we mark with great precision each birthday and anniversary, we turn them into premonitions and memories that allow us to recover what we are in danger of losing. Earlier generations could find reassuring images of the good family life beyond time in eternity or in the timeless archetypes provided by community. But because we insist on thinking of ourselves as temporal beings, each with his or her own biography, each with a unique family history, we can never escape our finitude and are tempted to turn all our events into ritual and image, all history into myth, in order to give ourselves some of the sense of permanence and connection that modern time denies us.

Family time is not without its contradictions, however. Ironically, it is precisely on such occasions and in such family places that family tensions often flare. The phenomenon of "holiday trauma" is now recognized in both Europe and North America. Voluntary hospitalizations increase as Christmas approaches, and in northern California hot lines are installed in anticipation of the mental disturbances the season produces.[137] It turns out that family time is experienced more positively in anticipation and in memory than in the moments of actual togetherness.

Because these are non-negotiable times, there is little real communication among family members. They are highly staged performances in which individuals are so involved in playing out their assigned parts that they have little chance to respond to one another in the here and now. At such times the mother is Mother, the father is Father, and the children are all Children, regardless of their age or marital status. In effect, family members have even less time for one another at these times than they do in other circumstances. Because family occasions are often disappointing and frustrating, families are compelled to try again the next day, the next week, the next year. And so family time turns, endlessly repeating but also producing the need for yet more family time. In this modern age, we never seem to have enough of it, but its rituals take time, especially women's time, adding to the sense of time famine that, without some significant redistribution of linear time, no amount of cyclical time can ever fully compensate for.

CHAPTER 6

No Place Like Home

It seems hard to believe that people cannot grasp the two most significant things about the little word *home*. The first, as I discovered quite painfully, is simply that one can't go home again: people change, places change, and what one remembers is often a mirage. The second is that home is not so much a physical space but a concept of mind, and, perhaps, a community in which one is at ease, a concept or community that we must forge for ourselves—no one else can create it for us.

Susan Groag Bell, *Between Worlds*[1]

THE VICTORIANS WERE NOT the first to realize that you can never go home again, but they did initiate the modern notion that home is something you must create for yourself. For centuries Europeans had thought of home as a destination, but they had never dared think of it as something they could make here on earth. For them, heaven was home, the one place that promised a peace of mind that could not ordinarily be found in their crowded residences. And they looked to church and the community to provide them with homes away from home. It was not until the middle of the nineteenth century that people began to think of home as something families could make for themselves. It was only then that home became identified with the place of residence and the modern quest for a homeplace began in earnest. But trying to find a house that could also serve as home proved a much more difficult task than anyone ever imagined. Over the past century and a half, the quest has led Europeans and Americans to build and rebuild their houses several times over, and when they have failed to find home at home, to move on, hoping to find in a second home what they cannot find in their primary residence.

Henry Glassie tells us that we are still in the midst of a revolution second only to mankind's transition from the nomadic life of the hunter-gatherer to the sessile existence of the first agriculturalists, a change that took place some ten thousand years ago. The first of these great transformations profoundly altered humanity's relation to nature; the second changed its relationship to itself.[2] This latest revolution began in the late eighteenth and early nineteenth centuries and continues today. It has transformed the meanings of time and space, producing an entirely new understanding of the relationship of house and home, creating new maps, as well as new myths, that still shape the rhythms and movements of families in the late twentieth century.

The modern revolution began quite unnoticed on Clapham Common just outside London in the 1790s. There a group of earnest English evangelicals created what can rightly be called the first modern suburb. They were intent on removing their families from the city in order to create a better spiritual environment, but the world they created for themselves bore little resemblance to the privatized existence that was ultimately to develop in the suburbs. The residents of Clapham Common were inspired by a much older notion of Christian community. Marianne Thornton later remembered of her childhood that "our houses and grounds were almost common property."[3] Doors stood open to adults as well as children, and once the Common was improved, it served to connect the households, which in their collectivity were remembered as home to all. Life flowed through these houses. Bible readings and prayers, as well as leisure, linked young and old, women and men, family and servants, all of whom came and went without ceremony. It was the light and heat of the spirit rather than that of the hearth that oriented movement in a Clapham Common household. "These families," notes Robert Fishman, "knew very little of that segregation by sex and age which was to mark the Victorian Age later in the nineteenth century. One is struck at Clapham with how much of their lives these families spent together; not only are men and women constantly in each other's company, but children were equally included in the adult world."[4]

The menfolk of Clapham Common journeyed each day to work in the metropolis, but their comings and goings went as unmarked as those of the women and children. Visitors entered directly into the main room of the house—then called the library—which was used for work and play, eating and worshiping.[5] The kitchen, with its large hearth, had ceased to be the center of the household's life, but there was as yet no formal drawing or sitting room, and no dining room as such. All rooms were multi-generational and ungendered; while beds had been removed from the downstairs common rooms, the bedrooms upstairs remained cold, unadorned, impersonal spaces with very little privacy, for beds were shared not only with family members but with visitors and servants.

There was nothing cozy about the houses on Clapham Common or those of similar evangelical enclaves on this side of the Atlantic. Placing spiritual before material comforts, these householders invested in their lives rather than in their residences. They spiritualized the household, but in doing so stripped it, as they had their churches, of all symbolic function. Nothing was allowed to stand between the believer and his or her God. In this, nineteenth-century evangelicals were like their Puritan ancestors of the sixteenth and seventeenth centuries, who had been no more tolerant of attachment to home than they were of worship at roadside shrines or holy wells. Their innerworldly asceticism reduced all space, as well as all time, to a single dimension—the path of lifelong pilgrimage whose only destination was union with the Almighty.[6]

During the great moments of religious revival in the nineteenth century, Protestants readily abandoned their dwellings and churches to preach in the fields and streets. During the 1830s and 1840s, they evangelized every available space, sending even women out into the world to do what they saw as God's mission. This wave of Christian revival, taking the form of perfectionism, gave rise to innumerable reform and communal movements that totally ignored the distinction between public and private, between families, generations, and even genders. It seemed for a moment that the Protestant vision of an "interlocking federation of godly households" might actually come into being.[7]

By the 1840s, however, the Protestant middle classes were feeling a good deal less at home in the world. In part their unease was a result of the capitalist transformation, which had made the world a much more amoral place in which to wander. However, there was also the fact that the journey of life was no longer taking place within the context of a community of believers. Now that it was a highly individualized, lonely quest for material success, the journey of life had lost its original meaning. As the image of God waiting at journey's end in the heavenly home faded, the direction of the journey changed abruptly. As Gwen Neville has described this change,

> The Protestant pilgrimage becomes one in which individualized new urban residents move periodically away from their industrial urban universe and back again into the universe associated with the tight-knit kin groups of rural past semifeudal times. The actual repeated journey made by the Protestant pilgrim is one not of going *out* but of going *back* periodically as a way of escaping individuation and depersonalization experienced as a member of a scattered, mobile, and often anonymous urban industrial society.[8]

The house, previously a mere way station, took on features that had been reserved for the heavenly destination. By the 1850s the daily, weekly, and annual homecomings of its inhabitants began to be talked about in terms that the older Protestantism would have regarded as idolatrous. Described as a shrine or altar, the house took on the attributes of a mecca, a storehouse of relics and souvenirs that brought the past magically into the present. And as the middle classes began to describe their domiciles in heavenly terms, heaven itself came to be imagined as a celestial suburb.[9]

The early nineteenth–century Protestant vision of a world transformed by mass conversion gave way to a notion of Christian nurture, which assigned to the family prime responsibility for future generations. The vision of a home beyond history and nature that had previously motivated lifelong pilgrimage through the world now became a reason for retreat from it.[10] "Home," declared Mrs. C. A. Riley in 1851, "there is magic in this simple word. . . . With it comes bright memories of happy hours spent with loved ones, endeared by ties of consanguinity and affections, hours of sweet and holy communion in this blest retirement from a cold and calculating world."[11] Home had lost its association with destination and taken on its modern meaning of retreat or return. Not by accident, this happened precisely at the time when capitalist society began to endorse the myth of competitive individualism, endowing the mobile male with heroic stature while assigning women and children to a sessile existence at home.[12]

The household had been the master metaphor for all living arrangements prior to the midnineteenth century.[13] Political as well as social order depended on it, for household residents were subject to the head of the place in which they dwelled in the same way that each was subject to the royal house under whose sovereignty they found themselves. Rights and duties varied by place in a social and political landscape that was notable for its irregularities. Great and small households coexisted in a terrain where power and status were distributed very unevenly; a majority of persons, men as well as women, had no house or authority to call their own.

The revolutions of the late eighteenth and early nineteenth centuries introduced a whole new way of thinking about social and political order. They not only toppled royal houses but eliminated the metaphor of the house as such, replacing it with that of the home. On the political level, order was reconceived in terms of the "homeland," of states rooted in national territories with clear temporal and spatial boundaries rather than as sovereignties transcending time and space. One's rights depended no longer on occupying a particular place in a hierarchical vertical order but on being a citizen of a nation conceived of as rooted in a particular territory.[14]

Simultaneously, the metaphorical landscape was leveled: the polity ceased to be understood as a hierarchy of households and became a mythic democracy of homes, sharing common characteristics by virtue of being rooted in the same territory. From the midnineteenth century onward, it was common to talk of the English home, the German *heimat*, or the Swedish *holm*, as if all homes, large or small, rich or poor, within a national territory had more in common with one another than with homes elsewhere.[15] *Home* and *homeland* were now paired in the spatial imagination in such a way that one was inconceivable without the other. Home functioned as a symbol promoting the unity of the family in the same way that homeland promoted the unity of the nation. Every nation began to imagine itself as more home-centered than the next. It was not enough for people to be housed; now they had to have homes of their own for the good of the homeland. This assumption prompted Britain's registrar general to declare in 1851: "The possession of an entire house is strongly desired by every Englishman; for it throws a sharp and well-defined circle around his family and hearth—the shrine of his sorrows, joys, and meditations."[16]

Americans attributed public and private virtue to the explicitly gendered home owner: "Such a man is, of necessity—we might say selfishly, a good citizen; for he has a stake in society."[17] The suspicion of the lodger or the renter that originated at this moment only increased with the passage of time. In a housing debate in the late 1930s, a British member of Parliament was moved to declare flats "an abomination . . . never meant for human beings. . . . Flats make Communists while cottages make individuals and, incidentally, make good Conservatives. . . . Any sensible Briton would sooner live in a little wooden shack of his own with a quarter of an acre, than in the finest flat or hotel."[18] His views were echoed by the American suburban developer Bill Levitt, who declared in 1949: "No man who owns his house and lot can be a Communist. He has too much to do."[19]

The home was an imagined community in the same way as the homeland. As symbols they became modernity's spatial points of reference, essential to individual and collective orientation and identity. The very elasticity of the term "home" in the Germanic languages allows it to mean different things to different people while acting as a powerful integrator.[20] Because it is a multivalent symbol with the capacity to reconcile class, gender, and age differences, home has become perhaps the most powerful source of identity in the modern era.[21] "The true home [is] the one spot on earth when man and woman may meet and each freely, fully exercise the rights of each, and so by fulfilling the law of their own being, fulfill also the will and law of their God," declared the Reverend J. Max Hark, an American clergyman, in 1888.[22]

Imagined homes and homelands have effectively collapsed difference into similarity, thereby disguising otherwise evident inequalities. In our time, memories and dreams of home provide a bond between women and men, old and young, rich and poor, that the actual housing supply can never provide. We pretend that the ideal may somehow be within reach of everyone. The Victorians, who were more realistic in such matters, were fully aware that the importance of home was symbolic. Mrs. E. B. Duffey had no illusions that everyone could own their own home when she wrote to her American audience in 1873: "The true home is a world within a world. It is the central point of the universe around which things revolve. It is the treasure-house of affections, the one serenely bright spot in all the world, toward which its absent members always look with hope and anticipation."[23]

In light of the Victorian middle classes' strong commitment to home, it surprises us to learn that, for most of the nineteenth century, they were renters rather than home owners. We like to think of them as the quintessential property owners, but just because they believed every man's house is his castle did not mean they stayed in one place very long. This fact, however, was itself one reason that, for them, "'home' was as much a social construct and a state of mind as a reality of bricks and mortar."[24] For most of the nineteenth century, both sexes felt reasonably at home in the expanding cities, where clubs, lodges, and the newly invented department store provided plenty of respectable homes away from home. Women found the proximity of shops and services particularly appealing.[25]

The fact that middle-class home ownership did not begin to increase until the last decades of the nineteenth century cannot be explained entirely in economic terms, for affordability had not been an issue.[26] The move to the single-family house in the suburbs was initiated by men rather than women. For the latter, homemaking was a business best served by the city, with all its conveniences and amenities.[27] But for men, for whom the home was refuge, these practical concerns were secondary. Even the extended commute enhanced the mythic status that home had come to have in their minds. The suburbs provided the appropriate setting for the naturalization of the home and the work that went on there. As far as men were concerned, homemaking would remain a great mystery. Meals and clean shirts appeared as if by magic.

> With fond longings does he turn toward the bright paradise, his home. . . . With what refreshing gladness does he retire from the noise, and strife, and selfishness of the gentle court, into this *sanctum sanctorum* of the world's vast temple. As he settles into his easy chair, and hears sweet voices call him father, . . . and his heart receives the endearing caresses of her who calls him husband, what delicious, holy pleasure melts and fills his soul![28]

From midcentury onward, the open, spare qualities that had characterized the Clapham Common houses were replaced by the closed, densely furnished interior spaces we associate with Victorianism. As middle-class residence shifted from the inner city to the suburbs, the preferred architectural style became the freestanding or semidetached house. The expanding bourgeoisie could no longer afford the spacious grounds enjoyed by the Clapham pioneers in suburban living, and the houses built after the 1840s were likely to stand side by side, uniformly oriented toward the street, each with its small yard front and back—the model for all subsequent suburban developments. In nineteenth-century America, landscaping was used to give the appearance of a freestanding house, for this became the symbol of individual independence that an apartment or attached house could not provide.[29]

This change occurred simultaneously with the transformation of the traditional connecting places—fields, streets, and marketplaces—into "empty" space, mere conduits for people and things.[30] The street was no longer a place to be and became something to cross or traverse. Likewise, the fields and marketplaces became agoraphobic, perceived as especially dangerous to women and children, but uncomfortable even for middle-class men who traveled them going to and from work.[31] In the cities there remained a few of the "great good places" that had traditionally provided homes away from home for women as well as men, but in the newly developing suburbs the journey between work and home was more likely to be uninterrupted.[32] Victorian middle-class males were fated to be the world's first commuters. In the early nineteenth century, many had lodged near their work as a matter of convenience, but this practice had largely ceased by 1900. Aware that commuting meant that they forfeited "some associations and friendships, some privileges," they were nevertheless convinced by the argument that "you have gained a *home*—that which you never truly have in a hired city lodging."[33]

To home was transferred all the meanings of comfort and rest that had once been associated only with heaven. In John Ruskin's words:

> This [is] the true nature of home—it is a place of Peace; the shelter, not only from all injury, but from all terror, doubt, and division. In so far as it is not this, it is not home; so far as the anxieties of the outer life penetrate into it, and the inconsistently minded, unknown, unloved, or hostile society of the outer world is allowed by either husband or wife to cross the threshold, it ceases to be a home; it is then only a part of that outer world which you have roofed over, and lighted fire in.[34]

Home had become a sacramental site, complete with the redemptive qualities previously associated with holy places: "bright, serene, restful, joyful nook of heaven in an unheavenly world."[35] As an American publication put it: "One of the holiest sanctuaries on earth is home. The family altar is more venerable than any altar in the cathedral. The education of the soul for eternity begins by the fireside. The principle of love, which is to be carried through the universe, is first unfolded in the family."[36] The parlor had become "the family temple . . . a shrine into which is placed all that is most precious," not only a ceremonial site but a museum.[37]

In Henry Glassie's words, the transformation of the house into the home represented the triumph of "comfort over generosity, personal aspirations over communal participation"; in these new domestic interiors, "manmade objects were ordered to class people."[38] Architecture was henceforth the means of creating boundaries of class, gender, and generation. Initially, class segregation took place within the house. Servants did not disappear from middle-class households until the 1930s in most Western countries. Yet such lower-class persons were effectively segregated architecturally and ritually from the midnineteenth century onward. They belonged to one part of the dwelling, still defined as the house, while the family belonged to another, now defined as the home. The residents of house and home had their own separate times and places, as if they existed in entirely different worlds.[39] This change effectively reclassified related as well as nonrelated persons. Now there was a clear distinction between the nuclear family (at home) and kin (just visiting); between children and women (always at home) and youth and men (strangers in their own homes); and between the renter and the home owner—all distinctions unknown in earlier periods.

Home had indeed become the mythic place where life began and ended. Home birth and home death became the middle-class norm, and it was only the poor who were born and died in hospitals. In earlier periods, birth and death had disrupted the household; now they consecrated it. The Victorians developed great attachment to the places where their children had been born and their ancestors had died, and by the end of the century they were investing in houses they meant to "keep and die in."[40]

Of course, many would never realize this dream. Middle-class people also ended up in the poorhouse, but they fended off their worst fears by reimagining old age in domestic terms. As Stephen Foster's popular 1851 song "Old Folks at Home" testified, Victorians had difficulty imagining the old as anywhere but at home. In the nineteenth century, the poorhouse would be renamed the "old people's home," further reinforcing the myth of a good old age, to which only a minority of the population would ever have access.[41]

What life could not ensure, death now guaranteed. In the reconstructed cemeteries of Europe and North America, the middle classes replicated their homes literally and symbolically. Tombs were referred to as "homes for the dead," and cemeteries came to look like suburbs.[42] But as if that were not sufficient reassurance, heaven was also reimagined as a place of single-family dwellings, dream houses awaiting their absent family members.[43]

The Victorians set the precedent not only for moving from house to house in search of home but also for creating within their houses a series of distinctive homes capable of maintaining the class, age, and gender distinctions they regarded as vital to social order and progress. As the house had once served humanity's need to master the elements, the home was conceived as mastering human nature. During the Victorian era, the house was perceived for the first time as a force of nature itself, with its own character. It was anthropomorphized, imagined to have a spirit capable of animating the world as no other place could. In earlier centuries, nature was seen as animated, as capable of speaking to man through rocks, trees, and animals. Now that nature had been brought so completely under man's dominion, it was silenced and the spirits that once animated the outdoors were moved indoors, where they took on a whole new life. Moreover, having condemned peasant animism as superstition, the Victorians now treated their domesticated pets and plants as if they had distinctive personalities.[44] The household interior, previously a purely functional space, became alive, every object capable of speaking to the inhabitants. To Winifred Foley, these were "no longer inanimate objects, but *friends*."[45]

Imagined in this anthropomorphic way, every house was expected to have a presentable face and less presentable lower and back areas.[46] Now that it was reoriented to the street, the front was simultaneously the bourgeois family's window on the world and the face it wished to present to that world. The houses of the wealthy elites had always had representative functions, but the ordinary eighteenth-century middle-class row house had been symmetrical and inscrutable, with no name or number. By the middle of the nineteenth century, however, a variety of styles—including Gothic and Italianate—had replaced the uniform classical fronts to give each house its own identity, connecting it firmly to the past.[47]

In Britain the bourgeoisie personalized their suburban villas, naming them, giving each a distinctive character. As Gervase Wheeler, a major Victorian architect, put it: "The genuine Englishman so loves his home and its belongings, that he gives even the most uncouth arrangements a certain charm, by investing them with individuality, and nameless and numberless evidences of habitableness, so that our houses which have been long occupied by the same family, appear pleasant to the visitor."[48] American as well as British housefronts were renowned for their finicky, idiosyncratic detail, which later generations would find ugly and pretentious but which, the architect Calvert Vaux argued, transformed even the most ordinary house into a true home.[49]

The backs of Victorian houses had much less personality; these were meant to be the functional side of the dwelling, the tradesmen's and servants' entry, where the comings and goings were routine and unceremonial. Front doors were reserved for family and important visitors. They were formal, equipped with knockers or bells, the site of ritualized comings and goings. These doors no longer opened into the kitchen, as was still the case in country cottages and working-class dwellings, but onto what the Victorians now called the hall, a well-defined transitional space where visitors were greeted, waited to be announced, and, if the inhabitants were out or did not wish to see them, left their calling cards. The hall was meant to be warm and cheerful; more than a mere passage, it was meant to "suggest habituary and domestic use."[50] It constituted a true threshold, demarcating not just the physical boundaries of the house but also, through newly invented threshold rituals, the distinctions between various persons who presented themselves there. "None of the family come to the door to meet you," it was noted. "The servant shows you into a Parlour—drawing-room was the proper word now."[51]

Back doors gave more direct, informal access to the interior, but only to the kitchen and work areas of the house, not to those areas now defined as "home." Back doors deserved no halls or special furnishings. The kitchen remained the one space in the middle-class house still connected to the world, but it was no longer a place where life flowed, joining one house to every other. Servants and tradespeople may have felt at home in other people's kitchens, but middle-class housewives certainly did not.[52] In large houses, kitchens remained "below stairs," places not for family but for servants. But even in houses where wives were more involved in cooking, kitchens lost their warm, welcoming character when the hearth was replaced by the coal-fired range and the open fire migrated to other parts of the house, where the newly invented fireplace became the focus of home, distinguishing family from not-family.

Only in working-class houses did the kitchen continue to be the locus of family life. In these cramped quarters, there was no place for a separate dining or living room. Cooking, eating, working, playing, even sleeping took place there. By the end of the nineteenth century, some working-class homes had set off one room as a parlor, but it functioned very differently from the middle-class drawing room. It was reserved for special occasions—such as illness or death—or for the occasional visitor, but it was not the center of home life. The kitchen continued to generate the greater light and warmth, and what the working classes could not find there, they still sought in their homes away from home: the pub, the tavern, and the café.

The idea of comfort was the Victorians' great contribution to modern living. Previously, comfort had been associated with the spiritual (consolation) and the social (mutual aid or support) and was traditionally provided by institutions. The Victorians were the first to domesticate comfort and associate it with physical well-being. As Witold Rybczynski notes, "'Comforter' in secular Victorian England no longer referred to the Redeemer, but to a long woolen scarf."[53]

Yet the physical and symbolic comforts of home were not always easy to reconcile. On both sides of the Atlantic, the hearth in the parlor was seen as a requirement of the latter but not necessarily conducive to the former. Fireplaces were attractive but wasteful and dirty, adding to the costs of heating and cleaning. Gervase Wheeler built them into his houses but had to admit that they made large drawing rooms uncomfortable; to compensate, he added "comfortable nooks and bays, free from draught, not far from the fire, nor near the door, wherein the members of the family circle may dispose themselves without formality."[54] The British continued to sacrifice physical to spiritual warmth until well into this century, and even Americans, who took to central heating earlier, would not give up the open flame. Henry Hudson Holly called the hot-air furnace "an abomination grievous to be borne by those who remember fondly the ancient symbol of domestic union and general hospitality."[55] Even as working fireplaces disappeared, they were replaced by symbolic hearths. Everywhere "the fireside image gained prominence even as the fireside proper was disappearing from the home."[56]

The parlor and the dining room became the semipublic places where family entertained invited guests; the only truly private spaces existed upstairs, where no stranger was allowed to penetrate. Staircases were now positioned so that "direct communication with the upper floor may not be seen."[57] Yet for most of the nineteenth century, bedrooms remained cold, austere, "hollow," backstage places in which to sleep, dress, and make ready for the elaborate ritual presentations that took place frontstage in the parlor and dining room.[58] The personalizing of bedrooms, and our contemporary notion of bed as the ultimate home of one's own, were wholly unthinkable to the Victorians before the 1880s. Belonging to the house more than the home, they were decorated with cheap religious prints rather than treasured family pictures.[59]

House and home jostled for priority for most of the nineteenth century, but it was clear by the 1870s and 1880s that home was winning. Initially, notions of homey comfort did not extend much beyond the parlor. As Dennis Chapman noted, families with servants "created two or more homes within a single house and left permanent marks on our domestic architecture ... the contrast between the kitchen and the living room, for example." The parlor was the first room to be decorated and furnished, the kitchen the last, and only gradually did comfort enter the dining room and the bedrooms.[60] Before 1850 only adults had beds of their own; children were expected to sleep with servants. However, by the 1880s providing children with rooms of their own was seen as vital, for "without it, it is only their father's house, not theirs. . . . But, by giving them their own apartment, they themselves become personally identified with it."[61]

To create its version of family space, the Victorian house used doors and passageways to divide front from back, upstairs from downstairs. Mrs. Hall, the representative Victorian wife, was told to create

> a comfortable fire-side, well-cooked meals, no disorder, no litter of any kind . . . let no smell of washing and ironing pervade the home, no talking of Susan's [the servant] shortcomings; or of the baby's ailments—baby should be in bed when Mr. Hall returns, and then be sure that no

basket of stocking-mending or household needlework be introduced to
his notice, under the idea that he may see how industrious you are.[62]

Separating the kitchen from the dining room prevented "exposure of the
domestic economy to guests" but also kept it hidden from the family itself.[63]

As a result, the kitchen was the one part of the house that remained
unincorporated into the home. Middle-class families retreated from the
kitchen to avoid contact with the disorder associated with servants, tradespeople, and the productive operations carried on there. After the invention
of the coal range in the 1780s, there were precious few improvements in
kitchen technology until the twentieth century, and most such improvements were achieved by people like the Shakers, who abhorred servant-
keeping.[64] Americans, who faced a servant shortage earlier than did Europeans, were the first to experiment with new technologies, but their houses
also bore the mark of class as well as gender division.

The narrow horizons that had given earlier generations such a clear, if fixed,
sense of place were disappearing by the 1850s. Set adrift by the industrial
and political revolutions to conquer vast new territories, middle-class men
turned to home as a point of orientation, as a source of psychic as well as
social order.[65] Many were convinced that civilization itself depended on the
creation of a nation of home-dwellers. Andrew Jackson Downing wrote that
"when smiling lawns and tasteful cottages begin to embellish a country, we
know that order and culture are established."[66]

Home was put forward as a cure for the newly discovered malady of ago-
raphobia, but there were those who held the home responsible for claus-
trophobia, also unique to the late nineteenth century.[67] In fact, many Americans and Europeans were highly ambivalent about this latest incarnation of
home. Henry David Thoreau built his Walden cabin, "a house which you
have got into when you have opened the outside door and the ceremony is
over," as a challenge to the homes he saw going up all around him. He
invoked an earlier Christian tradition in his transcendental meditations on
the virtues of homelessness. "We no longer camp as if for a night, but have
settled down on earth and have forgotten heaven. . . . We have built for this
world a family mansion, and for the next a family tomb."[68]

But as Christian and secular transcendentalism lost its appeal, this kind
of ambivalence became muted, though it never entirely disappeared.
Mobility increased, but absence only seemed to make the heart grow
fonder. As adult males exited their houses in pursuit of worldly success,
they became ever more attached to their mental image of home. At the

point when one in five Americans were changing residence every year, sales of samplers evoking "Home, Sweet Home" reached their peak.[69] Now that family members found themselves increasingly separated by the demands of capitalist economies and nation-states bent on promoting rapid change and mass mobility, simply occupying the same house was not sufficient to convey a sense of identity. Even as work and learning left the house and the lives of men and women, adults and children, went in different directions, the symbolism of home became ever more powerful. What had once been conceived of as father's house now became everyone's home, imagined, as Mrs. Duffey would have it, as the "point in the universe around which all things revolve." Just as the new family times coordinated the disparate schedules, providing family members with a common sense of anticipation as well as a store of collective memories, the symbols of home provided a domestic mecca that, wherever family members might be physically, brought them together in a shared mental terrain.

The Victorians invented a whole new way of seeing and talking about domestic space. The word *homemaking* came into parlance only in the mid-nineteenth century.[70] The term *homelike* first entered English in 1817, displacing the older word *homely*, with its meaning of simple or plain, which today we use to refer to people but rarely to homes. The term *homey* was first used in 1856, referring to those highly personalized spaces the Victorians liked to call "cozy," an eighteenth-century word that in the nineteenth century became virtually synonymous with home.[71] *Homemaking* came to mean something very different from *housekeeping*. A housekeeper could be hired; a homemaker could not. A house could be kept in repair by the expenditure of money, but to keep a home was thought of as a labor of love involving the creation of the symbols, myths, and rituals that made a house a home. And from the very beginning of the use of the term, "homemaking" was gendered, based on the assumption that a man could build and repair a house but only a woman could make a home. It was not just the labor of women but their presence that was required. As Josiah Condor wrote to his fiancée: "'Tis where thou art, is home to me/And home without thee cannot be."[72]

In the eighteenth century, it was the presence of its male head (what the Germans called *Hausvater*) that made a mere dwelling a real house. A woman could stand in as his surrogate, but in the eyes of the law, as well as popular opinion, the house was a masculine domain. Most men were deeply involved in the day-to-day running of the house, including child care, activities that were fully consistent with the prevailing definition of masculinity.[73] By the end of the nineteenth century, however, perceptions had turned 180 degrees. Homemaking, declared Frances Power Cobbe, a leading British feminist, was "a right which no man can take from us; for a man can no more make a home than a drone can make a hive. . . . It is a woman, and only a woman—and a woman all by herself, if she likes, and without any man to help her—who can turn a house into a home."[74] Similar views were being expressed on this side of the Atlantic. "Home is the wife's province," it was agreed. "It is her natural field of labor. It is her right to govern and direct its interior management."[75]

The ownership of a house was no longer sufficient to make a man feel at home. That required the presence of a woman—if not a wife, then a dutiful sister, daughter, or, as in Charles Dickens's case, a devoted sister-in-law.[76] Women's status and reputation for "true womanhood" depended on association with homes they could not legally own, while a man's respectability was increasingly vested in ownership and disassociated from actual involvement with day-to-day homemaking. Men who were too much involved in domestic affairs were regarded as "homebodies" and in danger of forfeiting their masculinity. A real man was the breadwinner who journeyed into the world, not in the *communitas* of the pilgrimage, but as an individual competing for wealth and power. For men, journey gave a whole new meaning to home. It was the place where they were not, the place they were always coming from or returning to. Many men continued to spend a good deal of time at home—some were even involved with housekeeping and child care—but because they were supposed to be more in the world than at home, their comings and goings were always marked in the same way as those of strangers, thereby ritually maintaining the symbolic distance necessary to true manhood.[77]

In earlier centuries, everyone had been more at home in the world, even if that world extended not much beyond the parish boundary. Now no one was at home in the world, even the men whose "nature" was assumed to fit them for worldly endeavors. As a consequence, home came to have a special and compelling meaning for men that it did not have for women of the same class. The Victorians were fully aware that "home is a business for women, haven for men."[78] It became the middle-class male's secular mecca, a mythic place that sustained him in the same way that the imagined Holy Land sustained the pilgrim.

Women approached the home in a more matter-of-fact way, for after all, it remained for most of them a place of long, hard hours of work. While men's comings and goings were marked daily, one threshold ceremony sufficed for women. Carrying the new bride across it had no precedent in any earlier ceremonies but had become an obligatory part of the middle-class wedding tradition by 1900.[79] Wives and daughters were less physical than symbolic captives of their homes, however. They were not nearly as closely confined or chaperoned as legend would have us believe, but home was something that no respectable woman could ever afford to leave behind symbolically. Wherever she went on her charitable or social rounds, the Victorian woman carried home and family with her. They were her one and only excuse for visiting or shopping. Her card represented her home and family just as a man's represented his firm or profession.[80]

Home had become a mythic place for men, and mythic places require keepers. Victorian daughters stayed home longer than sons. They were more likely to be married "from home," and embarking on a respectable marriage meant having a home of one's own. The idea of home as destiny drew women into marriage only to overwhelm them in what the Victorians called the "marriage trauma."[81] Men, on the other hand, were propelled into the world at an early age. They too dreamed of home, not, as women did, as destiny, but in nostalgic terms, as a place of return and refuge. As James Anthony Froude put it, "The very things which one must search for in the business of life, we must go back to home to find the healthiest types."[82]

Over the course of the century, middle-class men became ever more incapable of making a home for themselves. Undomesticated as children, they tended to turn their wives into mother figures and their children into playmates, with the result that the Victorian father figure became a curious combination of contradictory images: the stranger, the intruder, the clown, and the biggest child in the family.[83] Dora Montefiore remembered that, as a child of the 1850s, "every evening we were dressed to go down to the drawing room for the children's hour, between six and seven, when my dear father had returned home, and we small children were made joyful by his sunny smile and the way he entered into our fun and games and devised glorious surprises for us."[84]

Even as the old patriarchal *Hausvater* figure faded, the mother figure became more sharply defined and foregrounded. In the eighteenth century, no house could get along without a father; by the end of the nineteenth century, a home without a mother was a "broken" home, lacking in the essential quality of homeyness.[85] Wherever she went, it went with her; wherever she might be resident was automatically the "homeplace," the mecca for all pilgrimages, the site of daily, weekly, and annual family reunions. Even in death the mother was the "central point of the universe around which all things revolved." Her grave invariably became the family plot, the best kept, the one most frequently visited.[86]

On both sides of the Atlantic, the matrilocal homeplace was described as "a shrine more sacred than that of Mecca or Jerusalem."[87] It would seem a paradox that sons and daughters felt compelled to leave their own houses in order to feel truly at home, but ritual journeys to Grandmother's house or the old homestead allowed the divergent paths of family members to cross in ways that they no longer did in everyday life. The very anticipation of a homecoming or a reunion, together with the memories such an experience produced, provided a symbolic unity that physical proximity could no longer supply.[88]

By the end of the nineteenth century, home was more likely to be a memory than an actual place. The pace of change was rapidly obliterating old homeplaces, so that it had become literally impossible ever to go home again. Instead, images and symbols of the "old homestead" began to appear in parlors everywhere throughout the Western world, as these became the archives for the family's vanishing past. By the twentieth century, the homeplace, even when all that remained was a vacant lot, had an enduring attraction and haunting effect. "I went over there a year or two ago," remembers a North Carolina woman. "Well, I went on out there; and seemed like the memories poured out. Oh mercy. Seemed like they just came meeting me."[89]

Women became the prime keepers of family memories, but in the absence of actual homeplaces, they also became the objects of memory.[90] Memories of childhood, no longer able to attach themselves to a particular place, focused increasingly on mothers, who, wherever they might be, were regarded as home. "Home is the peculiar sphere of woman," wrote the Reverend John Ware. "With the world at large she has little to do. Her influence begins, centers and ends in her home."[91] The home was described as the "workshop for the mother. It is not only where she is to live, to love, but where she is to care and labor. Her hours, days, weeks, months and years are spent within its bounds; until she becomes an enthroned fixture, more indispensable than the house itself."[92]

Even as women became more physically mobile toward the end of the nineteenth century, they became more symbolically sessile. "A real home-loving person is a kind of sun," wrote a Swedish architect. "Whether she sits in her corner, smiling generally or walks from house to house, spreading warmth, she is always at home, radiating cosiness. Such a person is invincible."[93] Over the course of this century, home has become ever more matrilocal, symbolically if not literally. "Freed from the bonds of place, Mother can now be more truly at home," writes David Sopher.[94] While women's freedom of movement has undoubtedly increased, the pressures on them to "be there," culturally and psychologically, remain, binding them mentally to home in ways that men find difficult to appreciate.[95]

The Victorians were the first to animate domestic space, to use it for the cultural production of a feeling of connection, security, and peace that still attaches specifically to home and nowhere else. Ruskin described home as "a sacred place, a vestal temple, a temple of the hearth watched over by Household Gods."[96] Middle-class life became characterized by what an American observer called "beneficent estheticism in the matter of form and ceremony itself." The visual became the preeminent sense, and domestic architecture became for the first time an instrument of redemption.[97] The favored style of middle-class villas, Gothic revival, was assumed to imbue the house and its inhabitants with moral character. Its cross-shaped design, stained-glass windows, parlor organ, and Gothicized furniture all contributed to this effect.[98] Earlier Protestant generations had refused to sanctify their residences, but now W. J. Loftie could write: "We in England have decorated our churches sometimes perhaps a little too much. And it is surely time we turned to that second church, the temple in which even the old heathen place a family altar, and would give our homes a little more of the beauty which comes of order and purity."[99]

The home had never before been sanctified in the way it was in the nineteenth century.[100] Baldwin Brown would argue that home was a reflection of the "divine original."[101] All the talk of "home sweet home" led G. K. Chesterton to remark later that the Victorians had managed to create "almost the first irreligious home in all of human history," by which he meant that they had transferred the sacred to a realm that earlier generations had regarded as profane: "Theirs was the first generation that ever asked its children to worship at the hearth without the altar. This was equally true, whether they went to church at eleven o'clock, . . . or were reverently agnostic or latitudinarian."[102]

Catholics were somewhat slower to attribute a sacred quality to domestic space. They called on the priest to bless their houses, but the presence of pictures of the Blessed Mary and souvenirs of pilgrimages taken in the name of the faith were meant to remind them that true sanctity lay elsewhere. Not until the end of the nineteenth century did the urban Catholic home become its own source of redemption, but, once this revolution had occurred, the church itself had to struggle to remain the central place of Catholic devotion.[103] The pattern was much the same among Jews, for whom home also took on a sacred aura around the turn of the century. By then the "Jewish home," defined by an increasingly dense round of domestic holidays, objects, and food, was displacing the synagogue itself as the center of Jewish life, a trend that proved irreversible.[104]

Victorians on both sides of the Atlantic took great comfort in arranging their furniture into permanent groupings, abandoning the functional practice of placing chairs and tables against the walls, ready for deployment according to the number of people present. The middle classes abhorred open spaces, and their heavy, immobile furniture fixed the parlor's capacity and transformed it into a stage set for a prescribed set of family actors. The same was true of the other archetypal Victorian family space, the dining room, which provided only a set number of places for the rituals that took place there. As family time became more rigidly scheduled, family space also became more fixed and enclosed.[105]

The parlor and the dining room had to serve dual purposes, however. Initially designed in a fairly uniform and stylized manner, they were public as well as family rooms. They gave the house its "character," a term that carried heavy moral implications and, at first, left little room for personal taste or style.[106] Visiting became a highly ritualized affair, testing the social acceptability of both host and guest. Proper visits were made at certain set times, were of fixed duration, and followed a scripted drama of gracious greetings and farewells in which every respectable middle-class person was well schooled.[107]

As we have already seen, the parlor was the stage where the family put itself on display. It was there that it represented itself to itself in death as well as in life. Until the end of the nineteenth century, it was the place where the deceased were laid out for viewing. When it became the practice for undertakers to remove the dead from the house to the newly designated funeral parlor, the parlor was renamed the "living room"; it would remain the place where the middle classes entertained their guests and showed their best face to the world.[108]

Until this century, working-class people had too little space to be able to devote even part of it to representational purposes. When an additional room became available, it was usually converted into a parlor, the one place in the house kept for "privacy, for courtships or business or social intercourse which does not appeal to the whole of the family." As late as the 1950s, the working-class parlor remained "a place for the reception of the stranger or the official visitor, a defence in depth against the outerworld."[109] The parlor's window was the family's face to the world, a display case for the signs of its respectability and status. Normally, it was kept shut and child-proof. "Yet, however crowded we were, we never dreamed of sitting in our one tolerably large room except on special occasions," remembered a man who grew up near London during the 1920s. "The 'front room,' like every other in our street, was sacrosanct. Its green venetian blinds were pulled down on sunny days to preserve the colours of the carpet, its lace curtain drawn back just enough to reveal a thriving aspidistra in an art pot."[110] The front room indicated not only social status but domestic order. It was the face that family showed not only to the world but to itself. "Its most distinctive feature," noted Alwyn Rees, is the number of family photographs that adorn the chest-of-drawers and the mantle-pieces. It is a kind of museum or sanctum—the repository of things which have, or which once had, an emotional significance: wedding dresses and other old clothes in the chest-of-drawers—some of them belonging to the departed—wedding groups in out-moded fashions along the walls. . . . Its peace is seldom disturbed for any length of time save when a member of the family suffers a prolonged illness.[111]

The importance of the working-class parlor increased rather than decreased over the course of the century. In a survey of British housing completed in the late 1940s, Dennis Chapman found that,

in its ideal form, the parlour contains the portraits of parents, children, and friends; it houses souvenirs, each of which serves to remind its owner of some incident in the social life of the family, and gifts which are a memorial to the social relationships of the past. In some families articles of religious connotation find a place in the parlour; in Roman Catholic families a corner may be set aside as a shrine.[112]

As late as the 1970s, what the people of Ballymenone called "the Room" was still the place where "photographs of ancestors and children, emigrants and the home's inhabitants in youth, will widen attendance past time, space, and flesh. Mirrors will create portraits of the living next to those of the dead, who stare in an endless blessing down on the few major occasions that open up the Room to life."[113]

Today "the Room" survives in only the rural cottages and townhouses that have not been gentrified over the course of the twentieth century.[114] To middle-class housing experts, "the habit of keeping shut-up parlors for occasional company is so absurd that it is difficult to give people who practice it credit for ordinary common sense."[115] From the 1920s onward, domestic reformers turned their efforts to reconfiguring the relationship between the functioning house and the symbolic home; they did eventually succeed in reintegrating the two, a result with important implications for family life and for age and gender relations. This shift was largely attributable to the disappearance of servants on both sides of the Atlantic, necessitating an integration of spaces previously separated by class while maintaining a gendered division of house and home. The woman of the house had to take on all the tasks and spaces of housekeeping in addition to her already assigned roles and places of homemaking. In the absence of the cook, the housemaid, and the nanny, a new and much more demanding definition of wife and mother emerged in the interwar period. To assist the middle-class housewife with her increased burden of cleaning, cooking, and child care, the new science of "home economics" promoted smaller, more efficient kitchens that were not so cut off from the rest of the house.[116] The new "living room" was easier to clean, though the culturally obligatory fireplace remained a source of cold draughts and dirty carpets.[117]

After the Second World War, the interior spaces of houses were opened still further. The doors and walls between the kitchen, dining, and living rooms came down, and new "family rooms" were attached to the kitchen. As houses were built for a mass market, they became smaller and rooms were forced to serve multiple purposes.[118] Children did their homework at the dining room table, and the kitchen was "brought out of its ancient obscurity and [made] into a room—or part of a room—with social standing equal to all other rooms."[119] In American houses the kitchen returned to the front of the house, where, as Clifford Clark puts it, "the woman could run the house without ever leaving the kitchen. She could cook a gourmet meal for guests and still talk with them as she prepared the food. Or she could do the laundry and still keep an eye on the children."[120] In Europe as well, cooking, an activity left to the servants for the previous hundred years, suddenly regained prestige, thus enhancing the kitchen as mecca, while at the same time binding women even more closely to it. In the 1960s the British magazine *Women's Own* announced: "The kitchen has become the most important room in the house. This is the room which, more than any other, you love to keep shining and bright. A woman's place? Yes. For it is the heart and centre of the meaning of home. The place where, day after day, you make with your hands precious gifts of love."[121]

The last vestige of the old household had finally been incorporated into the symbolic space of the modern home. With servants gone, it was now family territory, but the immense costs of this repossession, not noticed at the time, were borne mainly by women, who became the occupying power symbolically as well as materially. As we have already seen, women's time had been appropriated by family. Now their space was at its disposal as well.

PART III

Mythic Figures
in the
Suburban Landscape

CHAPTER 7

The Perfect Couple

Nature yields nothing without ceremonies.
Ernst Cassirer, *The Philosophy of Symbolic Forms*[1]

MARRIAGE AS AN INSTITUTION may seem to be on the rocks, but romantic love has never been more valued than right now. The conjugal has become the standard for all relations, the premarital as well as the marital, the homosexual as well as the heterosexual. Children play at it, and teenagers practice it. Establishing a romantic relationship with another person, of different or same sex, is the sign of adulthood in modern Western culture.[2] Yet all this is a relatively recent development, for it was not really until the last century that the perfect couple assumed a central place in the Western imagination.

Romance is not new, but never has it been so exclusively symbolized by the love between just two people. In earlier centuries, it had been possible to imagine love in other ways—in relationships between friends, in bonds with spiritual figures, in various kinds of religious and secular communities.

For its first twelve centuries, Christianity showed a decided preference for love that transcended marriage and family; even when the church finally created its own marriage rite at the Fourth Latern Council in 1215, its ambivalence about equating love exclusively with the conjugal continued.[3] The Reformation of the sixteenth century gave full spiritual sanction to marriage, but Protestantism also taught that love of another was secondary to love of God. Not until the nineteenth century was conjugal love talked about as divine.

Today the perfect couple is as likely to be found outside as inside marriage. Once the conjugal became an idealized image, it could justify leaving marriage as well as entering it. However, the mythic bond tends to outlast the physical.[4] Modern conjugality endures much longer in the mind than it does in reality, even beyond death itself. Elisabeth Kubler-Ross recently told Jonathan Rosen that she intends to join her ex-husband in heaven despite the fact that he remarried before his death. "To my mind, when you're married, you're married for life," she said. "That's my philosophy. Even after he married that young Loulou, he was still my husband. That was his problem, not mine."[5] It seems that conjugality has been granted an immortality that singlehood has not, for when Europeans and Americans imagine life after death, they imagine only couples.[6]

For centuries conjugal love was more feared than celebrated; it was viewed as too volatile and insubstantial to sustain either individual identities or the social order. "In premodern Europe marriage usually began as a property arrangement, was in its middle mostly about raising children, and ended about love," writes John Boswell, who contrasts this expectation to the modern one, in which "marriage begins about love, in its middle is still mostly about raising children (if there are children), and ends—often—about property, by which point love is absent or a distant memory."[7]

Our ancestors were careful to restrict formal nuptials to those who were economically independent through access to a farm or a trade. People made the decision to marry before they had any particular mate in mind.[8] They married late, and the poorest among them never married at all. Fortunately for the celibate, there was still room for love outside marriage. As in many cultures where household formation is restricted, various forms of lesser unions, concubinage, and common-law arrangements were considered quite licit. Even same-sex unions, though they lost the sanction of the church after the fourteenth century, continued an underground existence, offering yet another variation of love.[9] Those who had no prospects of establishing a household could love as they liked as long as they were discreet about it, but those who would be masters and mistresses of households had less choice. Church and community could be counted on to extract the price of admission to this privileged position: conformity to the rules. As a consequence, there was very little romance in the way people courted and wed before the nineteenth century.

By modern standards, premodern courtships were hasty and matter-of-fact, wholly lacking in the process of self- and mutual discovery we have come to associate with romance. Prospective mates usually got to know one another in the normal course of work and play; in premodern society the sexes mixed freely in the markets, streets, and fields, and courtship was inseparable in its rhythms and locations from the rest of life. In Europe men sought out women where they worked. In Yorkshire this practice was called "going-a-sitting," while elsewhere it went by the name of "night visiting."[10] In America, "quiltings" and "huskings" provided similar occasions for getting to know the opposite sex. While these activities were rarely supervised by adults, premature pairing off was frowned upon by peers, who substituted their authority for that of parents.[11] The result was a quite astonishing degree of freedom and familiarity between young men and women, but always in the presence of others. It seems that they were in and out of one another's houses, even one another's bedrooms, with great frequency and informality. In Pamela Brown's account from rural Vermont in the 1830s, she and her friend Elmina had "laid abed very late" one Sunday: "We had hardly got the [house] work done before James Merill, Joel Slack and Thomas Fletcher came in. They staid and talked and sang an hour or two. Then we all walked down to the 'Five Corners' where we met Solomon Carlisle, H. Willis, the two Briggs and Charlotte Duncan."[12]

Contrary to myth, few premodern marriages, apart from those of the aristocracy, were arranged. Young women as well as young men enjoyed a very large measure of choice.[13] Lines of gender and age were not so clearly drawn then as they are now, and because they did not marry until their mid to late twenties, brides and grooms were far more mature, accomplished, and independent. Indeed, the late age of marriage was "in itself a measure of that maturity and of the recognition of the heavy responsibilities that wedlock invoked."[14] Many men had already established their manhood by going through the rites of passage associated with the trades. The female life course was less likely to be marked in the same manner, but years in service away from home had ensured that women's transition to the adult status of the goodwife, while swift, was not necessarily traumatic.[15]

Before marriage young people made and unmade relationships with bewildering rapidity, keeping open their options for a much longer period of time than young people do now. Today children play at marriage and teenagers "go steady," but in those times such behavior was met with great disapproval, not just from parents but from the young people themselves. Peers had a vested interest in keeping all the eligible parties in circulation; those times, like Valentine's Day, that we think of as for lovers were considered communal, with everyone getting and giving a gift.[16] Just as young people used coins called "god's pennies" to symbolize their acceptance or rejection of employment agreements, they used small gifts as tokens to make and unmake their most personal relationships. At the Pudsey hiring fairs, it was noted that:

> The lads get among the lasses, passing familiar jokes; some of them behave rather rudely. . . . If a young man prevails upon a young woman to accept a "tiding," which means accepting a brandy snap and nuts, the ice is broken, and it is looked upon by young and old as a kind of "god's penny," for the girl feels laid under some obligation to him.[17]

Symbolizing attachments in this mundane way had its advantages, not the least of which was the way it kept relationships open and flexible. Those who had the opportunity to get to know each other well as coworkers and members of the same communities and churches did not need an extended period of time to get acquainted. We think of love as something that needs time to develop; because we regard love as something deeply personal, as a disembodied feeling that comes from within, we are inevitably shocked by the haste with which people married before the nineteenth century. However, early modern people understood love as a physical phenomenon, which could be communicated more immediately. Their manner of expressing affection seems to us crude, even violent: "First they exchange glances, then casual remarks, then heavy witticisms. The young man shoves at the girl, thumps her hard on the back, takes her hand and squeezes it in a bone-cracking grip. She responds to this tender gesture by punching him in the back."[18] In Wales it was not unknown for a boy to urinate on a girl he was particularly fond of, and everywhere kisses were more like bites, for the drawing of blood was, like any commingling of body fluids, a powerful symbol of attachment.[19]

Love was not about self- and mutual discovery but about giving and receiving something understood to be very tangible. Everyone knew that love could be induced or exorcised by potions and charms, but they were also aware of the power of the black magic that could be invoked by jilted suitors and jealous siblings. They therefore resorted to the services of healers and magicians to prevent and cure the various forms of lovesickness they encountered. Believing that love was affected by the cosmos, they also resorted to astrologers and fortune-tellers to learn their lucky stars and pick out the right dates for their betrothals and marriages.[20]

As men and women approached their mid to late twenties, they became eligible for marriage, though their prospects were rarely certain because of the vagaries of inheritance and occupational opportunity. For seventeenth-century Lancashire bachelors like Roger Lowe, the two main topics of conversation were "tradeing and how to gett wives," activities that were practically as well as metaphorically inseparable.[21] The language of spinsters was not very different, for neither sex was particularly romantic.

Only when access to a farm or a trade was within reach were potential mates allowed any time or space to themselves, and even then only very briefly. We think of love as depending on the amount of time a couple spends together, but in those days its meaning was determined more by place than time. In addition to the marketplaces, which had a long association with the making and breaking of relationships of all kinds, certain landscape features, such as wells, upright stones, and bridges, served as trysting spots.[22] The early phase of mating was called "walking out," descriptive of the way lovers used space to display themselves to the world and thereby test the reactions of peers, parents, and community. In Wales this testing took a ritual form:

> The first few times a young man and a young woman appeared together at fairs, one of a group of young men was sent to "fetch" (*mofyn*) the young woman away on behalf of another member of the group. Her suitor had to buy her fairings in order to keep her, while the young man who tried to draw her away had to buy her fairings in order to entice her.[23]

Everywhere suitors from beyond the locality could expect much rougher treatment; many were forced to pay entry fees called "footings" before being allowed to visit regularly. But even local lads endured ritualized hazing before their rights to courtship were "protected ever after."[24]

These rites of passage, presided over by peer groups with the tacit approval of the larger community, entitled the couple to move on from "walking out" to "keeping company," the next and more serious stage of the courtship process. At this point they were given a surprising degree of latitude, being allowed to court at night under the cover of darkness and even under the covers themselves. In both Europe and North America, night visiting and bundling were recognized as legitimate steps in the marriage process because they allowed couples to test their compatibility even to the point of sexual intimacy.[25] It was said in Wales that "everyone who knows the ways of country people is aware that courting throughout the night was the custom and a young man going courting was terrified lest anyone see him in 'broad daylight.' "[26] In Henry Best's wonderfully detailed account of courtship in seventeenth-century Yorkshire, we are told that in the course of the man's visits to the woman's house, he "giveth her a ten-shilling piece of gold, or a ring of that price; or perhaps a twenty shilling piece, or a ring of that price, then the next time, or the next time after that, each other time, some conceited toy or novelty of less value."[27]

If accepted, such attentions constituted what were called "private spousals." William Whiteway recorded his in his diary on April 6, 1620: "Was concluded the marriage betwix me WM Whiteway and Eleanor Parkins, my best beloved which I pray God to bless and prosper."[28] We find it strange that he used the word *marriage* to describe what we would call engagement, but until the eighteenth century, the vows that William and Eleanor made to one another were considered as good as marriage in England and elsewhere.[29] When a Leicester couple, Elizabeth Cawt and Robert Hubbard, made their spousals in 1598, they went immediately to bed and "the next morning after giving and receiving of the said gold piece she the said Elizabeth did send for certaine of her frends to come to her house and there declared before them that they viz said Robert and Elizabeth had concluded a marriage betweene them."[30]

Even Puritans like Robert Cleaver praised spousals for allowing couples time "for the learning of the traill of all the lets and impediments, whereby promised marriage might be hindered."[31] As his colleague William Gouge put it, the espoused were "in a middle degree betwixt single persons and married persons; they are neither single, nor actually married."[32] If either party backed out and the other agreed to dissolve the partnership, they were free to return to the homosocial world of spinsters and bachelors without penalty.

In the view of the Christian church, consent had always constituted the essence of marriage. For centuries it had defended the rights of consenting parties against the interests of family and community; even as the church began insisting in the seventeenth and eighteenth centuries that only its own or (in the case of Puritan New England) civil ceremonies made marriage legal, ordinary people clung to the old notion that spousals constituted the real beginnings of marriage, which was then completed by arrangements between families culminating by a big public wedding.

And so William Whiteway recorded in his diary on May 6 that he and Eleanor were "betrothed in my father Parkins his hall about 9 of the clock at night, [by] Mr. John White in the presence of our parents."[33] In Best's account, the prospective bride and her father visited the groom's family, "and there doth the younge mans father meete them to treat of a dower, and likewise of a joynture and feeoffment for the woman; and then they all-soe appoint and set downe the day of the marriage."[34] This ritual, which the Welsh called "appointing the day," also had its parallels in North America, where the families celebrated the completion of their business with drink-ing and feasting. In Puritan New England, this part of the marriage rivaled the wedding itself in the scale and significance of its festivities.[35]

The time between betrothal and wedding was short by our standards. "The longer you court, the shorter you'll live together," was the standard wisdom. William Whiteway records that his church wedding took place on June 14, a little more than two months after the first spousals: "I William Whiteway was married to Eleanor Parkins by Mr. John White in the Church of the Holy Trinity in Dorchester, in the presence of the greatest part of the Town."[36] This time span was probably about average. Many would have married more quickly had it not been for the church require-ment that the couple's intentions be publicly announced—the so-called banns—on three consecutive Sundays before the wedding ceremony.[37]

Courtship was not for premoderns, as it has become for us, a time of self- and mutual discovery. Nor did marriage function, as it does today, as a rite of passage into adulthood. Maturity was a prerequisite, not a product, of the premodern wedding. It was a time to put right all the social relations that were inevitably disturbed by the creation of a new household, a rite of tran-sition for the community itself. Before the nineteenth century, the wedding was more a collective than a personal rite of passage. A very public occasion, the wedding began in parts of Britain with the groom and his friends going to "fetch" the bride from her house. According to an account of Welsh wed-dings in the eighteenth century, the groom, after entering the bride's house, "takes her by the hand, and sayeth, 'Mistis, I hope you are willinge,' or else kisseth her before them, and then followeth her father out of doors."[38] In Wales fetching took a very dramatic form: the groomsmen and the bride's people staged a mock battle: "They demand the Girl as a promised wife, and abuse another to all Intents and purposes, one party within the house and the other out of doors, to the Great Diversion of the Company."[39]

The script required that the groomsmen ultimately gain entry to search for the bride, who was sometimes hidden or disguised. Once she was located, "the Father appears, and welcomes his new Guests and they are desired to sit down to a cold Collation, and a Mug of ale is given to each." But then further drama ensued: "The Girl makes great moans & lamenta-tions, and if she can Counterfeit tears & Tearing of hair it is reckoned a meritt." Finally, she is put on a horse behind one of her company, who races off pursued by the groom and his men, the final act of separation of the bride from her household.[40]

Mothers and fathers did not accompany their daughters to church but stayed behind to perform the last rites of leave-taking—the throwing of old shoes, which symbolized the relinquishing of parental authority—or the scrubbing of the threshold, another sign of letting go.[41] The bride's family's involvement ended at this point. Fathers did not give away their daughters, and the family was under no obligation to hold a reception. Kin received no special invitations and, unless they were members of the community, rarely attended.

It was neighbors and friends who provided or sent gifts, for it was the community that provided the big wedding and, in the case of poor folk, also made the new household possible. In seventeenth-century Essex, Ralph Josselin recorded that at one neighbor's wedding, "Frends offd freely [and] he tooke above 56 pounds."[42] As late as the early nineteenth century, small-holders were still depending on one another to raise enough to get a start on a new household. In Wales they sent out a "bidder," who would invite the entire neighborhood to the wedding, asking them to "send a waggon or a cart, a horse and a colt, a heifer, cow and calf, or an ox and a half, or pigs, cocks, geese, goslings, ducks, turkeys, a saddle or bride, or a child's cradle, or what the house can afford," reminding one and all that *a great many can help one, but one cannot help a great many.*" Each gift would be noted and paid back in due time, for it was the custom that "all the payments (*pwython*) due to the young woman's father and mother, grandfather and grandmother, aunts, brothers and sisters, and the same due to the young man's father and mother, etc etc must be returned to the young people."[43]

This communal reciprocity was often sufficient to start a small farm or business. Where a bidden wedding tradition did not exist, a young couple might raise their own wedding portions by auctioning off prizes and selling food and drink to the crowd thus attracted to their wedding.[44] Guests were also ready to pitch in to erect so-called one-night houses on wasteland. In the north of England and Wales, it was said that people were "always ready to help one another . . . [and] would assemble about dawn at the appointed spot, and labouring with good will, each at an allotted task, would erect, long ere sunset, the clay walls of a dwelling for some young couple." Similar house and barn raisings were held in North America, especially on the frontier, where everyone pitched in to help create a new household.[45]

Weddings highlighted community, not conjugality, and for that reason the part played by the couple was relatively inconspicuous. They married in their best clothes, but neither bride nor groom stood out from their peers, who were similarly attired. Brides had no special costume, and there were no designated wedding attendants apart from the crowd of peers who set the tone and directed the drama. The religious ceremony was the least important part of any wedding day, and as soon as the newly married pair left the altar, they faced a series of tests of their fitness to fulfill the public roles of master and mistress of a household. In some places it was the custom "always [to] lock the wedding party into the church till they have pushed gold under the church door."[46] In Yorkshire the reason given was that "the twain should meet and overcome their first trouble or obstacle in life, within the precincts of the church."[47]

Other tests followed. In many parts of England, the couple was forced to jump an obstacle called the "petting stone." Those who jumped willingly earned the cheers of the crowd, but if a bride "pouted or hung back, or made a difficulty of observing the custom, she was said to have 'taken a pet,'" and "the poor husband was to be commiserated on the possession of a shrew."[48] Along the way from Yorkshire churches, wedding parties regularly encountered "hustlers," gangs of young men, "gaily dressed, and with blackened faces. The captain of this band cried a halt, he declared that he and his merry men were in need of wives, and unless the bridegroom paid them instantly 'bride guest money' his bride and every bonny bridesmaid would be kidnapped."[49] Made up of friends of the groom and former suitors of the bride, the "hustlers" were easily appeased. It was a ritualized way of letting out pent-up feelings of jealousy and envy, thereby ensuring the social harmony of the community. Such a rite also reminded the husband of his newly acquired patriarchal responsibility, not only to protect his wife but to show generosity to everyone, especially his former peers.

Arrival at the household initiated another round of challenges that required the new master to demonstrate his largesse while symbolically investing the bride with the symbols of her new mistress status—a broom, fire tongs, and, of course, the distaff.[50] Together they were supposed to provide a feast, the ultimate measure of their hospitality. Afterward the teasing and testing continued well into the night when the final act of the big wedding concluded with the traditional bedding—or as it was called in New England, "chambering"—ceremony. The crowd invaded the bedroom, demanding yet another offering. "A judicious present of money [which] was the only way to shorten the cacophonous serenade which otherwise lasted for hours."[51]

Big weddings were not allowed to interfere unduly with the normal rhythms of everyday life in the seventeenth and eighteenth centuries. "In early America, the transition to marriage was a smooth seam in the fabric of everyday life," Ellen Rothman has written. "A wedding meant a brief pause, not a disruption, in daily routine."[52] It was a celebration of the house, its master and mistress, rather than of the couple, and until the late nineteenth century, there was no word or concept for "newlyweds."[53] From the moment they were married, husband and wife were expected to take up their places in the community, symbolized by their being seated in church in one of the pews reserved for householders.[54]

The speed with which spinsters and bachelors were transformed into masters and mistresses must astound us. William Lloyd Garrison took only one week in 1834 to "settle down into domestic quietude."[55] Elizabeth Carter was ready to receive visitors the day after her marriage in 1821: "To look at her in her rocking chair, you would imagine her an old housekeeper."[56] While it was not uncommon for couples to take what was then called the "bridal trip," the purpose was to visit friends and distant kin, not to be alone with one another. For this reason, it was the custom for the pair to take their closest companions along—hardly the honeymoon as we know it.[57]

Weddings were memorable moments for communities, but they were rarely commemorated by the couples themselves. Apart from the aristocracy, no wedding anniversaries were celebrated; wedding gifts were entirely practical, meant for immediate use rather than as mnemonic devices. The wedding ceremony validated the identity of the community, not that of the couple, and licensed its authority over the household and all its inhabitants. After the wedding day, the household was subject to even closer inspection by friends and neighbors, who assumed the right to intervene at any time to correct the behavior of those whom they had wedded.[58] In seventeenth-century England, it was said that "every citizen is bound by oath to keep a sharp eye on his neighbor's house, as to whether the married people live in harmony"; in colonial New England this task was carried out by the local authorities.[59] Quarreling couples were subject to gossip, and, when this did not bring peace to the household, they were visited with ritual shaming in the form of the charivari, which in the Anglo-American world was known variously as "rough music," "shivaree," or "skimmingtons." Directed at brutal husbands as well as scolding wives, skinflint mistresses and greedy masters, these rites of redress endured in many rural areas well into the nineteenth century.[60] Congregations exercised similar discipline, stepping in when marriages failed or were broken by death, correcting abuses and supporting survivors.[61]

The same understanding of marriage as a public institution inspired the mutual aid associations that sprang up in the early nineteenth century. During the 1830s and 1840s, socialists and feminists invented a plethora of ceremonies that also preserved the basic features of the traditional wedding. "Make a new ceremonial for yourselves—a rival ceremonial—which shall win the people to your side," enthused the Owenite James Morrison.[62]

Owenite "halls of science" were sites of new secular rituals that underlined the collective responsibility of marriage. Couples had to obtain the consent of the community to marry, but once given, consent guaranteed vital public goodwill. In the case of death or separation, spouses and orphans were taken care of by the community.[63] Women were particularly in favor of this updated version of the big wedding, for, as Margaret Chappelsmith put it, "under such circumstance, infidelity and jealousy are not likely to arise."[64]

Eventually the European and American middle classes would create a whole new ceremonial for themselves, but it would not be a continuation of but a break with all that had gone before. In the new rites that developed in the second half of the nineteenth century, conjugal love became a prerequisite rather than a consequence of marriage. What had been a relatively short courtship became an extended symbolic process during which the couple created not only the material basis for a home but the mental world they would jointly inhabit. At a time when the lives of men and women were diverging and each family culture was unique to itself, time was needed for the couple to create out of the materials of dream and memory a world all their own. What the common ground of the everyday experience of work and leisure once provided had now to be created symbolically. Marriage was no longer a matter of "stepping into new roles, but, beyond this, stepping into a new world."[65]

In the past, marriage had been a joint project, with the man contributing as much, if not more, of the material needs of the household. Men continued to be the providers, while the symbolic world became the work of women. For the first time, courtship came under the direct control of the woman's family; with the head of the house absent on most days, it fell to the women to supervise love's initial stages. As the place of courtship shifted, so did its rhythms. Love's old public calendar—the first of May, Valentine's Day, the harvest festivals—gave way to a much more private cycle of family occasions: Sundays, Christmas, summer family holidays.[66] Courting males learned to abide by the house rules. Once they had presented their cards, they waited nervously in the hall until invited into the parlor to undergo the initial screening.[67] Mothers did most of the scrutinizing, but in due course serious suitors would be invited to join the family for Sunday dinner or to accompany them on a holiday excursion, where the father could render his judgment.[68]

The parlor became the seat of judgment, but it was also the window on the family's status and the museum of its history, offering a text for suitors to peruse as they sat over tea in polite conversation. In earlier periods, men had felt very much at home in other people's houses, but most men now found this phase of courtship extremely awkward—"the most embarrassing part of the affair," one called it—because it brought them from a man's world into unfamiliar, highly feminized territory, subordinating them not only to women's space but to women's time, a position that constituted a threat to their masculinity.

Men were eager enough to "fall in love" but liked to think of love as something that happened to them rather than something they were responsible for nurturing.[69] As with so many other aspects of Victorian life, the labors of love were unequally divided. Boys learned to expect love from women, and girls were trained to give and sustain it. While it was men who were expected to call, it was women who made the tea and kept the conversation going. Men also initiated the exchange of love letters, but women kept it going.[70] In an era when sexual passion could no longer be expressed publicly or physically, letters offered a symbolic substitute. Letters read in the privacy of the bedroom were kissed, fondled, and anthropomorphized. Nathaniel Hawthorne never read Sophia Peabody's letters without first washing his hands. "[I] locked my door, and threw myself on the bed, with your letter in my hand," he told her. "I read it over slowly and peacefully, and then folding it up, I rested my heart upon it, and fell fast asleep."[71]

Under these circumstances, it is not surprising that middle-class lovers developed very idealized images of one another, and of love itself. Men had the tendency to project onto the women they loved all the purity and virtue they had experienced in their relationship with their mothers.[72] Through the idealized vision of their bride-to-be, they worked out an image of themselves as devoted lovers without having to give up their old haunts and pursuits, including in many cases their whores and mistresses. Women also nurtured visions of ideal husbands, but because they were responsible for most of the labors of love, their dreams were always tempered by reality.[73]

Men also seem to have been the more romantic sex when it came to dreaming of the home the two would share together. Eldred Simpkins wrote to his fiancée Eliza Trescot in the 1860s that "visions of future years fraught with happiness passed before me when we should sit together by ourselves in 'our home' on the winter evenings by our bright fireside and talk about those years of separation and trial! And when I would come in tired and worn out my fair would meet [me] at the door and charm away fatigue and care." Like most women, Eliza held a more realistic view of her future abode. "Did you never reflect upon the chance of getting tired of seeing the same old face day after day, especially if the scene should not be varied and enlivened by some other?" she replied. "It would be unfortunate to tire of it for you couldn't get rid of it."[74] No doubt, Eldred also allowed reality to intrude on his reveries from time to time, but the dream house, together with the perfect couple, already occupied a central place in the modern male imaginary.

Courtship did not always lead to a decision to marry, but when it did, couples entered into what was by then called "engagement," a status so different from the old spousals that English-speaking people had to borrow a foreign term to describe it.[75] Middle-class people no longer confused betrothal with marriage. Engagement had become a family occasion by the 1860s, confirming the couple's right to one another's company but simultaneously spiritualizing the relationship.

While the Victorians were by no means as passionless as we have been led to believe, most seem to have heeded the injunction against premarital sex. Among the middle classes, premarital pregnancy rates fell sharply in the nineteenth century. Men, most of whom were already sexually active, found intimacy without physicality to be especially frustrating and wanted engagements to be as short as possible, but women enjoyed long engagements as the only time in their lives when they had a certain amount of leeway with their parents and a measure of the individuality they would lose once married. For men, the ability to provide for a family, was a prerequisite for any engagement, but for Victorian middle-class women, engagement was the only time when they could explore their "true selves" and establish an adult identity. Even as men pressed for them to set the wedding date, women hesitated, sometimes to the point of seeing their marriage chances vanish.[76]

Over the second half of the century, the period of engagement lengthened. Women rightfully defended long engagements on the grounds that marriage required time and preparation. For marriage had become more than just a matter of finding a house and provisioning it with the necessary items. A marriage had also to be stocked with dreams and memories, which it was the woman's responsibility to supply. In addition to the clothes and bed linens, there was now a symbolic trousseau to be gathered—a process that became so complicated by the end of the century that, as a woman doctor remarked in 1912, a "trousseau was as essential to the prospective bride as an outfit to the explorer of the arctic or tropical wilds, or, rather it was like the equipment of a traveler who sets out for an unknown Oriental country."[77]

Marriage was indeed a foreign land, approached with much greater apprehension than in earlier periods. The anxiety felt by middle-class women had become so substantial that it acquired its own name—"marriage trauma." Caroline Barrett described the eve of her marriage in 1851 as "the last night of my girl life. . . . A new life is to begin tomorrow—a life less free—more anxious—more responsible."[78] For men, putting down a deposit on a house or filing for a first mortgage was also the occasion of a certain anxiety, but since these acts affirmed their adult masculinity, the wedding day itself meant less to them than it did to their brides.[79]

The wedding was now the foremost female rite of passage. The groom stepped into the background, allowing the bride to occupy the center of attention. If men had had their way, weddings would have remained the limited affairs they were in earlier times; indeed, "any kind of wedding is dreadful" has been the male view of weddings since the late nineteenth century.[80] But when weddings became the province of women, men's views became largely irrelevant.

Since the midnineteenth century, nuptials have grown ever more elaborate and female-centered. In this century, it is accurate to say that "every girl likes to get married in white."[81] The white wedding, now standard throughout North America and Europe and popular in African and Asian nuptials as well, is perhaps the most enduring of all Victorian innovations.[82] Everywhere the ceremony focuses on the bride in pure white, "given away" by her father and then whisked off to the honeymoon. When a woman remembers the most important day of her life, the white wedding is usually regarded as "the time of her life."[83] It is what women dream of and plan for years. Men find it difficult to remember their weddings, but for a woman it is the moment that anchors her life, her sense of self. By the late Victorian period, men were becoming spectators at their own nuptials. As one English groom put it in 1875, he felt himself to be "the coolest and most unconcerned one of the whole party . . . unable to understand he was being married."[84] But the experience was entirely different for his bride. Dressed in the newly invented bridal costume—the luminous gown, veil, and matching bouquet—that set her off from all the other women present, she was the center of attention, symbolizing romance, as the groom in his dark suit could never do.

Weddings had previously been accommodated to the times and places of the everyday world. Until the midnineteenth century, most American weddings took place at home, accentuating their uneventfulness. But by the 1850s, marriage was returning to the churches of both North America and Europe, not because of growing religiosity but because churches represented the appropriate ritual space even for those who were no longer regular churchgoers.[85] Weddings were also becoming associated with special times and being held more often on weekends and holidays rather than on weekdays, times that highlighted their symbolic importance. This new calendar allowed families to gather from afar for the first time. Weddings became more familial and less communal; the ancient practice of calling banns to announce the nuptials gave way to newspaper notices and personal invitations.[86] Gifts to the couple ceased to be of a useful nature, and the wedding itself no longer culminated at the new domicile but was celebrated in a place specially rented for the occasion.[87]

When relations with neighbors became irrelevant to the success of marriages, houses no longer played a central role in big weddings. The only reminder of the old threshold ceremonies was the rice thrown as the couple left the church, but even this was an innovation, Indian rice having been introduced only in the Victorian period.[88] The reception, yet another Victorian invention, was paid for by the parents. The newlyweds had neither opportunity nor desire to demonstrate their capacities as householders. Instead of being conducted to their new home, they departed immediately on what was called from the 1860s onward the "honeymoon," to distinguish it from the old bridal trip. Couples no longer traveled with friends or family but journeyed alone to places like the Riviera or Niagara Falls, which by this time had already earned their reputations as romantic destinations.[89] And even their return was an essentially private moment. On the threshold, where the master and mistress had once stood to greet the great crowd of guests, the groom now quietly lifted the bride, symbolizing not the establishment of a household but the beginnings of a home. Henceforth, only the husband's comings and goings required further ritual treatment. From that day onward, the wife was forever the symbol of home, however many times she might cross the same threshold herself.[90]

By 1900 white weddings had become the great event in the lives of middle-class families, displacing even the funeral as the most obligatory moment for family gathering. It was the most frequently photographed event, with the wedding album representing the pair to themselves and their offspring forever after as a perfect couple, an image refurbished on each subsequent wedding anniversary. These were the images and rituals that Victorian spouses lived by, even when the marriages they lived with told a very different story.

In reality, the lives of middle-class husbands and wives were quite unconjugal. Men's lives continued to revolve around an exclusively male world of work and leisure. In their careers, they rarely encountered women except as subordinates, and, until the turn of the century, their leisure worlds were also largely homosocial. Men had their clubs and fraternal organizations, which in the late nineteenth century absorbed an enormous amount of their time, becoming virtually alternative families to many. Given the prevailing gender divisions, often compounded by large age differences between husbands and wives, it was not surprising that men's relations with their best friends were often more intense than those with their wives, whom they saw mainly on weekends and with whom they did not even vacation until late in the century. Many nineteenth-century men continued to keep up their extramarital affairs, and some also carried on liaisons with other men, hiding the nature of these relationships behind the accepted norms of male friendship.[91]

As for middle-class women, they too sustained intense, sometimes erotic same-sex relations, even as they lived under the protective sign of the perfect couple. Victorian women traveled and vacationed together. They had their own clubs and homes away from home every bit as comfortable as those their husbands frequented. The bonds they formed with sisters and best friends were often more intimate and intense than those they formed with their husbands. Often such relationships were as romantic as anything that had led up to marriage, and some more erotically satisfying than marriage itself.[92]

Homosocial and even homosexual relations posed no immediate threat to the image of the perfect married couple, however, for the Victorians accepted the compatibility of the homosocial and heterosocial worlds. Marriages could easily survive homosexual as well as heterosexual affairs, for much less weight was placed on companionship and sexual pleasure within marriage. It was simply assumed that men would have their extramarital affairs and that women would also find intimacy, even passion, outside marriage, chiefly, though not exclusively, with other women. In an era before effective birth control, these arrangements served middle-class marriages reasonably well. It was not until after the First World War that anyone thought seriously of trying to bring companionship and pleasurable sex into marriage itself. And it was then that what has become marriage's modern malady, feelings of unfulfilled expectations, began to manifest itself in the first, though still modest, increases in divorce.[93]

The 1920s brought courtship out of the parlor and into the commercialized spaces of the cinema balcony, the dance floor, and the backseat of the automobile, with the result that males regained much of the initiative they had lost during the Victorian era. They no longer had to wait for permission to visit but could now ask a woman out on a "date," as long as they were willing to pay for it. The dating game reinforced the images of men as providers and women as the passive objects of male attention. In what has been described as the Western world's first sexual revolution, young people gained considerable autonomy. Although most did not go beyond petting in their courtships, when they did engage in intercourse it was usually with the person they intended to marry.[94]

The rules of the dating game were designed to keep young people in circulation, but sexuality became even more conjugal. Resort to prostitutes declined dramatically in the twentieth century as sex became ever more central to the construction of the self in Western culture. The formation of an adult identity now depended more completely than ever before on establishing a relationship with a member of the opposite sex, and intercourse eventually became the ultimate sign of intimacy and maturity. As heterosexuality became ever more the norm, bachelors and spinsters of a certain age gained the reputation of being immature, "sick" individuals.[95] Passionate homosocial friendship became associated with homosexuality and suffered as a consequence of the homophobia that developed so virulently in this century.[96]

Romantic love became ever more firmly associated with marriage to the extent that until the 1960s it was almost impossible to imagine love taking any other form.[97] Working-class people continued to court and marry in ways much closer to those of the premodern era, however. For a very long time, pomp, ceremony, and custom mattered very little to them. When British researchers went hunting for a sense of tradition among the general population in the 1940s, they found that it was quite strong among the middle classes, but weak among working people.[98] It was not just that working-class families could not afford the big white wedding, but their daughters had much less need of a special rite of passage to validate an adulthood they had already achieved through work or, in some cases, through maternity. Until the early twentieth century, many working-class women still arrived at the altar pregnant.[99] They had not had the luxury of the "girl life" to begin with, and it did not make much sense to spend money on a white wedding when it was needed to set up housekeeping. In the 1920s and 1930s, most working-class brides were pleased to be married in their best dresses. The wedding was more likely to be on a weekday, with few attendants and only a small reception, often at home or in the corner tavern. Honeymoons were not something working people could afford, nor did they seem to desire them.[100] As late as the 1950s, these class distinctions were still clearly evident: at a time when 57 percent of British marriages were big church affairs, people of the professional class were almost twice as likely to be married that way as those of the unskilled classes.[101]

By the 1950s, however, there were signs that the white wedding was catching on among all classes; since that time, it has become almost universal. Prebridal pregnancy rates of the 1950s were at their lowest point in modern times, and for the next three decades marriage rates reached an all-time high, as did the number of big church weddings. The time and money expended on weddings increased astronomically so that by 1960, when the median American family income was only $4,970, the average wedding was estimated to cost $3,300.[102] Since that time the costs have gone even higher; many weddings now cost more than $30,000. Despite all the talk about modern marriages being in trouble, today's weddings are bigger than anything earlier generations can remember. Even though many couples have been cohabiting for months and even years prior to marriage, they still want an engagement followed by as big a wedding as possible. In the 1980s three-quarters of all American brides had been engaged, and 85 percent had a formal wedding. And the pattern in Europe, while it varied from country to country, was no different.[103]

White weddings used to be reserved for virgins and first-time marriages. Now they appeal to women of all ages who wish to affirm their identities and claim a place in the conjugal world. Today even those who have cohabited and have children want to be married in white. Brides prefer Victorian-style gowns, and the oldest, quaintest churches are overbooked by couples wanting the most memorable settings for their nuptials. Even the most exotic (some might say, bizarre) locations are chosen by couples determined to make this life's most important moment.

In 1988 the *New York Times* could announce that "the traditional wedding is back, in many cases with unprecedented lavishness," without ever reflecting on the fact that the appeal of the big wedding is actually quite recent. With engagements stretching out to almost a year, modern couples have had "plenty of time to ruminate on the rites of wedlock." By 1988 the average wedding cost over $10,000, and the three-day or weekend wedding was already becoming popular. Because couples are now older and have often been living together, they think of their wedding as a party for their friends and families. Dates are sometimes chosen to coincide with family anniversaries or birthdays, and it is not uncommon for couples to make a wedding tour, touching base with those who were unable to attend the ceremony. The honeymoon, previously a rite of separation, has become again a means of recognizing connections.[104]

In premodern times, courtship and marriage left little to the imagination. Today it seems as if there is little if any reality left when it comes to the phantasmagoria of contemporary weddings. They carry the burden of symbolizing love, not just for the couple but for all those who are attracted by their magic. As long as love was multivalent and could find refuge in a variety of other relationships, getting married was a relatively straightforward, practical matter, and weddings played only a very small part in the Western imaginary. Today weddings are our most popular ceremonial because they represent to us what nothing else can. Once the stuff of romantic literature only, they have become the major symbolic resource for film and television, providing the images, metaphors, and narratives for everything and anything, from corporate mergers to international peacemaking. Everyone loves a wedding, and the high rates of divorce guarantee an inexhaustible supply for a culture that cannot get enough of perfect couples, even as it encounters ever greater difficulty in maintaining marriage itself.

"Romantic love is still alone in producing the wonderful sense of well being, the ecstatic feelings which transfigure both lover and beloved, but we are finding that it disregards all the important realities when people decide to live together for a lifetime," writes one observer of this modern paradox.[105] In the late twentieth century, when lifetimes are as much as one-third longer than they used to be, it becomes very difficult to sustain romance for the duration of a marriage. The situation is made even worse by the fact that the standard of conjugality has risen so dramatically. The perfect couple now must be everything to one another—good providers, super sexual partners, best friends, stimulating companions—roles that earlier generations turned to others to fulfill.[106]

Since the 1980s, however, it has been possible to imagine romantic love in more than just one form. Today we acknowledge that it can take place outside marriage, and that people can fall in love more than once in a lifetime. Most of us are now quite willing to accept that romantic love can take a homosexual as well as a heterosexual form. But this broadening of the spectrum of romance has not diminished the appeal of the big wedding. Paradoxically, the big wedding flourishes even as cohabitation and divorce become more frequent and marriage as an institution becomes more fragile. To be sure, weddings have changed somewhat. Even royal brides now refuse to vow obedience, and grooms dress more colorfully than they once did. Yet there is no denying that courtship and marriage have never been more ritualized, never so productive of images for which we seem to have an unlimited appetite. It seems that we are relying more and more on big weddings to sustain our faith in love. The fact that it no longer matters that the bride is pregnant, that the pair coming down the aisle is gay or lesbian, or that the couple are both on their third or fourth marriages, is indicative of just how much the perfect couple still matters in Western culture.

CHAPTER 8

Mothers Giving Birth to Motherhood

There have always been mothers but motherhood was invented.
Ann Dally, *Inventing Motherhood*[1]

Because we assume that the physical act of giving birth naturally produces the desire and ability to nurture, we are stunned when we learn of birth mothers abusing or murdering their children, even though almost two of every three infants who die violently are killed by their own parents. When Susan V. Smith of South Carolina drowned both her sons in 1994, many of her neighbors found themselves searching for the answer to the question: "How could a mother do that to her children?"[2] We simply cannot believe that in giving birth a woman does not also give birth to herself as a mother. Yet many cultures make a distinction between maternity and motherhood, and even in Western society the connection between giving birth and giving nurture is surprisingly recent. It was not until 1875 that

English-speaking people began talking about "true motherhood" as if maternity and motherhood were one and the same. Only in our own century have these terms become so completely identified that we have felt compelled to invent a new vocabulary—surrogate mothers, adoptive mothers, foster mothers—to describe those who do not combine maternity and motherhood in the prescribed manner.

The meanings of motherhood and fatherhood are never stable or transparent but forever contested and changing. Whatever may be universal about the biology of conception, pregnancy, and birth, maternity has no predetermined relationship to motherhood, and paternity no fixed relationship to fatherhood; both vary enormously across cultures and over time.[3] The many meanings of motherhood and fatherhood are not only reflected in the various images, symbols, and rituals associated with birth but are shaped by them. Faced with the ultimate mystery of human reproduction, we turn to rituals to provide us with a sense of meaningfulness. Birth has always been marked culturally, but whereas its rites once served to create and sustain a distinction between maternity and motherhood, today they underline the identity between these concepts. When a woman gives birth in the late twentieth century, she does so not once but four times: to the child, to herself as mother, to the man as father, and to the group that in our culture we are most likely to call family.[4]

Our equation of maternity with motherhood is not only relatively recent but historically unprecedented by the standards of the Western world. In earlier centuries, giving birth and giving nurture were often incompatible for demographic and economic reasons as well as cultural ones. Because of the high levels of both fertility and mortality that prevailed in Europe and North America until the nineteenth century, there was simply no way that all women who gave birth could also mother all their children. Maternal mortality never fell below 7 percent until this century. Until about a century ago, infant mortality rates, calculated as the percentage of infants who die before they reach their first birthday, ranged from 15 to 25 percent; only about half of all those born lived to the age of twenty-one. To replace these losses, women's fertility rates remained very high. Children came so quickly that it was often impossible for a woman to nurture all who were born to her, and she was likely to die before all her children left home.[5] The lifelong, intensive involvement with the individual child that has become the standard of motherhood in our own times was simply impossible for many women before the twentieth century. As a consequence, maternity and motherhood were understood as quite separable, not unlike the current understanding of fatherhood, in which the term "to father" means merely to generate and implies none of the nurturing capacities that currently attach to the words "to mother."[6]

Children in earlier periods did not lack for mothering, however. There existed a wide range of alternative sources of nurture. Wet-nursing had always been practiced and seems to have increased in the seventeenth and eighteenth centuries.[7] Placing out infants to women who would suckle them for an extended period was common not only among upper-class women, many of whom considered breast-feeding distasteful and unfashionable, but among working women who had neither the time nor the energy for the task.[8] Until Jean-Jacques Rousseau and his followers managed to convince the literate public that using wet-nurses was a violation of the laws of nature, deciding how to nurse an infant was usually done on the basis of convenience, with no particular symbolic value attached to the maternal breast. It was not until the nineteenth century that wet-nursing went into a precipitous decline, which began when infants were no longer being sent out to nurse and nurses were required to live in under close maternal supervision. Eventually, the very idea of the nonmaternal breast became incompatible with good motherhood, and by 1900 the wet-nurse had become a thing of the past, associated with so-called primitive cultures but having no place in civilized society. Mothers either suckled their own infants or bottle-fed, a method made safe by the milk pasteurization techniques developed late in the nineteenth century.

The convergence of maternity and motherhood proceeded fastest among the middle classes, but even at that social level it was still common in the nineteenth century for older children to be informally adopted by relatives.[9] This practice remained quite widespread among the working classes well into the early decades of this century.[10] In neighborhoods where kin lived nearby, children often took meals and slept apart from their biological parents; in families with many offspring, older siblings were frequently sent to live with more distant relatives—to "claim kin," as it was called in England—a form of intrafamily relief.[11] This was merely an extension of the ancient practice of circulating children for their own good, which in earlier times had been more likely to involve movement among unrelated households. In sixteenth-century England, 60 percent of those between the ages of fifteen and twenty-four were living apart from their parents, mainly as servants.[12] From the early nineteenth century onward, however, the movement of the children of the poor into the households of the better-off began to slow down. Girls continued to be sent away into domestic service, but working-class boys stayed closer to home. Still, it was not until the interwar period of the twentieth century that parents could expect most if not all of their children to be their responsibility until they saw them married, and even then the newlyweds were likely to return to one of the parental homes until they could find a place of their own.

As John Boswell has shown, Christian culture in earlier times never held parents wholly responsible for bringing up all their children. Giving up a child to the church through the medieval institution of oblation was regarded as an act of both piety and good sense. Protestants eliminated this practice but established foundling hospitals and orphanages, which served a similar purpose. They too saw nothing immoral or unnatural about giving up one's children to the "kindness of strangers." In the eighteenth century, one-quarter of all the children born in Toulouse, France, were turned over to the care of others.[13]

In this country as well, the foundling home and the orphanage remained vital institutions until the early twentieth century, housing large numbers of children—mainly for short rather than permanent placement, however. It was only after the Second World War that these institutions were closed down and Western societies turned to adoptive families and foster homes as the exclusive means of caring for displaced children. This change followed the general shift in thinking of parenting as an individual rather than a collective responsibility, one best carried out by one set of parents rather than several. Even now we assume that foster or adoptive mothers are second-best to what we call "real" or "natural" mothers. There has always been a certain suspicion of stepmothers, but the fine lines we draw between different kinds of mothers, always maintaining biological motherhood as the norm, is a distinctly recent phenomenon. Stepmotherhood and grandmotherhood were not sharply defined categories until the nineteenth century, when, as Ann Dally points out, motherhood itself finally emerged "as a concept rather than a mere statement of fact."[14] Until that time, anyone who mothered was called "Mother," regardless of biology. The term was applied to the mistresses of brothels and to the keepers of journeymen's hostels. In colonial New England, all older women, whether they had children or not, were called mothers.[15] In Europe it was common to call midwives "good mothers."[16] Mothering knew no age, race, or gender boundaries. Older sisters who brought up their siblings were referred to as "little mothers"; slave women who nursed white children were called "mammies"; and nurturing qualities were attributed to men as well as to women throughout the medieval and early modern periods.[17] Until the nineteenth century, the term "to father" still retained nurturing as well as generative connotations.[18] Only in this century has maternity come to bear all the weight of the symbolic as well as practical meanings that were once attached to all who mothered rather than to the one particular person who gave birth.

Our contemporary notion that individual mothers are wholly responsible for the physical, spiritual, and emotional well-being of their children had no place in earlier understandings of reproduction. For most of human history, birth has been one of those things, like death, for which no human could claim responsibility, for the organs of reproduction, like the body itself, were seen as part of a larger cosmos that determined the timing and nature of all human events. Some human control over life and death was attributed to magical practices, which may not have been effective but were symbolically important: they gave people a feeling of predictability and security. While hostile to pagan magic, Christianity incorporated many of these practices into its own rites of birth, marriage, and death; until the Reformation, combinations of sacred and secular magic provided the symbolic reassurance lacking in the real world.[19] Magical notions of the cosmos were not overcome easily, and the Protestant project of disenchantment was only partially effective before the nineteenth century. Likewise, older understandings of the body changed only very gradually.

In the ancient world, a variety of mother goddesses provided the sense of security and comfort that real mothers often could not offer their own children. Their relics and images became pilgrimage sites for infertile women as well as orphaned children, for Christians as well as pagans. Mother goddesses continued to hold sway during the first millennium of Christendom, for "the insecurity and real dangers of medieval childhood created powerful, persistent fantasies of protection and rescue by an omnipotent, loving mother."[20] Nor was fantasy directed only toward female figures: Jesus was often portrayed as having maternal features, and monks were known to present themselves in similar terms.[21]

A plethora of maternal figures, male and female, were required to meet these needs, because until the twelfth century Christianity had no central mother figure. In her earliest representations, Mary was associated more with virginity than maternity, and the mother of Jesus was envisioned by the church more as the queen of heaven than as a mother as such. Only when Mary began to be represented as a mother in the late Middle Ages did she attract the devotion previously attached to pagan goddesses. For the first time it became possible to envision maternal as well as virgin saints. "In the Virgin," writes Clarissa Atkinson, "Christians discovered and made manifest in art and worship the powers of a sacred female common to many of the world's religions."[22]

In Mary, mother of Christ, late medieval Christians found a symbolic mother to live by. Her cult reached its apogee during the fourteenth and fifteenth centuries, when, as we have already seen, the Holy Family also became central to Catholic devotions, offering safe storage for the ideals of an emerging family system in which the nuclear unit was conceived for the first time as a moral core. It was at this time that Jesus acquired a father as well as a mother; for the next three centuries, the father figure was to compete with the mother figure for the right to symbolize nurturance. This was particularly true in Protestant lands, where the Reformation of the sixteenth century brought the Holy Family down to earth, finding new sources of symbolic reassurance within its own communities of godly households. A similar shift was apparent in Catholic countries, where the Holy Family also ceased to have a sacramental value and became a model for real families. The cult of Mary would continue to be a source of comfort to Catholics right up to the present day, but everywhere there was an increased emphasis on the heads of households providing the sense of protection and security that had once been sought elsewhere, at the roadside shrine or in monastic institutions.

Until the nineteenth century, nurturing capacity was thought of as an acquired talent more than as a sex-specific natural quality. Seventeenth- and eighteenth-century books on parenting were directed more to fathers than to mothers.[23] That there was as yet no equation between womanhood and motherliness was also evidenced in the witch persecutions of the sixteenth and seventeenth centuries. At no time before or since have so many women been associated with "the image of the witch as anti-wife and anti-mother—a sexual threat instead of a helpmate, a frightful danger to reproduction and the Christianization of children."[24] It was not accidental that in both Europe and North America many of those who were condemned and killed as witches were older women, many of them midwives and women past their childbearing years, onto whom could be projected the negative feelings of those who felt in some way deprived of nurture and protection.[25] Although patriarchs were the logical targets of such anger, they were too powerful to be confronted with these feelings. Instead, 80 percent of all those tried and executed for witchcraft were older women, most of them widowed, poor, and living on their own.

Midwives were particularly targeted because they were suspected of having knowledge of the old magic that Protestants wished to banish from their theocentric universe. The power to do good, traditionally assigned to these women, was easily stigmatized as the power of frightful evil.[26] Christina Larner's profile of the accused witch of the seventeenth century bears a striking resemblance to negative stereotypes of women in our own time: "She is assertive; she does not require or give love (though she may enchant); she does not nurture men or children, or care for the weak."[27] Accusations were rarely directed against wives and birth mothers as such, or even against wet-nurses or other women involved in child-rearing. Perhaps the anger was amplified by the guilt some fathers and mothers felt about not providing sufficiently for their own children. In any case, the patriarch and his goodwife were much too powerful to be criticized directly. If early modern Europeans and Americans could find nurturance in a much wider community than we can, they were also capable of wreaking vengeance on people they scarcely knew, persons onto whom it was easy to displace violently negative fantasies.

From the sixteenth through the early nineteenth centuries, motherhood was still subordinated to wifehood. As Clarissa Atkinson has described it, Protestantism placed a greater premium on "woman's role as a wife, consort, helpmeet, and lover—like Eve before the Fall, a central figure but secondary and complementary to her husband."[28] In the household economy of the commercial phase of capitalism, women were often partners, though normally junior partners, in farming and proto-industrial enterprises. Even as employment outside the household became closed to them, they were increasingly active in production both for household use and for the expanding market economy. Our notion of "housework," a term invented only in 1841 to describe domestic tasks, is incapable of encompassing all the skills acquired and practiced by women prior to the mid-nineteenth century.[29] The demands on a wife's time and energy were such that many found it difficult, if not impossible, to mother full-time. Until very late, the goodwife took precedence over the good mother.

Premodern rituals of pregnancy and birth reflected the tensions between wifehood and motherhood and reconciled the two by representing maternity as an episode in a woman's life rather than the beginning of an all-consuming career. Contrary to what we have been led to believe, birthing rites in earlier periods were not necessarily more elaborate than those of the modern era. Today women are the subject of intense and highly ritualized attention from conception onward, culminating with hospitalized birth, which Robbie Davis-Floyd has described as an "event more elaborate than any heretofore known in the 'primitive' world."[30] Through this modern rite of female passage a modern woman is left with few doubts about her primary identity. She may be a wife, consort, helpmeet, and lover, but she is above all a mother.

All societies mark birth and give it a meaning consistent with their material conditions and cultures. The birthing rites of the seventeenth and eighteenth centuries acknowledged maternity but reconciled it to women's other roles. They did so by representing pregnancy and maternity as something that happened to a woman, as an episode in her life in which she was more the object of natural and supernatural forces than a subject in control of her own body. As Jacques Gelis reminds us: "To the country mind, in times gone by, men had to wait for nature to accomplish her work within the time she herself had set. It could be neither hindered nor precipitated. In a word, nature must go at her own pace, and the child 'come' in its own time."[31] When Protestants substituted the will of God for the whim of nature, they did not grant any additional agency to mothers. Indeed, their completely theocentric universe deprived women of access to the charms and potions that had provided comfort to Catholics. In America as well, the Protestant woman "could only throw herself on the mercy of God, and the midwife dared do nothing that might appear magical."[32] As a result, the prospect of birth became more rather than less terrifying.

Like all rites of passage, birth during this period consisted of three stages—separation, transition, and reincorporation.[33] But unlike our contemporary version of the birthing ritual, which heavily emphasizes the social separation of the pregnant woman, the premodern birth process placed the most symbolic weight on the final phase, the incorporative rites of baptism of the child and the churching of the woman. These are best described as communal rites of progression rather than as individual rites of passage, for their purpose was not to underline the separateness of mother and child but to restore the household and communal relationships disrupted by the arrival of the little stranger.[34]

Traditional rites made little of the preparation for birth and a great deal of its consequences. Prior to the nineteenth century, births were hardly anticipated, for it was thought unlucky to preempt either nature or divine will by preparing for birth in too overt a manner. There was no sure way of confirming pregnancy until the woman felt the movement of the fetus, the so-called quickening, though much effort was put into divining conception by various magical means. According to the contemporary understanding of fertilization, male seed was endowed with the greatest generative powers. The position of intercourse was said to determine the sex of the child, and men believed they could tell at ejaculation whether or not conception had occurred. But there were myriad other ways to divine pregnancy, none of which required medical attention.[35]

Prenatal medical care was in fact quite rare, though there was a great deal of lore about how a woman should conduct herself either to ensure a healthy birth or, if the baby was unwanted, to end the pregnancy. Her thoughts and actions were assumed to affect the child in her womb, though it was also believed that others, especially the father, could also influence it.[36] As for what we would call the fetus, it was thought of as a fully formed child from the seventh month onward, with a will of its own, just biding its time before entering the world. Although the child was thought to be influenced by its mother's behavior, it was assumed to have as much, if not more, control over the woman's body as did the woman herself, lending further credence to the notion that pregnancy was something that happened to her rather than a condition she was entirely responsible for.[37]

There is evidence that husbands monitored the health of their wives very closely, keeping diary records, as did the Reverend Ralph Josselin.[38] But for the most part, pregnancy went unmarked. There were no changes in behavior or dress, no efforts to collect baby clothes or pick out a name; such acts were thought to be presumptuous, even unlucky.[39] Indeed, there was as much to fear as to celebrate since, as mentioned earlier, the maternal death rate never fell below 7 percent and often went higher.[40] There was no way to avoid morning sickness or labor pains, which doctors, midwives, and mothers alike still thought of as either naturally or divinely ordained, brought upon women by Eve's misconduct and therefore something they should accept rather than resist. From the fourteenth century onward, maternal suffering replaced virginal status as a way of demonstrating female holiness. "The definition of a good mother as a suffering mother was firmly lodged in the ideologies of sanctity and of motherhood," notes Atkinson.[41] And this was as true of Protestantism as of Catholicism, though Catholic women still had the sufferings of Mary to give them psychological comfort.

Not that women did nothing to ward off natural or supernatural torments. For centuries pagans had resorted to charms and potions to ease the pains of childbirth, and the Catholic church had offered its own shrines and relics for the same magical purposes. From the late Middle Ages onward, the girdle of Mary and the relics of other mother saints were the object of female pilgrimage. When a Catholic woman could not go herself, she would send a "traveling girl" to bring back some of the magic.[42] Their Protestant sisters were deprived of these means, but many visited holy wells and sacred stones clandestinely. Their primary resource was prayer, often offered as a kind of incantation designed to provide some measure of comfort.[43]

Most women continued their normal routines right up to the moment of labor. In the ordinary language of the seventeenth and eighteenth centuries, pregnancy and birth were described not as a condition but as an activity—"breeding"—not all that different from a housewife's other enterprises.[44] While many women sought a little rest and indulgence during their pregnancies, eighteenth-century medical advice books encouraged them to remain active in everyday tasks, for they were thought to be plethoric, requiring leaner diets and more rather than less exercise.[45] In any case, a pregnant woman hardly stood out in a population in which virtually all married women were bearing children until illness or death prevented it. As Jacques Gelis has noted, "This simultaneous and permanent presence of pregnancy was an essential element of the 'human landscape' in past centuries. The community was perpetually pregnant with itself."[46]

Few women did much in anticipation of birth itself. A few who could afford to leave their busy households seem to have returned to their mothers; in England aristocratic women "went to Town," London being the favorite place to deliver.[47] But most households could not afford to dispense with their female members even for a short period. Thus, most women were at or near home when birth pains began, and often as surprised by the onset of labor as were their husbands and neighbors. The beginning of labor was interpreted as the child's efforts to get out of the womb. The flurry of activity that it precipitated may strike us as chaotic, even careless, but it was consistent with the traditional understanding of the body as subject to natural and supernatural forces beyond human control.

The first step once birth was imminent was to call for the midwife and to separate and isolate the birthing mother.[48] A "lying-in chamber" was designated and closed off, the doors shut and the windows draped, so that none of the normal sounds, smells, or activities of the household could penetrate.[49] Sometimes birth would take place in the warmest place, normally the kitchen. If a bedroom was chosen, it was completely rearranged so as to deconstruct its familiar features, including the bed itself. Few women gave birth in their own beds, for the birthing position of the time was either standing or squatting, and it was normal to substitute a special cot or birthing chair.[50] Suddenly and deliberately removed from her role as wife and helpmeet, the expectant mother was as isolated as if she had been removed to a birthing hut in the African rain forest.[51]

The midwife was joined by a half-dozen "gossips," neighborhood matrons who were there to witness the birth and assist as best they could. They busied themselves preparing special food and drink, usually a caudle of either hot wine or spiced porridge, sharing birth stories, and praying for a safe delivery. Birth was considered a women's affair, and only when the life was threatened was the male doctor called in.[52] Every effort was made to prevent husbands from seeing or hearing what was often a painful and sometimes a lethal process. They awaited news in the company of male friends, drinking the "groaning malt," drowning the anxiety that birth invariably evoked—the fear of losing not only a mother and child but their indispensable helpmeet and companion.[53]

The father's absence from the birthing room might suggest the lack of a concept of paternity, but in reality the opposite was the case. Men were said to feel a pregnancy, to share morning sickness and suffer the so-called husband's toothache, even experiencing labor pains.[54] The rituals of couvade, common to virtually all societies, constituted a parallel rite of progression in which paternity was formally acknowledged by the father and the community. In addition, the law recognized paternity by assigning rights in the child to the father rather than to the mother.[55]

Once the ritual separation had been accomplished, the waiting began. Little effort was made to hasten nature's pace or to substitute human for divine will. Midwives sometimes liked to hurry events for their own convenience, but medical opinion prior to the nineteenth century was against inducing labor. In fact, midwives were no more sensitive or tolerant of the mother's wishes than were male doctors.[56] The common language of the time—"with child," "brought to bed," "lying-in"—reinforced the notion of the mother as an object of forces beyond her control.[57] Birth was the moment of greatest danger to her, to the child, and to everyone attending her. It had once been a moment when every available magical means would be brought to bear, but by the eighteenth century these were largely unavailable to women of the middle and upper classes. In Protestant America it was said that "no midwives can do what angels do," a reference to the fatalism that attended birth during this period.[58]

Once the child was delivered, it was the task of the midwife to cut the umbilical cord, separating the child symbolically as well as physically from the mother. Instead of being brought immediately to the breast, the child was often taken to the hearth, symbolically identifying it with the house rather than with the mother.[59] It was then swaddled and shown to the father, his friends, and the other neighbors gathered at the house at the news of the event. The neglect of the mother in the immediate postpartum period was not as cruel as it may seem. She was regarded as out of danger and needing rest, but, of equal significance, she was not supposed to show too much affection toward the child. The mother love that is so much celebrated in our own day was regarded with great suspicion during the eighteenth century.[60] Any display of emotion suggested that the woman was still under the control of the natural and supernatural forces associated with birth. Both she and the child needed protection from these; both needed a time and a space to gain, or regain, the full measure of their humanity before reincorporation into family and community.[61]

The birthing ritual did not end with the biological event but continued for some days and even weeks until all its most important phase, the rites of incorporation, were complete. For the child this meant a second birth through the rite of baptism. Ralph Josselin wrote at the birth of his first child in 1642, "God wash it from it[s] corruption and sanctify it and make it his owne."[62] Cleansing was one of the traditional functions of baptism, but even before the child was brought to the font it had ordinarily undergone several folk rites of purification, separating it symbolically from the womb and forces of nature that had brought it into the world. Great attention was given to shaping the child's head, as if it had to be remade in a human image.[63] Swaddling served similar symbolic purposes, for it "was these clothes which made the child human, just as the wider ceremony of childbirth of which swaddling was a part made the delivery an act of culture, not merely of nature."[64]

In the traditional narrative of birth, the wife "presented" the husband with the child, who in turn re-presented it to the world with great flare and ceremony. Among the eighteenth-century gentry, birth, especially of a first-born son, was celebrated with bonfires, feasting, and distribution of largesse. Among the middle classes, patriarchal rites were more restrained but followed a similar pattern of celebrating with family and friends.[65]

Until a child was given this second birth, it was deemed very important to keep it isolated from all natural or supernatural influences. Even its name was not made known for fear that external powers would take possession of it.[66] The haste to baptize newborns reflected the same fear. When a child was in danger of dying, midwives had the right to baptize it themselves.[67] Naturally, Protestant theology's rejection of infant baptism posed a problem for those who regarded the rite as vital to the making of a human being; the great mass of the population continued to bring infants to the church font, while educated Protestants opted for private christenings, which avoided the appearance of infant baptism but still represented a symbolic second birth, providing the newborn with a name and a social identity. On all social levels, this was a time for communal feasting and gift-giving. "The birth was a convivial affair, welding the family and the community together round the child."[68]

Mothers, still confined to the lying-in chamber by the strict conventions of the day, were rarely present at the church when their children were baptized.[69] They played little part in the immediate postpartum festivities, which were presided over by the paterfamilias. If the infant was to be wet-nursed, the mother might get only a brief glimpse before it was taken away, not to be seen again for months, sometimes even years. In the meantime, she had entered into her period of "lying in," a ritualized period of up to a month when she was in a transition state, betwixt and between, neither fully a wife nor fully a mother. The physical act of giving birth was not at that time deemed sufficient to endow her with the wholeness and sanctity we now see as naturally conferred by maternity. Maternity was an event, not a cultural category capable of endowing a woman with motherhood as we would understand it. Indeed, seeing birth as something that happened to her allowed a woman to return to her household roles relatively unchanged by the biological experience.

Restoring a new mother to the fullness of womanhood required a period of several weeks, called "her month"; this final stage of the traditional ritual of progression would return her to her role as wife and coworker. For the first week the new mother was supposed to remain immobilized in bed, drinking the special caudle and eating a restricted diet. She would receive a carefully orchestrated series of visitors—women relations first, later female friends—sharing caudle with them.[70] The husband was the first male to enter the lying-in chamber, but it was thought dangerous to have sex during "her month," and even the mother's breast, which has such erotic meaning in modern culture, was then regarded with distaste, even fear.[71] Gradually the lying-in chamber would be opened up and restored to its original order, and the new mother would venture into the other rooms of the house. She would not leave the house, however, until the end of the month, which was normally marked by the religious rite of "churching," the religious ceremony of purification and thanksgiving to which was attached so much significance during this period.[72]

It was popularly assumed that the unchurched mother, sometimes known as the "green woman," was so dangerous that she could kill the grass she stepped on, induce unwanted pregnancies, and bewitch both people and animals.[73] In the sixteenth century, churching involved a public procession from the house to the church, the mother surrounded by her "gossips," sometimes led by the midwife herself. It was not until a woman had received the priest's blessing that "she may now put off her veiling kerchief, and look her husband and neighbors in the face again," wrote Henry Barrow, who, like other reformers, saw too much pagan and papist magic in the churching ritual.[74] Protestant sects substituted the simple rite of thanksgiving prayers for the older purification rites, but these were not always satisfactory to ordinary women who demanded that parsons church them in the old manner; when they refused, some women were known to church themselves.[75]

Even as the literate classes turned increasingly to private thanksgiving, public churching remained extremely popular throughout the eighteenth and nineteenth centuries, kept alive by women who valued it for its power to reconnect them with their households and communities.[76] During "her month," the domestic order was turned upside down, and husbands took on many of the wifely duties. New mothers were even spared their usual sexual duties until they were churched, a rite of incorporation that, as David

Cressy writes, "established a ritual closure to this state of affairs, allowing the resumption of sexual relations between husband and wife and the restoration of normal domestic order."[77] According to John Brand's eighteenth-century description, "on the day when such a Woman was Churched, every Family, favoured with a call, were bound to set Meat and Drink before her."[78] In America this event was called the "groaning party." While the womenfolk rejoiced indoors, the men drank and fired off guns in recognition that a moment of danger had passed and their symbolic universe was once again in proper order.[79]

It is not surprising that churching remained popular among women of all classes throughout the eighteenth century. The upper classes differed from the lower only in their preference that it be a private ceremony, performed at home.[80] For all women, however, it signaled a return to their primary identity as wife and helpmeet, and as part of the community of women. Today we think of birth (and especially first birth) as a new beginning that initiates motherhood and starts a family, thereby bringing a woman into the fullness of her femininity. Earlier generations, who did not equate maternity with motherhood or insist that nurturance was the sole responsibility of the individual mother, endowed birth with an entirely different meaning, making of it less a rite of individual passage and more a rite of progression for the entire community.

Rituals like these did not simply reflect behavior, they shaped it. The traditional rites of churching and baptism incorporated mothers and children into the community in a way that underlined, not a woman's own individual motherhood, but her connection to all mothers, and her children's connection to all children. The rites encouraged women to see their offspring as separate from themselves and to see mothering as one task among many, one that could be shared with others, including men. This is not to say that they did not care deeply about their children. It was precisely because parents were so concerned with the well-being of their offspring under conditions of high mortality and economic uncertainty that they were willing to entrust them to the kindness of strangers for both the short and the long term.[81] Taking care of children was central to a house mistress's duties, but in the era of the patriarchal household the role of wife subsumed that of mother. Until the nineteenth century, children looked beyond their own natural families for mothering and fathering. In turn, mothers and fathers looked to children who were not their own to fulfill their duty and desire to be good parents.

As long as a distinction was maintained between maternity and motherhood, mother figures, both idealized and demonized, were by no means confined to the domestic sphere. In the Middle Ages, maternal icons had populated the cosmos. By the seventeenth century, they had been brought down to earth but were still associated with godly households. It was not until the nineteenth century that "true motherhood" came to be associated with all women by virtue of giving birth. For the first time, motherhood was fully sacralized. "Human mothers had been honored before, but not in such an inflated manner. Flesh-and-blood mothers had never been held up to the standards of the Virgin Mary. Even the Virgin Mary had not been held to her own standards." In earlier centuries, the mother of Jesus had been allowed a certain freedom from the domestic role, but now she too was "completely redomesticated into a Victorian mother."[82] In Catholic countries, her cult grew in strength, providing women with a powerful representation of domesticated motherhood. But in Protestant lands, it was mothers themselves who would be fashioned into icons of true motherhood. By the end of the nineteenth century, they were objects of worship in both North America and Europe.

The symbolic treatment of pregnancy and birth was already showing some changes in the early nineteenth century. Middle-class women were beginning to treat their pregnancies differently: they were less likely to discuss what they called their "condition" with their husbands, and more likely to seek out male doctors for prenatal attention. Beginning their withdrawal from the world much earlier, most would no longer leave home during the period they now referred to as their "confinement."[83] These changes were anticipated in the new language of maternity that had appeared among the educated classes of Europe and North America at the end of the eighteenth century. In 1791 the *Gentleman's Magazine* reported:

> All our mothers and grandmothers, used in due course to become *with child* or as Shakespeare has it, *round-wombed* . . . but it is very well known that no female, above the degree of chambermaid or laundress, had been with child these ten years past . . . nor is she ever *brought to bed* or *delivered* but merely at the end of nine months, has an accouchement; antecedent to which she informs her friends that at a certain time she will be confined.[84]

Lady Sarah Napier could write in 1818 that "no one can say 'breeding' or 'with child' or 'lying-in' without being thought indelicate. . . . 'In the family way' and 'confinement' have taken their place."[85] In the new United States, the term "pregnancy" was eclipsed by a whole series of euphemisms—"in the family way," "expecting," and "in a delicate condition."[86]

The term "expecting" conveyed a notion of anticipation that had been absent earlier. Birth ceased to be an event, something that happened to a woman, and became a condition women were expected to internalize and represent to the larger world. The ritual of birth itself was changing, with more attention paid to the first phase of separation and less to the last phase of incorporation, which became truncated, even nonexistent, among middle-class women. Pregnant women were now advised to refrain from travel and exercise, and while working-class women had no choice but to continue their everyday activities, those who could afford to remove themselves from contact with the world did so. A pregnant woman was no longer welcome in public places, and she was discouraged from participating in many social occasions. She was not subject to these new prohibitions because, as in the past, she was considered too much under the influence of nature and dangerous to herself and others, but rather because, as Ludmilla Jordanova has observed, women were now seen as "the carriers and givers of life, and as a result, a pregnant woman was both the quintessence of life and an erotic object."[87] As such, she needed the protection afforded by domestic seclusion.

A rite that had taken only a few days now stretched over months. By the time the child arrived, middle-class women were fully prepared and had made all the necessary arrangements. Whereas upper-class women had previously traveled to their mothers, mothers now came to them.[88] The lying-in chamber was a thing of the past, for the birthing room, now normally the bedroom, was to be kept as nearly as possible in a normal state, with doors and windows open. There was no rearrangement of furniture, but rather an effort was made to maintain a homelike atmosphere. The conjugal bed replaced the birthing stool, emphasizing the compatibility between the roles of wife and mother and minimizing the strange and dangerous aspects of the female body in labor.[89]

The Victorian middle classes were the first to insist on home birth. "Thus confinement for childbirth was withdrawal to the supreme source of a woman's identity and purpose, the home," write Richard and Dorothy Wertz. "There, in her domain, a woman relearned who she was and, in maternity, performed her essential duty. Thereafter she might return, richly renewed, to society."[90] The symbols of home and motherhood were mutually reinforcing. No longer did a middle-class woman have need of an extended period of lying-in culminating with churching. Birth itself was capable of sanctifying a woman; it was a redeeming experience, a defining moment in the life of all women, a performance in which the mother was now the central actor. "Labour is a drama, painful to the individual, and exerting a painful interest in those around her," wrote W. Tyler Smith in the 1848 *London Lancet*.[91]

The pain and suffering of labor had not yet been eliminated, and even though anesthesia had been available as early as the 1840s, many women scorned it until the very end of the century, preferring instead to act out the suffering that Christians still associated with true motherhood. Despite the deadly realities of continued high infant and maternal mortality rates, birth had lost its ancient symbolic association with death. Birth was now antici- pated with joy rather than dread. Middle-class women were more likely to prepare the baby's layette than their own winding sheets.[92]

It is all the more significant therefore that women were choosing to have men present at births rather than the "gossips" who had been the tradi- tional witnesses. By the 1840s and 1850s, not only were most middle-class home births attended by male doctors, but for the first time husbands were present in the birthing room.[93] Elaborate precautions were taken to pre- serve women's modesty, and doctors were trained to deliver by touch rather than by sight.[94] While most birth mothers were never entirely comfortable having male doctors present, and the doctors seem to have been wary of the presence of husbands, middle-class women and the medical profession appear to have worked out an arrangement that met the requirements of all concerned. As historians have suggested, the women's willingness to have men in attendance had less to do with medical concerns than with the cul- tural imperative to have a "guaranteed performance. . . . They may have wanted a representative male to see their pain and suffering in order that their femininity might be established and their pain verified before men."[95]

And men seem to have been drawn to birth for similar cultural reasons. For William Gladstone, the birth of his first child in 1840 was

> a new scene & lesson in human life. . . . I have seen her endure today . . . yet six times as much bodily pain as I have undergone in my whole life. . . . How many thoughts does this agony excite. . . . Certainly the woman has this blessing that she may as a member of Christ behold in these pains certain special means of her purification with a willing mind, & so the more cheerfully hallow them by willing endurance into a thank offering.[96]

Guilt seems to have replaced fear as the primary paternal emotion in the nineteenth century. Previously afraid to be present during the mysterious moment of birth, middle-class men now felt a powerful need to support their wives at their moment of greatest pain and danger.[97] Unlike working- class fathers, who continued to experience their wives' travails in the traditional form of couvade well into this century, middle-class men could no longer imagine their bodies as functioning like those of women. Among them, the term "to father" had already taken on its modern meaning: to inseminate. They were increasingly detached during the nine months of gestation and played virtually no role at all in the preparations for birth. The old rites of passage to fatherhood, the groaning malt and the ritual presentation of the child to its *pater*, had all but fallen away by the nineteenth century. Perhaps the middle-class man eagerly accepted the invitation to enter the birthing room for the first time because the only remaining symbolic connection to his child was through the mother.

Women were the central actors in the transformed rites of birth. Previously, maternity was something that happened to a woman, her maximum moment of vulnerability and suffering. Now the test of true womanhood was not only how well a woman bore physical suffering but how she responded emotionally to her newborn. This shift coincided precisely with the redefinition of women as the more delicate, more feeling sex, and with the reevaluation of mother love, which ceased to be seen as so dangerous it required a lying-in period to recover from and became instead central to "true motherhood," born of the sacred moment of birth.[98] Melesina Trench described the birth of her first child in 1787 in terms that were to become standard in the next century: "When I looked in my boy's face, when I heard him breathe, when I felt the full pressure of his little fingers, I understood the full force of Voltaire's declaration: Le chef d'oeuvre d'amour est le coeur d'une mere. . . . My husband's delight of his son nearly equalled mine."[99] In Mrs. Gaskell's Victorian novel *Ruth* (1853), the initial interaction between mother and child is rendered in precisely the same terms: "That baby touch called forth her love; the doors of her heart were thrown wide open for the little infant to go in and take possession."[100]

Until the moment of giving birth, a woman's femininity had been only potential; afterward, she was a true woman. Gone was the ritual separation of mother and child, the head shaping and the swaddling. The new mother was no longer considered a danger to herself and others, to be immobilized and quarantined until she underwent rites of purification. The breast, simultaneously naturalized and eroticized, became identified with both nurturance and pleasure; for middle-class Victorian women, breast-feeding became a symbol of true motherhood.[101] Doctors recommended it because it made women "more soft and beautiful," more rather than less attractive to their husbands.[102] In Dickens's novel of the same name, David Copperfield dreams that "a baby smile upon her breast might change my child-wife [Dora] into a woman."[103] In the traditional birth ritual, the postpartum period had served to symbolically disconnect mother and child, returning the woman to her multiple roles as wife and helpmeet. Now this time was used to symbolize fusion, as if, as Judith Lewis has put it, "the experience of motherhood presumably began only after the child's birth—precisely when it was thought to have ended a century earlier."[104]

Having ceased to be a moment of supernatural and physical danger, birth was represented as magical, transformative of the identities not just of the mother but also of the father and child. And what had once been a moment of communal reaffirmation now served primarily as a celebration of female kin connections. Attending their daughters' confinements became for older women a source of renewal of their own sense of motherhood. Queen Victoria set the example, insisting that her daughters wear her maternity gown and give birth in the same bed where they themselves had been born.[105] Few women were able to symbolize their connections in quite so dramatic a manner, but in time a whole set of all-female celebrations, including the baby and bridal shower, would arise.[106]

The old rites had emphasized incorporation; the new underlined separation. With birth symbolically disassociated from death and danger, the traditional practices of baptism and churching seemed neither necessary nor proper. Infant mortality rates remained relatively high, but among the middle classes the sickly child was no longer hastened away to be given the magical protection of baptism but was immediately placed under a doctor's care. Baptism could wait until the child and mother were physically ready. In the eighteenth and early nineteenth centuries, this ceremony was likely to take place at home, but after 1850 church christenings regained their popularity among the middle classes; they did not regain, however, their communal aspect or the magic that was still a part of working-class baptisms.[107] It was now the mother and child who provided the focus for these family ceremonials; they have remained the center of attention ever since, virtually displacing the father from his previous role in the baptism ceremony.

Churching went the way of the traditional baptism. Educated women recited prayers of thanksgiving in the privacy of their homes, leaving the public ceremony to the working classes.[108] The doctor now determined when a woman was ready to end her confinement. The new rite of passage, focused on separation, dispensed with all the old symbols of incorporation.[109] Maternity by itself had become sufficient to establish not only true motherhood but also fatherhood. In the absence of the old rites of paternity, fathers came to rely on birth to give meaning to their fatherhood, and they were drawn to the bedside by the powerful symbols present there. In the rescripted drama of birth, the husband became a father when he beheld mother and child together, joined by the powerful icon of the breast. For Amos Alcott, a new American father, this sight was an almost religious experience that made "it seem that I was, indeed, a Father."[110]

By the end of the nineteenth century, middle-class women were congratulating themselves on having mastered the natural and supernatural forces that still made birth such a mysterious and deadly process to many working-class women. "We can take care of our bodies, study them, worry about them, treat them, in short, much as one does a favorite horse, and then demand that they serve us absolutely," one American woman wrote in *Good Housekeeping* in 1915.[111] But this sense of control over nature had been achieved largely through science and in collaboration with the male medical establishment. By 1900 middle-class women were ready to take the step of demanding painless birth, an option that had been available since the 1840s but that they had been unwilling to adopt because suffering remained so closely identified with true motherhood. But now a generation of "New Women," many of them feminists eager to enter the wider world, were ready to dispense with what they regarded as an outmoded superstition. By the 1920s a variety of anesthetics, including "twilight sleep," had become popular in middle-class circles.[112] The physicality of birth was thereby separated from suffering as women asserted the superiority of mind over body.

Ironically, women's heightened desire to control their own bodies increased their dependency on the male medical profession and led directly to the hospitalization of birth, which began after the First World War and had become almost universal by the 1950s. In the nineteenth century, only the destitute went to hospitals to give birth. They were dangerous places until the 1880s, and the stigma attached to them was reflected in the fact that in 1900 only 5 percent of American births took place there. By 1939, however, one-half of all births took place in hospitals and three-quarters of all urban births were hospitalized. The middle classes led the way in placing themselves under medical care; the working classes followed when they could afford it.[113]

Beginning in the 1920s, middle-class women were coming to hold the medical view of their bodies as machines, prone to breakdown and failure. This was the rationale for hospitalization, inspiring the *Century Illustrated Magazine* to give its own version of the contemporary colloquy between a woman and her doctor:

> "But is the hospital necessary at all?" demanded a young woman of her obstetrician friend. "Why not bring the baby at home?"

"What would you do if your automobile broke down on a country road?" the doctor countered with another question.

"Try and fix it," said the modern chaffeuse.

"And if you couldn't?"

"Have it hauled to the nearest garage."

"Exactly. Where the trained mechanics and their necessary tools are," agreed the doctor. "It's the same with the hospital."[114]

Doctors had begun to see all birth as potentially pathogenic and to establish what they believed to be scientifically valid procedures to ensure the health and safety of both mother and child; middle-class women, increasingly taught to think scientifically about their own bodies and those of their children, readily accepted this rationale. Intensified prenatal care placed them in the category of patients, inducing them "to regard themselves as objects."[115] Saved from suffering but denied the central role in the drama of birth that their mothers and grandmothers had claimed, these otherwise liberated women found themselves subjected to procedures that initially had been designed to promote hygiene but that rapidly became rigidly routinized, denying the very humanity of mother and child that hospital birth was supposed to protect and enhance.[116]

Hospitalization's emphasis on separation began at the moment of admission. The woman was immobilized in a wheelchair and whisked away from her escort to be "prepped"—gowned, her pubic hair shaved, given an enema, bedded, sedated, and monitored, usually in splendid isolation. She was now on hospital time; should labor come too slowly, it was likely to be induced. (In the twentieth century, noticeably few births occur on weekends, normally a doctor's free time.)[117] Once labor began, the routines become even more invasive. The birth mother's sense of vulnerability was enhanced by the so-called lithotomy position, "her buttocks at the table's edge, her legs widespread in the air, her vagina totally exposed."[118] Other technological procedures, none of which had been proven to enhance the birthing process, were then deployed and, indeed, continue to be used to this day. In the United States episiotomy has become an almost universal practice, used in 90 percent of all births. Almost one-quarter of all American births are now performed by cesarean section, which places a woman's mind and body at an even further remove. Mirrors are provided so that the woman can observe the whole process, placing her in the position of witnessing herself, the ultimate reminder that in the modern scientific construction of birth it is the doctor, not the mother, who delivers the child.[119]

In the hospital, birth ceased to be a family event. The father's role was reduced to that of the nervous bystander, pacing the halls during labor, glimpsing the newborn through the glass of the nursery, his visits strictly limited. But the mother's access to the baby was also drastically restricted. It was handed by the doctor to the nurses, who washed and bundled it, a kind of secular baptism signifying the child's incorporation, not into the family or community, but into a technological world claiming full credit for its birth.[120] From the 1920s onward, mothers' access to their infants was governed by notions of "scientific motherhood," which emphasized scheduled feeding and sleeping and gave little support to breast-feeding or to the mothers themselves. It has been noted that, "while child experts became more sensitive to baby . . . they were increasingly insensitive to mother."[121]

Women's efforts to transcend nature through science began as part of a progressive effort to gain equal access to the men's world of work, education, and political power. By the 1940s, however, some women were questioning "twilight sleep" and anesthetized birth, along with other tenets of scientific motherhood like scheduled feeding. Margaret Mead demanded of her doctor, Benjamin Spock, that he assist her in achieving the fullest possible consciousness during the birth of her children. She also insisted on breast-feeding on demand, another radical departure from the technological model of child-rearing.[122] Educated women had been the first to internalize an image of themselves as machines, but by the 1950s they were beginning to complain of the factorylike conditions of the delivery wards. "The practice of obstetrics is the most modern and medieval, the kindest and the cruelest," wrote one mother of three. "Women are herded like sheep through the obstetrical assembly line, are drugged and strapped on tables while their babies are forceps-delivered. Obstetricians today are businessmen who run baby factories. Modern painkillers and methods are used for the convenience of the doctor, not to spare the mother."[123]

By this time a small number of middle-class women on both sides of the Atlantic had become followers of Grantley Dick Read's "natural childbirth" movement. They eschewed drugs out of a fear of possible damage to their infants' brains and began to listen to Spock's notions about a more flexible, commonsensical approach to child-rearing. Accepting that their own feelings and those of their children might be a better guide than the doctors and child care experts, they began to challenge the doctrines of scientific motherhood through their own experiences of mothering.

Although this new attitude upset the medical profession, the natural childbirth and child-rearing movements were no threat to postwar conventions of marriage and family. In fact, the followers of the Read, Lamaze, and Bradley methods were all concerned about restoring birth to its place as a family ritual, enhancing the "togetherness" that was so highly prized in the postwar era.

All were staunch defenders of the conventional nuclear family, with its gendered division of labor. No unwed fathers were admitted to Read's natural childbirth classes, and the training provided to properly married couples reinforced the highly gendered notion of childbirth and child care that assigned to fathers the role of secondary parent.[124] Fathers' supportive role still ended at the admissions desk, for the entry of fathers into the delivery room was resisted until the 1970s. But even when this barrier fell, fathers were subjected to a gendered set of rules and procedures that reduced them largely to the role of bystander and often left them feeling frustrated and alienated by the experience. Natural childbirth managed to restore women to a central role in the drama of birth but failed to provide symbols of the father's connection to the newborn. Birth continued to be defined as a female rite of individual passage, underlining the gendered nature of parenthood and reinforcing the connection between maternity and motherhood, while emphasizing the distinction between paternity and fatherhood.

Aware that hospital procedures, even when administered with the greatest consideration, are inevitably alienating and discomforting, many people had begun by the 1980s to advocate a return to birthing at home or, as the next best thing, in homelike birthing centers. This movement, together with the parallel return to midwife-assisted births, continues to grow in both Europe and the United States but has yet to displace medicalized childbirth procedures as the modern rite of passage for most women. In the United States, more than 85 percent of all births continue to occur in hospital settings, with only 1 percent taking place at home; in Europe the percentages of home births are higher but the symbolic construction of motherhood has not changed very much. Scientific motherhood continues to hold sway. Robbie Davis-Floyd has estimated that 70 percent of all American births conform to what she calls the technocratic model, with standard procedures of modern medicine constituting the rite of passage preferred by most women.[125] Even when they choose birthing centers, women insist on medically trained assistance, so that, whether under the bright lights of the delivery room or in the softer ambience of the birthing center, mothers still struggle to achieve the illusive sense of true motherhood under the sign of science.

Despite all the changes in location, little has altered over the two hundred years since birth ceased to be something that happens to a woman and became the ultimate source of adult female identity. Never have the rituals surrounding birth been so extended or elaborate; never has birth played so central a role in our imaginings of what family should be; never has so much time and effort been devoted to its anticipation and to its memory. But it remains a rite of individual passage, separating the new mother and underlining her singular relationship to the child. In earlier centuries, mothers certainly experienced postpartum depression, but there is evidence that the current absence of incorporative rituals leads to an overwhelming sense of isolation, a feeling of being "lost and alone."[126] Men are once again part of the birthing scene, but largely as witnesses, with their still and video cameras at the ready. It is still women who give modern family life's most demanding performance. It is something they most eagerly anticipate and look back on with a great deal of satisfaction. While they are going through their rite of passage, however, many find themselves overwhelmed, even to the point of becoming destructive to themselves and to their children.

Women give birth not only to children but to their husband's fatherhood, their own motherhood, and the family itself.[127] Weddings create couples, but it is birth that makes a family. We say that a young couple expecting their first child are "starting a family." We celebrate not only wedding anniversaries but children's birthdays; indeed, the latter have become the most important rites of progression for modern families, moments to synchronize calendars and symbolize unity. Childless couples are considered less than complete, and we talk about a family whose children have grown up as if it is no longer really a family.[128] While fathers as well as mothers experience this change, it is women who are most affected by "empty nest syndrome," a sense of loss only a little less painful to them than the onset of menopause, which until recently was equated with the loss of purpose in a woman's life.[129]

In the past, when maternity was separable from motherhood, it was possible to imagine motherless families and familyless mothers. Then, it was the absence of a patriarch that endangered the household, while today a family without a mother is the one most likely to be placed under the jurisdiction of the state. Prior to the nineteenth century, custody of children, even of infants, was invariably assigned to fathers; today mothers almost always seek and are assigned the responsibility for children.[130] We have no trouble imagining fatherless families, but a motherless family is unthinkable. In the twentieth century, law, psychology, and the social sciences have combined to declare the mother-child bond primary. Mothers are assigned all the credit when children turn out well, and all the blame when they turn out badly, for never has motherhood loomed so large in Western culture's sense of its own well-being.

Mother's voice, mother's smile, and mother's love first became central symbols in the Victorian period. But we can also detect the beginnings of modern mother-blaming in the same period, suggesting that idealization and demonization are two sides of the same coin. It was then that mothers first became the objects of intense nostalgia, particularly among sons who were forced to leave family behind in their quest for success in an uncertain, fragmented world that made the wholeness and certainty mothers stood for so unattainable and therefore so attractive. Daughters were also drawn to their mothers, but in a somewhat different way. They were more likely to remain within her orbit and to experience her as a real person rather than an idealized icon. Today, as more daughters enter careers, they too have found it harder to recognize the real woman behind the powerful image of motherhood. Daughters seem to find it as difficult to separate fantasy and reality when it comes to motherhood. As they have entered the world of work and politics, they have had increasing difficulty in seeing the human dimension of mothers, including their own.[131]

Fantasies about mothers have spread in proportion to the increasing complexity and difficulty of modern mothering. In the nineteenth century, when servants and kinfolk were more likely to be involved in the upbringing of children, the praise and blame were more likely be divided among several mother figures. The British upper classes have been notoriously fond of their nannies, but just as apt to project negative feelings onto them.[132] Today, when mothers are more likely to raise their own children, they are also more likely to be the objects of both idealization and demonization. The higher the standard that mothers set for themselves, the more likely they are to be blamed, and to blame themselves. As Ann Dally has put it: "In our times, there has been less idealization of women and wives, but idealization of the mother has reached unprecedented proportions. The result is that we now face a crisis of motherhood."[133]

In a world largely emptied of a sense of place, mothers have become fixed points in our mental landscapes. They must always be there for us, even in their physical absence. By 1900 it had become difficult to imagine any mother substitutes. Hymns composed for the new Mother's Day, invented just before the First World War, extolled mothers' singularity and centrality: "We find no second mother/We find no second home."[134] Today Europeans and Americans still return to mother's for Sunday dinner and at Christmas. It is her memory that is most honored and her grave that is most visited. Mother's Day is still a far more important occasion than Father's Day, which was invented in North America in 1908.[135] The spread of Mother's Day in the twentieth century testifies to the greater symbolic power of motherhood, which has been appropriated by all kinds of commercial, religious, and political movements. But the desire to honor the idea of motherhood has too often been accompanied by a neglect of the plight of actual mothers. Regimes like Nazi Germany, which placed huge burdens on women, were the most zealous in their promotion of Mother's

Day. And in our own country, in the current debates about welfare, the same idealization goes hand in hand with neglect of the dire conditions facing many real mothers.[136]

There is really no role in modern society quite like motherhood. Wifehood and husbandhood are disposable through divorce, and fathers can practice a kind of serial fatherhood in which they are allowed to try again when they fail with their first set of children.[137] But mothers are forever the mothers to the children they bear in a culture that privileges blood tie as its primary symbol of permanence and connection.[138] Motherhood is considered a full-time, lifelong career, and child-rearing, which was once understood as a set of learned tasks, is seen as an instinct that comes as naturally to women as the sex drive does to men.[139] While it could be argued that the physical burdens of child-rearing have diminished, the psychological and cultural work of motherhood has increased enormously. No longer a set of well-defined tasks that can be shared with others, modern mothering demands, as John Bowlby, the leading advocate of mother-child bonding, formulated it in 1951, "constant attention day and night, seven days a week and 365 in the year."[140]

For much of this century, the ideology of true motherhood demanded that women stay at home to meet the supposedly insatiable needs of their children; even now, as women cope with the equally greedy claims of the workplace, their time and presence are more in demand than those of men, even when both parents are earning the same salaries. Studies have shown that women have much greater difficulty mentally separating work and home than men. Even the physical separation of home and work does not automatically create cognitive distance for women in the same way that it does for men. Mothers who are thousands of miles from home remain responsible for its day-to-day operations. Studies show that they are more likely to check in by calling home and that they worry more than men.[141] Mothers are always mentally at home in ways that fathers are not. They do not have access to the rituals that allow men to create mental distance, for much more fuss is still made over men's home leavings and comings than women's. By and large, the symbols and images of both home and workplace underscore men's claims to the role of principal breadwinner, disguising and even erasing working women's contributions. Thus, even as the conditions of men's and women's work change, the cultural constructions remain the same, sustaining the image in the absence of reality.

Today motherhood is given far more ritual attention than fatherhood. It is something of a paradox that birth should have become such an elaborate rite of passage in an era of declining fertility and at a time when only about one-quarter of the average woman's life is involved with active childbearing and child-rearing. In the days when a married woman's life span was entirely taken up with mothering, there was no need to underline that basic function. Today our culture demands that motherhood be honored even at the expense of mothers themselves. All our private and public celebrations of motherhood—birthdays, anniversaries, Mother's Day—reflect our need to find through symbol and ritual a sense of nurture and protection that mothers by themselves can never fully provide. In earlier periods, society was able to turn to holy mothers and exemplary members of the community to reassure itself of the enduring qualities of good motherhood. Today we look to mothers themselves, who are placed in the unenviable position of having to live up to an ideal that only a superwoman could fulfill.

Unable to accept their own humanity and the shortcomings this inevitably entails, many women feel a disconnection between the idealized motherhood they are expected to live up to and the realities of everyday mothering. Modern culture has thus added yet another task to mother's work: representing herself to herself and to others as something she can never completely be. Never before has this cultural imperative taken up so much space and time in women's lives. Never have mothers been so burdened by motherhood.

CHAPTER 9

Bringing Up Fathers:
Strangers in Our Midst

The most important thing a father can do for his children is to love their mother.

Father Theodore Hesburgh[1]

FATHERS OCCUPY a very modest place in our symbolic universe—always at the threshold of family life, never at its center. Men pay for their autonomy by remaining strangers in their own homes. Perceived as liminal figures, fathers sometimes appear threatening, but usually they are just out of place, rather ridiculous in the domestic setting. As a consequence, the subject of fathers has been more likely to produce laughter than serious discussion. For most of our century, the treatment of fathers in film, fiction, and television has been satiric, if not dismissive. Fathers have not fared much better at the hands of scholars, who have had trouble taking fatherhood as seriously as motherhood. You will search in vain in advertisements

179

and media for creditable father figures. Fathers are treated as absent even when they should be present. The illustrated warnings about prenatal drinking and smoking that now adorn the walls of bars and restaurants depict only the maternal figure, despite the proven fact that sperm damaged by the same risky behavior can endanger the child. Our culture simply will not take paternity as seriously as maternity.[2]

To be sure, fatherhood has become much more visible in the past couple of decades, but this change was more the byproduct of our preoccupation with motherhood than of any appreciation of fathers as such. Sometime in the 1970s, medical sociologists began to notice a stranger in the delivery room, and it was only then that studies of fatherhood began to multiply.[3] The readmission of fathers to the birthing scene after a half-century of exclusion stimulated this interest, but researchers found that this new dimension of fatherhood was as strange to fathers as it was to them. By the late 1980s, a majority of fathers were attending the births of their children, but many were finding it an unnerving and alienating experience, not at all the reassuring beginning that the advocates of father-assisted births had hoped for.[4]

The feelings fathers have about themselves are consistent with the images of fatherhood generally held by Americans and Europeans. These are very thin images, without the emotional pull of the contemporary mother figure. As we have seen, mothers are supposed to be responsible for all the good that happens to children, and all the bad, but little is expected of fathers. Although there has been a growing concern over fatherless families in recent years, it too often has reinforced the image of fathers as strangers; we underestimate the desire of men to be involved in the lives of their children at the same time that we exaggerate the mother's role.[5] Historians have contributed to this misperception by concentrating almost exclusively on motherhood, virtually ignoring fathers.[6] Despite the fact that most history writing is about men, fathers are either absent from representations of the past or treated in an idealized manner. Any notion of "good fatherhood" seems to retreat deeper and deeper into history.

Today, when the panic over absent fathers and deadbeat dads has reached one of its periodic peaks, this sense of loss and regret is overwhelming. But before we succumb to the prevailing nostalgia, it would be well to remind ourselves that absent fathers have been a repeated theme in European and American cultures since the early nineteenth century, when the cult of the forefathers first appeared in its modern guise. From that point on, the best that Western societies have hoped for is the revival or revitalization of fatherhood, a project that, for all its religious, social, scientific, psychological, and, most recently, men's movement incarnations, has consistently failed to achieve its goals, largely because it has treated father-hood as a problem to be solved by the conscientious efforts of fathers them-selves. In reducing the problem of fatherhood to the individual level, the revitalizationist approach has ignored the degree to which the problem of fatherhood is built into the very political, economic, and cultural constitu-tion of the modern world. To paraphrase Ann Dally, one might say that there have always been fathers, but fatherhood has never been invented.[7]

Fatherhood's relationship to the biological act of paternity is neither fixed nor universally consistent. It is rather a social construction appropri-ate to the material and cultural conditions of the time and place where the fathering takes place. As the anthropologist Carol Delaney reminds us, fatherhood and motherhood are "not derived from the 'facts' of reproduc-tion, but are instead intimately related to a theory of reproduction, and this theory is itself embedded in a wider corpus of beliefs about the world."[8] If modern culture has conflated maternity with motherhood, it has separated paternity and fatherhood. Today the *genitor* is no longer automatically the *pater*.

Historically, motherhood and fatherhood have switched places in our symbolic universe. Before the nineteenth century, when Europeans and Americans thought about family and home, they almost exclusively con-jured up father figures. Today people imagine family and home using pri-marily images of mothers. Mothers are always there for them, a fixed point in their mental landscapes, but fathers are either absent or only dimly per-ceived, strangers in their own homes. Mother and father figures function in our culture to represent the familiar and the unknown. Invariably, mothers are perceived as close, and fathers as distant. Together they set the boundaries of the family, but neither is true to the real people who are our parents.

The cultural history of Western fatherhood is as complex, uneven, and con-voluted as that of Western motherhood. Until the fourteenth century, Christian iconography paid as little attention to Joseph as father as to Mary as mother. Until then, his image was that of the senile, cuckolded husband, the subject of artistic satire and folk humor, denied both saintly character and plausible paternity. It was not until the early modern period that Joseph emerged as a father figure worthy of respect and emulation in Catholic countries; although Protestants paid much less attention to holy fathers generally, it was in the same period that they began to fashion their own emblems of fatherhood out of the lives of the patriarchs of their godly com-munities.[9] The reformers raised fatherhood to an unprecedented symbolic level when they returned Christianity to the Judaic monogenetic notion of a single masculine creator. They swept the cosmos clear of the enlivening presence of maternal figures, including the Virgin Mary, leaving only one God and his earthly counterpart, the godly father.[10] Perhaps never before, and certainly never since, has fatherhood carried more symbolic if not actual weight than between the sixteenth and nineteenth centuries.

During this era, patriarchal figures took on nurturing as well as protective qualities. Until the mideighteenth century, it was even possible to imagine fathers as giving birth. Stories about cases of pregnant men circulated widely at a time when the male and female bodies were still seen as superior and inferior versions of the same thing rather than as fundamentally different.[11] A house without a *Hausvater* was not a proper family. Orphans were defined by their fatherlessness, and hospitality was the responsibility of males rather than females.[12] It was fathers who reached beyond the grave to haunt the living.[13] Being the head of a household endowed a male with the rights of fatherhood regardless of paternity. While becoming a householder usually coincided with marriage, bachelors could also be fathers by virtue of their propertied status. In the language of the eighteenth century, all the members of a man's household, whether related or not, were spoken of as "his family."[14]

Not every man would become a *Hausvater*, and many would give up their offspring to the care of other men in a period when richer households attracted the children of poorer families. But neither fathers nor mothers seem to have felt any threat to their identities in giving up their children. Possessiveness was defined as spoiling, and good parenting was understood to be an extensive rather than intensive enterprise, involving fathers as well as mothers. Fathers were active in all the major nurturing and educational functions we now associate with motherhood. They oversaw the wet-nursing of infants and knew how to clothe and doctor children. In the eighteenth century, it was still men who carried on the bulk of family correspondence. In matters of death as well as life, men were involved to a degree that has become rare in modern times. Evidence from letters and diaries suggests that fathers were every bit as affected by the illnesses and deaths of their children as mothers were.[15] And when the signers of the American Declaration of Independence wrote of their childhoods, it was their fathers rather than their mothers they remembered.[16]

Of course, the fatherly presence varied by class. It was weakest at the highest and lowest ends of the social scale, for the search for work sent poor men into the households of others, and thus away from their families, while aristocratic fathers were often away in military or civil service.[17] It was at the middling level that the household economy gave fathers a prominent place in family life. Not only artisans and farmers but business and professional men conducted much of their work in the house, assisted by their wives and children. Marriage was a working partnership until the middle of the nineteenth century, and a man's vocation was not allowed to interfere with his fatherly responsibilities. When it did, it was not uncommon for middle-class men to opt for early retirement, clearly indicating the priority they put on domestic life.[18]

The time and space of the *Hausvater* were inseparable from those of the family. As long as the rhythms of life were set by household tasks, there was no difference between his time and that of his wife, children, and servants. They all ate and prayed together; they got up and went to bed on the same schedule. Males felt no need for a special place of retreat because domesticity posed no threat to their masculinity.[19] They were as comfortable in the kitchen as women, for they had responsibility for provisioning and managing the house. Until the nineteenth century, cookbooks and domestic conduct books were directed primarily to them, and they were as devoted to decor as they were to hospitality.[20] Even in his absence, the *Hausvater's* presence was always felt.

The centrality of father figures in the early modern period is attributable in part to the existence of a set of reproductive rituals that transformed genitors into paters in a way that has no contemporary counterpart. Paternity by itself was no more capable of making a social father than it is now; poor men often failed to achieve the status of paterfamilias that was guaranteed to heads of households by virtue of the care they were able to give, both before and after a child was born. But this separation of fatherhood from paternity had its advantages for the children of the poor, who had no real choice but to find nurturance someplace other than in their natural families.

Fatherhood began with conception, for it was believed that it was possible for the male to know through his sexual organ when fertilizaton occurred. This belief lingered among the working classes even into this century. In the 1890s, when a doctor ridiculed a man's contention that he knew the date of conception because he had felt ill at the time, the father shot back, "You may laugh, Doctor, but I always know when that happens without my wife saying anything about it, and why shouldn't I, as I am the father."[21] According to the Aristotelian notion of reproduction dominant until the eighteenth century, the male was the more active partner in fertilization, the giver of human life, supplying both reason and soul. He was thought to provide the greater heat necessary to conception, and good sex was associated with successful fertilization.[22] There was as yet no distinction between sex and reproduction; as a consequence, men imagined themselves to be central to the generative process. The female was seen as passive, providing a material environment; she was essentially a vessel for carrying the child. As Carolyn Merchant has formulated it, the understanding current at the time was "of the man as parent and the woman as incubator."[23]

The father was seen as having the dominant role in shaping the child. William Harvey, for instance, believed that the reproductive system worked to guarantee that "the female produces an offspring like the father."[24] Coital positions were said to determine the sex of the child; the connection between father and child was viewed as visceral, as if they were part of one flesh. It was commonly believed that the natural resemblance between fathers and their children was sufficient to identify men who denied paternity. Paternity was felt to be so transparent that even threatening to use this method of divining it was often sufficient to bring men to marry the women they had made pregnant.[25]

Evidence from diary sources suggests that early modern fathers were very involved with pregnancy, monitoring the mother's condition and giving advice on diet and exercise.[26] Men also expressed their sense of fatherhood through the forms of couvade that are common to all cultures in which men regard the pregnancy as theirs as much as the mother's.[27] There is little direct evidence of couvade in the historical record, but reports of instances of the practice in the rural and urban working classes suggest that it must have been quite widespread. The notion of the "husband's toothache" was common enough, and some men became so overcome by morning sickness as to be unable to work.[28] Furthermore, it was commonly believed that a mother's pains could be transferred to the father. In rural Cheshire during the First World War, a woman was reported to have announced: "Oh, I am all right. J—— [her husband] is bearing the little one this time, and he is awfully bad."[29]

This kind of sympathetic magic was frowned on by the early modern clergy, who regarded a woman's suffering as the will of God. But their views made little progress against the prevailing understanding of the body as open and vulnerable to the influence of other bodies, a notion that persisted even among educated circles until the mideighteenth century, when the scientific image of the body as a self-regulating machine became dominant. In the sixteenth and seventeenth centuries, Catholic mothers-to-be still had the option of praying to the Virgin or using the relics of maternal saints to ward off the terrors of birthing, but Protestants like Ann Platter had no choice but to place their faith entirely in father figures. "Oh, I trust in the true God; he will help me through this," she prayed to the Almighty. She also seems to have placed great faith in her husband Thomas, who we know to have been with her throughout her birthing ordeal.[30]

Thomas Platter's presence at birth is an exception in the historical record, however; as we have already seen, birth remained a woman's affair until the early nineteenth century. Yet most early modern fathers had been sufficiently involved in the pregnancy to want to be nearby when the birth actually happened. By all accounts, they were the ones who sent for the midwife and the gossips and rearranged the household for the birth. Once they had assured themselves that they had done all they could, they stepped aside physically, but not necessarily psychologically. Oliver Heywood retreated to his chamber in 1683 to pray vigorously, a common practice among expectant fathers.[31] But he remained on call in case the birth became difficult and a doctor was needed. He could have expected to remain in charge of the household during the month or so of Mrs. Heywood's lying-in, after which time everything would finally be restored to its usual order.

Fathers could not attend the birth, but they were the center of the attention while it was taking place. Men prayed with their friends, but as long as the birth seemed to be going well, they also kept a more convivial vigil, drinking and eating. In Scotland there was a special "groaning malt" for such occasions, but everywhere the announcement of a successful birth meant a celebration. In some places the new father would be toasted; in others he would be served a special birthing cake called the "kenno."[32] The child would be placed in his arms and he would show it off to the gathered company. He was also the one who carried it to the baptismal font or, if he did not believe in infant baptism, presided over a domestic christening. On such occasions, the "father invites home his friends & ye Parson to drink ye health of ye woman in ye straw," it was reported, underlining the prominence of the father and the absence of the mother in postpartum celebrations.[33] The scale of the festivities differed by class, but if the baby was the firstborn of a gentry family, "bonfires gleamed through the countryside, oxen were roasted whole, and the customary paraphernalia of joy usual to rich Britons on such occasions were gone through with wondrous éclat."[34] Among the poor, there would be little publicity, but new fathers, like new husbands, could expect to be congratulated by their workmates for passing the ultimate test of virility.

After the birth, the child was symbolically, if not physically, in the hands of men, receiving its second birth from them.[35] In Catholic Europe the second birth was institutionalized as baptism, a rite of passage from nature to culture symbolized by the passing of the infant into the hands of holy fathers who delivered it to its spiritual family, the godparents. Catholics believed that baptism guaranteed them a place in heaven, but it was also commonly believed in the sixteenth and seventeenth centuries that it had the magical effect of ensuring the health of the child and protecting it from evil spirits. Protestantism objected to the magical dimensions of infant baptism and insisted that the spiritual rite be postponed until the child was mentally ready. Christenings thus moved from the church to the home in many places, especially colonial America, but this change did not prevent many of the faithful from continuing the old rites of paternity in the new setting. In fact, the loss of belief in the magical effects of baptism caused Protestant fathers to take their duties as caregivers even more seriously, for now the child's salvation depended on his spiritual guidance.[36] In effect, fatherhood had been extended to be coextensive with the whole life of a child.

Defined as giving birth but not life, motherhood ended in early modern Europe and North America at just that point in a woman's life when we would expect it to begin.[37] On the other hand, fatherhood began when we would now see it as ending. There was no closure to paternity, as there tends to be today when, after handing out cigars to their workmates, men return to their normal duties as husband and breadwinner.

Historians have now established that men took their fatherly duties very seriously.[38] The domestic treatises of the seventeenth and eighteenth centuries were directed mainly to them, and they were involved not only in the provisioning and medicating but in the catechizing, educating, and disciplining of children from infancy onward. "The bond between father and child was understood to be as intimate and as enduring as that between mothers and children," writes Steven Ozment in *When Fathers Ruled*.[39] The father's relationship to the child was not only close but full-time. It is highly significant that Protestantism defined fatherhood as work, as an essential dimension of the innerworldly asceticism men owed to God. Luther himself insisted that "when a father washes diapers and performs some other mean task for his child, and someone ridicules him as an effeminate fool . . . God with all his angels and creatures is smiling."[40]

Luther's language makes it abundantly clear that Protestant fatherhood was not only wholly compatible with but necessary to manliness. Moreover, fathers gave life to all the children placed in their care, not just to their own biological offspring.[41] On the plantations of the American South, slaves took their master's name and identified themselves as a part of his family. In turn, the master talked of his family, "white and black."[42] In colonial New England, no child, not even older youths, was allowed to be fatherless. In both North America and Europe, attitudes toward unwed motherhood and bastardy hardened, and laws were passed that attempted to ensure that there would be no fatherless families. Of course, this ideal was never achieved. High rates of adult mortality meant that in England only one-third of all children would reach marriage age with a father living.[43] Economic conditions compelled many fathers to migrate in search of work. Desertion was frequent, but often communications were so difficult that men simply lost touch with their families.[44] Yet these grim realities had little effect on the ideal. The image of the caring father remained central to the imagined family well into the nineteenth century.

However, before we begin to romanticize this *Hausvater* culture, it is important to keep in mind that this belief system sustained the manhood of some men by effectively denying it to others. In the household-based economy of proto-industrial capitalism and plantation slavery, natural fatherhood was never enough to qualify a man for true fatherhood. In the prenational patriarchal political order, which imagined itself to be a hierarchy of caring fathers from the monarch on down, only male householders counted as true fathers.[45] Until the late eighteenth and early nineteenth centuries, true fatherhood was a career that could be entered only through the narrow gate of the rites of passage reserved mainly for men of property. But those who experienced the profound transformation that ritual accomplished evinced an absolute assurance about their relationship to their children that stands in sharp contrast to the uncertainty and lack of felt connection characteristic of modern democratic fatherhood.

The world that fathers ruled would receive a seismic shock in the late eighteenth and early nineteenth centuries with the advent of the Industrial Revolution and the political revolutions that accompanied it. By the middle of the nineteenth century, the office and the factory had replaced the household as the point of production. And even when families still worked together in these new settings, the manager and the foreman usually usurped the power of the father. As time went on, the number of families working together shrank. Sharing work space and time continued longer among the working classes, but the practice disappeared almost entirely among the middle classes of Europe and North America. Among them, the only work fit for a man was outside the home; the only work proper to a woman was within it. This gendered division of labor effectively terminated the old notion of domesticated fatherhood. Now male generativity was associated almost entirely with the material world. In a secular scientific age, the notion of a pregnant man now seemed wholly impossible, but it became increasingly common to assign men credit for giving birth to everything having to do with the economy and polity. In the era of the market economy and the nation-state, men were imagined to father ideas, inventions, and nations. But their generativity was now confined to the public sphere; no longer the animators of family life, they were assigned the role of chief provider for the women and children who were now the family's imagined core.[46]

For their part, women lost their association with production and became wholly identified with reproduction. Female generativity came to be exclusively identified with the biological. In the view of Jacques-Louis Moreau, "If it is correct to state that the male is only male in certain moments, but the female is female all her life, it is principally to this [uterine] influence that this must be attributed; it is this influence that continually recalls woman to her sex and gives all her conditions such a pronounced physiognomy."[47] Women were now said to be captives of their bodies, while men were imagined to exercise mind over matter. Thus, the first phases of the capitalist industrial revolution did much more than remove fathers from the home physically; more important, it detached them symbolically, removing them to the world of the marketplace, from which they would return as strangers.

The French and American Revolutions had the parallel effect of dethroning fathers literally and symbolically. No longer could the polity be conceived of as a hierarchy of patriarchal households. New nations would henceforth conceive of themselves as fatherless families, emphasizing horizontal sibling bonds over vertical paternal ones.[48] For the next two hundred years, it would be difficult to imagine nations as anything but bands of brothers, young and male, defending their mothers and sisters against rival brotherhoods. In the French Revolution, notes Lynn Hunt, "there was never a father present in the new representations of the Republic, and mothers, except very young ones, also are largely absent. The parents had disappeared from this family, leaving the brothers to create a new world and protect their now orphaned sisters."[49] Fathers were relegated to a support role in the family romance of the new nation-state, whose gender and generational order was visible as early as 1793 in the French call for levée en mass: "Young men will go to fight, husbands will forge weapons and manage the transport services, wives and daughters will make tents and uniforms and will serve in hospitals; old men taking their stands in public places will inflame the patriotism of our soldiers."[50] Henceforth, when men were called to battle, it was as sons rather than as fathers. Even when fathers fought, they were first refashioned into "boys."[51]

The new American republic left some room for fathers, but only as Founding Fathers; from the early nineteenth century onward, fatherhood always loomed larger in the past than in the present, reflecting the perpetual sense of inadequacy that has dogged fathers since that time. It was mothers who were expected to raise future citizens. Robert Griswold has noted that the new model nation-state effectively "politicized motherhood and marginalized fatherhood."[52] In the new doctrine of "republican motherhood," the patriotism of sons was seen as dependent on maternal love.[53] Even while initially denying women active citizenship, the reimagined nation gave mothers the same exalted role as the nurturers of civic spirit. In the reinvented family of the Victorian era, males produced while females reproduced. The royal father was replaced by the sovereign fatherland, an abstraction that justified the conscription of real fathers—who were sent from home to the front in times of war and effectively removed from their paternal duties—and simultaneously assigned females to new roles of imperial and national motherhood.[54] By the end of the nineteenth century, monarchies and empires had become as symbolically matricentric as republics.

Initially, the high moral standards expected of patriotic motherhood were used to justify the exclusion of women from immoral politics. Nations understood as families, writ large justified an all-male military and the exclusion of women from suffrage. Eventually, feminists would use the image of moral womanhood to bolster the case for female voting rights, but even today women in the military are denied access to direct combat roles on the grounds that female virtue would be undermined. When Major Marie Rossi was killed during the Gulf War in 1992, her husband could find no other way to express her heroism than in the most traditional gendered terms: "I prayed that guidance be given her so that she could command the company, so that she could lead her troops into battle. . . . And I prayed to the Lord to take care of my sweet little wife."[55]

We have become so accustomed to thinking of the nation in family terms that we take this gendered language for granted, but while it was developing, the changing meaning of fatherhood and motherhood did not go unnoticed or uncontested. Not surprisingly, conservatives defended the rule of the fathers and attempted to restore the old patriarchal hierarchy. But radicals objected to the definition of fathers' rights and duties in purely public terms. In the wake of the American and French Revolutions, there were many attempts to fuse the new civic virtues expected of the male citizen with the old sense of domestic duty.[56] In England radicals like William Cobbett yearned to regenerate the household economy, with fathers taking renewed pride in every aspect of home life as well as politics. During the 1820s and 1830s, socialists and feminists experimented with alternative household and family arrangements designed to provide more equal participation in both private and public life. These attracted large numbers of middle-class women and men eager to reorganize both motherhood and fatherhood on the basis of greater freedom and equality. They experimented with housing and child care arrangements that would free women from sole responsibility for cooking, cleaning, and child-rearing, while allowing men the time and space to return to their previous prominence in domestic life. But by the 1840s, these movements, together with those of radical republicanism, which imagined public duty and private virtue to be compatible, were faltering.

From that time on, the doctrine of "separate spheres" reinforced the notion that morality belonged at home and the amoral world of marketplace and politics was no place for women and children. It had become difficult even to imagine men and women sharing the same space and time; by the midnineteenth century, men were exiting from the household, an absence that did not go unnoticed. "It seems to me, at times, as if there were no more *men* left in the world, they have all become *citizens*," complained one American wife and mother, who went on to note: "Their humanity seems merged in some presidency or secretaryship. They are good trustees, directors, cashiers, bankers, but they are very indifferent husbands and fathers."[57]

Middle-class men were indeed "indifferent" husbands measured by the old husbanding standards of the small farm or workshop, where men were very much involved in provisioning and maintaining the household. But middle-class husbands did meet the new market economy's standard of being the primary earner. As breadwinners, they continued to be biological genitors but ceased to be the kind of social paters their own fathers and grandfathers had been. The domestic advice books and child-rearing manuals that had been directed to men were now aimed exclusively at women.

The role of husband, now disconnected from domestic work, became the middle-class man's primary familial identity, subsuming that of fatherhood. Husbandhood provided a man's link to his children to the extent that it now became difficult, if not impossible, to imagine a bachelor father. But now a man's connection to his offspring was mediated through the mother, and middle-class fathers became distant figures, strangers even to their own children. Reportedly, one venerable Victorian, the Reverend Sabine Baring-Gould, the father of sixteen, failed to recognize his own daughter at a parish Christmas party: "And whose little girl are you?" he is said to have asked, to which the miserable child replied: "I am yours, Daddy."[58] To be sure, Baring-Gould's was an exceptional lapse, but there is no doubt that the close contacts fathers once had with their children were declining. By the end of the nineteenth century, working-class fathers were far more familiar with their children than most middle-class men.[59]

The rites of fatherhood that had once connected fathers to their children from conception onward continued longer among the urban and rural working classes but virtually disappeared in middle-class circles. The latter could no longer imagine a pregnant man, for science had finally located the reproductive processes firmly within the female body. In the 1840s, spontaneous ovulation was discovered in animals, opening the way for the discovery of the human ovum and the recognition of women's independent role in reproduction. Although the absolute proof of human ovulation did not come until the 1930s, science had already decided by the 1860s that the father's role in giving life ended with the contribution of his sperm. From that point on, the mother was now understood to be wholly responsible.[60]

As doctors became more involved in antenatal care, fathers became less so. As the expectant mother came to be a more fully developed role, the role of expectant father virtually disappeared. The ancient rites of couvade, which still provided working-class men with a way of symbolizing their paternity, were not an option for middle-class males, who often were not even informed of their wives' "condition" until near the time of birth.[61] Women's choice of confidant was their male doctors, who by the 1850s had largely replaced the midwife in the middle-class reproductive ritual. This was also the time when husbands gained admission to the birthing room, but only "to comfort, encourage and aid in sustaining his wife through the conflict of parturition; and to calm and compose her in the excitement or ecstasy to which she is often subject upon delivery."[62] It was made very clear that the father was there not by right but by invitation. Doctors were reluctant to admit him and had done so only at the behest of women. "The husband may be there or not, as the wife prefers," wrote one leading British obstetrician.[63]

It is very clear that middle-class males gained entry to birth as husbands, not as fathers. They were in the birthing room in their newly defined provider role, and as emotional support to the mother, but not to receive the child as their own. In the past, the newly delivered child was ceremoniously separated from the mother and passed to the father, who delivered it to its second birth. Now it was immediately brought to her and given the breast, the epiphany of the new motherhood and the moment that was supposed to have a transforming effect on men, making them into fathers. For many men it had just that result, but this brief moment was no replacement for the extended rite of passage that had previously constructed fatherhood.[64] They no longer felt as sure of their fatherhood as earlier generations had been.

Paternity had lost its publicity. It had become a private moment taking place in the bedroom, in the conjugal bed (itself a modern symbol of the bond between husband and wife), a purely sexual act disconnected from the instinct for nurture, which was attributed entirely to women. The privately circulated birth announcement replaced public celebrations, and even the baptism, which had regained favor in the second half of the nineteenth century, was a family affair in which the central figure was the mother rather than the father. New fathers did not have the support of other men before and during birth. Instead, the prospective father had to bear the jibes of his male friends, who, fearing the loss of his companionship, did everything they could to steer him away from domesticity. No wonder that many men, finding the role of expectant father lonely and unrewarding, looked forward to restoring bonds with their fellows.[65]

Fathers had conceded their place to mothers and indeed seemed to prefer it that way, for paying too much attention to children earned a man the label of "mollicot" and challenged his masculinity. The old customs of fatherhood were now reduced to passing out cigars and standing drinks, rites in which new fathers gave rather than received gifts, as if they had to earn their right to return to the world of real men. These customs emphasized their ability to provide but did little to connect them with their children.

Paternity's inability to sustain fatherhood became even more evident when birth was hospitalized in this century. Fathers were reduced to pacing the halls while mothers underwent their ultimate rite of passage. Wholly marginalized by the new medical routines, fidgeting fathers found themselves the butt of jokes, which further distanced them from their own fatherhood. The American male's experience of hospitalized birth was scarcely different from that described in Britain in the 1930s:

> Mother, both grandmothers, nurse, and even the doctor, traitor to his own sex, . . . all seem to manifest cruel delight in making the father feel what a rank outsider he is; allowing him only to peep at his small son or daughter, or to hold the tiny bundle for a moment, while they watch fearfully lest his hands slip and drop the baby. The father finds it so much easier to slip into the background entirely that the chances are he is soon completely out of the picture.[66]

Some working-class men continued to symbolize their feelings of paternity through forms of couvade, but they now found themselves competing with their mothers-in-law. One Lancashire man remembered his to claim that she "had aches and pains . . . [and that] she was 'feeling' for her daughter. I was called a great clown, it was all my fault."[67] The appearance of grandmaternal couvade is not as surprising as it may sound, for by this time mothers of all classes were very involved in their daughters' pregnancies and marriages; the newly invented bridal and baby showers, which had become a ritual bond among women, marginalized fathers still further.[68]

The more women reminded men that their sex was the cause of female suffering, the more men experienced a profound sense of helplessness, which they assuaged by striving to be the best providers they could be, a role that enhanced their husbandhood but did not necessarily close the gap between themselves and their children. The calls for a "new fatherhood" heard on both sides of the Atlantic after the 1920s enhanced the conjugal bond but fell short of altering the image of fathers as distant figures, for by this time middle-class fatherhood had become an activity for evenings, weekends, and certain calendar occasions like Christmas.

The diminished definitions of fatherhood were reflected in the law, which in the nineteenth century had begun to assign the custody of children entirely to mothers.[69] Fathers remained more involved with their older children, who were now staying home longer, but it was mothers who symbolized home and with whom children were expected to stay. Too intimate a relationship with one's children had become unmanly, likely to call into question not only a fellow's masculinity but also his maturity.[70] By the 1920s, fathers were trying to find time for family on weekends and holidays, transforming themselves into "fun dads," entering into their children's worlds, behaving very much like kids themselves.[71] In this respect, fathers behaved very differently from mothers, who rarely entered into child's play and sometimes found themselves the center of competition between men and children for their attention.[72]

Yet most of the formal family occasions that emerged in the nineteenth century emphasized male distance, as opposed to the closeness that was expected of women. Whether seated at the head of the table or in retreat in his "den," father was represented as the stranger in the house, a powerful, mysterious presence whose authority was always there to discipline unruly children and servants. Fathers were expected to be present on all family occasions, but their role was conspicuously different from that of mothers. At birthdays they were assigned the role of principal gift givers, a reinforcement of their image as providers.[73] This image was further reinforced in the middle-class rites of Christmas, which had redirected gifts from the poor to the children of the family.[74] Like the newly invented Santa Claus, fathers were imagined to be from another time and another place, arriving and departing into a world from which supposedly innocent middle-class women and children were protected.

In the iconography of Victorian genre painting, the figure in home-leaving and homecoming scenes is invariably a father or son. When a female appears at the threshold, she is always a fallen woman.[75] The message conveyed by these images, and by the daily, weekly, and annual rites of passage that had become the set pieces of middle-class life, was that the world was not simply physically distant but morally compromised. Mrs. Sarah Ellis worried that if men simply came and went, something precious to the family would be lost.[76] She need not have worried, for only three decades later the threshold ceremony had become standard in both Europe and North America, captured in the American poem "Father Is Coming":

> The clock is on the stroke of six,
> The father's work is done.
> Sweep up the hearth and tend the fire,
> And put the kettle on
>
> He's coming o'er the world apace,
> He's stronger than the storm.
> He does not feel the cold, not he,
> His heart, it is so warm.
>
> Hark! hark! I hear his footsteps now;
> He's through the garden gate.
> Run, little Bess, and ope the door,
> And do not let him wait.
> Shout, baby, shout! and clap thy hands
> For father on the threshold stands.[77]

As Eric Leed tells us, "events of arrival do not simply perform established harmonies and meanings of culture, but *create* those harmonies and meanings."[78] Fathers at the threshold, like strangers at the gate, defined the borders between home and the world. Threshold rites gave expression to male ambivalence, reflecting the tension between men's longing for home and their anxiety not to be too closely identified with that feminine domain. A young Maine man gave clear expression this ambiguity: "Two forces act upon me with equal power[:] the centripetal—which draws me towards my father and mother and friends—the centrifugal which acts as a repellant and drives me to seek wealth and distinction in foreign lands."[79]

Homecoming rites ensured the mental home-centeredness of the middle-class male but at the same time maintained the symbolic distance required to be a real man of the world. The new market economy and nation-state compelled men to detach themselves from the home and its values. Home-leaving and homecoming rites were an explicit recognition of that necessity. They elaborated the image John Demos has called the "father as intruder," which lingers into the present day.[80]

In the nineteenth century, working-class males were less likely to be given the ritual threshold treatment. The working-class family was still much more dependent on the earnings of all its members, and all were involved with the world to some degree. The desire for a "family wage" sufficient for a man to support his wife and children was articulated in the midnineteenth century, but it had been realized by only a minority of workers by 1900 and would remain elusive for many until after the Second World War.[81] Judged exclusively in terms of the breadwinning standard, most working-class men were failures as fathers, but by more traditional measures they remained good fathers to the limits of their economic capacities.

The superior ability of middle-class men to be good providers made their fatherhood seem less problematic in some ways, but it also cut them off from the psychological satisfactions of the old father role. Elite males sought compensation for this loss through their status as factory owners, as founders of new nations and parties, as father figures to colonized peoples in Africa and Asia. These men, single as well as married, and of all ages, were thus able to maintain a strong sense of paternity, even as their careers distanced them from their own children.[82] But even during the heroic era of industrial capitalism, nation-building, and imperialism in the nineteenth century, a certain yearning for lost fatherhood was evident.

During this same period, middle-class men were attracted to various fraternal organizations and military and paramilitary organizations that enabled them to act out their generative fantasies through elaborate rituals that constituted all-male versions of birth.[83] In effect, these Victorian fraternal orders and military organizations were symbolically, if not actually, men's families, separate from and complementary to the women-centered families of the era. Until early in this century, it was perfectly acceptable for men to have their own version of domesticity, to dine, lodge, and vacation together. Today these men's families are only a memory, nostalgically recalled by some, like Robert Bly, but no longer compatible with the twentieth-century ideals of companionate marriage and family togetherness.[84] In fact, the lodges and fraternal orders were already in decline by the 1920s, and male companionship was fast becoming reduced to the "boys' night out." Working-class men held on longer to their versions of men's families, the trade union and the pub or tavern, but after the Second World War they too abandoned these homes away from home, becoming as family- and home-centered as the middle-class male.[85]

The ideal of companionate marriage that became dominant after the 1920s has made for better husbands but only complicated the attainment of ideal fatherhood. Good mothering continues to be seen as a skill that comes so naturally to women that they need not be given credit for all the hard work that goes into it. In contrast, when men parent well, special notice is taken of their accomplishments.[86] When they parent badly, the law is ready to punish them, but even the worst father is in little danger of forfeiting his manhood, which is at risk only if he fails to establish relationships with women. The gateway to manhood is still, for most men, their demonstrated heterosexuality.[87] As old sources of masculinity, such as physical strength, have fallen away, this has come to mean more to men than ever.

In contemporary Western culture, men can do without children but not without women. Brought up almost entirely by women and heavily dependent on them, men tend to turn all women into mothers. Women also begin life in a female world, but unlike sons, daughters are taught to reproduce and nurture.[88] Women can do without men in Western culture, but not without children. A childless woman feels herself to be incomplete in a way that a childless man does not. A study that found that English men experience infertility as a blow not to their manhood but to their husbandhood concludes: "Since it was important for the woman to *be* a mother, it was vital for the husband to *become* a father."[89] Having a child secures a man's bond to the mother figure he was forced to separate from, but it also restores his "lost" childhood, placing him in a position of rivalry with his own children.[90] Thus, modern Western fatherhood has the paradoxical effect of bonding men to women while distancing them from their children.

Since the 1920s, it has been argued that men need to be more involved in rearing their children, especially their sons, who, it is said, have become "sissies" owing to a lack of fatherly involvement. The fear of effeminization has been a moving force behind the new fatherhood movement of the twentieth century, but it has also underlined perceived gender differences, which have been the cause of father absence in the first place.[91] All the talk of being "real men" has added to their detachment from the feminized domestic sphere. Despite their best intentions to reconnect with their children, men's relations with their children have become even more dependent on the quality of their relationship with their wives. As motherhood has become more of a lifetime career, fatherhood seems more than ever like a part-time occupation. From the beginning of this century, Americans were aware that "the suburban husband and father is almost a Sunday institution."[92]

Fathers find themselves vying for mothers' attention, rivals to their own children, and the twentieth century has witnessed a noticeable infantilization of male behavior as boyishness has become increasingly acceptable among adult men.[93] As the trend toward companionate marriage and family togetherness has intensified, the contradictions between good husbandhood and good fatherhood have became more evident. And as each successive "new fatherhood" movement of this century has failed to overcome these contradictions, increased concern and ever more desperate measures have followed.[94]

Today, even as marriage rates falter, the modern cult of motherhood holds remarkably firm, reflected throughout the West in the high and growing rates of single motherhood, not just among poor but among better-off women, and among heterosexual as well as lesbian. In the United States today, 25 percent of all births are out of wedlock, with only one-half of these fathers legally known. Illegitimacy rates in all Western countries are higher than they have been since the eighteenth century.[95] But nowhere do we see any voluntary move toward single fatherhood. Only one-half of all American children now live with their biological fathers. If unwed motherhood is still regarded by some as a tragedy, single fatherhood continues to be considered a joke, source material for film and television comedies.[96] Single fatherhood is not something society feels it must take seriously, for the male who wants children too much is not a real man.

Increasingly frustrated by the incidence of deadbeat dads and absent fathers, an alliance of moralists and social scientists has now emerged, constituting itself as the arbiter of "family values." They call for ever more punitive measures against delinquent fathers, who, they hold, together with single mothers, are responsible for what they perceive as the decline of the Western family.[97] What this powerful movement ignores is the fact that in the restructured global economy of the late twentieth century, the breadwinner role, never completely accessible to all fathers, has become difficult even for middle-class men. Since the 1970s, families expecting to maintain a middle-class standard of living have come to rely on two and sometimes more earners. To be sure, women's entry into high-paying careers has been the excuse for many men to divest themselves of the breadwinner role.[98] Yet there is no evidence of men wishing to escape the family as such. In fact, every indicator points toward the conclusion that marriage has never been held in such high esteem and never have men been so desirous of family life.[99]

This development is not at all surprising, because in most of those areas in which men previously created a sense of generativity all their own— men's colleges, fraternal organizations, the military—are no longer exclusively male domains. The roles in the economy and the polity that previously satisfied men's desires for social fatherhood are also no longer a male monopoly.[100] In an increasingly rationalized and bureaucratized world, the home is the only available sphere where fatherhood can be exercised, but men face tough competition there, their creativity usually confined to the garage or the cellar in an otherwise feminized household.[101]

This situation contributes to what the sociologist Frank Furstenberg calls the "good dads–bad dads complex."[102] More men want to be good fathers, but standards of good fatherhood, defined as something more than breadwinning, have had to keep pace with the standards of good mothering, which have risen spectacularly in the same period.[103] Trying to meet a single standard for parenthood is admirable, but men are far less prepared than women to achieve it. Girls are socialized for parenting in ways that boys are not. Their passage to motherhood begins even before pregnancy, whereas males experience fatherhood mainly at the moment of birth. Efforts to involve men at earlier stages appear to have been only partially successful, producing among them an even greater sense of inferiority and frustration.[104] Since the 1970s, fathers' attendance at birth has become almost obligatory, yet, because they have been there mainly to assist, they still feel marginal at best and sometimes wholly useless, with the result that the bonding between father and child is often only temporary.[105]

Fathers tend to retreat soon after birth into the old definitions of fatherhood—showering mother and child with attention and material support but, in order to do so, working longer hours and being even less available than before. The unwillingness of men to take advantage of even the most generous paternal leave policies in Denmark and Sweden must be attributed to the persistence of the old definition of fatherhood, which judges men largely in terms of how well they can provide. The fact that they can better fulfill their breadwinner responsibilities by returning to work as soon as possible means that fatherhood remains brief and episodic in most Western countries.[106]

Despite their best intentions, modern fathers still do not measure up to Luther's vision of diaper-washing dads of almost a half-millennium ago. Recent studies show that little has changed in the domestic division of labor since the 1960s, and that most of the menial tasks of child-rearing still fall to women.[107] The so-called new fathers of the 1980s and 1990s have a better image, but it is not at all clear whether their pattern of behavior has really changed. Furstenberg's view that "it is possible that fathers in the recent past did more than they got credit for and today less than we think" finds plenty of support in these studies.[108] But it would be wrong to think of this behavior as bad faith, especially when men struggle to achieve society's definition of good fatherhood, however limited that may be. When men fail to live up to the good breadwinner standard, they do not give up on fatherhood but rather try again with a new wife and a new set of children. In an era of readily available divorce, this option has led to what might be called serial fatherhood.[109]

Men want children, but not necessarily their own children. For them, marriage and fatherhood are a package.[110] Women are able to separate marriage and motherhood, often at great risk to themselves; however, while they are now allowed to be single mothers and serial wives, no option of serial motherhood is open to them. As the current legal controversies suggest, women who give up their children (even to day care) are at risk of losing their womanhood. Men who give up their children may be condemned as bad dads, but given our current notions of gender and generation, their manhood is never in danger.

Despite all this century's talk of a new fatherhood, Western culture finds itself unable to imagine a fatherhood that can give as well as provide for life. The current promoters of family values are fond of saying that our problems are "at heart cultural, not political or economic," but their solutions do not cut to the heart of the matter, which lies in the modern culture of reproduction itself.[111] Change is not just a matter of "parent training" but of altering the worldviews deeply embedded in the capitalist economy, the nation-state, and the scientific view of the body, which assigns the sexual instinct to men and the nurturing instinct to women. Those who wish to revitalize fatherhood would place the whole burden of transformation on individual men, but the changes required amount to a revolution in our social and political systems, a development they are reluctant to contemplate.

Yet there are changes afoot that may force just such a radical reconsideration. Changed by the evolving global capitalist economy, the postnational state, and reproductive technology, the family no longer stands as a refuge from the heartless world but is itself increasingly subject to market and technological forces.[112] Reproduction itself has become commercialized as men sell their sperm, and women their wombs. Even the once-sacrosanct notion of motherhood is under pressure as the new reproductive technologies transform the fetus into an "unborn patient"; a wholly new being, the "unborn child" is now a little person invested with a biological and legal identity separate from the mother's.[113]

In today's scientific understanding of reproduction, the egg has gained a kind of parity with the sperm, giving a woman equal rights with the man in the child. But as Barbara Katz Rothman has been at pains to point out, this new understanding threatens to separate maternity from motherhood just as paternity was long ago symbolically separated from fatherhood. When the term "to mother" becomes, like the term "to father," a function of the biologicial or genetic contribution alone, women become "father equivalents," with the same sense of strangeness and distance as that experienced by men.[114]

Technology has had the unintended effect of making the male and female experiences of birth more alike, reducing both to the status of spectators. The effect of the medicalization of reproduction has been to reinforce the image of the doctor as a "ritual elder" giving birth to a child independently of both mother and father. The potential for medical and legal authorities to step in to take the place of both mother and father is enormous. In many places, laws concerning fetal and child abuses have already established the state as the ultimate parent. In effect, mothering and fathering have been transformed into what Rothman rightly calls "background factors." There is the very real possibility that both sperm and egg will come to be seen as having a greater value to society than the people who produce them.[115] In the name of the perfect child, there are those who would have us focus all our attention on nature to the total neglect of nurture. The fantasy of perfecting reproduction, the dream of the eugenics movement at the beginning of this century, appears to be returning under the guise of saving children from parents who it is claimed cannot care for them before or after birth. We can now imagine perfecting children in the test tube, the incubator, and the orphanage, but we still cannot imagine perfecting society to the extent that all parents will have the resources to bring up their own offspring.

Not everyone has given up on the idea that both men and women can participate fully in the rearing of their offspring. The new birth movements that sprang up in the 1960s have tried to reconnect paternity with fatherhood in a way that will not have the effect of disconnecting maternity from motherhood.[116] In the face of myths of gender and generation that would place fatherhood and motherhood in opposition, they have attempted to reconstruct rites of fatherhood that will give symbolic recognition to the expectant father and make him a part of the birthing process, an effort that goes hand in hand with the project of reconstructing the rites of motherhood so as to give fuller expression to the many different roles women play in contemporary society. Clearly, this is no easy task, but it is equally evident that the reimagining of fatherhood cannot take place in the absence of a reconsideration of motherhood.

CHAPTER 10

Haunting the Dead

Maintaining the dead as members of society maintains the continuing life of the living. The living's assurance of life everlasting is dependent on keeping the dead live.

W. Lloyd Warner, *The Family of God*[1]

C ULTS OF THE DEAD are supposed to belong to other times and other places, yet we are a culture that denies death and does everything symbolically possible to keep our dead live. This is a departure from earlier European and North American practices, which kept the dead at a distance, confining their encounters with the living to certain times and places. Today we haunt our absent family members with an energy and determination that our ancestors would have found unbecoming, even sacrilegious. The dead have become part of our extended imagined family and are often felt to be as close, even closer, than its living members.

Virtually all known societies have made use of death to serve life. The living need the dead at least as much as the dead need the living. Today the dead are everywhere, occupying expensive real estate, taking up the time as well as the space of the living. "We live in a society in which entrepreneurs market space on an orbiting mausoleum," notes Michael Kearl.[2] Monuments and cemeteries constitute a significant part of the modern landscape. They are, as Lloyd Warner pointed out many years ago, a "substantial and visible symbol of this agreement among men that they will not let each other die."[3] But we also provide space for the dead closer to home, turning our residences into mini-mausoleums, featuring the photos and mementos of the deceased, refusing to let them depart. Few have gone as far as the Boston man who managed to keep the body of his wife hidden in his apartment for nine years, but with the growing popularity of cremation, it is not unknown for ashes to remain in the house for months, even years.[4]

Throughout the Western world, people report contact with the dead, usually with deceased family members. In the United States, 40 percent of adults report such experiences, and in Europe the findings are similar.[5] These are not the hauntings that turn profits for the horror film industry, but the sensed presence of deceased loved ones, what Gillian Bennett has called the "good dead," whom we find confirming and comforting. The presence is usually felt in a domestic setting, the chosen place of efforts to contact the dead, a practice that is far more common than is generally acknowledged. Neither the visits nor the séances are survivals of some premodern system of belief, however. Both are wholly modern phenomena, dating back only to the Victorian era and coinciding with the emergence of other modern forms of imagined families. "Belief in the supernatural allows the continuation of relationships of mutual love—parent and child, husband and wife—even when one of the partners is separated by distance or death," Bennett notes.[6] In one American study of widows, almost one-fifth had fantasies of being reunited with their dead spouses, actually experiencing the presence of the deceased. As Michael Kearl has suggested, the immense popularity of mediums and ghost photography indicates the degree to which the dead continue to serve as significant others for the living.[7]

What sets us apart from other cultures, and, indeed, from our own history, is what we use the dead to symbolize. The cemetery, once a place where the community gathered, is now used, except on Memorial Day, mainly for family reunions. Once the most public and communal of places, it has become, next to the home, society's most private domain. The modern "city of the dead," as Warner called it, is laid out in a manner quite different from the country graveyards of earlier centuries. In the old village of the dead, the deceased intermingled in death as they did in life. Few family plots existed, and most people were buried without respect to origins.

The modern cemetery, which had its beginnings in the early nineteenth century, reflects a very different sociability. Laid out with streets and sections reflecting the residential segregation of the modern city and suburb, it reproduces not only the class and ethnic divisions of modern society but the boundedness of private life. From the Victorian period onward, family tombs, plots, and graves came to reflect not only the increasing importance of the nuclear family but the emerging gender and generational relationships characteristic of the Protestant middle classes on both sides of the Atlantic. Warner found that in the 1950s the city of the dead operated on the same middle-class assumptions as the bourgeois city of the living. The layout of the plots, together with the inscriptions, reflected the superior respect given to adult males, the devotion expected of women, and the dependence and innocence of children. Disinterments were not uncommon; sometimes done for religious reasons, they more often symbolized changes in families' understanding of themselves. Just as people changed houses to reflect improved status, they moved their dead, providing them with new, often larger tombs, for the same reasons. No one thought this odd or ostentatious. Instead, the practice elicited praise: "He's a-doing this for his pa and ma. Just what any decent American would do."[8]

There was nothing new in honoring one's ancestors, but what Warner described was more complicated. The cemetery had come to occupy an unprecedented position in the family life of modern Europeans and Americans, not just through the funerals and visits that occurred there but, more importantly, as a space for the symbolic construction of family itself. In a highly mobile, fast-paced world, the dead were in many ways better suited than the living to serve this purpose. There, "at home" in its plot, the family of the dead was immune to the depredations of time and space that had made it so difficult for the living family to represent itself to itself in an appropriate manner. As Warner noted, the cemetery was a "firm and fixed social place" that provided certainty in an otherwise uncertain world.[9] But even safer was the domesticated heaven above, which was also being invented in the nineteenth century and to this day provides most Europeans and Americans with imagined families to live by.

Birth and death are existential moments that all cultures use to represent themselves to themselves. In medieval and early modern Europe, the moment of dying was the pivot on which individual and family lives turned. It was the one occasion that required a family gathering. Birth had no similar power of attraction; it was the deathbed that called family members together, for the end rather than the beginning of life held the greater significance at that time. All the years of one's life were considered equidistant from eternity, and everyone, the young as well as the old, felt close to death and attracted to the dying. The deathbed was portentous, a source of signs and omens. Last words were attended to not only for their practical significance for the survivors but for their symbolic meanings. It was on the deathbed that patriarchs gave their last instructions, inheritances were settled, and the fate of the next generation determined.[10] But even when there was no property to distribute or authority to exercise, there was a symbolic legacy to be considered. A good death was considered a sign of grace, a sign that the deceased was surely with his or her God in heaven.

Until the midnineteenth century, Protestant dying was the occasion of the ultimate "holy conversation" among family members, the daily version of which was still the centerpiece of Protestant family life. Protestants had long since dispensed with the last rites of the Catholic church; no other rituals, images, or litanies were allowed to interpose themselves between the dying and the Almighty. The Protestant middle classes were well practiced at what they called "daily dying," exercises often recorded in their diaries. William Gladstone called his "an account book of the all precious gift of Time," for he, like his contemporaries, believed that life could be terminated by God at any moment.[11] By perpetually preparing to meet their maker and participating in so many deathbed scenes, even the very young were ready to give a polished performance.

Prior to the nineteenth century, death happened not just to the old but to all ages, and children were introduced to death early on. It was the practice to christen orphaned infants over their dead mother's coffin.[12] Birth may have been a dark secret that divided age groups and families, but death was familiar to everyone, a topic of holy conversation. Louisa Hawes began to discuss death with her daughter Mary when she was eight in order to turn her "more to the sober realities of life." From that point on, Mary's birthdays were a time not of recall but for looking forward to the "sweet deliverance from life."[13] Children played at death, building toy coffins, rehearsing dying words, and making contributions to their own burial clubs; after all, they were responsible for their own dying.[14] In earlier centuries, the church had obligated children to attend funerals, but even in the absence of this requirement later on, they were drawn to the deathbed and the wake, where it was still the custom for everyone to touch or kiss the corpse.[15] Children's dying words were listened to as attentively as those of adults, and they were given the same burial.[16]

Symbols of death entered into life just when we would least expect it—at birth and again at marriage. Events that would direct our attention to origins focused the minds of earlier generations on destinations. A burial shroud had long been a part of a bride's trousseau, and the groom also brought his winding sheets into marriage. Mary Hughes's wedding pin, a reminder of her two dead siblings, was not thought of as morbid but as a proper reminder of mature women's special responsibility toward death, for after all, it was they who "laid out" the dead, washing and dressing them for burial.[17] Women were symbolically identified with the body and men with the soul. In Protestant culture, bodies were understood to be the prison of the soul and were to be disposed of as quickly as possible so as to facilitate its liberation.

Rural funerals of the seventeenth and eighteenth centuries were communal rather than family affairs. In Wales it was common well into the nineteenth century to hire a "bidder" who went around announcing the time and place of the funeral and requesting that each household send a representative. As with bidden weddings, donations of food and money were customary, allowing even the poorest to avoid the shame of being buried in a pauper's grave. The amounts given were remembered and reciprocated, so that a certain equality was guaranteed over several generations.[18] The wake, like the wedding, was given to the deceased by the community. Sitting with the corpse was a festive occasion, with "all the neighbours and Friends of ye Deceased" eating, drinking, smoking, praying, and playing "little comical mountebank tricks" on themselves and the corpse to keep themselves awake.[19] Even immediately after death, the dead person was still regarded as a presence. The corpse, regarded as existing in a condition somewhere between life and death, had to be attended to, "watched" or "waked," until final disposal.[20] At no other point would the body contain and convey such a powerful range of messages or evoke such powerful emotions. Familiar with the dying and with death, those who attended the corpse showed no fear or disgust. The avoidance behavior so typical in our times was absent in theirs.

The next day there would be a "walking funeral," involving a large public procession to the church or graveyard; the coffin was carried from the house by the family and "given up to the community, to which it now belonged." After a short service, the members of the community would return to the house for a meal. Only the gentry had private funerals in which hearses transported the coffins to the graveyard. Among ordinary people, "to have a private funeral, with paid bearers who may also be strangers, is to shock and outrage the social instincts and sensibilities of the community."[21]

As with weddings, funerals gave the community a chance to represent itself to itself, to redefine itself in the absence of one of its members. Funerals were therefore important moments of symbolic negotiation between friends and neighbors as well as family. It was a time of rendering judgment: a small turnout indicated low esteem. "What a poor funeral he had; he was not the man he was supposed to be," it was said in one case.[22] But it was also a time for the friends and family of the deceased to redefine their communal relations. The scale of the postburial repast at the house could raise or lower status. Positive esteem could be influenced by providing a large feast after the services, a tradition that lasted in some places into the twentieth century.[23] Edwin Grey remembers one old woman remarking: "It was a very poor set out, there was only biscuits and such; why, I've buried three 'usbands and I buried 'em all with 'am [ham]."[24]

In the seventeenth and eighteenth centuries, Protestants were taught not to overvalue earthly relationships or to confuse them with the divine original. "Family celebrations could contribute to the building of a little kingdom of heaven on earth," wrote one Essex Quaker in 1846, emphasizing that festivities were not an end in themselves but a means for "the looking forward to the building of heaven above."[25] Death was not a mirror held up to this world, but a window through which the next could be glimpsed. The Reformation had banished the sacraments of dying and dismissed the notion of purgatory in the belief that there was nothing the living could do for the dead. Puritans on both sides of the Atlantic discouraged wakes and urged that burials be swift and simple, "without any Ceremony." They were convinced that postmortem rituals "are in no way beneficiall to the dead . . . and have proved many wayes hurtful to the living."[26] They eliminated candles and prayers for the dead from the burial service, paring it down to a sermon after which the body was disposed of as quickly as possible in a grave that was unpretentious and untended.[27] Outward signs of mourning were also regarded as a pagan or papist survival. Until the midnineteenth century, there were no special clothes, no annual visits to the graveyard, no mementos of the deceased. As the Reverend Ralph Josselin reminded his congregation in a 1651 funeral sermon: "God would have us forget the dead. . . . This forgetfulness is not of the graces and vertues of the dead . . . but is of their persons."[28] What was to be remembered was not the individual but the values he or she represented. Biographies and eulogies also dwelled not on the person but on the kind of person.

In the seventeenth century, Protestant iconoclasm had been carried to the point that it seemed to some that "nothing will be shortly left to continue the memory of the deceased to posteritie."[29] In the eighteenth century, antiritualism had eased somewhat, and Protestants on both sides of the Atlantic began to mark their graves again. Yet the ambivalence about memorialization remained; in the early nineteenth century, dissenters and evangelicals still thought that the memory of the deceased should be "per-

petuated rather in the loving hearts" and lived out in the lives of the survivors rather than preserved in monuments.[30]

Protestantism rejected the old communal rites of death, but it did not
prohibit collective forms of bereavement. In the seventeenth-century Puritan community, and later among dissenting sects, no family mourned alone.
Christians were warned that it was dangerous to grieve too much for other
nuclear family members; doing so was a rebellion against God's decision to
call them to his heavenly home.[31] During the era of waves of evangelical
revival, the practice of good dying flexed outward to embrace a larger community. Congregations, friendly societies, fraternal organizations, and
utopian communities were all deeply involved with the final moments of
their members. Their last words were recorded, and good deaths were
widely publicized.[32]

In the early nineteenth century, stories of dying were retold often in
both private and public. Obituaries skipped over a person's early years to
concentrate on his or her last days. Biographers treated their subjects the
same way, assigning much greater significance to the later than the early
years, to endings rather than origins. The corpse was of little interest to
Protestants; they made no effort to preserve hair or other mementos.
Instead, the body was disposed of as quickly and simply as possible. There
were no tombs or subsequent memorial services, for it was understood that
the deceased was with God.[33]

Yet the image of the person whom families wished to remember was
much more likely to be captured at death than at any other time of life.
Death masks and portraits painted immediately after death were common
in middle-class houses in the late eighteenth and early nineteenth centuries. When, in the 1840s, the newly invented daguerreotype made it possible to capture a likeness soon after death, memorial photography continued the painterly tradition, allowing families to remember the moment of
death itself; some posed themselves with the corpse as close to the moment
of death as possible. Southworth and Hawes advertised in 1846: "We make
miniatures of children and adults instantly and of Deceased Persons either
at our rooms or at private residences."[34]

In the archives of postmortem photography we see wives posing with
dead husbands (husbands with dead wives are rarer), and parents with dead
children. The images were sometimes used by artists commissioned to do
family portraits, but more often families had black-bordered cards made up
to send to relations and friends. Postmortem photographs were very much
a part of the earliest forms of the family album, for the immediate postmortem moment was still thought of as the best representation of a person.
They are not very pretty pictures, however; in many cases rigor mortis won

the race with the photographer. Bodies look rigid and faces contorted, but no one made any attempt until the second half of the nineteenth century to cosmetize or beautify the dead, to make them look lifelike. In a culture that highly valued the good death, the living still felt quite comfortable with the recently deceased, and even its uglier aspects were no cause for revulsion.

Good dying occupied an unprecedented place in the public and private life of the early nineteenth century. The old fear of death had fallen away to the point that dread seemed almost to have been replaced by longing. In the eighteenth century, hell had ceased to be a vivid reality, and everyone could imagine a place for themselves in heaven. The epitome of the good death was no longer a violent struggle—the medieval notion of wrestling with death—but a peaceful passing. As death was reimagined as a beautiful lover, marriage became its metaphor. Just as the shroud was disappearing from the trousseau, the wedding gown became the preferred burial dress.[35]

The images of what Philippe Ariès has called the "beautiful death" were not necessarily more faithful to the realities of dying, but they were part of the naturalization of the life processes during this period, rendering them more attractive to the spectator if not to the birthing or dying person. Among educated people, dying was now imagined as a peaceful process, not unlike going to sleep, "an easy transition to a happier state, a natural metamorphosis to be accepted, even welcomed."[36] The intense grief the Puritans had distrusted was now a valued emotion, a means of redemption for the survivors. Rituals could no longer do anything for the dying, but they were a godsend to the living. "I love to think that our separations, griefs, and our improvement under them, will make us love each other intensely when we love again," proclaims the father in one of the best-selling American consolation novels of the 1850s.[37]

A good death was still regarded as an indication of a good life, but by the middle of the century a significant shift in emphasis had occurred. The roles of the dying and the living were reversed as death became more naturalized and aestheticized and attention shifted to the survivors. The death of the self became less important than the death of the other, the other now defined narrowly as a member of the nuclear family. As Ariès has described the change:

> Affectivity, formerly diffuse, was henceforth concentrated on a few rare beings whose disappearance could no longer be tolerated and caused a dramatic crisis: the death of the other. It was a revolution in feeling that was just as important to history as the related revolutions in ideas, politics, industry, socioeconomic conditions or demography.[38]

Dying had ceased to be a public event, but the last moments of the dying were still carefully recorded, talked about, and even publicized in local newspapers and pious magazines. William Gladstone found accounts of his sister Anne's dying quite enthralling.[39] Death was a frequent subject of family conversation, as familiar to children as to adults. While dying continued to offer an occasion for family gatherings, it was now the family itself at the center of attention. When Lucy Warren was dying in the 1830s, she played the role of the dutiful daughter, more concerned with her parents' grief than her own death. According to her mother, she "wished to avoid giving trouble" and never mentioned death throughout her ordeal.[40] The best death was one that evoked the most family feeling; this seventeen-year-old managed to keep the family's attention on their loss rather than on her own dying. In turn, the Warrens struggled to demonstrate their perfect love, not only for Lucy but for one another, believing, as their contemporaries did, that "the chain of family love on earth becomes much more strong and enduring, when some of its precious links are in heaven."[41]

Narrowed to the circle of the nuclear family, the survivors' grief began to take precedence over the dying person's anguish. "The modern attitude toward death is an extension of the affectivity of the nineteenth century," writes Ariès.

> The last inspiration of this inventive affectivity was to protect the dying or the invalid from his own emotions by concealing the seriousness of his condition until the end. When the dying man discovered the pious game, he lent himself to it so as not to disappoint the others' solicitude. The dying man's relations with those around him were now determined by a respect for this loving lie.[42]

As Lucy Warren's death demonstrates, it was possible for the dying and the family to create a collective representation of family togetherness at the very moment of family separation.

In the early nineteenth century, families confined their grief to the moment of death itself. Dying could be a protracted period, but once declared dead, the body was disposed of and the memory of the person kept only in the hearts and minds of the survivors. There was no extended period of bereavement, no "inability to surrender the past—expressed, for instance, by brooding over memories, sensing the presence of the dead, clinging to possession," as Peter Marris put it.[43] But after the 1850s, the dying moment turned ugly and the deathbed lost its attractions. Mourning, previously synonymous with grief itself and limited to the duration of the feelings of loss, now took on a life of its own, going well beyond the moment of deepest grief to become a ritual extending over months, even years.

In part, the disenchantment with the dying was due to the increasing medicalization of aging and death in the second half of the century. Most dying was still done at home, for only the destitute died in hospital; those who could afford it died in their own beds, though their dying moments were now likely to be supervised by doctors who found the presence of the family a nuisance. Once naturalized, aging and dying were readily reinterpreted as diseases. What had previously been seen as the will of God, and therefore holy, was transformed into something profane, even repugnant.[44] In the late nineteenth century, our modern taboos about dying, amounting to a denial of death, began to accumulate. The way was also prepared for the eventual hospitalization of dying in this century, when death has been placed entirely under the control of medical science. Middle-class Victorians gave priority to health over immortality, the result of which was the distancing of the living from the dying.[45] They avoided the deathbed and abandoned the traditions of watching and waking the corpse. The working classes kept these customs well into the twentieth century, when they too came under the spell of scientific thanatology.

Medicalization gave life a sharper definition and new intensity, but in marking its end so definitively, science created a sense of separation and loss that was all the more overwhelming. Knowing the dead could not return to haunt the living, the Victorian middle classes began to haunt the dead, visiting them in cemeteries and communicating with them through spiritualist mediums. Caught between the contradictory impulses to avoid the dying and to keep the dead alive, the Victorians shifted the emphasis from the good death to the proper funeral, the right cemetery, and the appropriate signs of mourning.

As dying has become a medical matter, Europeans and Americans have become less and less acquainted with dying. This lack of exposure began with the exclusion of children from the deathbed. The very young were gradually exempted from viewing, touching, or kissing the corpse; while they continued to attend funerals, they were the only age group released from deep mourning, allowed to wear white rather than black. By the 1880s, children were relieved of even this obligation, and in the twentieth century the very young have ceased to attend funerals altogether.[46] While working-class children remained close to death well into the twentieth century, the middle classes could no longer tolerate such proximity. For them, the child had become the favorite symbol of life, and by 1900 the death of a child had come to be grieved more intensely than the death of any adult.[47] Photographs of dead children were the first to be beautified, eliminating all memory of painful or violent dying.[48] In time other Victorian emblems of life, the pregnant woman and the new mother, would also be excused from close association with death, thus creating the illusion of distance between life's beginning and its ending, another part of the life course revision already in progress.[49] People no longer prepared themselves to die. The young and old were no longer regarded as equidistant from death, and by 1900 dying was associated almost exclusively with old age, even though mortality at all age groups remained relatively high. As long as dying was something you prepared for daily, it was sudden death that was feared most. But when people put death out of sight and mind, "natural death"—quick, easy, requiring no preparation—became the preferred form of dying.[50]

In our century, death has become the great unknown. Many adults have never seen anyone die. Just as birth previously took place out of sight and mind, now death comes quietly and secretly behind closed doors. In the 1850s and 1860s, middle-class women still laid out the dead, but soon thereafter they were beginning to give this task up to the professional undertaker. The corpse had come to be seen as polluting, and the bourgeoisie now preferred representations of the dead person to the real thing. Embalming and cosmetizing the corpse served this end, and by 1900 undertakers had perfected the art of making the corpse seem more "life-like."[51]

Until the First World War, it was still the practice to display the dead in the parlor, the one room where life and death were allowed to coexist. Sometimes the deceased's bedroom was kept just as it had been at the hour of death. Queen Victoria made a daily ritual of laying out Prince Albert's clothes and shaving water, but there was not enough space for this variation on the cult of the dead in most middle-class households, which settled for less elaborate forms of commemoration organized around pieces of clothing, locks of hair, and photos.[52] Shepard Mount had his dead granddaughter, Camille, painted in 1868. She is imagined as an angel, enveloped by a white cloud, with a watch stopped at the hour of her death visible in the foreground. "I have framed it and hung it up for all to see and love—for next to the dead babe herself—it is now the idol of the family. Alas! how everything fades from us."[53]

Every parlor became a gallery and a museum, but the memorial photography displayed there now portrayed the deceased as the family had known them in life rather than at their dying moment. "In every home there is an enshrined memory, a sacred relic, a ring, a lock of shining hair, a broken plaything, a book, a picture, something sacredly kept and guarded, which speaks of death, which tells as plainly as words, of someone long since gone."[54] Victorian children were invariably struck by the parlor's haunting atmosphere, its eerie silence and dark secrets. It was the last refuge of the unspeakable, the one place in the house where it was possible to converse not only about the dead but with them, for it also became the favored location for spiritualist séances, a movement that had begun in the 1840s in North America and spread rapidly in middle-class circles on both sides of the Atlantic.[55]

The parlor was to remain a liminal place in middle-class homes until the editor of the *Ladies' Home Journal* declared in 1910 that in modern houses there was space only for "living rooms." The best room continued to perform its old functions in many working-class homes until well into the present century, but the commercial funeral parlor, first established around 1885 to cater to transients, began to have a role in middle-class life by 1900. By the 1930s the middle classes were making full use of its "slumber rooms."[56] By that time funeral directors had not only removed the dead from the house but were thinking of eliminating the viewing entirely. A British etiquette book of the period recommended that the dead be "protected from unnecessary display," and that if anyone asked to view the body, "a refusal can always be mollified by remarking that the deceased would prefer to be remembered as he [or she] was in life."[57] Memory was no longer focused on the hour of a person's death but on the early years of his or her life. By the 1930s postmortem photography was regarded as perverse, and albums were purged of all reference to death.[58] People now wished to be remembered only as they had lived, not as they died.

Long before dying was removed to the hospital and the dead to the funeral home, the good death had been displaced by the proper funeral. As we have already seen, the early nineteenth–century middle classes made little of the funeral, preferring to concentrate their grief at the very moment of death and rejecting all ritual. "The truth is," counseled the American Reverend Orville Dewey in 1825, "these trappings of grief seem to me indifferent and childish where there *is* real grief; and where there is not, they are a mockery." British evangelicals also upheld the case against elaborate funeral rites until the 1850s: "We do not hesitate to denounce the present accumulation of ceremony and outlay at funerals as not only ridiculous but sinful."[59] Their protests suggest, however, that the "trappings" were already beginning to take hold. By midcentury the living had upstaged the dying in concentrating all attention on their loss. What we now regard as the "traditional" funeral was a Victorian invention. The fancy casket replaced the old wooden coffin, and a hearse rather than a wagon carried the body from the house to the church and then to the place of burial, where a specially prepared vault awaited. Family and community pallbearers were replaced by black-garbed professionals, who provided assurance of a flawless funeral, allowing the family to concentrate on their roles, to present themselves in perfect family formation to the watching world.[60]

The commercialized funeral came in several different forms, with appropriately varied prices. It quickly established itself as the "rite of passage *par excellence* by which to assert financial and social position—a secular last judgment which had as its goal the exhibition of worldly respectability."[61] The place of burial, previously a matter of indifference, had also gained heightened importance. The old churchyard, with its jumble of unmarked and untended graves, would no longer suffice. While the poor continued to be buried there, the middle classes now preferred the "cemetery," which had become separated from the church and was often located outside of town, where more space was available. The first of these was Mount Auburn, built in Cambridge, outside of Boston, in 1831. Soon there were hundreds of new cemeteries on both sides of the Atlantic, under secular as well as religious management, where middle-class families could purchase a plot suitable to their social standing. The new cemeteries coincided with the rise of middle-class home ownership and represented perfectly the emerging Victorian social order, which excluded the poor and allowed the middle classes to represent themselves to themselves as they wanted and could afford. A 1914 ad in the *London Times* read: "A family vault for sale (under cost) in the best part of Highgate Cemetery."[62]

Once the right place was secured, many people erected tombs—sometimes designed to look like their own residence on a smaller scale—which they referred to as "perpetual homes"; here it was imagined that the dead could be at "home . . . with their friends, and . . . blest by the communion with them."[63] The family vault was indeed the ultimate home: the combination of rail transportation and the new embalming technology developed during the American Civil War made it possible for loved ones to be brought from long distances. Family burial became possible for the first time, bringing families closer in death than they had been in life. Most Victorian family plots were also fitted out with cemetery furniture—benches, chairs, even tables—that made the living family feel equally at home.[64]

In rural areas the old walking funerals continued until the beginning of this century; and in many poor urban neighborhoods the old practice of the community chipping in to give the dead a proper send-off continued as well. But over the course of the nineteenth century the poor also became increasingly dependent on commercial funerals to provide that small degree of dignity in death they had been deprived of in life.[65] Where the body lay was also for them a test of social standing, for the class segregation of the cities of the dead mirrored the residential patterns of the cities of the living.

In the new cemeteries, private plots were maintained and visited by families in a way the old collective graveyard had never been. The visit to the cemetery became a regular part of middle-class Sundays in the second half of the nineteenth century. Until the practice faded around the First World War, whole families would spend hours communing with their dead, fulfilling what was expected of the bereaved. In North America, what was commonly called Decoration Day varied by region but usually consisted of a family reunion that began with the sprucing up of the grave and was followed by a picnic at the site, complete with songs and storytelling.[66] The modern cemetery was designed to be a pleasant place where the living could find the same repose they imagined the dead to enjoy. The natural setting suggested a timeless place where the present was joined to the past and the future. In fact, the visit to the cemetery anticipated in many ways the family vacation. And it is not surprising that the cemetery landscape was the model for places of urban recreation like New York's Central Park, for the city of the living mirrored the city of the dead and vice versa.[67]

The visit to the cemetery was only one aspect of the practice of extended mourning, which reached its peak in the 1880s and did not fully disappear until after the First World War. Mourning had previously referred only to the emotion of grief, but by midcentury it had become a performance, lasting months, even years, and requiring special clothes and paraphernalia. Prior to that time, "weeds" referred to all clothing; thereafter, the word meant the black garb supplied by emporia devoted entirely to the needs of mourners.[68] While Victorians mourned for certain public figures—presidents and monarchs—they no longer grieved for the community at large. The good funeral and proper mourning were strictly family affairs in which the codes of dress and behavior created and maintained a much stricter distinction between family and friends, even friends of a lifetime.[69]

Mourning became concentrated entirely on what Philippe Ariès has called "those few rare beings whose disappearance could no longer be tolerated." The nuclear family deserved the most elaborate performance; uncles, aunts, and cousins received less attention. The rules were rigidly adhered to, regardless of the actual experience of family life or the real feelings of those involved. The ritual expression of family loss was the responsibility of women rather than men. It was assumed that they suffered most when a child or relative died, and that men were much less vulnerable to the loss of the other. As a result, mature women automatically became the family's chief mourners, just as they had once been responsible for "laying out" the corpse. It was the widow, not the widower, who was forbidden to leave the house for a month, had to wear mourning for two years (including a veil for the first year), and could not marry. A woman would wear full mourning for her parents, spouse, children, grandchildren, and siblings; moreover, she would wear half-mourning not only for uncles, aunts, cousins, and intimate friends but also for her husband's close relations, even if she had never met them.[70]

Before the good death was replaced by the proper funeral and extended mourning, grief had been everyone's responsibility and was shared by both sexes and all ages, even household servants. Men were the first to be exempted; children and servants were then also released from deep mourning, leaving adult women to carry the full weight of symbolic representation. "The custom of mourning presses far more heavily on women than men," noted London's *Women's World* in 1889. "In fact, so trifling are the alterations made in a man's dress . . . that practically the whole burden of mourning wrappings could seem to have fallen on women."[71] In postmortem photography, it was women who appeared with dead children and husbands. When the picture is of a woman, she lies alone.[72] It was always her mourning that was a sign of true family feeling, and her death that marked the end of the family cycle. A woman who refused to do her duty ran the risk of forfeiting not only her respectability but her place in family life. A young English widow was told by her neighbors that "if I would not wear a bonnet, *it proved we were never married*."[73]

It has been common to interpret the rise of conspicuous funerals, elaborate cemeteries, and extended mourning as either status-seeking on the part of the new middle classes or the commodification of death by the newly emerging funeral industry. Yet the entrepreneurs of death were only providing what families had already developed for themselves. Furthermore, funerals and mourning became largely private affairs, not particularly suitable occasions for showing off to society. In reality, families were as much concerned with representing themselves to themselves as to the world at large. Funerals and extended mourning were their ways of providing a family to live by, proving to themselves the absolute love and loyalty that they were afraid they had not been able to provide one another in real life. The objectification and commodification of feelings that the funeral industry catered to but did not invent served the invaluable function of closing the gap between the ideal and the real by displacing intense emotions onto objects, where, as Grant McCracken suggests, they were "kept within reach but out of danger."[74]

The cemetery was a place where the Victorians' imagined family could be kept within reach but out of danger, but as society became more physically mobile, only heaven could guarantee completely safe storage. Just as the free-floating golden age of the past was one place of safe repository for family ideals, so the dream of family reunion in the afterlife offered another. In some ways, the future proved to be an even more attractive repository for imagined families because, unlike the past, it presented a blank slate.[75] Heaven had always served as a projection screen, but until the nineteenth century the images it carried were theocentric rather than anthropocentric. The life early Protestants imagined there was "a life free not only from the pains of the earth but from everything earthly. Not only do sorrow, illness, death, and labor cease, but friends, family, change, and human understanding are utterly unimportant." In the heaven of the seventeenth and eighteenth centuries, all traces of human time and space had been transcended. The saved were imagined to be engaged in perpetual worship of God, whose presence abolished all the usual temporal and spatial requirements, including family itself. Heaven was an eternal Sabbath, one great congregation, timeless time and placeless space, in which the mundane arrangements of human life lost all meaning.[76] As Alan Macfarlane has put it, "Death was the end to everything imaginable."[77]

While the popular imagination of the seventeenth and eighteenth centuries may still have been capable of conjuring up heavens and hells populated with real bodies, Protestantism regarded such imaginings as rank superstition, unworthy of true Christians. According to their belief system,

> . . . in heaven, God dominates. On earth, change, growth and decay make everything impermanent. Since only the perfect exists in heaven, there is no need for change. On earth, work, struggle for knowledge, and family commitments draw our attention away from God. In heaven, the saints are free from labor. Since they receive immediate wisdom, God's elect are even spared the troubles of research and study. Families also never interfere with divine meditations.[78]

As the reformers saw it, there was no need for family in heaven; it could only stand between the believer and God. Calvin proclaimed that even spouses "will be torn apart from each other."[79] The Puritans were particularly insistent on the ephemeral nature of family ties in the presence of the Almighty. As the sixteenth-century puritanical Anglican bishop Joseph Hall put it, "When we meet before the glorious throne of the God of Heaven, all the respects of our former earthly relations must utterly cease and be swallowed up of that beatifical presence, divine love, and infinitely blessed fruition of the Almighty." He insisted that "nature has no place in glory; here is no respect of blood; none of marriage: this grosser acquaintance and pleasure is for the paradise of Turks, not the heaven of Christians."[80] As late as the midnineteenth century, it was still possible for American Protestants to assert that a husband "would be so enraptured with the Lord Jesus that [his wife] might be at his side for ages before he would think of looking at her."[81]

By the late eighteenth century, this radical separation of earth and heaven was softening somewhat. Under the influence of Emanuel Swedenborg, William Blake, and other romantics, heaven gradually became more anthropocentric, sensual, and dynamic. By the middle of the next century, love of family was competing successfully with love of God. Marriage and parenthood had become substitutes for God's eternal love, gaining the status of what Anthony Giddens has called "pure relationships"—relationships based on a "trust [that] can be mobilized only by a process of mutual disclosure" and sustained by nothing outside the symbolic interaction of the parties themselves.[82] Given the difficulty of sustaining pure relationships, it is not surprising that the Victorians sought safe storage for their unrequited loves in their homes, cemeteries, and heaven above. There they were able to sustain the symbolic interactions rendered difficult or impossible by real life.

By the midnineteenth century, it was possible to imagine the most intimate aspects of family life beyond the grave. The romantics had even had the temerity to project sexuality into a space that previously had been thought of as having no corporeal existence. But the Swedenborgian and Blakean visions of the ultimate pure relationship—true love outside marriage—went a step beyond where the Victorians were willing to go. After the midnineteenth century, sex would enter the pearly gates only with a marriage license. A fuller, more anthropomorphic vision of heaven was permitted, but only after it had been domesticated.[83] Heaven at the end of the nineteenth century was a far more conventional place than the one the romantics had imagined at the beginning of the era.

The midcentury heaven was like the cemetery, a projection of the world as the middle class wished it could be. Heaven was represented spatially as a busy city, complete with streets and urban institutions like schools and concert halls but also with separate dwellings. The one great mansion of the Almighty gave way to single-family homes when heaven ceased to be understood as one great congregation and came to be seen as many different family groups, each practicing holiness in a domestic rather than a church setting. Heaven became the ultimate family reunion, a vision that disturbed those who still held to a more theocentric notion. As one Anglican cleric remarked: "So, these pious ladies desired to go to heaven, not as St. Paul did, 'who desired to depart and be with Christ,' but to be with their 'John' or their 'Roy' amid all the old amusements of earth and senses."[84]

When the space of the heavenly city came to be imagined as so similar to its earthly counterpart, it became possible to think of communicating, even commuting, between them. The rise of spiritualism in the 1840s and 1850s reflected a diminished sense of distance between the living and the dead, an idea that would have been unimaginable in earlier centuries. Spiritualists were convinced that, as a spiritualist epitaph of 1893 put it, "death is merely a change of conditions," and that, as far as families were concerned, the living and the dead existed in the same spatial and temporal continuum.[85] As earth and heaven were imagined to be more spatially similar, they were also seen as more temporally alike. In earlier periods, Christians had imagined heaven to be one endless Sabbath, an eternity beyond the spectrum of ordinary time. Now, however, heaven was endowed with temporality, a place where change, growth, and progress were all equally present.

By the midnineteenth century, heaven had ceased to be seen as a place of repose, worship, and contemplation of the divine and taken on all the attributes of the bourgeois ethic of hard work and ceaseless striving. It had become a place to complete those projects left undone in life, a kind of extension of the lifetime. Even the new terms for heaven—the "afterlife," or "everlasting life"—suggested a temporal continuity that had been absent when time and eternity had been two quite different realms and heaven and earth spatially distant. By the midnineteenth century, the idea of temporal continuity was so entrenched that the Last Judgment, signifying an end of time, had become unthinkable.[86] Life, once seen as a "small parenthesis" in the vastness of eternity, had itself become eternal. Those aspects of life that earlier generations had regarded as ephemeral—sexuality, family, work—were now seen as God-ordained, a means of experiencing the divine both in this life and in the next.

God was pushed into the background, and Christ's role was reduced to that of an official greeter at the pearly gates, a presence otherwise indistinguishable from the family and friends who now populated the heavenly city. Heavenly families served the same function the Holy Family did in earlier periods: supplying the symbolic affirmation, the archetypes, that earthly family life could not provide but needed to live by. Now earthly families provided their own archetypes, which, safely projected into the afterlife, provided the comfort missing in this life. Existing in a time and space immune to the forces that rendered the family ideal unattainable in the here and now, these imagined families provided both a powerful legitimization of the ideal and an opportunity for family to reinforce its sense of unity through ongoing symbolic interaction with the deceased by way of hauntings and séances. As Colleen McDannell and Bernhard Lang describe it: "The weak barrier between heaven and death permitted both the imagination of a heaven which was a perfected earth, and the hope that earth would imitate heavenly conditions."[87]

Seventeenth-century Puritans had urged spouses to love one another but to reserve their heart for God, for death severed all human relations, even marriage.[88] In the nineteenth century, divine love was displaced by human love. The good Christian no longer had to contemplate giving up family upon death; on the contrary, he or she "merely moved from one loving home to another. Meeting one's departed family became a more pressing concern than union with God."[89] The Victorians imagined their heavenly families to be nuclear, resident in single-family homes, located in what seemed suspiciously like a new garden suburban.

The good family life, which had once been thought of as a means to salvation, was now imagined to be its consequence. Everything was better in heaven. Houses never fell into disrepair, all the children acted like little angels, and loved ones never separated. As Ariès has put it, heaven became not so much a "heavenly home as the earthly home saved from the menace of time."[90] By the fourth quarter of the nineteenth century, the anthropomorphized paradise had become so familiar that Mark Twain could satirize "the little ten-cent heaven about the size of Rhode Island."[91] In the absence of a more concrete vision of the future of this world, middle-class Americans and Britons settled for what Ann Douglas has called their "celestial retirement village."[92]

While twentieth-century visions of heaven have been perpetually updated to keep pace with technological progress, paradise remains essentially the same as the Victorians imagined it: a place where the idealized family can find safe haven from the problems that beset real families. In the 1980s, 71 percent of Americans polled said they believed in a heaven where those who had lived the good life would be rewarded. Similar beliefs were held by Europeans. Catholics tended to hold onto theocentric notions of heaven longer than did Protestants, but by the twentieth century they too imagined heaven as a place where "God will be a personal character willing to be hugged, individuals will retain their personalities, families will reunite, and earthly activities will continue."[93] In the late twentieth century, theologians have retreated from the idea that heaven is a real place, preferring to regard it as a symbol behind which lie deeper truths. But the anthropomorphic vision of paradise they originally helped to promote is sustained at the popular level by a complex of near-death accounts, mortuary sculpture, and movie treatments that sustain a very Victorian vision of eternal love and reunited families, even in the face of the fragile and fragmented personal relations of a very post-Victorian era.

To be sure, our symbolic interaction with the dead has changed. The cemetery visit, which became a family tradition in the nineteenth century, has become more difficult as families have dispersed geographically. The times when whole communities used to visit family graves—Easter, All Souls' Day, Decoration Day, and Memorial Day—have been replaced by the special family reunion, which often takes place at or near an ancestral grave site.[94] But we have also found new ways to keep the dead alive. Modern technology has not only facilitated the bridging of time and space among the living but erased the distance between the living and the dead, if not between the living and the dying. Cryogeneticists deep-freeze corpses in the hope that once the fatal diseases they suffered from are conquered, they can be brought back to a healthier existence.[95]

Most families rely on less scientific means of keeping the dead alive. The home has become what Mary Douglas calls a "memory machine," providing a place for the dead as well as the living.[96] This function has been facilitated by modern photography and by video technology, which allows us to retain vivid images of the deceased. "I don't take flowers to the cemetery at anniversaries," an Englishwoman told Gillian Bennett. "I put them in the house, near the picture, and I say, 'This is where they are. They're with me.' "[97] Such icons allow us, even compel us, to focus "vivid attention on the dead or departed family members and the concomitant lost identity. In this way, mere personal memory is transformed into objective and constraining social fact."[98] Bennett found that, among the middle-class women she interviewed, the presence of the dead confirmed their feminine identity and attached them even more firmly to their homes. "I've been here forty-five years," one told her. "I wouldn't really like to leave here, because I always feel that my mother and father are here."[99]

Although their layout and architecture have changed considerably in the late twentieth century, cemeteries continue to function as cities of the dead. "The current obsession with keeping everything tidy, not accepting long grass and leaning tombs, and treating the funeral as a refuse disposal problem, reflects a deep malaise in society," writes James Curl, echoing the criticism Geoffrey Gorer has made of British death ways and Nancy Mitford's similar critique of Americans. He adds, "Death was never a tidy thing; it is foolish to try to make it so, and to compartmentalize it away from life and the living."[100] But such critiques ignore the ways in which the dead sustain the living. In fact, the care and attention we give to our cemeteries reflect the fact that we are on much friendlier terms with the dead today than were those earlier generations who let the grass grow and the monuments crumble.

However, our problem is not with the dead but with the dying, for whom there has been no social role in modern society. Those most prone to die, the elderly, have been treated as if they were socially dead, our way of coping with the fear of dying we inherited from the Victorians. Since their time the elderly have been increasingly left to face their end in social isolation. The invention of the modern lifetime, with its premise that longevity can be guaranteed by the proper application of medical science, encourages us to place death out of sight and out of mind. Today the death of a child or a young spouse is virtually unthinkable, an event for which none of us is prepared and that shatters the small worlds of the survivors as nothing else can. But the death of older persons is expected, even anticipated; too often we condemn them to a social death long before their physical demise, thereby depriving them of the possibility of a full life and the good death that earlier generations, though much less blessed in number of years, could count on.

But once again, our attitudes may be changing. Youthful violence and the AIDS epidemic have produced a death awareness among age groups that previously regarded themselves as virtually immortal. The hospice movement of recent decades has brought the living and the dying closer together than at any time since the early nineteenth century, and the controversy over medically assisted suicide has brought out of the shadows a whole set of previously taboo subjects.[101] Although four-fifths of Americans die in hospitals, surveys indicate that most want to die at home under conditions that they and their families can control. Within the past two decades, many people who had made no preparations for their own dying have begun to think about "living wills." Today one-fifth of adult Americans have put their wishes in writing and some 90 percent of Americans say that they do not want extraordinary measures taken to prolong their lives.[102]

Today's death awareness movement has become the death preparedness movement, suggesting that we may be at a turning point as major as the one that first segregated the living and the dying more than a century ago. If we want to, we can make the dying as much a part of our lives as the dead have been. But, to do so, we will also have to revise our myths and images of a family life that has relied so much on the dead for its sense of continuity.

PART IV

New Times and New Places
Myths and Rituals for a Global Era

CHAPTER 11

Conclusion: Remaking Our Worlds

> Myths convey values and expectations which are always evolving
> . . . but, and this is fortunate, never set so hard they cannot be
> changed again.
>
> Marina Warner, *Six Myths of Our Times*[1]

In December 1990, the *New York Times* announced, with evident relief, that "Even in the Frenzy of the 90s Dinner Time Is for the Family." A national phone survey of families with children under eighteen had revealed that 80 percent said they had eaten dinner together the night before; 46 percent had had seven meals together during the week. Even those who had not been able to be together as often said that they wished they could have done so. "Nearly all these people said eating dinner together provided a peaceful respite from the frenzy of their day. Without it, many said, they would no longer feel as though they were a family."[2] But two years later, the *Times* reported on another study that had less welcome news about family togetherness. Observed firsthand, only one-third of families with children were actually seen to sit down to eat together every night of the week.[3]

It was not that people had deliberately misled the phone surveyors. They were simply reporting the families they lived by rather than the families they lived with; they were unable to distinguish between the two. Family meals, holidays, and vacations are so much a part of modern mythology that we have great difficulty approaching them with any objectivity. On the other hand, when we reduce such things to facts and numbers, we lose sight of their meaning and function in modern family life. The fact that Americans want to believe they eat together more than they actually do tells us a great deal more than any statistic does. It reflects the very widespread feeling that there is never enough time for family, a fact of modern life that an overwhelming number of Americans now feel is "the core threat to American families."[4]

To listen to the prophets of family decline, one would think that the families we live with are all falling apart and that "family values" are on the verge of extinction. These are indeed hard times for the families we live with, but these same circumstances have stimulated an unprecedented level of creativity on the part of those who seek to sustain caring, cooperative relations with those they consider family. Since 1970 the percentage of children living with a single parent has risen from 12 percent to 27 percent. The same quarter-century has seen the number of persons who live alone increase from 13 percent to almost 26 percent. Such figures would seem to be very alarming, but they do not tell the whole story: they do not capture the bonds between the two groups that have been forming over the same period. What is now being called "para-parenting," which has long been practiced in working-class and minority communities, is now being adopted by the middle class as well. At all social levels, families are flexing rather than breaking.[5]

People are inventing new families to live by as well as with. The old images and rituals are changing even as new ones are coming into being. We have seen how fatherhood and motherhood are being reimagined. The life cycle is undergoing a major reritualization, and aspects of family life that received no recognition only two decades ago now have their appropriate symbolism. When Hallmark brought out its first divorce card in 1958, no one would buy it. The company tried again in the mid–1970s, but there was still no market. Today, however, divorce cards are a minor success, and a tradition of divorce ceremonies is beginning. In addition, there are now ceremonies appropriate to gay and lesbian relationships, and dimensions of the life cycle that previously went unmarked, such as menopause, now have their ritual treatments.[6]

The families we live by are no longer confined to real space and time. People now fall in love and mourn in cyberspace, giving a whole new meaning to the old idea of the kindness of strangers.[7] Men as well as women are coming to recognize the importance of ritual in their lives. Ronald Grimes, one of the leaders of the current renaissance of ritual, remembers that as a young man he responded to ritual with disdain. "Then, I recognized how badly I needed it, and I began to cultivate it."[8] Robert Fulghum presided over ceremonies for years during his career as a Unitarian minister, but he did not discover their value in his own life until he was in his fifties. "It's like finding my 'lost' glasses perched on the end of my nose," he writes. "So has it been with this search for an understanding of rituals. Right there in front of my face all along."[9]

Even the most affluent societies suffer from what is now known as time famine. In her recent book *The Overworked American*, Juliet Schor demonstrates that adults in this country worked on average a month longer in 1992 than they did in 1969.[10] The major part of this increase has been borne by women, but child labor is also on the increase, particularly in the teen years. To make things worse, Witold Rybczynski informs us, even our leisure time is becoming regimented and more like work.[11] Those who do time studies tell us that families have been the losers in the competition for scarce days, hours, and minutes. Time spent by Americans on housework began to fall in 1970 for the first time in this century, but parents still complain they do not have enough time for their children, much less one another. In the most recent study of American family time, it was discovered that fathers talked to their children an average of only eight minutes on weekdays. Mothers did only slightly better, managing eleven minutes of conversation. It turns out that mothers who stayed at home did no better than mothers who worked.[12]

Although most Europeans work fewer hours and have much more generous vacation time, they too are experiencing time famine. A transnational study of fathers found that they spent on average only forty-five minutes a day in the same room as their young offspring, and even less time with their older children. Parents spent more time with their children on weekends and holidays, but even then the quantity of time was meager.[13] As we have seen, mornings and afternoons have long since been lost to school and work. But now the evening is endangered as both parents arrive home late, with only minutes to spare before the children's bedtime. According to recent studies, children's bedtimes are becoming later, even as television programming is moved forward an hour to reduce the sleep deficits of over-worked parents.[14]

With hindsight, we can see that families have been exposed to ever greater time pressures since the 1960s, while during the same period their private space has been invaded to an unprecedented extent. The already blurred lines between public and private time, and between public and private space, apparently are in danger of being erased entirely, owing in part to the invasion of the home by so-called time-consuming durables, first the radio, then television, and more recently the videocassette recorder and home computers. By the 1990s the house had become its own entertainment and communications center. Moreover, "time-saving" durables like the washer and dryer returned to the home much of the labor that had left it a century and a half earlier, making the house of the 1990s a much busier place, more like a preindustrial household than the homes of the Victorian period.[15] "Then Home was to be a place of quiet, of repose," John Demos has written. "Now it must generate some excitement. Then the True Woman served as the appointed guardian of domestic values. . . . Now here is the figure of the 'Total Woman'—who, to be sure, keeps an orderly house and seeks consistently to help her man, but who is also sensual and assertive within limits."[16] Now, without servants, the woman of the house bears a much greater burden than ever before.

The squeeze on family time and space has produced significant cultural innovations however. Even as the quantities of time available have contracted, the cultural demand for quality time has increased. Both Europeans and Americans have found themselves wanting their houses to be homier, and when this cannot be achieved, they have turned in ever larger numbers to second homes to meet the felt need for quality space. Since the 1970s, families have been reimagining themselves in ways that require both new times and new places. As a consequence, new myths and rituals have begun to emerge, challenging the old without wholly displacing them.

We are now in the midst of the most intensive period of social and cultural change since the first era of industrial and democratic revolution two hundred years ago. Patterns of family behavior are undergoing massive alteration, but so too are family cultures. The current debate over family values is an expression of this historic moment. Self-styled advocates of family values claim to represent the only viable conception of what family can be when in fact they are simply, for the moment, the most audible voice in a debate that stretches back over centuries—the debate over the meaning of the complex and contradictory processes of human reproduction. We should be wary of concluding that those who get the widest media coverage represent the last word on the subject. The contemporary quest for family values is far more widespread and diverse, and its outcome far from certain.

Even those facts of life that earlier generations had convinced themselves were unshakable have in the last quarter-century become uncertain and contested. The very notion of a lifetime began to be questioned in the 1970s as new variations in age of schooling, marriage, family formation, and retirement began to surface. Precocity, something that had been discouraged since the midnineteenth century, began again to be acceptable, and bright children were encouraged to skip grades and seek early admission to college. But this time it was not just the prodigies but all children who were to receive a "Head Start."[17] What some have hailed as the era of the "superkid," and others have condemned as the generation of the "hurried child," had arrived, leading some to wonder whether childhood itself might be disappearing.[18]

There has also been concern that adolescence might vanish: since the 1970s, young people have been acting more adultlike. Not only do teens seem to be growing up faster sexually, but they are entering the culture of consumption previously reserved for older youths and adults. To pay for cars, vacations, and clothes, young people are working earlier, sometimes dropping out of school to do so. Not only are young people taking adult liberties, they were also assuming adult responsibilities. The startling rise in teenage pregnancies since the 1970s, and the refusal of some unwed young mothers to give up their children for adoption, has raised the specter of children having children.[19]

It has also been since the 1970s that the previously tight age grading of higher education has begun to show signs of loosening. Not only are college students no longer marching in lockstep through the traditional four years of undergraduate education, but many older persons (especially women) are returning to school, making colleges and universities far more age-heterogeneous. As professional and graduate schooling began to attract increasing numbers, the category "youth" began to be extended into the twenties.[20] The age of entry into full-time employment, marriage, and family formation all began to rise just as more and more young women and men found themselves postponing the traditional markers of adulthood. In the 1960s the popular definition of a young man was eighteen to twenty-two years of age; by the 1980s, it had stretched from eighteen to forty.[21]

The notion of "identity crisis" is no longer exclusive to adolescence but has become a metaphor for life at every stage.[22] We now organize our lives much more around crisis than normality; this may not be a bad strategy in an era when continuity has been displaced by change, when the college graduate can count on making six or seven career changes and more than one marriage and family in a single lifetime.[23] But these same conditions also demand new myths and rituals to cope with the resulting feelings of isolation and strain. It is against this backdrop that we must understand how the times of our lives have changed over the past twenty years.

The meaning of adulthood itself has changed. The Berkeley anthropologist Stanley Brandes made this discovery in the 1970s when he found himself becoming concerned about the approach of age forty.

> I began for the first time in my life to feel uneasy about my age. Uppermost in my mind was that forty represented a turning point, fraught with unfulfilled ambitions and severely limited opportunities. To be sure, I could reflect on what others might consider substantial achievements in professional and family life, but somehow these paled beside the imminent arrival of a date—my fortieth birthday—when disturbances would inevitably occur.

Prompted by his own anxieties, Brandes began to read widely in the literature of midlife crises, which suggested that ages fifty and sixty, even age thirty, were equally critical moments. Discussions with friends produced no reassuring consensus as to which age was most critical, but what Brandes did discover was that the meaning of forty had changed dramatically. What had once been a marker for the beginning of old age was now seen as the entry into middle age. Furthermore, what had been an age that mattered mainly to men was becoming worrisome to women. But apparently no biological factors could account for the meaning of forty to this generation.[24] Recent research has shown that there is no evidence that numerical age is a strong predictor of any of the physical or mental qualities that have traditionally been associated with particular stages of life.[25] Instead, what Brandes and others were finding was overwhelming evidence of the plasticity of human development.[26]

By the 1980s, midlife had lost its timeless quality and become one of the most rapidly changing and ambiguous periods in the lives of all adults. Changes in the length of life, career patterns, and familial relations were causing women as well as men to reach for symbols that would give meaning to the flux of middle age. One result was a sudden proliferation of adult birthdays. People began to celebrate the passage of the decennial ages forty, fifty, and sixty; even the elderly, a group that had been no friend of age, were making their birthdays into moments of collective celebration. Most adults would no doubt have liked to forget their birth dates, but they

were finding themselves fixated on years like forty and compelled to fashion such milestones into collective observances of ever greater significance.[27] As Brandes observes: "To take forty as representing middle age has
enabled people to situate themselves with reference to other, more clearly
defined age groups. It has provided a kind of anchor point, a frame of reference, which we seem to require in the increasingly age-differentiated
society in which we live."[28]

In the 1970s middle age ceased to be a state of being and turned into just
another stage of becoming. Some women raced the biological clock to have
babies before infertility set in, but more women than ever were remaining
single longer. Marriage was no longer governed by the temporal norms that
had prevailed in the 1950s and 1960s, when the number of ever-married
women reached its highest levels in the history of the West. By the 1980s
only 40 percent of women would follow the sequence of work, marriage,
childbearing, and homemaking that had been the norm in their mothers'
generation.[29] Many by then were cohabiting, even having children out of
wedlock. Although most who did so would eventually marry, there was no
longer any consensus about the right age. Surveys showed agreement over
the "best" age of first marriage dropping from 90 percent in the 1960s to
only 40 percent in the 1980s.[30] The growing rate of remarriage after the
1970s, owing to higher divorce rates, has only made the matter of timing
more ambiguous. Middle age, which used to be associated with stable marriages and housefuls of children, has become a period of painful divorces
and empty nests—no longer a timeless state but a period of frantic changes.
According to surveys in the 1980s, the time designated as the prime of life
has shifted from middle age to young adulthood.[31]
     The age of retirement has also come unstuck as more and more people,
especially men, have opted to retire before sixty-five.[32] Women, who have
tended in the past to subordinate the timing of their lives to the times of
men's lives, are both entering and exiting employment in much larger numbers today, with the result that the timing of retirement often becomes a
matter of negotiation for two-career couples.[33] Moreover, leaving employment, like entering it, has become a conditional rather than a final decision;
many older people find themselves employed part-time.
     Like midlife, old age has ceased to be a state of being and become a
stage of becoming. This is partly attributable to the remarkable increase in
longevity, but the circumstances of the elderly have improved as well: since
the 1960s, they have enjoyed better incomes, better living conditions, and
better health than any previous generation. By the 1980s it was possible for
Peter Laslett to declare that old age is not one stage but two, which he calls

the Third and Fourth Ages. His Third Age includes "young-old"—those in their sixties and seventies who are able and eager to live active, independent lives in retirement. To his Fourth Age belong the "old-old," those whose dependence and inactivity fit the traditional stereotype of old age.[34] Yet even this distinction now seems too rigid for those, like Gail Sheehy, who talk about a "second adulthood" and emphasize the creative possibilities open to all older people.[35]

We have reached a point where numerical age is no longer a reliable predictor of life circumstances.[36] It is not just the timing but the sequencing of the times of our lives that has become uncertain. Many people no longer act their age, with the result that the apparent natural laws of aging are being called into question in the social as well as the medical sciences.[37] Now that the unreliability of age as a predictor of a person's mental and physical capacities has been acknowledged, even more discrepancy has been generated between the old self-fulfilling images of age and actual behavior. One of Gail Sheehy's most consistent findings was the great disparity between people's numerical age and how old they feel. She found that both men and women feel eight to ten years younger than their birth certificates indicate.[38]

How do we account for these changes? They have certainly been influenced by the very institutions that used age as a standard for readiness and competency in the past and are now abandoning it. Many schools, for instance, are now more ready to promote students on the basis of achievement rather than age. Under increasing competitive pressures, both at home and abroad, large firms seem to be abandoning seniority in favor of promoting those with the greatest talent regardless of age. And modern nation-states, whose laws once used age as a proxy for a whole range of rights and duties associated with citizenship, seem also to be scrapping it as the struggle against age discrimination advances.[39] We have even reached the point where the military is no longer solely a young man's occupation. Not only is it now taken for granted that women can serve as well as men in most capacities, but the age range of those serving has vastly expanded. In the 1991 Gulf War, the allies fielded what was, in effect, a middle-aged army.[40]

We are entering what some have called the postmodern era of aging, which encourages everyone, regardless of age, to think of themselves in a perpetual state of becoming.[41] We are asked to retrain, reeducate, and "recycle," a word that suggests a very nonlinear view of the lifetime. No longer are women the only ones asked to adapt, change, and accept the condition of being relative creatures. Men too are now being told to keep their options open, to be flexible enough to meet the demands of the new global economy. Gail Sheehy gave the same advice to her adult readers in 1981 that was once given to children: "One of the worst mistakes in middle age is to define oneself—and continue to define oneself—by a single source of identity."[42] In her most recent book, Sheehy has abandoned entirely the notion of predictability and celebrates flexibility with even greater ardor, declaring that "the most successful and healthy now develop *multiple identities*, managed simultaneously, to be called upon as conditions change."[43]

Today many Europeans and Americans are turning away from the nineteenth-century linear notion of the journey of life and returning to the ancient resources of ritual and symbol to construct for themselves alternative chronotypes capable of coping with the new temporal uncertainties. The two groups that have been pioneering on this frontier since the 1960s are young people and the elderly. This is not at all surprising, for they are the ones whom the major institutions of society have had no time for, literally and metaphorically. After the tight scheduling of childhood, young people have found themselves in what society refers to as an "awkward age," a period betwixt and between; the anxieties of this time have been heightened by the fact that since the 1960s youth has expanded to encompass "thirtysomething." The simultaneous revolution in longevity left older people in a similar temporal limbo, what sociologists call the "roleless role" of facing their biological destinies without any transcendent purpose apart from the futile effort to control the body's inevitable decline.[44]

Rites and symbols of aging, which once clustered toward the beginnings of life, consequently shifted to older age groups. Retirement communities have invented their own rites of passage that serve to integrate newcomers. Increasing at an even faster rate are what Elizabeth Colson has called rites of age solidarity, exemplified by the collective birthday parties organized by senior citizens' centers: members celebrate not their individual ages but the all-encompassing symbol of "good old age." In these popular ceremonies, attended by families and friends, all those with a birthday in a given month celebrate it together. Each celebrant receives a round of applause, but the celebration is more of the community than of the individual, more of age itself than of the specific ages present. By combining birthdays, senior citizens have "celebrated their distinctive status and reassured themselves, and told outsiders, that it is good to be old."[45] Age is thereby transformed from something that divides and isolates into something that unites and comforts. Old age becomes more like a "season," extending across space as well as time, reaching backward and forward to encompass people from their sixties through their nineties. Together, elders of quite different ages form a convoy that will see them through the rough seas of time, providing a model for others.

It should not be surprising that it is women who have been the most innovative in reimagining old age. Barbara Myerhoff, who was the first to explore the cultural creativity of the elderly, noted that "as a group, men appear more worn-out and demoralized than women." The men she observed in the 1960s remained passive, accepting the inevitability of postretirement degeneration, an assumption that had been current for over a century. By contrast, the women quietly went about the work of making something positive of old age, becoming *bricoleurs* of time, reshaping it to give their lives, and those of the men in their lives, renewed purpose.[46]

Even as the old chronotypes have been challenged, the Western sense of place has been undermined by the new global economy, which has unleashed the greatest movement of people since the nineteenth century while also shifting the boundaries between public and private, thus once again undermining the fixed meanings of home.[47] Since the 1970s, the house has ceased to be a refuge and become again a very busy place. Life flows through it at an ever-accelerating pace. Parents complain that it is no more than a pit stop for children, while children rarely see their working parents. "We never get time to see one another—we merely pass coming and going," report the denizens of the American suburb.[48] But the situation is no different in Sweden, where Rita Tornborg asks: "Are there others in the world who have such an obsession with home life as we, with the same economic sacrifices and mental agonies? Housekeeping is a full-time job, which the citizen has to take care of during the few daytime hours left between work and sleep."[49]

There is very little that is relaxing about home ownership. The growing awareness of everything from domestic violence to the toxins lurking in our cupboards and basements has exposed the myth of the house as a refuge.[50] The women's movement has helped us to see some of the false distinctions between private and public life, while environmentalists encourage us to think of our homes as part of the larger world, which we should be treating as our true home if we are all to survive on this small planet. As a result, home is less and less a place of return and more a point of departure for the new social movements that would make the world a better place to live.

As home becomes busier, the consumer economy taps into our need for homes away from home. Families are going out more than they did twenty years ago. There seems to be a "family restaurant" on every corner, each offering its version of "home cooking."[51] Just about any product is marketable with the symbols of home attached to it—from soups (homemade) to videos (home entertainment).[52] In a similar manner, hotels and resorts advertise their homelike qualities, expanding their clientele beyond the lonely traveler to include the whole family. The success of Disneyland inaugurated the era of the commercialized "family vacation," and now even Las Vegas and Club Med lure their patrons with promises of fun for the whole family.[53] Today's tourists are looking for not only all the comforts of home but a more authentic version of what they have left behind. Houses as different as Lincoln's log cabin and the country seats of English lords attract millions eager to glimpse a home life they imagine to have once existed. What the Germans call the *Heimat* business thrives on this latest wave of nostalgia.[54]

If we could, we would turn everywhere into a home away from home. In the past two decades, there has been a strong tendency toward domesticating office and work spaces; we redecorate them with warm colors and family pictures. Large firms try to build corporate cultures around these homey settings, representing themselves to themselves and to the world at large as happy families. Yet these spaces lack the one quality that makes any place a home, namely, the control of space over time. While the definition of home has become increasingly flexible, people still find it hard to feel at home in corporate and other public settings. It is no coincidence that the appeal of working at home has grown by leaps and bounds over the past two decades. An increasing portion of the workforce is now working out of their residences on a part- or full-time basis. While this shift of location has solved some of the typical family's most pressing logistical problems, it has had no appreciable effect on people's sense of having neither time nor space enough for family life as such.[55]

Partly in response to the perceived need for a place for family, home has also been on the move within the house itself, establishing itself firmly in the kitchen. Among the working classes, family life never really left there, but for the middle classes this shift represents an important change, the latest phase of what began with the Victorian parlor and continued with the living and family rooms of the early twentieth century. The home within the house remains matrifocal, centered as firmly as ever on women, even as they gain access to the larger world. Women are now figures in perpetual motion, but modern housekeeping devices have not altered their greater identification with the home.[56] In fact, many of the time-consuming durables, like the telephone, have made it more rather than less difficult for women to detach themselves from domestic responsibilities. Even when they are away, women feel much more on call than men do.

Women's space, like women's time, continues to be at the disposal of the family in a way that men's time and space are not. Today's children claim total sovereignty over their bedrooms and often turn attics and basements into worlds of their own.[57] Fathers can also retreat to their backyard sheds and garages, but mothers have no place that is theirs alone now that the kitchen has become the new family room. They can find some privacy in the master bedroom, but now that it has become a place of sensual pleasure, it too is no longer the refuge it once was.[58]

The contemporary suburban house has opened up and become a staging area for all kinds of activities—work, school, and recreation. Over forty million Americans work out of their homes at least part-time; the number of "telecommuters," already seven million strong, is expected to expand immensely by the end of the century. One woman, a bank vice president who shares her home office two days a week with her four-year-old and eighteen-month-old children, noted that "at the office, I have one function. . . . At home, I'm a mommy and a banker . . . a wearing situation."[59]

Today, as public services shrink and good jobs are harder to get, home has become increasingly self-exploiting, especially for women. Previously, their task was to represent home to men and children. Now women find themselves representing it to themselves, even when doing so involves working the "second shift," with the attendant mental stress and overwork. "Virginia creeper and honeysuckle are not enough to dampen and conceal the vibrations that run through the houses," writes Rita Tornborg.

> Because inside the TV is on, and the radio is on, and the cassette deck is on, the electric beater is spinning, the dishwasher is hissing and sighing, the washing machine is bubbling, the stereo is on, the children's dog is on, and the blender is kneading dough for healthy bread, which is eaten standing up, because people are in a hurry.[60]

And in the midst of all this chaos stands Mother, the symbolic center of the frantic household.

The longing for home expands rather than diminishes. Europeans used to be apartment dwellers, but two decades of conservative privatization policies have turned almost all of them into avid home owners. In the United States, 80 percent of adults view "the traditional single-family detached home with a yard as the ideal place to live," although actual home ownership declined slightly in the 1980s. As a goal, home ownership outranks a happy marriage and an interesting job.[61]

In Western society, you must still leave home in order to prove you are an adult, and you must have a home if you are to keep that coveted status. But the stock of housing suitable to proper homemaking is limited, and young people (especially men) are living in their parents' home more now than twenty years ago.[62] Some of these "boomerang kids" envy the older home owners, who hold tenaciously to their houses as a source of psychological as well as economic security, dreading the moment when they must move out, even if doing so will lead to greater convenience and physical comfort.[63] But a rise in home-centeredness is only to be expected in a period of global economic dislocation, unprecedented migrations, and massive levels of exile. It is precisely because such vast numbers of us cannot go home again that the nostalgia for roots is increasing everywhere.[64]

Even as they make a place for their returning children, many people find themselves caring for their elderly parents. Recent studies have found that the bonds between generations are very strong, refuting the notion that American families have become uncaring and unsupportive of the elderly. In fact, only about 6 percent of the elderly live in institutions, and these are often the very old (often women) who have outlived all their kin.[65] As public assistance is cut back by states eager to trim their budgets, the family must bear the ever-heavier burden of caring for an aging population. Most of this work falls to women, who remain the primary caregivers within the household and end up taking care of the sick and the elderly, becoming homemakers for life.[66] With the increase in the number of the elderly who prefer to die at home, this task has become more demanding than ever. The Victorians were the first to domesticate birth and death, but they had servants, spinster aunts, and dutiful daughters who could help them care for the young and the old. In today's servantless household, women are stretched to their limits to fulfill family needs and desperate for time and space even when there is no sick child or elderly relative needing their attentions.

There has always been a certain tension between the functional requirements of the house and the symbolic comforts of the home. Premodern Europeans and Americans turned elsewhere to find homeyness, and we are doing the same. In recent years, Americans in particular have been working longer hours to pay for second homes and to maintain "homeplaces," most of which sit unoccupied for much of the year. In the hills of North Carolina, Michael Ann Williams finds people abandoning the houses they grew up in to live in modern dwellings. These moves are consistent with their long-standing practice of moving house each generation; what is new is their refusal to sell the old places. They prefer to leave them empty, even if doing so causes them to fall into ruin. Williams found that "people keep an eye on them from a trailer next door, a ranch house across the road, or a modern home in town," returning periodically to make a personal visit or to organize a family reunion.[67]

Serving a similar purpose for urban and suburban dwellers is the weekend or vacation house, an expensive and time-consuming mecca for the dispersed family, a symbol of home even for those who never have time to spend there. A study of New Yorkers with places in Vermont found that most are likely to be married with children. They see their second homes as "ideal [places] to be with the children," making up for what they cannot seem to do in the city. "Here is the place to play out family dramas, to permit the more uninterrupted assumption of family roles."[68] Amy Cross, who has studied summer houses in North America, observes that people have a greater attachment to them than they do to their regular residences. "Not real estate, it is more a state of mind that can be packed and moved about— to any woods or seaside. And many of us travel through life with a memory of a perfect place waiting for our return."[69] Summer places are equally popular all across Europe. In Sweden, "the journey to summer is for many people also a journey through time, back to childhood."[70] There, too, home-places have become a way of life over the last quarter-century.

The summer house becomes the one fixed point in time and space. The photographs and films taken there are viewed throughout the long winter months, an invaluable symbolic resource for family members who may not see one another again until the next summer season. In the late twentieth century, our family life has become more hectic and our households less habitable as women have joined men in working longer hours and commuting greater distances so as to afford a weekend or summer place. In many Western countries today, millions of such places stand empty for most of the year while the needs of the truly homeless go unmet.

The British sociologist Jan Bernardes estimates that there are as many as two hundred different arrangements that Europeans and Americans now regard as legitimate "family."[71] Some see this diversification as a recent development, but it is clear that variation has always been a part of Western family history. This makes even more astonishing the power that the notion of "The Family" continues to exercise over the modern imagination.[72] This idol of family life sustains our economy and dominates our politics, holding us hostage to the "culture wars" currently being waged in the name of family. When the self-appointed legislators of family values survey Western society, they see little but chaos and degeneration. The emotional appeal of this position is enormous, but it obscures the diversity of family forms and inflicts real pain on those who do not conform to a single, narrowly defined notion of family.

On the other side of this debate are many who, out of frustration, see all the talk of family values as mystifying and oppressive. Yet if the family values movement systematically disregards the material problems that real families struggle with, their opponents too often underestimate the appeal of home and family as sources of meaning and comfort. Families today are beset by a poverty of time, space, and money, but they are no less threatened by a poverty of cultural resources. They do not find the diversity and complexity they live with every day reflected in either the media or the conventional wisdom of those social sciences that are supposed to provide us with the truth about family life but instead promote norms that are out of touch with current realities.[73]

We all have an enormous stake in providing every family with the material resources, including adequate income, time, and space, to meet its most pressing needs. It is equally important that we guarantee education and health services to all families. There must be flexible conditions of employment not just for the corporate few but for everyone who needs time for family. And it is high time that our laws reflected the diversity of family arrangements. These must be changed so as to support caring and nurturing gay and lesbian relationships as well as heterosexual unions. We also need to realign our health, housing, and social security systems with the new realities of aging. The families we live with can no longer be regarded as a private matter; they must be given the highest priority in our thinking about the public well-being.

No less pressing is the task of cultural reconstruction, involving the creation of new languages, symbols, and rituals. It is time to abandon once and for all the idol of "The Family" and to validate the great variety of families that people are actually living by. Mainstream culture has yet to acknowledge the creativity we see all around us. It promotes a set of images of family and home that no longer bear much relation to either reality or the imaginings of a large part of the population. It is time to recognize the richness of our contemporary family cultures and to explore the possibilities that these open to all of us regardless of our class, race, or gender. It is time for men to enter fully into the creation of myth and ritual, not, as Robert Bly would have it, in isolation with women but in cooperation with them.[74] No man or woman can afford to be a passive observer; the families we live by are everyone's responsibility. We must strive toward new family cultures that will not unduly burden or privilege either sex or any age group, or ignore the creativity of any class or ethnic group. Men must be willing finally to pick up their share of the cultural work involved, but women must be prepared to make a place for them in this endeavor.

I have no recipe for families' future; if I did, I would be contradicting everything I believe about the nature of family life. In opposition to those advocates of family values who would impose their prescriptions on others,

I would insist that we keep our family cultures diverse, fluid, and unre-
solved, open to the input of everyone who has a stake in those futures.[75]
This democratizing endeavor should extend across families of all kinds, gay
and lesbian as well as heterosexual, and bring together different ethnic and
racial groups in the understanding that, whatever our differences, we are all
involved in the age-old quest for relations that are caring, supportive, and
enduring. If history has a lesson for us, it is that no one family form has ever
been able to satisfy the human need for love, comfort, and security. Our rituals, myths, and images must therefore be open to perpetual revision,
never allowed to come under the sway of any orthodoxy or to serve the
interest of any one class, gender, or generation. We must recognize that
families are worlds of our own making and accept responsibility for our own
creations.

NOTES

INTRODUCTION

1. Jane Collier, Michelle Rosaldo, and Sylvia Yanagisako, "Is There a Family? New Anthropological Views," in *Rethinking the Family: Some Feminist Questions*, eds. Barrie Thorne with Marilyn Yalom (New York: Longman, 1982), p. 34.
2. Ibid., p. 35.
3. Ibid., p. 38.
4. On symbolic worlds, see Tamotsu Shibutani, "Reference Groups as Perspectives," *American Journal of Sociology* 9, no. 5 (March 1955): 564.
5. Edward T. Hall, *The Dance of Life: The Other Dimensions of Time* (New York: Anchor Books, 1983); Hall, *The Silent Language* (Garden City, N.Y.: Doubleday, 1959).
6. See Jenna Weissman Joselit, *The Wonders of America: Reinventing Jewish Culture, 1880–1950* (New York: Hill and Wang, 1994); on Catholic family culture, see Colleen McDannell, *The Christian Home in Victorian America, 1840–1900* (Bloomington: Indiana University Press, 1986), pp. 85–91, 116–23, 150–55; Micaela Di Leonardo, *The Varieties of Ethnic Kinship, Class, and Gender among California's Italian Americans* (Ithaca, N.Y.: Cornell University Press, 1986).

CHAPTER ONE

1. Witold Rybczynski, *Home: A Short History of an Idea* (New York: Penguin, 1987), p. 9.
2. David Lowenthal, *The Past Is a Foreign Country* (Cambridge: Cambridge University Press, 1985), p. 122.
3. On American notions of community, see Thomas Bender, *Community and Social Change in America* (New Brunswick, N.J.: Rutgers University Press, 1978), chaps. 1 and 2; on Sweden, see Orvar Löfgren and Jonas Frykman, *Culture Builders: A Historical Anthropology of Middle-Class Life* (New

Brunswick, N.J.: Rutgers University Press, 1987), pp. 59–60; on Germany, see Mack Walker, *German Home Towns, Community, State, and General Estates, 1640–1871* (Ithaca, N.Y.: Cornell University Press, 1971), and Alon Confino, *Nation as a Local Metaphor: Wuertemburg, the German Empire, and National Empire, 1871–1918* (Chapel Hill: University of North Carolina Press, forthcoming); on England, see Robert Colls and Philip Dodd, eds., *Englishness: Politics and Culture, 1880–1920* (London: Croom Helm, 1986), and Anthony P. Cohen, *The Symbolic Construction of Community* (London: Routledge, 1985).

4. Eugene Rochberg-Halton, *Meaning and Modernity: Social Theory in the Pragmatic Attitude* (Chicago: University of Chicago Press, 1986), p. 188; Stephanie Coontz, *The Way We Never Were: American Families and the Nostalgia Trap* (New York: Basic Books, 1992), chap. 1.

5. Arlene Skolnick, *Embattled Paradise: The American Family in an Age of Uncertainty* (New York: Basic Books, 1991), pp. 47, 50–51, 77–78.

6. Paula Fass, *The Damned and the Beautiful: American Youth in the 1920s* (New York: Oxford University Press, 1977).

7. Quoted in Coontz, *The Way We Never Were*, p. 12.

8. David Lowenthal, "Past Time, Present Time," *Geographical Review* 65, no. 1 (1975): 2–3; John Demos, "Images of the American Family, Then and Now," in *Changing Images of the Family*, eds. Virginia Tufte and Barbara Myerhoff (New Haven, Conn.: Yale University Press, 1970), pp. 49–50; Löfgren and Frykman, *Culture Builders*, p. 39.

9. Quoted in Walter Houghton, *The Victorian Frame of Mind 1830–1870* (New Haven, Conn.: Yale University Press, 1957), p. 344; on the prevalence of nostalgia among males, see Fred Davis, *Yearning for Yesterday: A Sociology of Nostalgia* (New York: Free Press, 1979), p. 54.

10. Colleen McDannell, *The Christian Home in Victorian America, 1840–1900* (Bloomington: Indiana University Press, 1986), p. 5.

11. Alex Shoumatoff, *The Mountain of Names: A History of the Human Family* (New York: Simon & Schuster, 1985), pp. 213–24; see also Anthony Richard Wagner, *English Genealogy* (Oxford: Clarendon Press, 1972), pp. 3–4, 397–407.

12. Mary Jo Maynes, "The Contours of Childhood: Demography, Strategy, and Mythology of Childhood in French and German Lower-Class Adults," in *The European Experience of Declining Fertility, 1850–1970: The Quiet Revolution*, eds. John Gillis, David Levine, and Louise Tilly (Oxford: Basil Blackwell, 1992), pp. 101–24.

13. John Hajnal, "European Marriage Patterns in Perspective," in *Population in History: Essays in Historical Demography*, eds. D. V. Glass and D. E. C. Eversley (London: Edward Arnold, 1965); and Hajnal, "Two Kinds of Pre-Industrial Household Systems," *Population and Development Review* 8, no. 3 (1982): 449–94; Wally Seccombe, *A Millennium of Family Change: Feudalism to Capitalism in Northwestern Europe* (London: Verso, 1992), chap. 3; David Herlihy, *Medieval Households* (Cambridge: Cambridge University Press, 1985), chaps. 1–3.

14. Quoted in Alan Macfarlane, *The Origins of English Individualism* (Oxford: Basil Blackwell, 1978), p. 75.

15. Quoted in Laurel Thatcher Ulrich, *A Midwife's Tale: The Life of Martha Ballard, Based on Her Diary, 1785–1812* (New York: Vintage, 1991), p. 281.
16. Hajnal, "Two Kinds of Pre-Industrial Household Systems," pp. 449–94.
17. David Herlihy rightly argues that the Western family system enhanced the "poor man's chances of gaining a wife and producing progeny," but relative only to the ancient and Germanic worlds. *Medieval Households*, p. 158.
18. Lawrence Stone, *The Family, Sex, and Marriage in England, 1500–1800* (New York: Harper & Row, 1977), pp. 58–64.
19. Peter Laslett, *Family Life and Illicit Love in Earlier Generations* (Cambridge: Cambridge University Press, 1977), p. 169; see also Illana Krausman Ben-Amos, *Adolescence and Youth in Early Modern England* (New Haven, Conn.: Yale University Press, 1994), p. 48.
20. Herlihy, *Medieval Households*, p. 159.
21. Ben-Amos, *Adolescence and Youth in Early Modern England*, p. 69.
22. John Gillis, *Youth and History: Tradition and Change in European Age Relations, 1750 to the Present* (New York: Academic Press, 1975), pp. 5–12, 21–26.
23. Laslett, *A Fresh Map of Life: The Emergence of the Third Age* (Cambridge, Mass.: Harvard University Press, 1991), chap. 3; E. A. Wrigley and Roger Schofield, *The Population History of England, 1541–1871: A Reconstruction* (Cambridge, Mass.: Harvard University Press, 1981), chap. 8; on American rates, see Stone, *The Family, Sex, and Marriage in England*, p. 609; Seccombe, *A Millennium of Family Change*, pp. 225–26.
24. John Gillis, *For Better, For Worse: British Marriages, 1600 to the Present* (New York: Oxford University Press, 1985), chaps. 1–2.
25. Ulrich, *A Midwife's Tale*, pp. 138, 152–67; Gillis, *For Better, For Worse*, chap. 4.
26. Ulrich, *A Midwife's Tale*, pp. 138, 147, 155, 160.
27. Naomi Tadmore, "'Family' and 'Friend' in *Pamela*: A Case Study in the History of the Family in Eighteenth-Century England," *Social History* 14, no. 3 (October 1989): 289–306.
28. On the language of family, see Raymond Williams, *Key Words*, rev. ed. (New York: Oxford University Press, 1983); Petrus Spierenberg, *The Broken Spell: A Cultural and Anthropological History of Preindustrial Europe* (New Brunswick, N.J.: Rutgers University Press, 1991), p. 283; and Jean-Louis Flandrin, *Families in Former Times: Kinship, Household, and Sexuality* (New York: Cambridge University Press, 1979), pp. 4–10. On the languages of household and home, see Orvar Löfgren, "Family and Household: Images and Realities: Cultural Change in Swedish Society," in *Households: Comparative and Historical Structure of the Domestic Group*, eds. R. Netting, R. Wilk, and E. Arnould (Berkeley: University of California Press, 1984), pp. 457–58; and Lawrence Stone and Jeanne C. Stone, *An Open Elite? England, 1540–1880*, abr. ed. (New York: Oxford University Press, 1986), p. 212.
29. Mechal Sobel, *The World They Made Together: Black and White Values in Eighteenth-Century Virginia* (Princeton, N.J.: Princeton University Press, 1987); Herbert G. Gutman, *The Black Family in Slavery and Freedom, 1750–1925* (New York: Random House, 1977).
30. Sobel, *The World They Made Together*, p. 167.

31. Eugene Genovese, *Roll, Jordan, Roll: The World the Slaves Made* (New York: Vintage, 1976), bk. 1; Gutman, *The Black Family.*
32. Robert Darnton, *The Great Cat Massacre and Other Episodes in French Cultural History* (New York: Vintage, 1985).
33. Sobel, *The World They Made Together,* pp. 167ff.
34. Shoumatoff, *The Mountain of Names,* pp. 213–14.
35. As articulated by Mircea Eliade, *Myth and Reality* (New York: Harper & Row, 1974), p. 34.
36. For a general discussion of the modern cult of origins, see Barry Schwartz, "The Social Context of Commemoration: A Study in Collective Memory," *Social Forces* 61, no. 2 (December 1982): 374–402.
37. Alan Macfarlane, *The Family Life of Ralph Josselin* (New York: W. W. Norton, 1970), p. 83.
38. Keith Wrightson, *English Society, 1580–1680* (New Brunswick, N.J.: Rutgers University Press, 1982), pp. 44–51; Ben-Amos, *Adolescence and Youth in Early Modern England,* pp. 54–69.
39. According to Wrightson (*English Society*), the terms "friend" and "kin" were interchangeable (55); Macfarlane, *The Family Life of Ralph Josselin,* chap. 10; Ralph Houlbrooke, *English Family Life, 1576–1716: An Anthology from Diaries* (Oxford: Basil Blackwell, 1989), pp. 219–20.
40. On the language of friendship, see Ellen Rothman, *Hearts and Hands: A History of Courtship in America* (Cambridge, Mass.: Harvard University Press, 1987), p. 36; Macfarlane, *The Family Life of Ralph Josselin,* p. 150.
41. Quoted in Edmund Morgan, *The Puritan Family: Essays on Religion and Domestic Relations in Seventeenth-Century New England* (New York: Harper & Row, 1966), p. 52.
42. Quoted in ibid., p. 49.
43. Irene Quenzler Brown, "Death, Friendship, and Female Identity during New England's Second Great Awakening," *Journal of Family History* 12, no. 4 (1987): 367–87.
44. See Leslie Moch, *Moving Europeans: Migration in Western Europe since 1650* (Bloomington: Indiana University Press, 1992), p. 58.
45. Ulrich, *A Midwife's Tale,* pp. 128–29.
46. Ibid., pp. 218–19.
47. James Fentress and Chris Wickham, *Social Memory* (Oxford: Basil Blackwell, 1992), chap. 3.
48. Michael Ann Williams, *Homeplace: The Social Use and Meaning of Folk Dwellings in Southwestern North Carolina* (Athens: University of Georgia Press, 1993), pp. 48–49.
49. Felicity Heal, *Hospitality in Early Modern England* (Oxford: Clarendon Press, 1990).
50. Stone and Stone, *An Open Elite?* p. 212.
51. Ulrich, *A Midwife's Tale,* pp. 91–94.
52. E. M. Forster, *Marianne Thornton: A Domestic Biography 1797–1887* (New York: Harcourt, Brace, and Co., 1956), p. 32; see also Robert Fishman, *Bourgeois Utopias: The Rise and Fall of Suburbia* (New York: Basic Books, 1987), pp. 51–62.
53. Natalie Zemon Davis, "Ghosts, Kin, and Progeny: Some Features of Family

Life in Early Modern France," in *The Family*, eds. Alice Rossi, Jerome Kagan, and Tamara Hareven (New York: W. W. Norton, 1978), p. 92.

54. Williams, *Key Words*, pp. 140–42.

55. Ulrich, *A Midwife's Tale*, pp. 281–82.

56. Quoted in Fentress and Wickham, *Social Memory*, p. 14.

57. Quoted in Morgan, *The Puritan Family*, p. 20.

58. Stone, *The Family, Sex, and Marriage in England*, p. 56.

59. For a contrary point of view, see David Popenoe, "American Family Decline, 1960–1990," *Journal of Marriage and the Family* 55, no. 3 (August 1993): 527–42.

60. Marina Warner, *Six Myths of Our Time: Little Angels, Little Monsters, Beautiful Beasts, and More* (New York: Vintage, 1994), p. 20.

CHAPTER TWO

1. Judith Stacey, "Good Riddance to 'The Family': A Response to David Popenoe," *Journal of Marriage and the Family* 55, no. 3 (August 1993), p. 545.

2. David Popenoe, "A New Familism: Renewing Families, the Responsive Community," *Current*, no. 150 (February 1993): 36; and Popenoe, "The Family Condition of America: Cultural Change a Public Policy," in *Values and Public Policy*, eds. Henry J. Aaron, Thomas E. Mann, and Timothy Taylor (Washington, D.C.: Brookings Institution, 1994), p. 97.

3. Popenoe, "The Family Condition of America," p. 97.

4. David Popenoe, "American Family Decline, 1960–1990," *Journal of Marriage and the Family* 55, no. 3 (August 1993): 528.

5. Mark Mellman, Edward Lazarus, and Allan Rivlin, "Family Time, Family Values," in *Rebuilding the Nest: A New Commitment to the American Family*, eds. David Blankenhorn, Steven Bayme, and Jean Bethke Elshtain (Milwaukee: Family Service America Press, 1990), pp. 74–75; figures on marriage preference come from Andrew J. Cherlin, *The Changing American Family and Public Policy* (Washington, D.C.: Urban Institute Press, 1988), p. 4; on the value placed on marriage and parenting, see Dennis K. Orthner, "The Family in Transition," in Blankenhorn, Bayme, and Elshtain, *Rebuilding the Nest*, pp. 95, 103.

6. Marion Roberts, *Living in a Man-made World* (London: Routledge, 1991), pp. 9–10.

7. Mellman, Lazarus, and Rivlin, "Family Time, Family Values," p. 83.

8. David Herlihy, *Medieval Households* (Cambridge, Mass.: Harvard University Press, 1985), p. 3.

9. Ibid., pp. 19–27.

10. Clarissa Atkinson, *The Oldest Vocation: Christian Motherhood in the Middle Ages* (Ithaca, N.Y.: Cornell University Press, 1991), pp. 10–11.

11. John Boswell, *Same-Sex Unions in Premodern Europe* (New York: Vintage, 1994), p. 111.

12. The context of these teaching is discussed by Gilbert Meilaender, "A Christian View of the Family," in Blankenhorn, Bayme, and Elshtain, *Rebuilding the Nest*, 133–48.

13. Wayne A. Meeks, *The First Urban Christians: The Social World of the Apostle Paul* (New Haven, Conn.: Yale University Press, 1983).

14. Quoted in Peter Brown, *The Body and Society: Men, Women, and Sexual Renunciation in Early Christianity* (New York: Columbia University Press, 1988), p. 435.

15. Karl Barth, quoted in ibid., pp. 138–39.

16. Carol Delaney, *The Seed and the Soul: Gender and Cosmology in Turkish Village Society* (Berkeley: University of California Press, 1991), pp. 8–24.

17. Quoted in Herlihy, *Medieval Households*, p. 22.

18. Atkinson, *The Oldest Vocation*, chap. 3; Boswell, *Same-Sex Unions*, pp. 118–21.

19. Atkinson, *The Oldest Vocation*, pp. 102–15.

20. Yi-Fu Tuan, *Space and Place: The Perspective of Experience* (Minneapolis: University of Minnesota Press, 1977), p. 182.

21. Quoted by David E. Sopher from "The So-Called Letter to Diogetus," in "The Landscape of Home: Myth, Experience, Social Meaning," in *The Interpretation of Ordinary Landscapes*, ed. D. W. Meinig (New York: Oxford University Press, 1979), p. 135.

22. Gwen Kennedy Neville, *Kinship and Pilgrimage: Rituals of Reunion in American Culture* (New York: Oxford University Press, 1987), p. 17.

23. Victor Turner and Edith Turner, *Image and Pilgrimage in Christian Culture: Anthropological Perspectives* (New York: Columbia University Press, 1988), p. 15.

24. John Bossy, "Blood and Baptism: Kinship, Community, and Christianity in Europe from the Fourteenth to the Seventeenth Centuries," in *Sanctity and Security: The Church and the World*, ed. D. Baker (Oxford: Basil Blackwell, 1973), pp. 129–44.

25. John Bossy, *Christianity in the West, 1400–1700* (New York: Oxford University Press, 1985), chap. 2.

26. Ibid., p. 58.

27. Dorothy Owen, *Church and Society in Medieval Lincolnshire* (Lincoln: Lincolnshire Local History Society, 1971), pp. 124–27.

28. Herlihy, *Medieval Households*, chaps. 2–4.

29. Agnes Heller, *Everyday Life* (London: Routledge and Kegan Paul, 1984), p. 239.

30. Donald Gifford, *The Farthest Shore: A Natural History of Perception* (New York: Vintage, 1991), pp. 71–72.

31. This view still prevails in Islamic rural Turkey; see Delaney, *The Seed and the Soul*, p. 59.

32. Bossy, *Christianity in the West*, pp. 15–18; Bossy, "Blood and Baptism," pp. 133–37; Louis Haass, "Social Connections between Parents and Godparents in Late Medieval Yorkshire," *Medieval Prosopography* 10, no. 1 (1989): 1–21.

33. Mary Ann Clawson, *Constructing Brotherhood: Class, Gender, and Fraternalism* (Princeton, N.J.: Princeton University Press, 1989), pp. 34ff.

34. John Boswell, *The Kindness of Strangers: The Abandonment of Children in Western Europe from Late Antiquity to the Renaissance* (New York: Pantheon, 1988), p. 110; see also chaps. 4–5.

35. On the assistance provided by neighbors, see Keith Wrightson, *English Society, 1580–1680* (New Brunswick, N.J.: Rutgers University Press, 1982), pp. 54–57; Lynn Lees, *Solidarities of Strangers: The English Poor Law and the People, 1700–1948* (New York: Cambridge University Press, 1997); and

Katherine A. Lynch, "Some Long-term Continuities in the History of the Western Family: Individual, Family, and Community Relations," in *The History of Marriage and the Family in Western Society*, ed. Roderick Phillips (Toronto: Canadian Scholars Press, 1995).

36. Clawson, *Constructing Brotherhood*, pp. 30–34; John Gillis, *Youth and History: Continuity and Change in European Age Relations, 1750 to the Present* (New York: Academic Press, 1975), pp. 21–26.

37. Peter Laslett, "Family, Kinship, and Collectivity as Systems of Support in Pre-Industrial Europe: A Consideration of the 'Nuclear-Hardship' Hypothesis," *Continuity and Change* 3, no. 2 (1988): 153–75.

38. Marc Bloch, *Feudal Society*, vol. 1 (London: Routledge and Kegan Paul, 1962), pt. 3.

39. Atkinson, *The Oldest Vocation*, pp. 118, 137.

40. Ibid., p. 192.

41. Ibid., pp. 153, 160–61.

42. Bloch, *Feudal Society*, pt. 3.

43. Bossy, *Christianity in the West*, pp. 7–10.

44. Ibid., p. 11.

45. Thomas Cole, *The Journey of Life: A Cultural History of Aging in America* (Cambridge: Cambridge University Press, 1992), chap. 1; Steven Ozment, *When Fathers Ruled: Family Life in Reformation Europe* (Cambridge, Mass.: Harvard University Press, 1983).

46. Atkinson, *The Oldest Vocation*, pp. 194, 202–4.

47. Bossy, *Christianity in the West*, p. 95.

48. Ferdinand Mount, *The Subversive Family: An Alternative History of Love and Marriage* (London: Jonathan Cape, 1982), p. 27.

49. Edmund Morgan, *The Puritan Family: Essays on Religion and Domestic Religion in Seventeenth-Century New England* (New York: Harper & Row, 1966), chaps. 1–2.

50. Quoted in Charles Taylor, *Sources of the Self: The Making of Modern Identity* (Cambridge, Mass.: Harvard University Press, 1989), p. 226.

51. Ibid., p. 227.

52. Gordon Schochet, *The Authoritarian Family and Political Attitudes in Seventeenth-Century England: Patriarchialism in Political Thought* (New Brunswick, N.J.: Transaction Books, 1988).

53. Lyndal Roper, *The Holy Household: Women and Morals in Reformation Augsburg* (Oxford: Clarendon Press, 1989), chap. 1.

54. Atkinson, *The Oldest Vocation*, pp. 201, 214.

55. Sobel, *The World They Made Together*, Pt. 1; Eugene Genovese, *Roll, Jordon, Roll: The World the Slaves Made* (New York: Vintage, 1976).

56. Cole, *The Journey of Life*, pt. 1.

57. Neville, *Kinship and Pilgrimage*, p. 21.

58. Barry Levy, *Quakers and the American Family: British Quakers in the Delaware Valley, 1650–1765* (New York: Oxford University Press, 1988), pt. 1.

59. Colleen McDannell and Bernhard Lang, *Heaven: A History* (New Haven, Conn.: Yale University Press, 1988), chap. 6; on American Puritans' view of home, see Marilyn Chandler, *Dwelling in the Text: Houses in American Fiction* (Berkeley: University of California Press, 1991), pp. 6–7.

60. Cole, *The Journey of Life*, chap. 2.

61. Bossy, *Christianity in the West*, pp. 34, 117–18.

62. Keith Thomas, *Religion and the Decline of Magic* (New York: Scribner's, 1971), pp. 70–73.

63. Mary Douglas, "The Idea of Home: A Kind of Space," in *Home: A Place in the World*, ed. Arien Mack (New York: New York University Press, 1993), pp. 261–81.

64. On changing perceptions of the public and private, see Lyn Lofland, *A World of Strangers: Order and Action in Urban Public Space* (New York: Basic Books, 1973).

65. John Gillis, *Youth and History*, pp. 21–25; John Demos, *A Little Commonwealth: Family Life in Plymouth Colony* (New York: Oxford University Press, 1970), pp. 77–78.

66. Quoted in David Flaherty, *Privacy in Colonial New England* (Charlottesville: University Press of Virginia, 1972), p. 75; see also Maxine de Wetering, "The Popular Concept of 'Home' in Nineteenth-Century America," *Journal of American Studies* 18, no. 1 (April 1984): p. 18.

67. Leonore Davidoff and Catherine Hall, "The Architecture of Public and Private Life: English Middle-Class Society in a Provincial Town, 1750–1850," in *The Pursuit of Urban History*, eds. D. Fraser and A. Sutcliffe (London: Edward Arnold, 1983), pp. 340–41.

68. Raymond Oldenburg, *The Great Good Place* (New York: Paragon House, 1991), pp. 12–13.

69. J. E. Christopher Hill, *Society and Puritanism in Pre-Revolutionary England* (London: Secker & Warburg, 1964), pp. 443–81.

70. Atkinson, *The Oldest Vocation*, pp. 234–35.

71. William Gouge, *Of Domesticall Duties* (1622), as quoted in John Demos, "Images of the Family, Then and Now," in Demos, *Past, Present, and Personal* (New York: Oxford University Press, 1986), p. 27 (emphasis added).

72. Quoted in Laurel Thatcher Ulrich, *Good Wives: Image and Reality in the Lives of Women in Northern New England, 1650–1750* (New York: Vintage, 1980), p. 3.

73. Ibid.

74. John Lyons, *The Invention of the Self: The Hinge of Consciousness in the Eighteenth Century* (Carbondale: Southern Illinois University Press, 1978), p. 43.

75. David Lowenthal, *The Past Is a Foreign Country* (Cambridge: Cambridge University Press, 1985), p. 198.

76. Peter Berger, *The Sacred Canopy: Elements of a Sociological Theory of Religion* (New York: Anchor, 1967), pp. 37–38.

77. On the city as living memory, see Eugene Rochberg-Halton, *Meaning and Modernity: Social Theory in the Pragmatic Attitude* (Chicago: University of Chicago Press, 1986), chap. 9; on the use of rural landscapes as memory sites, see James Fentress and Chris Wickham, *Social Memory* (Oxford: Basil Blackwell, 1992), pp. 92ff.; on the rites of memory inscribed by the custom of "beating the bounds," see Bob Bushaway, *By Rite: Custom, Ceremony, and Community in England, 1700–1800* (London: Junction Books, 1982), p. 25.

78. The first diagnosis was that of Johannes Hofer (1688), cited in Lowenthal, *The Past Is a Foreign Country*, p. 10.

79. J. E. Christopher Hill, *The World Turned Upside Down: Radical Ideas during the English Revolution* (Harmondsworth, Eng.: Penguin, 1975).

80. Clifford Clark, *The American Family Home, 1800–1860* (Chapel Hill: University of North Carolina Press, 1986), pp. 12–13; Edit Fel and Tamas Hofer, *Baeuerliche Denkweise in Wirtschaft und Haushalt* (Goettingen: Otto Schwartz, 1972), p. 338. Working-class French people still treat their living space as functional; see Pierre Bourdieu, *Distinction: A Social Critique of Judgment and Taste* (London: Routledge, Kegan, Paul, 1984), p. 379.

81. On ghosts, see Gillian Bennett, *Traditions of Belief: Women and the Supernatural* (London: Penguin, 1987), chap. 6; and Theo Brown, *The Fate of the Dead: A Study of Folk Eschatology in the West Country after the Reformation* (Ipswich, Eng.: D. S. Brewer, 1979).

82. Michael Ann Williams, *Homeplace: The Social Use and the Meaning of the Folk Dwelling in Southwestern North Carolina* (Athens: University of Georgia Press, 1991), p. 58.

83. Henry Glassie, *Passing the Time in Balleymenone: Culture and History of an Ulster Community* (Philadelphia: University of Pennsylvania Press, 1982), p. 342.

84. Williams, *Homeplace*, p. 47.

85. Glassie, *Passing the Time in Balleymenone*, p. 238.

86. Clark, *The American Family Home*, pp. 12–16; Fel and Hofer, *Baeuerliche Denkweise*, p. 339.

87. Gillis, *Youth and History*, pp. 14–18.

88. John Gillis, *For Better, For Worse: British Marriages, 1600 to the Present* (New York: Oxford University Press, 1985), pp. 150–59; on American weddings, see Ellen K. Rothman, *Hands and Hearts: A History of Courtship in America* (Cambridge, Mass.: Harvard University Press, 1987), chap. 2; and Williams, *Homeplace*, pp. 48–49.

89. Gillis, *For Better, For Worse*, pp. 76–81, 211–19; Edward P. Thompson, *Customs in Common: Studies in Traditional Popular Culture* (London: Merlin, 1991), chap. 7.

90. R. L. Winstanley, ed., *The Ansford Diary of James Woodford*, vol. 1 (n.p., 1980), p. 20.

91. Berger, *Sacred Canopy*, p. 112.

92. Taylor, *Sources of the Self*, p. 211.

93. David Kunzle, "William Hogarth: The Ravaged Child in the Corrupt City," in *Changing Images of the Family*, eds. Virginia Tufte and Barbara Myerhoff (New Haven, Conn.: Yale University Press, 1979), pp. 99–140. The more innocent image of children was just beginning to emerge in the late eighteenth century; see James Steward, *The New Child: British Art and the Origins of Modern Childhood, 1730–1830* (Berkeley: University Art Museum and Pacific Film Archive, 1995), chap. 8.

CHAPTER THREE

1. John Bender and David E. Wellbery, eds., *Chronotypes: The Construction of Time* (Stanford, Calif.: Stanford University Press, 1991), p. 4.

2. Thomas R. Cole, *The Journey of Life: A Cultural History of Aging in America* (Cambridge: Cambridge University Press, 1992), p. xxx.

3. For a full discussion of chronotypes, see John Bender and David E. Wellbery, eds., *Chronotypes: The Construction of Time* (Stanford, Calif.: Stanford University Press, 1991), pp. 1–15. I owe the notion of the lifetime as a vector of time to Eviatar Zerubavel.

4. Barbara Adam, "Perceptions of Time," *Companion Encyclopedia of Anthropology*, ed. Tim Ingold (London: Routledge, 1994), p. 515.

5. Zygmunt Bauman, *Mortality, Immortality, and Other Life Strategies* (Stanford, Calif.: Stanford University Press, 1992), pp. 142, 163.

6. Cole, *The Journey of Life*, p. 5 (Cole's emphasis).

7. Quoted in ibid., p. 6.

8. Ibid., pp. 7–8.

9. Ibid., pp. xxviii–xxx.

10. Ibid., pp. xxvii–xxvii.

11. David Cheal, "Relationships in Time: Ritual, Social Structure, and the Life Course," *Studies in Symbolic Interaction* 9 (1988): 101.

12. Andrew J. Weigert and Ross Hastings, "Identity, Loss, Family, and Social Change," *American Journal of Sociology* 82, no. 6 (May 1977): 1175–76.

13. Eviatar Zerubavel, *The Fine Line: Making Distinctions in Everyday Life* (New York: Free Press, 1991), p. 1.

14. Eviatar Zerubavel, *Hidden Rhythms: Schedules and Calendars in Social Life* (Chicago: University of Chicago Press, 1981); Zerubavel, *The Seven Day Circle: The History and Meaning of the Week* (New York: Free Press, 1985).

15. Jacques LeGoff, *Time, Work, and Culture in the Middle Ages* (Chicago: University of Chicago Press, 1980), pp. 29–57; Edward P. Thompson, "Time, Work-Discipline, and Industrial Capitalism," in his *Customs in Common: Studies in Traditional Popular Culture* (London: Merlin, 1991), pp. 352–403; David S. Landes, *Revolution in Time: Clocks and the Making of the Modern World* (Cambridge, Mass.: Harvard University Press, 1983).

16. Quoted in Theodore Zeldin, *An Intimate History of Humanity* (New York: HarperCollins, 1995), p. 351.

17. Quoted in Cole, *The Journey of Life*, p. 4.

18. Ibid., p. 15.

19. Donald Gifford, *The Farthest Shore: A Natural History of Perception* (New York: Vintage, 1991), pp. 71–72.

20. R. Porter and D. Porter, *In Sickness and in Health: The British Experience, 1650–1850* (Oxford: Basil Blackwell, 1988), p. 77.

21. Colleen McDannell and Bernard Lang, *Heaven: A History* (New York: Vintage, 1990), chaps. 7–9.

22. David Lowenthal, *The Past Is a Foreign Country* (Cambridge: Cambridge University Press, 1985), pp. 20–34.

23. Jacques LeGoff, *History and Memory*, trans. Steven Rendall and Elizabeth Chamar (New York: Columbia University Press, 1992), pp. 68–80.

24. Gifford, *The Farthest Shore*, p. 72.

25. On the scope of the present in the past, see Robert Muchembled, *Popular Culture and Elite Culture in France, 1400–1700*, trans. Lydia Cochrane (Baton Rouge: Louisiana University Press, 1985), p. 48.

26. Henry Glassie, *Passing the Time in Balleymenone: Culture and History of an Ulster Community* (Philadelphia: University of Pennsylvania Press, 1982), p. 353.

27. Carlo Cipolla, *Clocks and Culture, 1300–1700* (London: Collins, 1957); Cole, *The Journey of Life*, p. 11.

28. Jeremy Rifkin, *Time Wars: The Primary Conflict in Human History* (New York: Henry Holt, 1984), p. 77.

29. Anthony Giddens, *Modernity and Self-Identity: Self and Society in the Late Modern Age* (Stanford, Calif.: Stanford University Press, 1991), pp. 16–17.

30. Quoted in *Notes and Queries*, 6th series, vol. 5 (April 15, 1882): 234–35.

31. *Reports and Transactions of the Devonshire Association*, 1917.

32. Winifred Foley, *A Child in the Forest* (London: Hutchinson, 1978), p. 133.

33. Stanley Brandes, *Forty: The Age and the Symbol* (Knoxville: University of Tennessee Press, 1985), pp. 16, 94–95.

34. George Bourne, *Memoirs of a Surrey Labourer* (London: Duckworth, 1907), p. 8.

35. Wally Seccombe, *A Millennium of Family Change: Feudalism to Capitalism in Northwestern Europe* (London: Verso, 1992), pp. 42–43, 188; Thomas Held, "Rural Retirement Arrangements in Seventeenth to Nineteenth Century Austria," *Journal of Family History* 7, no. 3 (Fall 1982): 227–54.

36. On the variation of life courses, see Harvey J. Graff, *Conflicting Paths: Growing Up in America* (Cambridge, Mass.: Harvard University Press, 1995), chap. 3; on Europe, see Illana Krausman Ben-Amos, *Adolescence and Youth in Early Modern England* (New Haven, Conn.: Yale University Press, 1994).

37. Held, "Rural Retirement Arrangements," pp. 227–54.

38. Quoted from Ben-Amos, *Adolescence and Youth in Early Modern England*, p. 32; see also Arthur Imhof, "Life-Course Patterns of Women and Their Husbands, Sixteenth to Twentieth Century," in *Human Development and the Life Course*, eds. Aage B. Sorensen, et al. (Hillside, N.J.: Erlbaum, 1985).

39. John Gillis, *Youth and History: Continuity and Change in European Age Relations, 1750 to the Present* (New York: Academic Press, 1975), p. 103.

40. Joseph Kett, "Curing the Disease of Precocity," in *Turning Points: Historical and Sociological Essays on the Family*, eds. John Demos and Sarane Boocock (Chicago: Chicago University Press, 1977), pp. 191–94.

41. Cole, *The Journey of Life*, p. 8.

42. Ibid., p. 33.

43. Philippe Ariès, *Centuries of Childhood: A Social History of Family* (New York: Vintage, 1965), chap. 1; Ben-Amos, *Adolescence and Youth in Early Modern England*, pp. 10–11.

44. Ben-Amos, *Adolescence and Youth in Early Modern England*, p. 34.

45. On the concept of postmaturity, see Michael Kearl, *Endings: A Sociology of Death and Dying* (New York: Oxford University Press, 1989), p. 34.

46. Ben-Amos, *Adolescence and Youth in Early Modern England*, p. 37.

47. Quoted in ibid., p. 23.

48. John Bossy, *Christianity in the West, 1400–1700* (New York: Oxford University Press, 1985), p. 97; Keith Thomas, *Religion and the Decline of Magic* (New York: Scribner's, 1971), pp. 603–6.

49. Cole, *The Journey of Life*, pp. 24–28.

50. Ben-Amos, *Adolescence and Youth in Early Modern England*, pp. 23–27.

51. On life planning, see Peter Berger, Brigitte Berger, and Hansfried Kellner, *The Homeless Mind: Modernization and Consciousness* (New York: Vintage, 1973), pp. 72–77.

52. Seccombe, *A Millennium of Family Change*, chaps. 3–4; Daniel Scott Smith, "Old Age and the 'Great Transformation': A New England Case Study," in *Aging and the Elderly*, eds. S. Spicker, K. Woodward, and D. van Tassel (Atlantic Highlands, N.J.: Humanities Press, 1978), pp. 285–302.

53. Natalie Zemon Davis, "Ghosts, Kin, and Progeny: Some Features of Family Life in Early Modern France," in *The Family*, eds. Alice Rossi, Jerome Kagan, and Tamara Hareven (New York: W. W. Norton, 1978), pp. 87–114.

54. Ben-Amos, *Adolescence and Youth in Early Modern England*, p. 15.

55. Even among Protestants, this change of attitude occurred very gradually and unevenly; see Philip Greven, *The Protestant Temperament: Child-Rearing, Religious Experience, and the Self in Early America* (Chicago: University of Chicago Press, 1977).

56. Bossy, *Christianity in the West*, pp. 109–12.

57. Porter and Porter, *In Sickness and in Health*, p. 77.

58. Thomas Cole, "The 'Enlightened' View of Aging: Victorian Morality in a New Key," in *What Does It Mean to Grow Old?* eds. Thomas Cole and Sally Gadow (Durham, N.C.: Duke University Press, 1986), p. 120.

59. David D. Hall, *Worlds of Wonder, Days of Judgment: Popular Religious Belief in Early New England* (New York: Alfred A. Knopf, 1989), chap. 5.

60. John Walzer, "A Period of Ambivalence: Eighteenth Century American Childhood," in *The History of Childhood*, ed. Lloyd de Mause (New York: Psychiatry Press, 1974), p. 358.

61. William Gladstone, *The Gladstone Diaries*, vol. 1, ed. M. Foot (Oxford: Clarendon Press, 1968), pp. ixx, 218.

62. Cole, *The Journey of Life*, p. 113.

63. Quoted in Porter and Porter, *In Sickness and in Health*, p. 251.

64. Hall, *Worlds of Wonder*.

65. Norbert Elias, *The Loneliness of Dying*, trans. Edmund Jephcott (Oxford: Basil Blackwell, 1985), p. 75.

66. Ruth Richardson, *Death, Dissection and the Destitute* (Harmondsworth, Eng.: Penguin, 1988), pp. 272–81; Thomas Laqueur, "Bodies, Death, and Pauper Funerals," *Representations* 1, no. 1 (February 1983): 109–26.

67. Elias, *The Loneliness of Dying*, p. 75.

CHAPTER FOUR

1. Gerald Handel and Robert D. Hess, *Family Worlds: A Psychological Approach to Family Life* (Chicago: University of Chicago Press, 1971), p. 1.

2. On the nature of symbolic universes, see Tamotsu Shibutani, "Reference Groups as Perspectives," *American Journal of Sociology* 60, no. 5 (March 1955): 564; David Unruh, "The Nature of Social Worlds," *Pacific Sociological Review* 22, no. 3 (July 1980): 271–96; Benita Luckmann, "The Small Life-Worlds of Modern Man," in *Phenomenology and Sociology*, ed. Thomas Luck-

mann (Harmondsworth, Eng.: Penguin, 1978), pp. 275–90; and Lyn Lofland, *A World of Strangers: Order and Action in Urban Public Space* (New York: Basic Books, 1973).

3. Peter Berger, *The Sacred Canopy: Elements of a Sociological Theory of Religion* (New York: Doubleday, 1967), p. 6; Peter Berger, Brigitte Berger, and Hansfried Kellner, *The Homeless Mind: Modernization and Consciousness* (New York: Vintage, 1974), p. 66.

4. Berger, *The Sacred Canopy*, p. 28.

5. Thomas Clarkson, *A Portraiture of Quakerism*, 3 vols. (London: Longman, 1806), vol. 1, pp. 296–97.

6. Ibid., vol. 2, pp. 30–41.

7. Mary P. Ryan, *The Empire of the Mother: American Writing about Domesticity* (New York: Haworth, 1982), p. 27.

8. Michael Curlin, "A Question of Manners: Status and Gender in Etiquette and Courtesy," *Journal of Modern History* 57, no. 3 (September 1985): 395–423.

9. Clarkson, *A Portraiture of Quakerism*, vol. 1, pp. 317–56, vol. 2, pp. 3–43; see also J. W. Frost, *The Quaker Family in Colonial America* (New York: St. Martin's Press, 1973); and Barry Levy, *Quakerism and the American Family: British Quakers in the Delaware Valley, 1650–1765* (New York: Oxford University Press, 1988), pp. 60–61.

10. Clarkson, vol. 1, pp. 312, 322–323; on Quaker language, see Richard Bauman, *Let Your Words Be Few: Symbolism of Speaking and Silence among Seventeenth Century Quakers* (Cambridge: Cambridge University Press, 1983), chaps. 2 and 4.

11. Ryan, *The Empire of the Mother*, p. 23.

12. Leonore Davidoff and Catherine Hall, *Family Fortunes: Men and Women of the English Middle Class, 1780–1850* (London: Hutchinson, 1987), chaps. 4 and 7.

13. Steven Ruggles, *Prolonged Connections: The Rise of the Extended Family in Nineteenth Century England and America* (Madison: University of Wisconsin Press, 1987).

14. Davidoff and Hall, *Family Fortunes*, chaps. 5–6.

15. Ibid., p. 221; Ryan, *The Empire of the Mother*, pp. 138–39.

16. Davidoff and Hall, *Family Fortunes*, pp. 219–21.

17. Quoted in ibid., p. 222.

18. On Quakers, see Levy, *Quakerism and the American Family*, pp. 70–75, 243–50; see also Davidoff and Hall, *Family Fortunes*, pp. 216–21.

19. Henry Makepeace Thackeray, "De Juvenete," *Roundabout Papers* (London: Smith, 1869), p. 232.

20. John Stuart Mill, "Spirit of the Age," in his *Essays in Politics and Culture*, ed. Gertrude Himmelfarb (Garden City, N.Y.: Doubleday, 1963), p. 3.

21. Henry Stowell, "The Age We Live In," in *Exeter Hall Lectures*, vol. 6 (London, 1850–51), pp. 45–46.

22. Quoted in Walter Houghton, *The Victorian Frame of Mind* (New Haven, Conn.: Yale University Press, 1957), p. 66.

23. Matthew Arnold, "On the Modern Element in Literature" (lecture given at Oxford, 1856), in *Essays by Matthew Arnold* (London, 1914), p. 468 (Arnold's emphasis).

24. Walter Pater, "Coleridge," quoted in Houghton, *The Victorian Frame of Mind*, p. 64.

25. John Stuart Mill, *The Letters of John Stuart Mill*, vol. 2, ed. Hugh Elliott (London: Longman, 1910), p. 359.

26. Early nineteenth–century Baptist, quoted in Ryan, *The Empire of the Mother*, p. 67.

27. Ibid., pp. 80–102; see also Deborah Valenze, *Prophetic Sons and Daughters: Female Preaching and Popular Religion in Industrial England* (Princeton, N.J.: Princeton University Press, 1989), chaps. 1–3.

28. *Mother's Monthly Journal* (1836), quoted in Ryan, *The Empire of the Mother*, p. 101.

29. John Gillis, *Youth and History: Continuity and Change in European Age Relations, 1750 to the Present* (New York: Academic Press, 1975), chap. 3; Joseph Kett, *Rites of Passage: Adolescence in America, 1790 to the Present* (New York: Basic Books, 1977), pp. 199–204; E. Anthony Rotundo, *American Manhood: Transformations in Masculinity from the Revolution to the Modern Era* (New York: Basic Books, 1993), pp. 61–74.

30. Ryan, *The Empire of the Mother*, chap. 3.

31. Mark Carnes, *Secret Ritual and Manhood in Victorian America* (New Haven, Conn.: Yale University Press, 1989).

32. J. F. C. Harrison, *The Second Coming: Popular Millenialism, 1780–1850* (New Brunswick, N.J.: Rutgers University Press, 1979), pp. 22, 28, 166–73.

33. On the Mormons and various antinomians, see John Gillis, *For Better, For Worse: British Marriages, 1600 to the Present* (New York: Oxford University Press, 1985), pp. 219–24.

34. Spencer Klaw, *Without Sin: The Life and Death of the Oneida Community* (New York: Allen Lane, 1993).

35. Owen quoted in Barbara Taylor, *Eve and the New Jerusalem: Socialism and Feminism in the Nineteenth Century* (New York: Vintage, 1983), p. 48.

36. Quoted in ibid., p. 34; for more on Owenite notions of family, see Gillis, *For Better, For Worse*, pp. 224–28.

37. On working-class kin ties, see Michael Anderson, *Family Structure in Nineteenth Century Lancashire* (Cambridge: Cambridge University Press, 1971), chaps. 8 and 10; Stephanie Coontz, *The Social Origins of Private Life: A History of American Families, 1600–1900* (London: Verso, 1988), chap. 8; and Wally Seccombe, *Weathering the Storm: Working-Class Families from the Industrial Revolution to the Fertility Decline* (London: Verso, 1993), pp. 64–69.

38. Ruggles, *Prolonged Connections*, chaps. 8 and 10; Coontz, *The Social Origins of Private Life*, chap. 9.

39. Davidoff and Hall, *Family Fortunes*, pp. 364–69.

40. Charles Taylor, "The Politics of Recognition," in *Multiculturalism: Examining the Politics of Recognition*, ed. Amy Gutman (Princeton, N.J.: Princeton University Press, 1992), pp. 31–37.

41. On the growing idealization, particularly of mothers, see Orvar Löfgren and Jonas Frykman, *Culture Builders: A Historical Anthropology of Middle-Class Life* (New Brunswick, N.J.: Rutgers University Press, 1987), pp. 118–25; see also Jonathan Gathorne-Hardy, *The Rise and Fall of the British Nanny* (London: Hodder and Stoughton, 1972).

42. On this crisis of faith, see Houghton, *The Victorian Frame of Mind*, pp. 58–60.

43. Baldwin Brown, *The Home Life: In the Light of Its Divine Idea* (London, 1866), and Charles Kingsley, *Letters and Memories of His Life* (London, 1877), both quoted in ibid., p. 347; see also Clifford Clark, *The American Family Home, 1800–1860* (Chapel Hill: University of North Carolina Press, 1986), pp. 29–30.

44. Berger, *The Sacred Canopy*, pp. 37–38.

45. Alain Corbin, "Backstage," in *A History of Private Life*, vol. 4, ed. Michelle Perrot (Cambridge, Mass.: Harvard University Press, 1990), p. 465.

46. For a discussion of the current phenomenon, see Mark Slouka, *War of the Worlds: Cyberspace and the High-Tech Assault on Reality* (New York: Basic Books, 1995), chap. 5.

47. Arlene Skolnick, "Public Images, Private Realities: The American Family in Popular Culture and Social Science," in *Changing Images of the Family*, eds. Virginia Tufte and Barbara Myerhoff (New Haven, Conn.: Yale University Press, 1979), pp. 297–315.

48. Viviana Zelizer, *Pricing the Priceless Child: The Changing Social Value of Children* (New York: Basic Books, 1985), chap. 1.

49. Peter Knobel, "Rites of Passage: Jewish Rites," in *The Encyclopedia of Religion*, vol. 12 (New York: Macmillan, 1987), p. 393; Lesley Hargreaves, "The Rites of Passage of Baptism, Marriage, and Death in Shotten Colliery" (B.A. thesis, Leeds University, 1982), pp. 37–39.

50. Jenna Weissman Joselit, *The Wonders of America: Reinventing Jewish Culture, 1880–1950* (New York: Hill and Wang, 1994), chap. 3; J. D. C. Fisher, *Confirmation Then and Now* (London: Society for the Propagation of Christian Knowledge, 1978), pp. 138–42.

51. Joan Kron, *Home-Psych: The Social Psychology of Home and Decoration* (New York: Crown, 1983), pp. 17–18, 148–52.

52. Joan Busfield and Michael Paddon, *Thinking about Children: Sociology and Fertility in Post-War Britain* (Cambridge: Cambridge University Press, 1977), pp. 134–66.

53. Lois Banner, "The Meaning of Menopause: Aging and Its Historical Contexts in the Twentieth Century," Working Papers, Center for Twentieth-Century Studies, University of Wisconsin at Milwaukee (Fall-Winter 1989–90), pp. 21–23; on fears of the indulgent grandparent in eighteenth-century America, see John Demos, *Past, Present, and Personal: The Family and the Life Course in American History* (New York: Oxford University Press, 1986), pp. 153–54.

54. Maurice Aughulon, *Marianne into Battle: Republican Imagery and Symbolism in France, 1789–1880* (Cambridge: Cambridge University Press, 1981); Marina Warner, *Monuments and Maidens: The Allegory of the Female Form* (London: Pan Books, 1985).

55. One of the Goncourt brothers, quoted in Anne Martin-Fugier, "Bourgeois Rituals," in *A History of Private Life*, vol. 4, ed. Michelle Perrot (Cambridge, Mass.: Harvard University Press, 1990), p. 322.

56. On the changing definition of *family*, see Raymond Williams, *Key Words*, rev. ed. (New York: Oxford University Press, 1983), pp. 131–34.

57. K. C. Phillips, *Language and Class in Victorian England* (Oxford: Basil Blackwell, 1984), pp. 160–72; Julie M. Gricar, "How Thick Is Blood? The Social

Construction and Cultural Configuration of Kinship" (Ph.D. dissertation, Columbia University, 1990), pp. 82–84, 271–72.

58. Benedict Anderson, *Imagined Communities: Reflections on the Origin and Spread of Nationalism* (London: Verso, 1983).

59. Alexander Shoumatoff, *The Mountain of Names: A History of the Human Family* (New York: Simon & Schuster, 1985), p. 123.

60. Martin-Fugier, "Bourgeois Rituals," pp. 324–25.

61. Corbin, "Backstage," p. 457.

62. Gricar, "How Thick Is Blood?" pp. 276–82.

63. On family Bibles, see Colleen McDannell, *The Christian Home in Victorian America, 1840–1900* (Bloomington: Indiana University Press, 1986), pp. 39–40, 103–4; see also Katherine Grier, *Culture and Comfort: People, Parlors, and Upholstery, 1850–1930* (Amherst: University of Massachusetts Press, 1988), pp. 8–15.

64. Shoumatoff, *The Mountain of Names*, pp. 213–24; Anthony Richard Wagner, *English Genealogy* (Oxford: Clarendon Press, 1972), p. 401.

65. Shoumatoff, *The Mountain of Names*, p. 214.

66. Lawrence Stone and Jeanne C. Stone, *An Open Elite? England, 1540–1880*, abr. ed. (New York: Oxford University Press, 1986), pt. 3.

67. Keith Thomas, *Religion and the Decline of Magic* (New York: Scribner's, 1971), p. 642.

68. Corbin, "Backstage," pp. 545–47.

69. Marcel Pagnol, *My Father's Glory; and, My Mother's Castle* (London: Picador, 1991).

70. Corbin, "Backstage," pp. 530–31; Löfgren and Frykman, *Culture Builders*, pp. 78–79; Gricar, "How Thick Is Blood?" p. 57; Marvin B. Sussman, "Pet/Human Bonding: Applications, Conceptual and Research Issues," in *Pets and Family*, ed. Marvin Sussman (New York: Haworth Press, 1985), pp. 1–30; Marc Shell, "The Family Pet," *Representations*, no. 15 (Summer 1986): 121–53.

71. Corbin, "Backstage," p. 530.

72. On America, see Karen Halttunen, *Confidence Men and Painted Women: A Study of Middle Class Culture in America, 1830–1870* (New Haven, Conn.: Yale University Press, 1982), chap. 6; on the staging of middle-class life in Sweden, see Löfgren and Frykman, *Culture Builders*, pp. 126–43; Clark, *The American Family Home*, p. 42; McDannell, *The Christian Home in Victorian America*, pp. 88–89; on the theatricality of Victorians more generally, see Nina Auerbach, *Private Theatricals: The Lives of the Victorians* (Cambridge, Mass.: Harvard University Press, 1990).

73. Jeanne Boydston, *Home and Work: Housework, Wages, and the Ideology of Labor in the Early Republic* (New York: Oxford University Press, 1992), p. 149.

74. Quoted without attribution in Martin-Fugier, "Bourgeois Rituals," p. 270.

75. Quoted in Jennie Calder, *The Victorian Home* (London: Batsford, 1977), p. 145 (Calder's emphasis).

76. Martha Vicinus, *Independent Women: Work and Community for Single Women, 1850–1920* (Chicago: University of Chicago Press, 1985).

77. Martin-Fugier, "Bourgeois Rituals," pp. 330–31. Recent research indicates that women are the family storytellers, though the stories are often about male

family "heroes"; Peter Martin, Gundhild Hagestad, and Patrick Diedrich, "Family Stories: Events (Temporarily) Remembered," *Journal of Marriage and the Family* 50 (May 1988): 533–41.

78. Harriet Blodgett, *Centuries of Female Days: Englishwomen's Private Diaries* (New Brunswick, N.J.: Rutgers University Press, 1988), pp. 37–40, 57–58.

79. Martin-Fugier, "Bourgeois Rituals," p. 266.

80. Steven Stowe, *Intimacy and Power in the Old South: Ritual in the Lives of the Planters* (Baltimore: Johns Hopkins University Press, 1987), pp. 3–4, 90–96.

81. Stephen Papson, "From Symbolic Exchange to Bureaucratic Discourse: The Hallmark Greeting Card," *Theory, Culture, Society* 3, no. 2 (1986): 99–111; William B. Waits, *The Modern Christmas in America: A Cultural History of Gift Giving* (New York: New York University Press, 1993), chaps. 4–5.

82. Martin-Fugier, "Bourgeois Rituals," pp. 263–64.

83. Susan Sontag, *On Photography* (New York: Delta, 1972), p. 9; see also Eugene Rochberg-Halton, *Meaning and Modernity: Social Theory in the Pragmatic Attitude* (Chicago: University of Chicago Press, 1986), pp. 166–67, 170; Gunhild Hagestad, "Dimensions of Time and the Family," *American Behavioral Scientist* 29, no. 6 (July-August 1986): 689.

84. David Cheal, *The Gift Economy* (London: Routledge, 1988), p. 7.

85. Martin-Fugier, "Bourgeois Rituals," pp. 264–65.

86. Margaret Deland, "Christmas Giving," *Harper's Bazaar* 38 (December 1904), quoted in William B. Waits, *The Modern Christmas in America: A Cultural History of Gift Giving* (New York: New York University Press, 1993), p. 71; on the symbolic meaning of Christmas today, see Theodore Caplow, "Rule Enforcement without Visible Means: Christmas Gift Giving in Middletown," *American Journal of Sociology* 89, no. 6 (May 1984): 1306–23; Caplow, "Christmas Gifts and Kin Networks," *American Sociological Review* 47, no. 3 (June 1982): 383–92.

87. Gwen Neville, *Kinship and Pilgrimage: Rituals of Reunion in American Protestant Culture* (New York: Oxford University Press, 1987), chap. 3.

88. Theodore C. Humphrey and Linda Humphrey, eds., *"We Gather Together": Food and Festival in American Life* (Ann Arbor, Mich.: UMI Research Press, 1988), pp. 20–25; on family rituals generally, see David Cheal, "Relationships in Time: Ritual, Social Structure, and the Life Course," *Studies in Symbolic Interaction* 9 (1988): 83–109. It is important to note that most kin and memory work has been done by women; see Micaela di Leonardo, "The Female World of Cards and Holidays: Women, Families, and the Work of Kinship," *Signs* 11, no. 3 (1987): 440–53; Carolyn J. Rosenthal and Victor Marshall, "Generational Traumas of Family Ritual," *American Behavioral Scientist* 31, no. 6 (July-August 1988): 669–84.

89. Shoumatoff, *The Mountain of Names*, pp. 12–13, 218.

90. Martine Segalen, *Historical Anthropology of the Family* (Cambridge: Cambridge University Press, 1986), p. 100.

CHAPTER FIVE

1. Michael Young, *The Metronomic Society: Natural Rhythms and Human Timetables* (Cambridge, Eng.: Cambridge University Press, 1986), p. 100

2. Edward T. Hall, *Dance of Life: The Other Dimensions of Time* (New York: Anchor Books, 1983). See also Eviatar Zerubavel, *Hidden Rhythms: Schedules and Calendars in Social Life* (Chicago: University of Chicago Press, 1981).

3. David Harvey, *The Post-Modern Condition: An Enquiry into the Origins of Cultural Change* (Oxford: Basil Blackwell, 1989), chap. 16.

4. David Cheal, "Relationships in Time: Ritual, Social Structure, and the Life Course," *Studies in Symbolic Interaction* 9 (1988): 101; see also Gunhild Hagestad, "Dimensions of Time and the Family," *American Behavioral Scientist* 29, no. 6 (July-August 1986): 679–94.

5. Andrew J. Weigert and Ross Hastings, "Identity, Loss, Family, and Social Change," *American Journal of Sociology* 82, no. 6 (May 1977): 1175–76.

6. Martin Kohli, "The World We Forgot: A Historical Review of the Life Course," in *Later Life: The Social Psychology of Aging*, ed. Victor Marshall (Beverly Hills, Calif.: Sage, 1986): pp. 271–303.

7. John Gillis, *Commemorations: The Politics of National Identity* (Princeton, N.J.: Princeton University Press, 1994), pp. 3–24; see also Michael Kammen, *Mystic Chords of Memory: The Transformation of Tradition in American Culture* (New York: Alfred A. Knopf, 1991); Mona Ozouf, *Festivals and the French Revolution* (Cambridge, Mass.: Harvard University Press, 1988), chap. 7; Zerubavel, *Hidden Rhythms*, chap. 3.

8. Kohli, "The World We Forgot," pp. 280–82.

9. Leonard Cain, "Aging and the Law," in *Handbook on Aging and Social Sciences*, eds. Robert Binstock and Ethel Scanas (New York: Van Nostrand Reinhold, 1976), pp. 342–68.

10. Joseph Kett, *Rites of Passage: Adolescence in America, 1790 to the Present* (New York: Basic Books, 1977), pt. 2; John Gillis, *Youth and History: Continuity and Change in European Age Relations, 1750 to the Present* (New York: Academic Press, 1975), chaps. 2–3.

11. Gerald Gruman, "The Cultural Origins of Present-Day 'Ageism': The Modernization of the Life Cycle," in *Aging and the Elderly*, eds. S. Spicker, K. Woodward, and D. van Tassel (Atlantic Highlands, N.J.: Humanities Press, 1978), p. 360.

12. John Modell, Frank F. Furstenberg Jr., and Theodore Herschberg, "Social Change and Life Course Development in Historical Perspective," *Journal of Family History* 1, no. 1 (Fall 1976): 7–32; Michael Anderson, "The Emergence of the Modern Life Cycle in Britain," *Social History* 10, no. 1 (January 1985): 69–87.

13. Anderson, "The Emergence of the Modern Life Cycle," pp. 85–87; Thomas R. Cole, *The Journey of Life: A Cultural History of Aging in America* (Cambridge: Cambridge University Press, 1992), pt. 3.

14. Peter Laslett, "Societal Development and Aging," in *Handbook of Aging and the Social Sciences*, eds. R. Binstock and E. Shanas (New York: Van Nostrand Reinhold, 1985), pp. 199–230.

15. Cole, *The Journey of Life*, chap. 5.

16. Don Gifford, *The Farther Shore: A Natural History of Perception, 1798–1984* (New York: Vintage Books, 1991), p. 73.

17. The term was first used in English in 1770; see Theodore Zeldin, *An Intimate History of Humanity* (New York: HarperCollins, 1995), p. 351.

18. Thomas Cole, "Aging, Meaning, and Well-being: Musings of a Cultural Historian," *International Journal of Aging and Human Development* 19, no. 4 (1984): 332–34; Gruman, "Cultural Origins of Present-Day 'Ageism,'" pp. 365–70.
19. Cole, *The Journey of Life*, chap. 9.
20. W. Andrew Achenbaum, "The Aging of 'The First New Nation,'" in *Our Aging Society: Paradox and Promise*, eds. Alan Pifer and Lydia Bronte (New York: W. W. Norton, 1986), p. 21.
21. Peter Laslett, *A Fresh Map of Life: The Emergence of the Third Age* (Cambridge, Mass.: Harvard University Press, 1991), chap. 3; on the cult of youth at the end of the century, see Robert Wohl, *The Generation of 1914* (Cambridge, Mass.: Harvard University Press, 1979), chap. 6.
22. Cole, *The Journey of Life*, p. 80.
23. Gruman, "Origins of Present-Day 'Ageism,'" p. 363.
24. On the renaming of old age shelters as "homes," see Cole, *The Journey of Life*, pp. 204ff.
25. As quoted in ibid., p. 144; see also Susan Tamke, "Human Values and Aging: The Perspective of the Victorian Nursery," in Spicker, Woodward, and van Tassel, *Aging and the Elderly*, pp. 63–87.
26. In the seventeenth century, middle-aged women were more likely than older women to be stigmatized as witches. By the nineteenth century, witches were invariably depicted as "old crones"; see John Demos, *Entertaining Satan: Witchcraft and the Culture of Early New England* (New York: Oxford University Press, 1987), pp. 391–92.
27. Gruman, "Origins of Present-Day 'Ageism,'" p. 363.
28. John Gillis, "Vanishing Youth: The Uncertain Place of the Young in a Global Age," *Young* 1, no. 1 (April 1993): 5–12.
29. Gillis, *Youth and History*, chap. 4.
30. John Gillis, *For Better, For Worse: British Marriages, 1600 to the Present* (New York: Oxford University Press, 1985), chap. 9.
31. Frank F. Furstenberg Jr. and Andrew Cherlin, *The New American Grandparenthood: A Place in the Family, A Life Apart* (New York: Basic Books, 1986); Gunhild Hagestad, "The Family: Women and Grandparents as Kin-Keepers," in Pifer and Bronte, *Our Aging Society*, pp. 141–160.
32. Ozouf, *Festivals and the French Revolution*.
33. Mrs. Taylor, *Practical Hints to Young Females on the Duties of a Wife, a Mother, and a Mistress of a Family* (1815), quoted in Leonore Davidoff and Catherine Hall, *Family Fortunes: Men and Women of the English Middle Class, 1780–1850* (London: Hutchinson, 1987), p. 176 (Davidoff and Hall's emphasis).
34. Cited in Lynn Mahoney, "'Order and Method': Visions of Housework in American Cookery Books, 1800–1860" (seminar paper, Rutgers University, May 1990), p. 17.
35. Mrs. Sarah Ellis, *Women of England, Their Social Duties and Domestic Habits* (London: Rischer, 1838), pp. 55–56.
36. Harvey, *The Post-Modern Condition*, p. 202.
37. Margaret Visser, *The Rituals of Dinner: The Origins, Evolution, Eccentricities, and Meaning of Table Manners* (New York: Grove and Weidenfeld, 1991), pp. 147, 277–80.

38. Quoted in Barbara Carson, *Ambitious Appetites: Dining, Behavior, and Patterns of Consumption in Federal Washington* (Washington, D.C.: American Institute of Architects Press, 1990), p. 122.

39. Visser, *The Rituals of Dinner*, p. 281.

40. Carson, *Ambitious Appetites*, p. 29.

41. Chevalier, quoted in Harvey Levenstein, *Paradox of Plenty: A Social History of Eating in Modern America* (New York: Oxford University Press, 1993), p. 8. The tradition of silent, quick eating remains in rural Ireland and Wales; see Henry Glassie, *Passing the Time in Balleymenone: Culture and History of an Ulster Community* (Philadelphia: University of Pennsylvania Press, 1982), pp. 358–60.

42. Charles Dickens, *American Notes for General Circulation* (1842), quoted in John Kasson, *Rudeness and Civility: Manners in Nineteenth-Century America* (New York: Hill and Wang, 1990), p. 186.

43. Visser, *The Rituals of Dinner*, p. 159.

44. Ibid., pp. 29–48; Davidoff and Hall, *Family Fortunes*, pp. 385–86.

45. Quoted in Kasson, *Rudeness and Civility*, p. 187.

46. Visser, *The Rituals of Dinner*, pp. 82, 147–49.

47. Ibid., p. 82.

48. Levenstein, *Paradox of Plenty*, p. 20.

49. Wolfgang Schivelbusch, *Disenchanted Night: The Introduction of Light in the Nineteenth Century* (Berkeley: University of California Press, 1988), pp. 158–62; Visser, *The Rituals of Dinner*, p. 160.

50. Carson, *Ambitious Appetites*, chap. 3; K. C. Phillips, *Language and Class in Victorian England* (Oxford: Basil Blackwell, 1984), pp. 24–27.

51. James Bossard and Eleanor Bell, *Ritual in Family Living: A Contemporary Study* (Philadelphia: University of Pennsylvania Press, 1950), p. 100.

52. Leonore Davidoff, "The Rationalization of Housework," in *Dependence and Exploitation in Work and Marriage*, eds. Diana Leonard Baker and Sheila Allen (London: Longman, 1976), pp. 124–35; Carson, *Ambitious Appetites*, pp. 74–75; Visser, *The Rituals of Dinner*, pp. 159–60.

53. Hugh McLeod, *Religion and the People of Western Europe* (Oxford: Oxford University Press, 1981), p. 109.

54. Quoted in Levenstein, *Paradox of Plenty*, p. 20.

55. H. Thompson (1880), quoted in Stephen Mennell, *All Manners of Food: Eating and Taste in England and France from the Middle Ages to the Present* (Oxford: Basil Blackwell, 1985), p. 206.

56. Visser, *The Rituals of Dinner*, pp. 345–46.

57. Levenstein, *Paradox of Plenty*, p. 163.

58. Nils-Arvid Bringeus, "Beten bei Tisch," in *Sozialkultur der Familie*, eds. A. C. Bimmer and I. Weber-Kellerman (Geissen, 1982), pp. 58–79.

59. For a discussion of how temporal regularity contributes to reification, see Zerubavel, *Hidden Rhythms*, pp. 42–43; and Davidoff, "The Rationalization of Housework," pp. 124–37. On the contrast between French working class and bourgeois eating habits, see Pierre Bourdieu, *Distinction: A Social Critique of the Judgement of Taste* (London: Routledge and Kegan Paul, 1984), pp. 195–202.

60. Visser, *The Rituals of Dinner*, p. 49; *New York Times*, December 5, 1990.

61. Ellen Ross, *Love and Toil: Motherhood in Outcaste London* (New York: Oxford University Press, 1993), pp. 31–36.

62. Kasson, *Rudeness and Civility*, pp. 206–7.

63. Quoted in Visser, *The Rituals of Dinner*, p. 240. On the didactic quality of Victorian family dinners, see Bringeus, "Beten bei Tisch," p. 70.

64. On ritualism, see T. Jackson Lears, *No Place for Grace: Antimodernism and the Transformation of American Culture, 1880–1920* (New York: Pantheon, 1981), pp. 194–96.

65. Marcel Proust, *Remembrance of Things Past*, quoted in Visser, *The Rituals of Dinner*, p. 29; on the connections between memory and food, see Sidney Mintz, *Sweetness and Power: The Place of Sugar in Modern History* (New York: Vintage, 1985), pp. 87–94.

66. Shlomo Deshen, "Domestic Observance: Jewish Practice," in *The Encyclopedia of Religion*, vol. 4 (New York: Macmillan, 1987), pp. 401–2; see also Jenna Weissman Joselit, *The Wonders of America: Reinventing Jewish Culture, 1880–1950* (New York: Hill and Wang, 1994), chap. 5.

67. Many working-class families in Britain lacked kitchen facilities until after the Second World War. They would send Sunday dinner to be cooked in a baker's shop, the same place where they bought their bread; Mennell, *All Manners of Food*, p. 219.

68. Anne Murcott, " 'It's a Pleasure to Cook for Him': Food, Mealtimes, and Gender in some South Wales Households," in *The Public and Private*, ed. Eva Gamarreikow (London: Heinemann, 1983), p. 87; Michael Bird and Pam Mills, "What People Eat," *New Society* (December 21, 1972): 684–85.

69. *New York Times*, December 5, 1990.

70. Juliet Shor, *The Overworked Americans: The Unexpected Decline of Leisure* (New York: Basic Books, 1991), chap. 1; Witold Rybczynski, *Waiting for the Weekend* (New York: Viking, 1991), pp. 19–20, 223–34.

71. Barbara Myerhoff, "Rites and Signs of Ripening: The Intertwining of Ritual, Time, and Growing Older," in *Age and Anthropological Theory*, eds. David Kertzer and Jennie Keith (Ithaca, N.Y.: Cornell University Press, 1984), p. 306; see also Carolyn J. Rosenthal and Victor Marshall, "Generational Transmission of Family Ritual," *American Behavioral Scientist* 31, no. 6 (July-August 1988): 669–84.

72. On other dimensions of this symbolic process, see Benedict Anderson, *Imagined Communities: Reflections on the Origins and Spread of Nationalism* (London: Verso, 1983).

73. This tendency toward exaggeration is reflected in the 85 percent of adults claiming to remember that, when they were young, their families always ate together. "The Struggle to Keep Family Time Quality Time," *New York Times*, December 5, 1990.

74. Lewis quoted in "The Struggle to Keep Family Time Quality Time," *New York Times*, May 12, 1988; see also Visser, *The Rituals of Dinner*, p. 97.

75. Schivelbusch, *Disenchanted Night*, pp. 157–86.

76. Helene R. Roberts, "Marriage, Redundancy, or Sin: The Painter's View of Women in the First Twenty-five Years of Victoria's Reign," in *Suffer and Be Still: Women in the Victorian Age*, ed. Martha Vicinus (Bloomington: Indiana University Press, 1973), pp. 45–76.

77. John Demos, *Past, Present, and Personal: The Family and the Life Course in American History* (New York: Oxford University Press, 1986), pp. 60–61; David Roberts, "The Paterfamilias of the Victorian Governing Class," in *The Victorian Family*, ed. Richard Wohl (London: Croom Helm, 1978), p. 64.

78. The term "quality time" was first used in the 1950s, but the notion dates back to the Victorian period; see Robert Griswold, *Fatherhood in America: A History* (New York: Basic Books, 1993), pp. 202–3.

79. Bossard and Boll, *Ritual in Family Living*, p. 101.

80. In two-earner families, bedtime has been pushed back by two to three hours over the past couple of decades; "The Battle of Bedtime: Children Won," *New York Times*, March 1, 1990.

81. Quoted in Demos, *Past, Present, and Personal*, p. 61.

82. Karen Hausen, "Mothers, Sons, and the Sale of Symbols and Goods: The 'German Mother's Day,' 1923–33," in *Interests and Emotions: Essays on the Study of Family and Kinship*, eds. Hans Medick and David Sabean (Cambridge: Cambridge University Press, 1984), pp. 371–413; Leigh Eric Schmidt, *Consumer Rites: The Buying and Selling of American Holidays* (Princeton, N.J.: Princeton University Press, 1995), chap. 5.

83. Vivien Hughes, *A London Child of the 1870s* (Oxford: Oxford University Press, 1977), p. 71.

84. Rybczynski, *Waiting for the Weekend*, pp. 71–74.

85. Ibid., p. 71.

86. Colleen McDannell, *The Christian Home in Victorian America, 1840–1900* (Bloomington: Indiana University Press, 1986), p. 93.

87. Rybczynski, *Waiting for the Weekend*, pp. 75–76, 105–7, 138; "Social Changes in Britain: The Full Survey," *New Society* (December 27, 1962): 29.

88. Rybczynski, *Waiting for the Weekend*, p. 230.

89. Davidoff, "The Rationalization of Housework," pp. 134–35; Kasson, *Rudeness and Civility*, pp. 206–7.

90. D. A. Reid, "The Decline of Saint Monday, 1766–1876," *Past and Present*, no. 71 (May 1976): 76–101.

91. Bossard and Boll, *Ritual in Family Living*, pp. 94, 160.

92. A. K. Hamilton Jenkins, *Cornish Homes and Customs* (London: Dent, 1934), p. 184.

93. John A. Pimlott, *The Englishman's Christmas: A Social History* (Atlantic Highlands, N.J.: Humanities Press, 1978), pp. 71–72; for an account of an eighteenth-century mumming, see *The Ansford Diary of James Woodforde*, vol. 2, ed. R. L. Winstanley (n.p., 1979), pp. 86–87. Guising did not completely disappear until World War I in Cornwall; A. K. Hamilton Jenkins, *Cornish Homes and Customs* (London: Dent, 1934), p. 184.

94. Bob Bushaway, *By Rite: Custom, Ceremony, and Community in England, 1700–1800* (London: Junction Books, 1982), pp. 24–25, 38–42, 149–59; see also Robert Malcolmson, *Popular Recreation in English Society, 1700–1850* (Cambridge: Cambridge University Press, 1973), p. 27.

95. Robert Myers, *Celebrations: The Complete Book of American Holidays* (Garden City, N.Y.: Doubleday, 1972), pp. 342–43.

96. As late as 1874, Henry Ward Beecher remarked: "To me Christmas is a foreign day"; quoted in Philip Snyder, *December 25th: The Joys of Christmas Past*

(New York: Dodd Mead, 1985), p. xiii; see also Pimlott, *The Englishman's Christmas*, chap. 7.

97. *Notes and Queries*, 1st series, vol. 12 (October 20, 1855): 298. One place where Christmas actually developed strength in the nineteenth century was Newfoundland; see Gerald Sider, "Christmas Mumming and the New Year in Ouport Newfoundland," *Past and Present* 71 (May 1976): 115–25.

98. Oliver Heywood, quoted in Hugh Cunningham, *Leisure in the Industrial Revolution, 1780–1880* (London: Croom Helm, 1980), pp. 101–2.

99. The paternalist rituals lasted longer in the countryside; see Pamela Horn, *Labouring Life in the Victorian Countryside* (Dublin: Gill and Macmillan, 1976), p. 158. Working-class rites are discussed in Eileen Yeo, "Culture and Constraint in Working-Class Movements," in *Popular Culture and Class Conflict, 1590–1914*, eds. Steven Yeo and Eileen Yeo (Brighton, Eng.: Harvester, 1981), pp. 155–86.

100. Quoted in Pimlott, *The Englishman's Christmas*, p. 89.

101. Pimlott argues that the new Christmas was an "essentially Christian Socialist institution," emphasizing charity rather than real social change; ibid., p. 88.

102. George Buday, *The History of the Christmas Card* (London: Spring Books, 1964), pp. 8, 44, 137–52, 187–88; on American practices, see William B. Waits, *The Modern Christmas in America* (New York: New York University Press, 1993), chaps. 1–5; Schmidt, *Consumer Rites*, chap. 3.

103. Hughes, *A London Child of the 1870s*, pp. 28–29.

104. "Santiclaus" was described as a new custom in *Notes and Queries*, 5th series, vol. 11 (January 25, 1879): 66.

105. J. M. Golby and A. M. Purdue, *The Making of Modern Christmas* (Athens: University of Georgia Press, 1986), p. 105.

106. Hugh F. Martyndale, *A Familiar Analysis of the Calendar of the Church of England* (London, 1830), p. 267 (Martyndale's emphasis).

107. Pimlott, *The Englishman's Christmas*, p. 94.

108. Ibid., p. 110.

109. *Notes and Queries*, 2nd series, vol. 6 (December 25, 1858): 535 (emphasis in original).

110. A discussion of different kinds of time is provided by Zerubavel, *Hidden Rhythms*, pp. 111–13; see also Adam Kuper, "The English Christmas and the Family: Time out and Alternative Realities," in *Unwrapping Christmas*, ed. Daniel Miller (Oxford: Clarendon Press, 1993), pp. 157–75.

111. On perceptions of Christmas past, see Raymond Firth, *Symbols: Public and Private* (Ithaca, N.Y.: Cornell University Press, 1973), p. 219; Waits, *The Modern Christmas in America*, chap. 2.

112. Charles Dickens, *Sketches by Boz*, quoted in Golby and Purdue, *The Making of Modern Christmas*, p. 13.

113. *Notes and Queries*, 2nd series, vol. 4 (December 26, 1857): 507.

114. Quoted in Gavin Weightman and Steve Humphries, *Christmas Past* (London: Sidgwick and Jackson, 1987), p. 88.

115. Clement A. Miles, *Christmas in Ritual and Tradition, Christian and Pagan* (London: T. Fisher Unwin, 1912), pp. 18, 27, 360. Whitsun was originally more important to children; see J. Barlow Brooks, *Lancashire Bred, An Autobiography* (Oxford: Church Army Press, n.d.), pp. 103–4.

116. Pimlott, *The Englishman's Christmas*, chap. 10; Golby and Purdue, *The Making of Modern Christmas*, pp. 73–75.

117. Roberts, "The Paterfamilias of the Victorian Governing Class," p. 64; Weightman and Humphries, *Christmas Past*, pp. 138–53.

118. James Anthony Froude, *The Nemesis of Faith* (London: Chapman, 1849), p. 104. Dickens remarked, "Happy, happy Christmas that can win us back to the delusion of our childish days"; Charles Dickens, *The Christmas Books*, vol. 1, ed. M. Slater (Harmondsworth, Eng.: Penguin, 1971), p. ix.

119. Leslie Bella, *The Christmas Imperative: Leisure, Family, and Women's Work* (Halifax, Nova Scotia: Fernwood Publishing, 1992).

120. Male cross-dressing remained a tradition in British working-class Christmas; see Weightman and Humphries, *Christmas Past*, pp. 50–53.

121. Quoted in Joselit, *The Wonders of America*, pp. 229–43.

122. Myers, *Celebration*, pp. 276–83; Mary Ryan, *Cradle of the Middle Class: The Family in Oneida County, New York, 1770–1865* (Cambridge: Cambridge University Press, 1981), p. 146.

123. Phyllis Bourne, "Going to the Countryside," *Cassell's Family Magazine* (1875), pp. 489–91; "Surviving Vacation (It's a Family Battle)," *New York Times*, August 1, 1991; on contemporary "retreats," see Rybczynski, *Waiting for the Weekend*, chap. 7.

124. On American summer communities, see Gwen Neville, *Kinship and Pilgrimage: Rituals of Reunion in American Protestant Culture* (New York: Oxford University Press, 1987), chap. 5.

125. John K. Walton, "The Demand for Working-Class Seaside Holidays in Victorian England," *Economic History Review*, 2nd series, vol. 24, no. 2 (May 1989): 249–65; see also John Burnett, *Destiny Obscure* (Harmondsworth, Eng.: Penguin, 1984), p. 249.

126. John Clarke and Chas Critcher, *The Devil Makes Work: Leisure in Capitalist Britain* (Urbana: University of Illinois Press, 1985), p. 171.

127. Gary Cross, ed., *Worktowners at Blackpool: Mass-Observation and Popular Leisure in the 1930s* (London: Routledge, 1990), pp. 37–70.

128. Ibid., pp. 40, 153, 157–58.

129. Ibid., p. 57.

130. Rybczynski, *Waiting for the Weekend*, chap. 7.

131. "A Summer Place," *New York Times*, August 7, 1986. Some 13 percent of Canadians surveyed return to the same summer cottage each year.

132. Dr. Mathild B. Canter, quoted in "Surviving Vacation (It's a Family Battle)."

133. "'Having a Great Time': Americans on Vacation," *New York Times*, June 6, 1990; see also *Americans on Vacation*.

134. Susan Sontag, *On Photography* (New York: Delta, 1972), p. 9; see also Eugene Rochberg-Halton, *Meaning and Modernity: Social Theory in the Pragmatic Attitude* (Chicago: University of Chicago Press, 1986), pp. 166–67, 170.

135. Amy Willard Cross, *The Summer House: A Tradition of Leisure* (Toronto: HarperCollins, 1992), pp. 125, 135.

136. Joan Busfield and Michael Paddon, *Thinking about Children: Sociology and Fertility in Post-War Britain* (Cambridge: Cambridge University Press, 1977), pp. 114–40.

137. Nils-Arvid Bringeus, "Bitte keine Feier, oder Das Fest als Trauma," *Hessische*

Blaetter fuer Volks und Kulturforschung 7, no. 8 (1978): 36–44; Jane Alexander, "Private Fiesta," *New Society* (December 21, 1972): 676; J. M. Pimlott, ". . . But Once a Year," *New Society* (December 20, 1962): 9; Orvar Löfgren, "The Great Christmas Quarrel and Other Swedish Traditions," in *Unwrapping Christmas*, ed. Daniel Miller (Oxford: Clarendon Press, 1993), pp. 217–34.

CHAPTER SIX

1. Susan Groag Bell, *Between Worlds: Czechoslovakia, England, America* (New York: Dutton, 1991), p. 226.
2. Henry Glassie, *Passing the Time in Balleymenone: Culture and History of an Ulster Community* (Philadelphia: University of Pennsylvania Press, 1982), p. 405.
3. E. M. Forster, *Marianne Thornton: A Domestic Biography, 1797–1887* (New York: Harcourt, Brace, and Co., 1956), p. 32.
4. Robert Fishman, *Bourgeois Utopias: The Rise and Fall of Suburbia* (New York: Basic Books, 1987), p. 56.
5. Leonore Davidoff and Catherine Hall, *Family Fortunes: Men and Women of the English Middle Class, 1780–1850* (London: Hutchinson, 1987), pp. 358–62; Clifford Clark Jr., *The American Home, 1800–1960* (Chapel Hill: University of North Carolina Press, 1986), pp. 11–12.
6. On Catholic home culture, see Colleen McDannell, *The Christian Home in Victorian America, 1840–1900* (Bloomington: Indiana University Press, 1986), chap. 3.
7. Doreen M. Rosman, *Evangelicals and Culture* (London: Croom Helm, 1984), p. 114; Maxine de Wetering, "The Popular Concept of 'Home' in Nineteenth-Century America," *Journal of American Studies* 18, no. 1 (April 1984); Davidoff and Hall, *Family Fortunes*, chap. 7; Gwendolyn Wright, *Building the Dream: A Social History of Housing in America* (New York: Pantheon, 1981), pt. 3.
8. Gwen Neville, *Kinship and Pilgrimage: Rituals of Reunion in American Protestant Culture* (New York: Oxford University Press, 1987), p. 20.
9. Ann Douglas, *The Feminization of American Culture* (New York: Alfred A. Knopf, 1977), pp. 223–26; Colleen McDannell and Bernhard Lang, *Heaven: A History* (New York: Vintage, 1988), pp. 273–75.
10. Clark, *The American Home*, p. 25; Wetering, "The Popular Concept of 'Home,'" pp. 6–15.
11. *The Family Circle and Parlor Annual*, quoted in Clark, *The American Home*, p. 31; see also McDannell, *The Christian Home in Victorian America*, pp. 19ff.
12. Marilyn Chandler, *Dwelling in the Text: The House in American Fiction* (Berkeley: University of California Press, 1991), pp. 4–6.
13. Orvar Löfgren, "Family and Household: Images and Realities: Culture Change in Swedish Society," in *Households: Comparative and Historical Structures of the Domestic Group*, eds. R. Netting, R. Wilk, E. Arnould (Berkeley: University of California Press, 1984), p. 458.
14. Shelly Errington, "Making Progress on Borobadur: An Old Monument in a New Order" (paper delivered at "The Culture of Ruins" Conference, Center for Cultural Studies, University of California at Santa Cruz, January 25, 1992);

see also Benedict Anderson, *Our Imagined Communities: Reflections on the Origin and Spread of Nationalism* (London: Verso, 1983), chap. 10; David Sopher, "The Landscape of Home: Myth, Experience, Social Memory," in *Interpretation of Ordinary Landscapes*, ed. D. W. Meinig (New York: Oxford University Press, 1979), pp. 130–46; Sopher, "The Structuring of Space and Place Names and Words for Space," in *Humanistic Geography: Prospects and Problems*, eds. D. Ley and M. S. Samuels (Chicago: Maaroufa Press, 1978), pp. 262–63.

15. Hermann Bausinger, "Auf dem Wege zu einem neuen aktiven Heimatsverständnis," in *Heimat heute*, ed. Hans-Georg Wehling (Stuttgart: Kohlmanner Verlag, 1984), pp. 11–15; see also Bausinger, *Folk Culture in a World of Technology* (Bloomington: Indiana University Press, 1990), pp. 54–55; Alon Confino, *Nation as Local Metaphor: Wuertemburg, the German Empire, and National Memory, 1871–1918* (Chapel Hill: University of North Carolina Press, forthcoming); in the United States, talk of a specifically Jewish home can be traced back to the 1880s and became more insistent over time; Jenna Weissman Joselit, *The Wonders of America: Reinventing Jewish Culture, 1880–1950* (New York: Hill and Wang, 1994), chap. 4.

16. Quoted in Löfgren, "Family and Household," p. 463.

17. Samuel Sloan, *City Homes, Country Homes, and Church Architecture*, quoted in Clark, *The American Home*, p. 24.

18. Quoted in Margery Spring Rice, *Working Class Women*, 2nd ed. (London: Virago, 1981), p. 16.

19. Chandler, *Dwelling in the Text*, p. 15.

20. Sopher argues that "English is indefinite not only as to the extent of home, but also as to its content, so that it is in fact understood to incorporate family—or at other scales, kin, neighbor, folk." He claims that Romance languages tend to be less flexible; "The Structuring of Space," pp. 130–31, 136.

21. On home as a symbol, see McDannell, *The Christian Home in Victorian America*, p. 45; and Patrick Wright, *On Living in an Old Country: The National Past in Contemporary Britain* (London: Verso, 1985), pp. 10–11.

22. Quoted in Clark, *The American Home*, p. 110.

23. Mrs. E. B. Duffey, *What Women Should Know* (1873), quoted ibid., p. 46.

24. Davidoff and Hall, *Family Fortunes*, p. 358.

25. On American women's fondness for the city, see Margaret Marsh, "From Separatism to Togetherness: The Social Construction of Domestic Space in American Suburbia, 1840–1915," *Journal of American History* 76, no. 2 (September 1989): 509–10; on London women's uses of the city, see Erika Rappaport, *The West End and Women's Pleasure: Gender and Commercial Pleasure in London, 1860–1914* (Princeton, N.J.: Princeton University Press, forthcoming).

26. M. J. Daunton, *House and Home in the Victorian City: Working-Class Housing, 1850–1914* (London: Edward Arnold, 1983), p. 194; Daunton, "Public Place and Private Space: The Victorian City and the Working-Class Household," in *Pursuit of Urban History*, eds. D. Fraser and Anthony Sutcliffe (London: Edward Arnold, 1983), pp. 212–18.

27. Marsh, "From Separatism to Togetherness," pp. 506–9.

28. Jesse Peck, *The True Woman* (New York, 1857), quoted in Jeanne Boydston, *Home and Work: Housework, Wages, and the Ideology of Labor in the Early*

Republic (New York: Oxford University Press, 1990), p. 146; see also Wetering, "The Popular Concept of 'Home,'" p. 25; Sopher, "The Structuring of Space," pp. 132–33.

29. J. Douglas Porteus, "Home: The Traditional Core," *Geographical Review* 66, no. 4 (October 1976): 65ff.; Clare Cooper, "The House as Symbol," *Design and Environment* 3 (1972): 30–37; Clare Cooper Marcus, *House as Mirror of Self* (Berkeley: Conari Press, 1995).

30. Daunton, *House and Home*, pp. 3, 14–15, 25.

31. Anthony Vidler, *The Architectural Uncanny: Essays on the Modern Unhomely* (Cambridge, Mass.: MIT Press, 1992), chap. 1.

32. On Vienna, see Robert Rotenberg, *Time and Order in Metropolitan Vienna* (Washington, D.C.: Smithsonian Press, 1992).

33. Henry Cleaveland, and William and Samuel Backus, *Village and Farm Cottages* (1856), quoted in McDannell, *The Christian Home in Victorian America*, p. 25; Antoine Prost, "Public and Private Spaces in France," in *A History of Private Life*, vol. 5, eds. P. Ariès and G. Duby (Cambridge, Mass.: Harvard University Press, 1991), pp. 1–143.

34. John Ruskin, *Sesame and Lilies* (1864), quoted in Walter Houghton, *The Victorian Frame of Mind, 1830–1870* (New Haven, Conn.: Yale University Press, 1957), p. 343.

35. Baldwin Brown, *Young Men and Maidens: A Pastoral for the Times* (London, 1871), quoted in Houghton, *The Victorian Frame of Mind*, p. 345.

36. Quoted in Clark, *The American Home*, p. 29.

37. Mary Gay Humphreys, "The Parlour," *Decorator and Furnisher* (1883), quoted in Mary W. Blanchard, "Oscar Wilde's America: The Aesthetic Movement and the Hidden Life of the Gilded Age, 1876–1893" (Ph.D. dissertation, Rutgers University, 1994), p. 278. Forthcoming from Yale Press.

38. Glassie, *Passing the Time in Balleymenone*, pp. 404–5.

39. Dennis Chapman, *The Home and Social Status* (London: Routledge and Kegan Paul, 1956), pp. 17–19.

40. Clark, *The American Home*, p. 123.

41. Andrew Achenbaum, *Old Age in the New Land: The American Experience since 1780* (Baltimore: Johns Hopkins University Press, 1978), chap. 4; on the rise of "old people's homes," see Carole Haber, *Beyond Sixty-five: The Dilemma of Old Age in America* (New York: Cambridge University Press, 1983), chap. 5.

42. Clark, *The American Home*, p. 128; John Morley, *Death, Heaven, and the Victorians* (Pittsburgh: University of Pittsburgh Press, 1971), chaps. 4–5.

43. McDannell and Lang, *Heaven*, pp. 264–73.

44. On the changing understanding of nature, see Keith Thomas, *Man and the Natural World: A History of Modern Sensibility* (New York: Pantheon, 1983); Orvar Löfgren and Jonas Frykman, *Culture Builders: A Historical Anthropology of Middle-Class Life* (New Brunswick, N.J.: Rutgers University Press, 1987), chap. 2.

45. Winifred Foley, *A Child in the Forest* (London: Hutchinson, 1978), p. 144 (Foley's emphasis).

46. Chapman, *The Home and Social Status*, pp. 17–21; Clark, *The American Home*, chap. 1.

47. Fishman, *Bourgeois Utopias*, p. 70.

48. Gervase Wheeler, *The Choice of Dwelling* (London: John Murray, 1871), pp. 128–29.

49. Clark, *The American Home*, p. 19; McDannell, *The Christian Home in Victorian America*, pp. 23–25.

50. Wheeler, *The Choice of Dwelling*, p. 207; Kenneth Ames, "Meaning in Artifacts: Hall Furnishings in Victorian America," *Journal of Interdisciplinary History* 9 (Summer 1978): 19–46; on visiting, see Leonore Davidoff, *The Best Circles: Society, Etiquette, and the Season* (London: Croom Helm, 1973), pp. 42–47.

51. R. Jeffries, *Hodge and His Masters* (1880), quoted in K. C. Phillips, *Language and Class in Victorian England* (Oxford: Basil Blackwell, 1984), p. 60.

52. Chapman, *The Home and Social Status*, p. 19; Clark, *The American Home*, p. 41; Alison Ravetz, "The Victorian Coal Kitchen and Its Reformers," *Victorian Studies* 11, no. 4 (June 1968): 435–60.

53. Witold Rybczynski, *Home: A Short History of an Idea* (New York: Viking Penguin, 1986), p. 20.

54. Wheeler, *The Choice of Dwelling*, pp. 217–18; Chapman, *The Home and Social Status*, p. 96.

55. Quoted in Clark, *The American Home*, p. 82.

56. Anne Martin-Fugier, "Bourgeois Rituals," in *A History of Private Life*, vol. 4, ed. Michelle Perrot (Cambridge, Mass.: Harvard University Press, 1990), p. 280.

57. Wheeler, *The Choice of Dwelling*, p. 208.

58. Barry Schwartz, "The Social Psychology of Privacy," *American Journal of Sociology* 73, no. 6 (May 1968): 741–52.

59. Yi-Fu Tuan, "Place: An Experiential Perspective," *Geographical Review* 56, no. 2 (April 1975): 154; Christa Pieske, "Wandscmuck im buergerlichen Heim um 1870," in *Wohnen im Wandel*, ed. L. Niethammer (Wupperthal: Hammer, 1979), p. 260.

60. Chapman, *The Home and Social Status*, p. 19. By the 1950s the bedroom had achieved first priority, and it was not until very recently that the kitchen was more than an afterthought.

61. Clark, *The American Home*, p. 35.

62. Eliza Warren, *A Young Wife's Perplexities* (1886), quoted in Jennie Calder, *The Victorian Home* (London: Batsford, 1977), p. 108.

63. Wheeler, *The Choice of Dwelling*, p. 210.

64. Leonore Davidoff, "The Rationalization of Housework," in *Dependence and Exploitation in Work and Marriage*, eds. Diana Leonard Barker and Sheila Allen (London: Longman, 1976), pp. 124–38; Christine Hardyment, *A History of Domestic Arrangements* (London: Viking, 1992), chaps. 9–10.

65. Sopher, "The Structuring of Space," pp. 135–37; Eric Leed, *The Mind of the Traveller* (New York: Basic Books, 1991), chap. 8; Hermann Bausinger, *Folk Culture in a World of Technology*, trans. Elke Dettmer (Bloomington: Indiana University Press, 1990), chap. 2.

66. Quoted in Chandler, *Dwelling in the Text*, p. 2.

67. Both terms came into common usage only in the 1870s and 1880s.

68. Quoted in Chandler, *Dwelling in the Text*, pp. 27, 40.

69. Sopher, "The Structuring of Space," p. 136.

70. A "housekeeper" had previously meant someone who stayed at home. On the etymology of *housework*, see Ruth Schwartz Cowan, *More Work for Mother* (New York: Basic Books, 1983), pp. 17–18.

71. The evolution of terms like *homely* can be traced through the *Oxford English Dictionary*. On *hominess* and *comfort*, see Rybczynski, *Home*, chap. 2.

72. Quoted in Davidoff and Hall, *Family Fortunes*, p. 178.

73. Naomi Tadmor, "'Family' and 'Friend' in *Pamela*: A Case Study in the History of Family in Eighteenth-Century England," *Social History* 14, no. 3 (October 1989): 289–306.

74. Cobbe, *The Duties of Women* (1881), quoted in Calder, *The Victorian Home*, p. 103.

75. Clark, *The American Home*, p. 32.

76. Calder, *The Victorian Home*, p. 117.

77. John Gillis, "Ritualization of Middle-Class Life in Nineteenth-Century Britain," *International Journal of Politics, Culture, and Society* 3, no. 2 (Winter 1989): 224–27.

78. Davidoff and Hall, *Family Fortunes*, p. 178.

79. John Gillis, *For Better, For Worse: British Marriages, 1600 to the Present* (New York: Oxford University Press, 1985), pp. 75, 124.

80. Davidoff, *The Best Circles*, p. 42; on the way turn-of-the-century department stores used homelike qualities to attract women customers, see Erika Rappaport, "Selling the City: The Promotion of Women's Pleasure in London's West End, 1909–1914" (paper delivered at Rutgers Center for Historical Analysis, December 10, 1991), pp. 32–35.

81. Ellen Rothman, *Hands and Hearts: A History of Courtship in America* (Cambridge, Mass.: Harvard University Press, 1987), pp. 172–75.

82. James Anthony Froude, *The Nemesis of Faith* (London: John Chapman, 1849), p. 104.

83. On contrasting male and female views of marriage, see Rothman, *Hands and Hearts*, chap. 10; on male nostalgia for the homes of their childhood, see Calder, *The Victorian Home*, p. 151; on the changing image of fathers, see John Demos, *Past, Present, and Personal: The Family and the Life Course in American History* (New York: Oxford University Press, 1986), chap. 3.

84. Quoted in Peter Gay, *The Bourgeois Experience: Victoria to Freud*, vol. 1 (New York: Oxford University Press, 1984), p. 102.

85. Sopher, "The Structuring of Space," pp. 144–46; Leed, *The Mind of the Traveller*, p. 221.

86. On the nineteenth-century origins of the family reunion, see Neville, *Kinship and Pilgrimage*, chap. 3; McDannell, *The Christian Home in Victorian America*, pp. 135–40; Michael Ann Williams, *Homeplace: The Social Use and Meaning of the Folk Dwelling in Southwestern North Carolina* (Athens: University of Georgia Press, 1991), pp. 130ff.

87. Quoted in Clark, *The American Home*, p. 4.

88. Neville, *Kinship and Pilgrimage*, pts. 2–3.

89. Quoted in Williams, *Homeplace*, p. 135.

90. Sopher, "The Structuring of Space," p. 136.

91. John Ware, *Home Life in America* (1864), quoted in Wetering, "The Popular Concept of 'Home,'" p. 13.

92. Quoted in Tamara Hareven, "The Home and the Family in Historical Perspective," in *Home: A Place in the World*, ed. Arien Mack (New York: New York University Press, 1993), p. 235.

93. Quoted in Orvar Löfgren, "The Sweetness of Home: Class, Culture, and Family Life in Sweden," *Ethnologia Europaea* 14 (1984): 49.

94. Sopher, "The Structuring of Space," p. 146.

95. Christema Nippert-Eng, *Home and Work: Negotiating Boundaries in Everyday Life* (Chicago: University of Chicago Press, 1996).

96. Quoted in Houghton, *The Victorian Frame of Mind*, p. 343; see also McDannell, *The Christian Home in Victorian America*, p. 22.

97. William B. Chisholm, quoted in T. Jackson Lears, *No Place for Grace: Antimodernism and the Transformation of American Culture, 1880–1920* (New York: Pantheon, 1981), p. 192; see also Asa Briggs, *Victorian Things* (London: B. T. Batsford, 1988), chap. 2; on different modes of communication, see Yi-Fu Tuan, *Segmented Worlds and Self: Group Life and Individual Consciousness* (Minneapolis: University of Minnesota Press, 1982), chap. 6; on the changing priority of the senses, see Alain Corbin, "Backstage," in *A History of Private Life*, vol. 4, ed. Michele Perrot (Cambridge, Mass.: Harvard University Press, 1990), pp. 457–547.

98. Clark, *The American Home*, p. 26; Kenneth Clark, *The Gothic Revival: An Essay in the History of Taste* (London: Constable, 1950).

99. W. J. Loftie, *A Plea for Art at Home* (1876), quoted in Briggs, *Victorian Things*, p. 213.

100. McDannell, *The Christian Home in Victorian America*, p. 2.

101. Baldwin Brown, *The Home Life: In the Light of Its Divine Idea* (London, 1866), quoted in Houghton, *The Victorian Frame of Mind*, p. 347; see also Clark, *The American Home*, pp. 29–30.

102. G. K. Chesterton, *The Autobiography of G. K. Chesterton* (New York: Sheed and Ward, 1936), p. 20.

103. McDannell, *The Christian Home in Victorian America*, chap. 3.

104. Joselit, *The Wonders of America*, chap. 4; Marion Kaplan, *The Making of the Jewish Middle Class: Women, Family, and Identity in Imperial Germany* (New York: Oxford University Press, 1991), chap. 2.

105. Peter Thornton, *Authentic Decor: The Domestic Interior, 1620–1920* (London: Weidenfeld and Nicolson, 1984), p. 221.

106. Karen Halttunen, "From Parlour to Living Room: Domestic Space, Interior Decoration, and the Culture of Personality," in *Consuming Visions: Accumulation and Display of Goods in America, 1880–1920*, ed. Simon Bronner (New York: W. W. Norton, 1989), p. 159.

107. Davidoff, *Best Circles*, pp. 42–46; Clark, *The American Home*, pp. 42–45.

108. Halttunen, "From Parlour to Living Room," p. 165; Clark, *The American Home*, pp. 132ff.

109. Chapman, *The Home and Social Status*, p. 113.

110. Quoted in John Burnett, *Destiny Obscure* (Harmondsworth, Eng.: Penguin, 1984), p. 225.

111. Alwyn Rees, *Life in a Welsh Countryside* (Cardiff: University of Wales Press, 1975), p. 46. A very similar account is provided by Glassie, *Passing the Time in Balleymenone*, pp. 338–43.

112. Chapman, *The Home and Social Status*, p. 112.

113. Glassie, *Passing the Time in Balleymenone*, p. 342.

114. Williams, *Homeplace*, p. 85.

115. Clark, *The American Home*, p. 144; Thornton, *The Domestic Interior*, pp. 113–16.

116. Christina Hardyment, *Dream Babies: Child Care from Locke to Spock* (London: Jonathan Cape, 1983), chaps. 3–4.

117. Chapman, *The Home and Social Status*, p. 96.

118. Ibid., pp. 27–31; Clark, *The American Home*, pp. 201ff.

119. Davidoff, "The Rationalization of Housework," pp. 147–51; Clark, *The American Home*, p. 204.

120. Clark, *The American Home*, p. 215.

121. Quoted in Stephen Mennell, *All Manners of Food: Eating and Taste in England and France from the Middle Ages to the Present* (Oxford: Basil Blackwell, 1985), p. 264.

CHAPTER SEVEN

1. Ernest Cassirer, *The Philosophy of Symbolic Form* (New Haven: Yale University Press, 1955), pp. 38-39.

2. Peter Berger and Hansfried Kellner, "Marriage and the Construction of Reality," *Diogenes*, no. 46 (1964): 5; on the persistence of the association of marriage with maturity and success, see Enid Nemy, "Society Looks Askance at the Family of One," *New York Times*, February 28, 1991.

3. John Boswell, *Same-Sex Unions in Premodern Europe* (New York: Vintage, 1995), p. 178.

4. Judith Wallerstein and Sarah Blakesee, *Second Chances: Men, Women, and Children a Decade after Divorce* (New York: Ticknor and Fields, 1989).

5. Jonathan Rosen, "Rewriting the End: Elisabeth Kubler-Ross," *New York Times Magazine* (January 22, 1995): 25. For further evidence, see Kenneth Gergen, *The Saturated Self: Dilemmas of Identity in Contemporary Life* (New York: Basic Books, 1991), pp. 71–72.

6. Colleen McDannell and Bernhard Lang, *Heaven: A History* (New York: Vintage, 1988), pp. 303–11.

7. Boswell, *Same-Sex Unions*, pp. xxi–xxii.

8. Edmund Morgan, *The Puritan Family: Essays on Religion and Domestic Relations in Seventeenth-Century New England* (New York: Harper & Row, 1966), p. 54.

9. Boswell, *Same-Sex Unions*, pp. 262–82.

10. John Gillis, *For Better, For Worse: British Marriages, 1600 to the Present* (New York: Oxford University Press, 1985), pp. 123–24; Hans Medick, "Village Spinning Bees: Sexual Culture and Free Time among Rural Youth in Early Modern Germany," in *Interest and Emotion: Essays on the Study of Family and Kinship*, eds. Hans Medick and David Sabean (Cambridge: Cambridge University Press, 1984), pp. 317–39; Edward Shorter, *The Making of the Modern Family* (New York: Basic Books, 1975), chap. 4.

11. Ellen Rothman, *Hearts and Hands: A History of Courtship in America* (Cambridge, Mass.: Harvard University Press, 1987), p. 23.

12. Quoted in ibid., p. 23.
13. Ibid., pp. 27–29; Gillis, *For Better, For Worse*, pp. 125–30.
14. Illana Krausman Ben-Amos, *Adolescence and Youth in Early Modern England* (New Haven, Conn.: Yale University Press, 1994), p. 237.
15. Ibid., chaps. 5–6.
16. Gillis, *For Better, For Worse*, p. 24.
17. Joseph Lawson, *Letters to the Young in Pudsey during the Last Sixty Years* (Stannington, Eng., 1887), pp. 13–14.
18. Martine Segalen, *Love and Power in the Peasant Family: Rural France in the Nineteenth Century*, trans. Sarah Matthews (Oxford: Basil Bláckwell, 1980), p. 16.
19. John Gillis, "From Ritual to Romance: Toward an Alternative History of Love," in *Emotion and Social Change: Toward a New Psychohistory*, eds. Carol Z. Stearns and Peter N. Stearns (New York: Holmes & Meier, 1988), pp. 90–92.
20. Ibid.
21. Roger Lowe, *The Diary of Roger Lowe*, ed. William Sachse (New Haven, Conn.: Yale University Press, 1938), p. 37.
22. On the mnemonic function of marketplaces, see Jean-Christophe Agnew, *Worlds Apart: The Market and the Theatre in Anglo-American Thought, 1550–1750* (Cambridge: Cambridge University Press, 1986), pp. 17–40.
23. David Jenkins, *The Agricultural Community of South-West Wales at the Turn of the Twentieth Century* (Cardiff: University of Wales Press, 1971), p. 147.
24. Lawson, *Letters to the Young*, p. 15.
25. Rothman, *Hearts and Hands*, pp. 48–50.
26. Trefor Owen, "West Glamorgan Customs," *Folk-Life* 3 (1965): 47.
27. *Rural Economy in Yorkshire in 1641, Being the Farming and Account Books of Henry Best of Elmswell in East Riding*, Surtees Society, no. 33 (1857): 116–17.
28. W. Barnes, "The Diary of William Whiteway," *Proceedings of the Dorset Natural History and Archeological Field Club* 13 (1892): 59.
29. Boswell, *Same-Sex Unions*, p. 15; Gillis, *For Better, For Worse*, pp. 43–45.
30. See A. Percival Moore, "Marriage Contracts or Espousals in the Reign of Queen Elizabeth," *Reports and Papers of the Associated Architectural Societies of 1909*, pp. 290–91.
31. F. J. Furnivall, *Child-Marriages, Divorces, and Ratifications in the Diocese of Chester* (London, 1897), p. xlviii.
32. Quoted in Peter Laslett, *The World We Have Lost* (New York: Scribner's, 1971), pp. 143–44.
33. Barnes, "The Diary of William Whiteway," p. 59.
34. *Rural Economy in Yorkshire*, pp. 116–17.
35. David Hackett Fischer, *Albion's Seed: Four British Folkways in America* (New York: Oxford University Press, 1989), p. 81; Morgan, *The Puritan Family*, pp. 32–33; Rothman, *Hearts and Hands*, pp. 29–30.
36. Barnes, "The Diary of William Whiteway," p. 59.
37. Gillis, *For Better, For Worse*, p. 43.
38. *Rural Economy in Yorkshire*, pp. 116–17.
39. Quoted in Gillis, *For Better, For Worse*, pp. 57–60.

40. Owen, "West Glamorgan Customs," p. 52; for the full text of this account, see Dayffd Ifans, "Lewis Morris ac Afrerion Priodi yng Nghheredigion," *Ceredigion* 8, no. 2 (1972): 194.

41. "Choice Notes," in *Notes and Queries* (London, 1859), p. 265. See also *Notes and Queries*, 4th Series, vol. 2 (October 10, 1868): 434; and (November 7, 1868): 450. American parents were also absent from their daughters' weddings; see Rothman, *Hearts and Hands*, pp. 76–77.

42. Quoted in Gillis, *For Better, For Worse*, pp. 98–99.

43. Trefor Owen, *Welsh Folk Customs* (Cardiff: National Museum of Wales, 1978), pp. 161–62; see also Gillis, *For Better, For Worse*, pp. 153–55.

44. Gillis, *For Better, For Worse*, pp. 155–58.

45. A. Craig Gibson, "Ancient Custom and Superstition in Cumberland," *Transactions of the Historic Society of Lancashire and Cheshire* 10 (1857–58): 103; R. U. Sayce, "Popular Enclosures and the One-Night House," *Montgomeryshire Collections* 47, pt. 2 (1942): 109–17.

46. W. Crooke, "Lifting the Bride," *Folk-Lore* 12 (1902): 228–29.

47. R. Blakeborough, "A Country Wedding a Century Ago" (Blakeborough MSS, Sheffield University Library).

48. On petting stones, see Gillis, *For Better, For Worse*, pp. 65–66.

49. Blakeborough, "A Country Wedding."

50. Margaret Baker, *Discovering the Folklore and Customs of Love and Marriage* (Aylesbury, Eng.: Shire Publications, 1974), p. 50.

51. Tom Minors, "Quaint Marriage Customs in Old Cornwall," *Old Cornwall*, vol. 1, pp. 23–24; on American ceremonies, see David Hackett Fischer, *Albion's Seed: Four British Folkways in America* (New York: Oxford University Press, 1989), p. 82.

52. Rothman, *Hearts and Hands*, p. 74.

53. The term "newlyweds" was first used in 1918; *Oxford English Dictionary*, 2nd ed., vol. 10.

54. Pews were distributed by house rather than family in the eighteenth century; John Demos, *Past, Present, and Personal: The Family and the Life Course in American History* (New York: Oxford University Press, 1986), p. 29.

55. Quoted in Rothman, *Hearts and Hands*, p. 83.

56. Quoted in ibid., p. 81.

57. Ibid., pp. 82–83.

58. Ibid., p. 74.

59. "Diary of the Journey of the Most Illustrious Philip Julius, Duke of Stettin-Pomerania through England, 1602," *Transactions of the Royal Historical Society*, vol. 6 (1892), p. 65.

60. Gillis, *For Better, For Worse*, pp. 76–81; Edward P. Thompson, "The Sale of Wives," in his *Customs in Common: Studies in Traditional Popular Culture* (New York: New Press, 1991), pp. 404–66.

61. On Quaker marriage discipline, see Barry Levy, *Quakers and the American Family: British Settlement in the Delaware Valley* (New York: Oxford University Press, 1988), pp. 72–80.

62. Quoted in Barbara Taylor, *Eve and the New Jerusalem: Socialism and Feminism in the Nineteenth Century* (New York: Pantheon, 1983), p. 225; Eileen Yeo, "Robert Owen and Radical Culture," in *Robert Owen: Prophet of the*

Poor, eds. S. Pollard and J. Salt (London: Macmillan, 1971), p. 98; Yeo, "Culture and Constraint in Working-Class Movements," in *Popular Culture and Class Conflict, 1590–1914: Explorations in the History of Labour and Leisure*, eds. Eileen Yeo and Stephen Yeo (Brighton, Eng.: Harvester, 1981), pp. 155–86.

63. Gillis, *For Better, For Worse*, pp. 225–27.
64. Quoted in Taylor, *Eve and the New Jerusalem*, p. 213.
65. Berger and Kellner, "Marriage and the Construction of Reality," p. 208.
66. On Christmas romance, see Tony Bennett, "Christmas and Ideology," in his *Popular Culture* (Milton-Keynes, Eng.: Open University Press, 1985), p. 65; see also Colin Bell, *Middle-Class Families: Social and Geographical Mobility* (London: Routledge and Kegan Paul, 1968), p. 94.
67. Beth L. Bailey, *From Front Porch to Back Seat: Courtship in Twentieth-Century America* (Baltimore: Johns Hopkins University Press, 1988), pp. 13–16.
68. Gillis, *For Better, For Worse*, p. 283.
69. Francesca Cancian, *Love in America: Gender and Self-Development* (Cambridge: Cambridge University Press, 1987), pp. 16–29; Rothman, *Hearts and Hands*, pp. 105–6.
70. Steven M. Stowe, *Intimacy and Power in the Old South: Ritual in the Lives of the Planters* (Baltimore: Johns Hopkins University Press, 1987), pp. 90–91, 96; Karen Lystra, *Searching the Heart: Women, Men, and Romantic Love in Nineteenth-Century America* (New York: Oxford University Press, 1989), chap. 1; on uses as evidence in court, see Ginger Frost, *Promises Broken: Courtship, Class, and Gender in Victorian England* (Charlottesville: University Press of Virginia, 1995), chaps. 1–2.
71. Quoted in Lystra, *Searching the Heart*, p. 23.
72. Orvar Löfgren and Jonas Frykman, *Culture Builders: A Historical Anthropology of Middle-Class Life* (New Brunswick, N.J.: Rutgers University Press, 1987), pp. 119–23.
73. Gillis, *For Better, For Worse*, pp. 278, 287.
74. Quoted in Lystra, *Searching the Heart*, pp. 195–96.
75. Boswell, *Same-Sex Unions*, p. 15.
76. Frost, *Promises Broken*, chaps. 5–6.
77. Quoted in Rothman, *Hearts and Hands*, p. 166.
78. Quoted in ibid., p. 174.
79. Gillis, *For Better, For Worse*, pp. 286–87; Rothman, *Hearts and Hands*, p. 279.
80. From "Pilot Questionnaire on Marriage, 1947," Family Planning Box 3c (Mass Observation Archive, Sussex University, England).
81. Ibid.
82. On the ways the same symbols can serve different purposes, see Miki Tanikawa, "Japanese Weddings: Long and Lavish (Boss Is Invited)," *New York Times*, February 26, 1995.
83. "Pilot Questionnaire on Marriage."
84. Quoted in Rothman, *Hearts and Hands*, p. 172.
85. Ibid., pp. 310–11; Gillis, *For Better, For Worse*, pp. 292–93.
86. Rothman, *Hearts and Hands*, p. 161.
87. Ibid., pp. 168–70; Gillis, *For Better, For Worse*, pp. 294–95.
88. Gillis, *For Better, For Worse*, p. 284.

89. Ibid., p. 311; Rothman, *Hearts and Hands*, p. 175.

90. Gillis, *For Better, For Worse*, p. 293.

91. Mark Carnes, *Secret Ritual and Manhood in Victorian America* (New Haven, Conn.: Yale University Press, 1989); Jeffrey Weeks, *Sex, Politics, Society: The Regulation of Sexuality since 1800* (London: Longman, 1981), chaps. 3 and 11; George Chauncey, *Gay New York: Gender, Urban Culture, and the Making of the Gay Male World, 1890–1940* (New York: Basic Books, 1994), pts. 1–2.

92. Cancian, *Love in America*, pp. 25ff.; Lilian Faderman, *Odd Girls and Twilight Lovers: A History of Lesbian Life in Twentieth-Century America* (New York: Columbia University Press, 1991), chaps. 1–2; Carroll Smith-Rosenberg, "The Female World of Love and Ritual: Relations between Women in Nineteenth-Century America," in Smith-Rosenberg, *Disorderly Conduct: Visions of Gender in Victorian America* (New York: Oxford University Press, 1985), pp. 53–76.

93. Elaine Tyler May, *Great Expectations: Marriage and Divorce in Post-Victorian America* (Chicago: University of Chicago Press, 1980); Cancian, *Love in America*, chap. 3.

94. Bailey, *From Front Porch to Back Seat*, pp. 25–56; Stephanie Coontz, *The Way We Never Were: American Families and the Nostalgia Trap* (New York: Basic Books, 1992), chap. 8; Gillis, *For Better, For Worse*, chap. 9; Paula Fass, *The Dammed and the Beautiful: American Youth in the 1920s* (New York: Oxford University Press, 1977), chaps. 3–6.

95. Coontz, *The Way We Never Were*, chap. 8.

96. On the history of friendship, see Theodore Zeldin, *An Intimate History of Humanity* (New York: HarperCollins, 1995), pp. 325–26.

97. Boswell, *Same-Sex Unions*, pp. 262–78.

98. Gillis, *For Better, For Worse*, pp. 285–86.

99. Gillis, *For Better, For Worse*, p. 277.

100. John Modell, *Into One's Own: From Youth to Adulthood in the United States, 1920–1975* (Berkeley: University of California Press, 1989), pp. 6–16; Gillis, *For Better, For Worse*, chap. 10.

101. Gillis, *For Better, For Worse*, p. 286.

102. Bailey, *From Front Porch to Back Seat*, pp. 75–76.

103. Rothman, *Hearts and Hands*, p. 310.

104. Linda Wells, "The Wedding," *New York Times Magazine* (February 14, 1988): 65, 78; Georgia Dullea, "Three-Day Weddings Join the Marriage Season," *New York Times*, June 9, 1986; "A Family Affair: Paying for the Wedding," *New York Times*, June 27, 1991.

105. Robert Brain, *Friends and Lovers* (New York: Basic Books, 1976), p. 246.

106. Lillian Rubin, *Just Friends: The Role of Friendship in Our Lives* (New York: Harper & Row, 1985).

CHAPTER EIGHT

1. Ann Dally, *Inventing Motherhood: The Consequences of an Ideal* (London: Burnett Books, 1982, p.17.

2. "Disillusioned Town Reviles Woman Accused of Killings," *New York Times*,

November 5, 1994; see also Susan Chira, "Murdered Children: In Most Cases, a Parent Did It," ibid.

3. Dana Raphael, "Matrescence, Becoming a Mother: An 'Old/New' Rite of Passage," in *Being Female: Reproduction, Power, and Change*, ed. Dana Raphael (The Hague: Mouton, 1975), pp. 65–71.

4. Robbie E. Davis-Floyd, *Birth as an American Rite of Passage* (Berkeley: University of California Press, 1992), pp. 13, 38.

5. Even among the relatively healthy American populations, rates of orphanage were very high; see Richard Wertz and Dorothy Wertz, *Lying-in: A History of Childbirth in America* (New York: Free Press, 1977), p. 3; Peter Laslett, *Family Life and Illicit Love in Earlier Generations* (Cambridge: Cambridge University Press, 1977), chap. 4.

6. Shari Thurer, *Myths of Motherhood: How Culture Reinvents the Good Mother* (Boston: Houghton Mifflin, 1994), p. 213.

7. Ibid., p. 177; Elisabeth Badinter, *Mother Love: Myth and Reality: Motherhood in Modern History* (New York: Macmillan, 1981), p. 48; Valerie Fildes, *Wet-nursing: A History from Antiquity to the Present* (Oxford: Basil Blackwell, 1988), chaps. 6–8.

8. Fildes, *Wetnursing*, chap. 8.

9. Leonore Davidoff and Catherine Hall, *Family Fortunes: Men and Women of the English Middle Class, 1780–1850* (Chicago: University of Chicago Press, 1987), pp. 222–23.

10. Ellen Ross, *Love and Toil: Motherhood in Outcast London, 1870–1918* (New York: Oxford University Press, 1993), pp. 133–37.

11. Carl Chinn, *They Worked All Their Lives: Women of the Urban Poor in England, 1880–1939* (New York: St. Martin's Press, 1988), chaps. 2–4; Michael Anderson, *Family Structure in Nineteenth-Century Lancashire* (Cambridge: Cambridge University Press, 1971), pt. 3.

12. Illana Krausman Ben-Amos, *Adolescence and Youth in Early Modern England* (New Haven, Conn.: Yale University Press, 1994), p. 2.

13. John Boswell, *The Kindness of Strangers: The Abandonment of Children in Western Europe, Late Antiquity to the Renaissance* (New York: Pantheon, 1988), p. 11.

14. Dally, *Inventing Motherhood*, p. 17.

15. Laura Thatcher Ulrich, *Good Wives: Image and Reality in the Lives of Women in Northern New England, 1650–1750* (New York: Vintage, 1980), p. 158.

16. Jacques Gelis, *History of Childbirth: Fertility, Pregnancy, and Birth in Early Modern Europe* (Cambridge: Polity, 1991), p. 105.

17. On the phenomenon of "little mothers," see Elizabeth Roberts, *A Woman's Place: An Oral History of Working-Class Women, 1890–1940* (Oxford: Basil Blackwell, 1984), pp. 24–25, 173; Chinn, *They Worked All Their Lives*, pp. 26–36; on the familial relationship of whites and blacks on American slave plantations, see Mechal Sobel, *The World They Made Together: Black and White Values in Eighteenth-Century Virginia* (Princeton, N.J.: Princeton University Press, 1987), chap. 10; on the nurturing qualities attributed to men, see Davidoff and Hall, *Family Fortunes*, pp. 329–35.

18. For a fuller discussion, see chap. 9.

19. Keith Thomas, *Religion and the Decline of Magic* (New York: Scribner's, 1971), chaps. 2–3.
20. Clarissa Atkinson, *The Oldest Vocation: Christian Motherhood in the Middle Ages* (Ithaca, N.Y.: Cornell University Press, 1991), p. 137.
21. Caroline Walker Bynum, "Jesus and Mother and Abbot as Mother: Some Themes in Twelfth-Century Cistercian Writing," in her *Jesus as Mother: Studies in the Spirituality of the High Middle Ages* (Berkeley: University of California Press, 1983), pp. 110–59; on the continuation of this trend, see David Leverenz, *The Language of Puritan Feeling: An Exploration in Literature, Psychology, and Social History* (New Brunswick, N.J.: Rutgers University Press, 1980).
22. Atkinson, *The Oldest Vocation*, pp. 115, 143.
23. Steven Ozment, *When Fathers Ruled: Family Life in Reformation Europe* (Cambridge, Mass.: Harvard University Press, 1983); Thurer, *Myths of Motherhood*, pp. 166–67; Mary Ryan, *The Empire of Mother: American Writing about Domesticity, 1830–1860* (New York: Haworth, 1982), pp. 18–22.
24. Atkinson, *The Oldest Vocation*, p. 232; Thurer, *Myths of Motherhood*, p. 157.
25. Atkinson, *The Oldest Vocation*, p. 232.
26. On the powers of midwives, see Gelis, *History of Childbirth*, pp. 105–10.
27. Christina Larner, *Witchcraft and Religion*, p. 84.
28. Atkinson, *The Oldest Vocation*, p. 220.
29. Thurer, *Myths of Motherhood*, p. 90.
30. Davis-Floyd, *Birth as an American Rite of Passage*, pp. 1–2.
31. Gelis, *History of Childbirth*, p. 65.
32. Wertz and Wertz, *Lying-in*, p. 23.
33. On rites of passage generally, see Arnold van Gennep, *Rites of Passage* (Chicago: University of Chicago Press, 1960).
34. On rites of progression, see David Cheal, "Relationships in Time: Ritual, Social Structure, and the Life Course," *Studies in Symbolic Interaction* 9 (1988): 98.
35. Audrey Eccles, *Obstetrics and Gynecology in Tudor and Stuart England* (Kent, Ohio: Kent State University Press, 1982), pp. 24–26, 60; Angus McClaren, *Reproductive Rituals: The Perception of Fertility in England from the Sixteenth to the Nineteenth Century* (London: Methuen, 1984), chaps. 1–2.
36. McLaren, *Reproductive Rituals*, pp. 13–30; Gelis, *History of Childbirth*, pp. 47–56, and chap. 6.
37. Gelis, *History of Childbirth*, p. 58.
38. Alan Macfarlane, *The Family Life of the Reverend Ralph Josselin* (New York: W. W. Norton, 1970), pp. 81–91.
39. Gelis, *History of Childbirth*, pp. 67ff.; American death records in the eighteenth century include many infants who died without names, Sandra Brant and Elissa Cullman, *Small Folk: A Celebration of Childhood in America* (New York: E. P. Dutton, 1980), p. 43.
40. Thurer, *Myths of Motherhood*, p. 171.
41. Atkinson, *The Oldest Vocation*, p. 193.
42. Gelis, *History of Childbirth*, pp. 70–75.

43. Thomas, *Religion and the Decline of Magic*, pp. 508, 516.

44. Ralph Josselin used this language; and it continued among the upper classes until the late eighteenth century; Macfarlane, *The Family Life of the Reverend Ralph Josselin*, pp. 84–85; see also Judith S. Lewis, *In the Family Way: Childbearing in the English Aristocracy, 1760–1860* (New Brunswick, N.J.: Rutgers University Press, 1986), p. 72; Madeleine Riley, *Brought to Bed* (South Brunswick, N.J.: A. S. Barnes, 1968), p. 4.

45. Eccles, *Obstetrics and Gynecology in Tudor and Stuart England*, pp. 45–47, 60–65; Ann Oakley, *The Captured Womb: A History of the Medical Care of Pregnant Women* (Oxford: Basil Blackwell, 1984), pp. 22–24.

46. Gelis, *History of Childbirth*, p. 45.

47. On aristocratic women, see Lewis, *In the Family Way*, pp. 52–54, 156–58.

48. Van Gennep, *Rites of Passage*, p. 41.

49. Eccles, *Obstetrics and Gynecology in Tudor and Stuart England*, pp. 94–95; Adrian Wilson, "Participant or Patient? Seventeenth-Century Chldbirth from the Mother's Point of View," in *Patients and Practitioners: Lay Principles of Medicine in Pre-Industrial Societies*, ed. Roy Porter (Cambridge: Cambridge University Press, 1985), p. 135; Wertz and Wertz, *Lying-in*, chap. 1.

50. Lewis, *In the Family Way*, p. 151; Wilson, "Participant or Patient?" p. 135; Edward Shorter, *The Making of the Modern Family* (New York: Basic Books, 1975), p. 145; Eccles, *Obstetrics and Gynecology in Tudor and Stuart England*, p. 92; Gelis, *History of Childbirth*, pp. 97–98, 130–32.

51. Wilson, "Participant or Patient?" pp. 132–35; Shorter, *The Making of the Modern Family*, pp. 48–56; Ralph Houlbrooke, *English Family Life, 1576–1716: An Anthology from Diaries* (Oxford: Basil Blackwell, 1989), pp. 129–30; Wertz and Wertz, *Lying-in*, pp. 12–14.

52. Shorter, *The Making of the Modern Family*, pp. 293–94.

53. Wilson, "Participant or Patient?" pp. 133–36.

54. Gelis, *History of Childbirth*, pp. 38, 155; Lisa Cody, "The Politics of Body Contact: The Discipline of Reproduction in Britain, 1688–1834" (Ph.D. dissertation, University of California at Berkeley, 1993), conclusion.

55. Nigel Lowe, "The Legal Status of Father: Past and Present," in *The Father Figure*, eds. L. McKee and M. O'Brien (London: Tavistock, 1982), pp. 26–28; Riley, *Brought to Bed*, pp. 68, 105–13.

56. Wertz and Wertz, *Lying-in*, pp. 20–23; Wilson, "Participant or Patient?" pp. 129–30; Shorter, *The Making of the Modern Family*, pp. 38–39; Gelis, *History of Childbirth*, pp. 134–35.

57. Riley, *Brought to Bed*, pp. 3–4; Lewis, *In the Family Way*, p. 72.

58. Quoted in Wertz and Wertz, *Lying-in*, p. 21.

59. Gelis, *History of Childbirth*, p. 163.

60. Ruth Bloch, "American Feminine Ideals in Transition: The Rise of the Moral Mother, 1785–1815," *Feminist Studies* 4, no. 2 (1978): 101–26; Badinter, *Mother Love*, pt. 1.

61. Gelis, *History of Childbirth*, p. 183.

62. Alan Macfarlane, *The Family Life of Ralph Josselin* (New York: W. W. Norton, 1970), p. 88.

63. Eccles, *Obstetrics and Gynecology in Tudor and Stuart England*, p. 83; Joseph Illick, "Childrearing in Seventeenth-Century England and America," in *The*

History of Childhood, ed. Lloyd deMause (New York: Psychohistory Press, 1974), p. 307; *Notes and Queries*, 5th series (September 14, 1878): 205, and (September 28, 1878): 255–26.

64. Wilson, "Participant or Patient?" p. 137.
65. Macfarlane, *The Family Life of Ralph Josselin*, pp. 88–89; Houlbrooke, *English Family Life*, p. 131; on folk rites, see John Brand, *Observations on Popular Antiquities* (London: Chatto and Windus, 1877), pp. 340–41.
66. Gelis, *History of Childbirth*, p. 195.
67. Houlbrooke, *English Family Life*, pp. 130–31; B. Midi Berry and Roger Schofield, "Age of Baptism in Preindustrial England," *Population Studies* 25 (1971): 453–63; Thomas, *Religion and the Decline of Magic*, pp. 36–7, 56.
68. Gelis, *History of Childbirth*, p. 188.
69. Wilson, "Participant or Patient?" p. 138.
70. Eccles, *Obstetrics and Gynecology in Tudor and Stuart England*, pp. 95–97; Wilson, "Participant or Patient?" pp. 137–38; Lewis, *In the Family Way*, pp. 194–99; van Gennep, *Rites of Passage*, p. 48; Gelis, *History of Childbirth*, pp. 188–94.
71. Linda Pollock, *Forgotten Children: Parent-Child Relations from 1500 to 1900* (Cambridge: Cambridge University Press, 1983), p. 215; Eccles, *Obstetrics and Gynecology in Tudor and Stuart England*, pp. 14, 98.
72. Wilson, "Participant or Patient?" p. 138; Lewis, *In the Family Way*, pp. 195–97.
73. Thomas, *Religion and the Decline of Magic*, pp. 15, 38–39; David Cressy, "Thanksgiving and the Churching of Women in Post-Reformation England," *Past and Present* 141 (November 1993): 115.
74. Quoted in Thomas, *Religion and the Decline of Magic*, p. 60.
75. Cressy, "Thanksgiving and the Churching of Women," pp. 123–32.
76. Peter Rushton, "Purification or Social Contract? Ideologies of Reproduction and the Churching of Women after Childbirth," in *The Public and Private*, eds. Eva Gamarnikow, et al. (London: Heinemann, 1983), pp. 124–31.
77. Cressy, "Thanksgiving and the Churching of Women," p. 115.
78. Brand, *Observations on Popular Antiquities*, p. 228.
79. Wertz and Wertz, *Lying-in*, pp. 5–10.
80. Lewis, *In the Family Way*, pp. 201–2; Adrian Wilson, "The Ceremony of Childbirth and Its Interpretation," in *Women as Mothers in Pre-Industrial England*, ed. Valerie Fildes (London: Routledge, 1990), p. 92.
81. Pollock, *Forgotten Children*, pp. 111–13; Boswell, *Same-Sex Unions*, pp. 428–34.
82. Thurer, *Myths of Motherhood*, p. 186.
83. Wertz and Wertz, *Lying-in*, pp. 79–80.
84. Quoted in Lewis, *In the Family Way*, p. 72.
85. Quoted in ibid.
86. Wertz and Wertz, *Lying-in*, p. 79.
87. Ludmilla Jordanova, "Naturalizing the Family: Literature and the Bio-medical Sciences in the Late Eighteenth Century," in her *Languages of Nature: Critical Essays on Science and Literature* (London: Free Association Press, 1986), p. 105.
88. Lewis, *In the Family Way*, pp. 53–54.

89. Ibid.; Pollock, *Forgotten Children*, p. 36; John Conquest, *Letters to a Mother, on the Management of Herself and Her Children in Health and Disease* (London: Longman, 1848), pp. 39–46; Shorter, *The Making of the Modern Family*, p. 145.

90. Wertz and Wertz, *Lying-in*, p. 80.

91. Quoted in Mary Poovey, "Scenes of an Indelicate Character: The Medical Treatment of Victorian Women," in Catherine Gallagher and Thomas Laqueur, *The Making of the Modern Body* (Berkeley: University of California Press, 1987), p. 157.

92. Pollock, *Forgotten Children*, pp. 204–8; among the working classes, birth and death were still associated until this century; see Mary Chamberlain and Ruth Richardson, "Life and Death," *Oral History* 11, no. 1 (Spring 1983): 31–43.

93. J. Jill Suitor, "Husbands' Participation in Childbirth: A Nineteenth-Century Phenomena," *Journal of Family History* 6 (1981): 278–93; Shorter, *The Making of the Modern Family*, p. 294; Lewis, *In the Family Way*, pp. 177–83; J. H. Walsh, *A Manual of Domestic Economy Suited to Families Spending from 100 to 1000 a Year* (London, 1857), p. 558.

94. Wertz and Wertz, *Lying-in*, pp. 85–87.

95. Ibid., p. 65.

96. Quoted in Poovey, "Scenes of an Indelicate Character," p. 157.

97. John H. Miller, "'Temple and Sewer': Childbirth, Prudery and Victoria Regina," *The Victorian Family*, ed. A. S. Wohl (London: Croom Helm, 1978), pp. 34–36; Riley, *Brought to Bed*, pp. 122–23.

98. Lewis, *In the Family Way*, pp. 58–59, 71–72; Miller, pp. 35–39; Jan Lewis, "Mother's Love: The Construction of an Emotion in Nineteenth-Century America" (paper delivered at the Pittsburgh Symposium, July 1988).

99. Quoted in Pollock, *Forgotten Children*, p. 206.

100. Quoted in Miller, "Temple and Sewer," p. 35; for other literary representations, see Riley, *Brought to Bed*, pp. 28–29.

101. Jordanova, "Natural Facts," pp. 50ff.; Thurer, *Myths of Motherhood*, pp. 199–200.

102. Conquest, *Letters to a Mother*, p. 93; Fildes, *Women as Mothers*, p. 401.

103. Quoted in Riley, *Brought to Bed*, p. 5.

104. Lewis, *In a Family Way*, pp. 73–74.

105. Miller, "Temple and Sewer," pp. 37–38.

106. David Cheal, *The Gift Economy* (London: Routledge, 1988), pp. 99–100.

107. James Obelkevich, *Religion and Rural Society: South Lindsey, 1825–1875* (Oxford: Clarendon Press, 1976), pp. 127–30.

108. Rushton, "Purification or Social Contract?" pp. 118–23; David Clark, *Between Pulpit and Pew: Folk Religion in a North Yorkshire Fishing Village* (Cambridge: Cambridge University Press, 1982), pp. 114–23.

109. Suitor, "Husbands' Participation in Childbirth," pp. 284–87; Miller, "Temple and Sewer," p. 36.

110. Quoted in Pollock, *Forgotten Children*, p. 205; see also Riley, *Brought to Bed*, pp. 115–24.

111. Quoted in Wertz and Wertz, *Lying-in*, p. 106.

112. Ibid., chap. 4.

113. Ibid., pp. 133–35.

114. Quoted in Davis-Floyd, *Birth as an American Rite of Passage*, p. 51.
115. Wertz and Wertz, *Lying-in*, p. 168.
116. Ibid., p. 173.
117. Gelis, *History of Childbirth*, p. 272.
118. Davis-Floyd, *Birth as an American Rite of Passage*, p. 123.
119. On the meaning of mirrors, see ibid., pp. 132–35.
120. Ibid., pp. 68–69.
121. Thurer, *Myths of Motherhood*, p. 255.
122. Wertz and Wertz, *Lying-in*, pp. 180–82.
123. Letter to the editor, *Ladies' Home Journal* (May 1958), quoted in ibid., p. 172.
124. Wertz and Wertz, *Lying-in*, p. 185.
125. Davis-Floyd, *Birth as an American Rite of Passage*, p. 282.
126. For a summary of these studies, see ibid., pp. 41–43.
127. Ibid., p. 38.
128. Joan Busfield and Michael Paddon, *Thinking about Children: Sociology and Fertility in Post-War Britain* (Cambridge: Cambridge University Press, 1977), pp. 134–56.
129. Carroll Smith-Rosenberg, "Puberty to Menopause: The Cycle of Femininity in Nineteenth-Century America," in Smith-Rosenberg, *Disorderly Conduct: Visions of Gender in Victorian America* (New York: Oxford University Press, 1985), pp. 182–96; Gail Sheehy, *The Silent Passage: Menopause* (New York: Random House, 1992).
130. Lowe, "The Legal Status of Father," pp. 28–42.
131. Orvar Löfgren and Jonas Frykman, *Culture Builders: A Historical Anthropology of Middle-Class Life* (New Brunswick, N.J.: Rutgers University Press, 1987), pp. 118–25; Nancy Friday, *My Mother/My Self: A Daughter's Search for Identity* (New York: Delacourte, 1977).
132. Jonathan Gathorne-Hardy, *The Rise and Fall of the British Nanny* (London: Hodder and Stoughton, 1972).
133. Dally, *Inventing Motherhood*, p. 17.
134. John Gillis, *For Better, For Worse: British Marriages, 1600 to the Present* (New York: Oxford University Press, 1985), p. 253; on the importance of symbols of the mother as nurturer, see Joan Brumberg, *Fasting Girls: The Emergence of Anorexia Nervosa as a Modern Disease* (Cambridge, Mass.: Harvard University Press, 1988), chap. 5.
135. Leigh Schmidt, "The Humbug of Modern Ritual: The Invention of Father's Day" (paper delivered at the Davis Center of Princeton University, November 1994).
136. Karen Hausen, "Mothers, Sons, and the Sale of Symbols and Goods: The 'German Mother's Day' 1923–33," in *Interest and Emotion: Essays on the Study of Family and Kinship*, eds. Hans Medick and David Sabean (Cambridge: Cambridge University Press, 1984), pp. 371–414.
137. Frank F. Furstenberg Jr., "Good Dads—Bad Dads: Two Faces of Fatherhood," in *The Changing American Family and Public Policy*, ed. Andrew Cherlin (Washington, D.C.: Urban Institute Press, 1988), pp. 193–216.
138. Barbara Katz Rothman, *Recreating Motherhood: Ideology and Technology in a Patriarchical Society* (New York: W. W. Norton, 1989), p. 32.
139. Ornella Moscucci, *The Science of Women: Gynaecology and Gender in*

England, 1800–1929 (Cambridge: Cambridge University Press, 1990), pp. 15–40.

140. Quoted in Dally, *Inventing Motherhood*, p. 101.

141. Christema Nippert-Eng is currently researching this question in a contemporary American context.

CHAPTER NINE

1. *The Harper Book of Quotations*, 3rd ed. (New York: HarperCollins, 1993), p. 155.

2. Despite recent advances showing that fetal health is affected by the condition of the sperm, the mother is invariably the one held responsible for fetal damage. For an analysis of how culture overrides science in this area, see Cynthia Daniels, "Between Father and Fetuses: The Social Construction of Male Reproduction and the Politics of Fetal Harm" (paper delivered at meetings of the American Political Science Association, 1993); see also Daniels, *At Women's Expense: State Power and the Politics of Fetal Rights* (Cambridge, Mass.: Harvard University Press, 1993).

3. John Nash, "Historical and Social Changes in the Perception of the Role of the Father," in *Role of the Father in Child Development*, ed. Michael Lamb (New York: Wiley, 1976), pp. 62–88; Sonia Jackson, "Great Britain," in *The Father's Role: Cross-Cultural Perspectives*, ed. Michael Lamb (Hillsdale, N.J.: Erlbaum, 1987), pp. 33–34; Lorna McKee and Margaret O'Brien, "The Father Figure: Some Current Orientations and Historical Perspectives," in *The Father Figure*, eds. Lorna McKee and Margaret O'Brien (London: Tavistock, 1982), p. 3; Charlie Lewis, *Becoming a Father* (Milton Keynes, Eng.: Open University Press, 1986), pp. 3ff.

4. Jackson, "Great Britain," p. 37; Charlie Lewis, "'A Feeling You Can't Scratch': The Effect of Pregnancy and Birth on Married Men," in *Fathers: Psychological Perspectives*, eds. N. Beaill and J. McGuire (London: Tavistock, 1982), pp. 46, 60; Lewis, *Becoming a Father*, pp. 57–78.

5. Shari Thurer, *Myths of Motherhood: How Culture Reinvents the Good Mother* (Boston: Houghton Mifflin, 1994), pp. 252–75.

6. An exception is Robert Griswold, *Fatherhood in America: A History* (New York: Basic Books, 1993). There are no comparable treatments as yet of European fatherhood.

7. Ann Dally, *Inventing Motherhood: The Consequences of an Ideal* (London: Burnett Books, 1982), p. 17.

8. Carol Delaney, *The Seed and the Soil: Gender and Cosmology in Turkish Village Society* (Berkeley: University of California Press, 1991), p. 26.

9. David Herlihy, *Medieval Households* (Cambridge, Mass.: Harvard University Press, 1985), pp. 127–30; Clarissa Atkinson, *The Oldest Vocation: Christian Motherhood in the Middle Ages* (Ithaca, N.Y.: Cornell University Press, 1991), chap. 5.

10. Thurer, *Myths of Motherhood*, chap. 5.

11. Lisa Ann Cody, "The Politics of Body Contact: Disciplines of Reproduction in Britain, 1688–1834" (Ph.D. dissertation, University of California at Berkeley, 1993), conclusion; see also Thomas Laqueur, *Making Sex: Body and Gender*

from the Greeks to Freud (Cambridge, Mass.: Harvard University Press, 1990), chaps. 4–5; Angus McLaren, *Reproductive Rituals: The Perception of Fertility in England from the Sixteenth Century to the Nineteenth Century* (London and New York: Methuen, 1984), chaps. 2–3.

12. On the role of males in hospitality, see Rhys Isaac, *The Transformation of Virginia, 1740–1790* (Chapel Hill: University of North Carolina Press, 1982), pp. 70–79.

13. Natalie Z. Davis, "Ghost, Kin, and Progeny: Some Features of Family Life in Early Modern France," in *The Family*, eds. Alice Rossi, Jerome Kagan, and Tamara Hareven (New York: W. W. Norton, 1978), pp. 87–114.

14. Naomi Tadmore, "'Family' and 'Friend' in *Pamela*: A Case Study in the History of the Family in Eighteenth-Century England," *Social History* 14, no. 3 (October 1989): 289–305.

15. Linda Pollock, *Forgotten Children: Parent-Child Relations from 1500 to 1900* (Cambridge: Cambridge University Press, 1983); see also John Demos, *Past, Present, and Personal: The Family and the Life Course in American History* (New York: Oxford University Press, 1986), pp. 68–91.

16. Thurer, *Myths of Motherhood*, p. 167.

17. Lawrence Stone, *The Family, Sex, and Marriage in England, 1500–1800* (New York: Harper & Row, 1977), pp. 451–62; John Gillis, *Youth and History: Continuity and Change in European Age Relations, 1750 to the Present* (New York: Academic Press, 1975), chap. 1.

18. Leonore Davidoff and Catherine Hall, *Family Fortunes: Middle-Class Women and Men* (Chicago: University of Chicago Press, 1987), pp. 225–27; see also Davidoff, "The Family in Britain," in *Cambridge Social History of Britain, 1750–1950*, vol. 2 (Cambridge: Cambridge University Press, 1990), pp. 77–79.

19. John Gillis, "Ritualization of Middle-Class Family Life in Nineteenth-Century Britain," *International Journal of Politics, Culture, and Society* 3, no. 2 (Winter 1989): 213–35.

20. Mary Ryan, *The Empire of Mother: American Writing about Domesticity, 1830–1860* (New York: Haworth, 1982); see also Nona Glazer-Mulbin, "Housework," *Signs* 1, no. 1 (Summer 1976): 910ff.

21. F. L. Newman, "Some References to the Couvade in Literature," *Folk-Lore* 3, no. 3 (September 1942): 156.

22. Thomas Laqueur, "Orgasm, Generation, and the Politics of Reproductive Biology," in *The Making of the Modern Body*, eds. Thomas Laqueur and Catherine Gallagher (Berkeley: University of California Press, 1987), pp. 1–16; Roy Porter, "A Touch of Danger: The Man-Midwife as Sexual Predator," in *Sexual Underworlds of the Enlightenment*, eds. George S. Rousseau and Roy Porter (Chapel Hill: University of North Carolina Press, 1988), pp. 206–32.

23. Carolyn Merchant, *The Death of Nature: Women, Ecology, and the Scientific Revolution* (New York: Harper & Row, 1980), p. 157.

24. Quoted in ibid., p. 161.

25. John Gillis, "From Ritual to Romance: Toward an Alternative History of Love," in *Emotion and Social Change: Toward a New Psychohistory*, eds. Carol Z. Stearns and Peter N. Stearns (New York: Holmes & Meier, 1988), pp. 90–96.

26. Diary entries of Ralph Josselin and John Dee, in *English Family Life, 1576–1716*, ed. Ralph Houlbrooke (Oxford: Basil Blackwell, 1988), pp. 104–5; Linda Pollock, ed., *A Lasting Relationship: Parents and Children over Three Centuries* (London: Fourth Estate, 1987), pp. 31ff., 204–6; Audrey Eccles, *Obstetrics and Gynecology in Tudor and Stuart England* (Kent, Ohio: Kent State University Press, 1982), pp. 45–47, 60–65; Ann Oakley, *The Captured Womb: A History of the Medical Care of Pregnant Women* (Oxford: Basil Blackwell, 1984), pp. 22–24; Judith Scheid Lewis, *In the Family Way: Childbearing in the English Aristocracy, 1760–1860* (New Brunswick, N.J.: Rutgers University Press, 1986), pp. 124–33.

27. Cody, "The Politics of Body Contact," p. 387; for accounts of what might well be couvade, see Pollock, *A Lasting Relationship*, pp. 31ff.; Houlbrooke, *English Family Life*, p. 102.

28. A. W. Smith, "An Introduction to East London Folklore," *East London Papers* 2, no. 2 (October 1959): 64; Norman Dennies, F. Henriques, C. Slaughter, *Coal Is Our Life* (London: Tavistock, 1956), p. 210; *Folk-Lore* 42 (1931): 293; Fletcher Moss, *Folk-Lore: Old Customs and Talk of My Neighbors* (Manchester, Eng., 1898), p. 7.

29. *Folk-Lore* 29 (1918): 320.

30. Steven Ozment, *When Fathers Ruled: Family Life in Reformation Europe* (Cambridge, Mass.: Harvard University Press, 1983), p. 110.

31. Houlbrooke, *English Family Life*, p. 130.

32. Madeleine Riley, *Brought to Bed* (South Brunswick, N.J.: A. S. Barnes, 1968), pp. 107–8.

33. Quoted in Trefor Owen, *Welsh Folk Customs* (Cardiff: National Museum of Wales, 1978), p. 146.

34. From a Trollope novel, as quoted in Riley, *Brought to Bed*, p. 8.

35. Baptism has no counterpart in Turkey, for Muslims believe that the second and higher birth comes with death; Delaney, *The Seed and the Soil*, p. 60.

36. Thurer, *Myths of Motherhood*, p. 162.

37. Laurel Thatcher Ulrich, *Goodwives: Image and Reality in the Lives of Women in Northern New England, 1650–1750* (New York: Vintage, 1980); Thurer, *Myths of Motherhood*, p. 186.

38. Griswold, *Fatherhood in America*, chap. 2; Demos, *Past, Present, and Personal*, p. 45; E. Anthony Rotundo, *American Manhood: Transformations in Masculinity from the Revolution to the Modern Era* (New York: Basic Books, 1993), chap. 1.

39. Ozment, *When Fathers Ruled*, p. 132.

40. Quoted in ibid., p. 8.

41. John Boswell, *The Kindness of Strangers: The Abandonment of Children in Western Europe from Late Antiquity to the Renaissance* (New York: Pantheon, 1988), chap. 12.

42. Eugene D. Genovese, *Roll, Jordan, Roll: The World the Slaves Made* (New York: Vintage, 1972), pp. 70–75.

43. Peter Laslett, *Family Life and Illicit Love in Earlier Generations* (Cambridge: Cambridge University Press, 1977), p. 162.

44. On the levels of desertion evident in the divorce records of France in the 1790s, see Roderick Phillips, *Putting Asunder: A History of Divorce in*

Western Society (Cambridge: Cambridge University Press, 1989), pp. 175–84.

45. If David Herlihy's studies of early modern Europe are right, two-thirds to three-quarters of all families could not bring up their children by themselves; *Medieval Households*, p. 159.

46. Rotundo, *American Manhood*, chap. 7.

47. Quoted in Lynn Hunt, "The Unstable Boundaries of the French Revolution," in *A History of Private Life*, vol. 4, ed. Michelle Perrot, trans. Arthur Gold-hammer (Cambridge, Mass.: Harvard University Press, 1990), p. 44; see also Thurer, *Myths of Motherhood*, chap. 6; Ornella Moscucci, *The Science of Women: Gyneacology and Gender in England, 1800–1929* (Cambridge: Cambridge University Press, 1990).

48. Lynn Hunt, *Politics, Culture, and Class in the French Revolution* (Berkeley: University of California Press, 1984), chap. 1; on fraternal bonds, see George L. Mosse, *Nationalism and Sexuality: Middle-Class Morality and Sexual Norms in Modern Europe* (Madison: University of Wisconsin Press, 1985).

49. Hunt, "The Unstable Boundaries of the French Revolution," p. 25.

50. Quoted in Geoffrey Best, *War and Society in Revolutionary Europe, 1778–1870* (Leicester, Eng.: Leicester University Press, 1982), p. 103.

51. On the increasing glorification of youth and the appropriation of boyhood by men, see Rotundo, *American Manhood*, pp. 257–59.

52. Griswold, *Fatherhood in America*, p. 13.

53. Initially, women were assigned the role of republican wifehood, which empha-sized their partnership in public affairs with republican men. But when this role was perceived by males as too radical, the role of republican motherhood was invented. On this shift, see Jan Lewis, "Motherhood and the Construction of the Male Citizen in the United States, 1750–1850," in *Construction of the Self*, ed. George Levine (New Brunswick, N.J.: Rutgers University Press, 1992), pp. 143–64; Jan Lewis, "The Republican Wife: Virtue and Seduction in the Early Republic," *William and Mary Quarterly*, 3rd series, 64, no. 4 (October 1987): 689; see also Hunt, "The Unstable Boundaries of the French Revolution," pp. 43–44.

54. Mary Ryan, *The Empire of Mother: American Writing about Domesticity* (New York: Haworth, 1982).

55. Quoted in John Gillis, "Vanishing Youth: The Uncertain Place of the Young in a Global Age," *Young: Nordic Journal of Youth Research* 1, no. 1 (February 1993): 4.

56. Hunt, "The Unstable Boundaries of the French Revolution"; see also Elisa-beth Badinter, *Mother Love: Myth and Reality: Motherhood in Modern History* (New York: Macmillan, 1981), pp. 257ff.; Jan Jewis, "Women and the Political Culture of Antebellum America" (paper delivered at Philadelphia Center for Early American History, May 1988).

57. Quoted in William H. Thayer, *Pastor's Wedding Gift* (Boston, 1854), p. 41. I owe this citation to Stephen Frank, "'Their Own Proper Task': The Construc-tion of Meanings for Fatherhood in Nineteenth-Century America" (unpub-lished paper, 1992), p. 70.

58. Cited in David Roberts, "The Paterfamilias of the Victorian Governing Class," in *The Victorian Family*, ed. Anthony Wohl (London: Croom Helm,

1978), p. 60; on the father as stranger, see Demos, *Past, Present, and Personal*, pp. 48ff.

59. Trevor Lummis, "The Historical Dimension of Fatherhood: A Case Study," in McKee and O'Brien, *The Father Figure*, pp. 43–56.

60. Laqueur, "Orgasm, Generation, and the Politics of Reproductive Biology," pp. 24ff.; see also Wertz and Wertz, *Lying-in*, p. 82; and Moscucci, *The Science of Women*, pp. 29–40.

61. Wertz and Wertz, *Lying-in*, p. 79.

62. J. Jill Suitor, "Husbands' Participation in Childbirth: A Nineteenth-Century Phenomenon," *Journal of Family History* 6, no. 3 (Fall 1981): 284.

63. Ibid., p. 284; Miller, "Temple and Sewer," pp. 34–35; Riley, *Brought to Bed*, pp. 113–23.

64. Pollock, *Forgotten Children*, p. 205; Riley, *Brought to Bed*, p. 5.

65. James Obelkevich, *Religion and Rural Society: South Lindsey, 1825–1875* (Oxford: Clarendon Press, 1976), pp. 128–30.

66. Quoted in Frank Howard Richardson, "Fatherhood," in *The Mother's Encyclopaedia*, Brit. ed., ed. Len Chaloner (London: Allen and Unwin, 1939), p. 217.

67. Oral interview with a working-class man born in 1910, Mr. D.2.P. File in the Elizabeth Roberts Oral History Collection, Lancaster University, England. I am grateful to Elizabeth Roberts for her generosity in sharing her research.

68. David Cheal, *The Gift Economy* (London: Routledge, 1988), pp. 99–100.

69. Nigel Lowe, "The Legal Status of Fathers: Past and Present," in McKee and O'Brien, *The Father Figure*, pp. 26–42; Griswold, *Fatherhood in America*, pp. 29–30.

70. The growing concern with homosexuality at this time is examined by Jeffrey Weeks, *Coming Out: Homosexual Politics in Britain from the Nineteenth Century to the Present* (London: Quartet, 1990); see also Rotundo, *American Manhood*, 278ff.

71. Demos, *Past, Present, and Personal*, pp. 50–51; and Griswold, *Fatherhood in America*, chap. 6. By the early part of this century, British fathers were often treated as the biggest child in the family; Standish Meachem, *A Life Apart* (London: Thames & Hudson, 1977), pp. 117–18; Chinn, *They Worked All Their Lives*, p. 62. The growing acceptance of boyish traits in adult men is also noted by Rotundo, *American Manhood*, p. 257.

72. This is underscored by a study of vacationers in Blackpool, England: *Worktowners in Blackpool: Mass-Observation and Popular Leisure in the 1930s*, ed. Gary Cross (London: Routledge, 1990).

73. Gillis, "Ritualization," pp. 227–30; Roberts, [oral interviews], p. 72.

74. John A. Pimlott, *The Englishman's Christmas: A Social History* (Atlantic Highlands, N.J.: Humanities Press, 1978), chap. 10; J. M. Golby and A. W. Purdue, *The Making of Modern Christmas* (Athens: University of Georgia Press, 1986), pp. 73–75, 88. It was noted in the 1930s that "some parents enjoy him [Santa] more than the children do"; C. Winifred Harley, "Santa Claus," in Chaloner, *The Mother's Encyclopaedia*, p. 525.

75. Helene R. Roberts, "Marriage, Redundancy, or Sin: The Painter's View of Women in the First Twenty-five Years of Victoria's Reign," in *Suffer and Be Still: Women in the Victorian Age*, ed. Martha Vicinus (Bloomington: Indiana

University Press, 1973), pp. 45–76; see also Robert Wheaton, "Images of Kinship," *Journal of Family History* 12, no. 4 (1987): 401–2; Christa Pieske, "Das Bild der Familie in Wandschmuck des 19. Jahrhunderts," in *Sozialkultur der Familie*, eds. A. C. Brimmer and I. Weber-Kellerman (Geissen, 1982), pp. 89–113; Davidoff, L'Esperance, and Newby, pp. 151–59.

76. Mrs. Sarah Ellis, *Women of England, Their Social Duties and Domestic Habits* (London: Fischer, 1838), p. 55.

77. From Mary Howitt, *The Children's Hour* (January 1868), quoted in Demos, *Past, Present, and Personal*, pp. 52–53.

78. Leed, *The Mind of the Traveler*, p. 87.

79. Quoted in Rotundo, *American Manhood*, p. 58.

80. Demos, *Past, Present, and Personal*, pp. 60–61.

81. Louise Tilly and Joan Scott, *Women, Work, and Family* (New York: Holt, Rinehart and Winston, 1978), pt. 2; Wally Seccombe, *Weathering the Storm: Working-Class Families from the Industrial Revolution to the Fertility Decline* (London: Verso, 1993), pp. 146–55.

82. Patrick Joyce, *Work, Society, and Politics: The Culture of the Factory in Later Victorian England* (Brighton, Eng.: Harvester Press, 1980), chap. 4; J. A. Mangan and James Walvin, *Manliness and Morality: Middle-Class Masculinity in Britain and America, 1800–1940* (Manchester, Eng.: Manchester University Press, 1987).

83. During the second half of the nineteenth century, these constituted a home away from home for most middle-class and many working-class men. On the nature of their rituals, see Mary Ann Clawson, *Constructing Brotherhood: Class, Gender, and Fraternalism* (Princeton, N.J.: Princeton University Press, 1989), chaps. 2–5; Mark Carnes, *Secret Rituals and Manhood in Victorian America* (New Haven, Conn.: Yale University Press, 1989); Rotundo, *American Manhood*, chap. 4.

84. Robert Bly, *Iron John: A Book about Men* (Reading, Mass.: Addison-Wesley, 1990).

85. Griswold, *Fatherhood in America*, chap. 6; Clawson, *Constructing Brotherhood*, chap. 7.

86. Thurer, *Myths of Motherhood*, p. 287.

87. David Owens, "The Desire to Father: Reproductive Ideologies and Involuntarily Childless Men," in McKee and O'Brien, *The Father Figure*, p. 82.

88. See Nancy Chodorow, *The Reproduction of Mothering: Psychoanalysis and the Sociology of Gender* (Berkeley: University of California Press, 1978).

89. Owens, "The Desire to Father," p. 82.

90. Martin Richards, "How Should We Approach the Study of Fathers?" *The Father Figure*, eds. L. McKee and M. O'Brien (London: Tavistock, 1982), pp. 68–70.

91. On the rise of fears of effeminacy dating from the 1890s, see Rotundo, *American Manhood*, pp. 276–83; Griswold, *Fatherhood in America*, pp. 171–83.

92. From *Harper's Bazaar* (1900), quoted in Demos, *Past, Present, and Personal*, p. 61.

93. Demos, *Past, Present, and Personal*, p. 62; on the psychodynamics of men's rivalry with their children, see Richards, "How Should We Approach the Study of Fathers?" pp. 70ff. On the boyishness of twentieth-century men, see

Rotundo, *American Manhood*, pp. 257–58; Chinn, *They Worked All Their Lives*, p. 52.

94. Griswold, *Fatherhood in America*, chaps. 9–11; for the most recent round, see David Blankenhorn, *Fatherless America: Confronting Our Most Urgent Social Problem* (New York: Basic Books, 1995); Susan Chira, "War over Role of American Fathers," *New York Times*, June 19, 1994.

95. Laslett, *Family Life and Illicit Love*, chap. 3; Stephanie Coontz, *The Way We Never Were: American Families and the Nostalgia Trap* (New York: Basic Books, 1992), chap. 10.

96. Demos, *Past, Present, and Personal*, pp. 41–67; E. Anthony Rotundo, "American Fatherhood: A Historical Perspective," *American Behavioral Scientist* 21 (1985): 7–25.

97. For the most recent expression of this position, see David Popenoe, "Family Decline in America," in *Rebuilding the Nest: A New Commitment to the American Family*, eds. David Blankenhorn, Steven Bayme, and Jean Bethke Elshtain (Milwaukee: Family Service America Press, 1990), pp. 39–52; for a critical assessment of the new family values movement, see Judith Stacey, "The New Family Values Crusaders," *The Nation* (July 25–August 1, 1994): 119–22.

98. Barbara Ehrenreich, *The Hearts of Men: American Dreams and the Flight of Men from Commitment* (Garden City, N.Y.: Anchor Books, 1983).

99. The latest survey results are provided by Mark Mellman, Edward Lazarus, and Allan Rivlin, "Family Time, Family Values," in Blankenhorn, Bayme, and Elshtain, *Rebuilding the Nest*, pp. 73–92.

100. These well-paying positions constitute only about 20 percent of all future jobs, according to Robert Reich, *The Work of Nations: Preparing Ourselves for the Twenty-first Century* (New York: Alfred A. Knopf, 1991), pp. 171–84.

101. On the increase in work within the household, see R. Pahl, *Division of Labour* (Oxford: Basil Blackwell, 1984); see also John Brinckerhoff Jackson, *A Sense of Place, a Sense of Time* (New Haven, Conn.: Yale University Press, 1994), chap. 10.

102. Frank F. Furstenberg Jr., "Good Dads—Bad Dads: Two Faces of Fatherhood," in *The Changing American Family and Public Policy*, ed. Andrew J. Cherlin (Washington, D.C.: Urban Institute Press, 1988), pp. 193–218.

103. Thurer, *Myths of Motherhood*, pp. 286–90.

104. Lewis, "'A Feeling You Can't Scratch,'" pp. 51ff.; Lewis, *Becoming a Father*, pp. 31–39, 60–67; Jackson, *A Sense of Place*, p. 42; recent findings on envious and destructive behavior by fathers is reported in Georgia Dullea, "Expectant Fathers' Symptoms," *New York Times*, September 6, 1982.

105. Sonia Jackson, "Great Britain," in *The Father's Role: Cross-Cultural Perspectives*, ed. Michael Lamb (Hillside, N.J.: Erlbaum, 1987), pp. 37, 58; Lewis, *Becoming a Father*, pp. 59–64.

106. Soren Carlsen, "Men's Utilization of Paternity Leave and Parental Leave Schemes," in *The Equality Dilemma: Reconciling Working Life and Family Life, Viewed in an Equality Perspective: The Danish Example*, eds. S. Carlsen and J. E. Larsen (Copenhagen: Munksgaard International Publishers, 1994), pp. 79–90; on Sweden, see Lewis, *Becoming a Father*, p. 189; on the increasing commercialization of fatherhood, see "Here Ye, Hear Ye, Our Baby Is Here," *New York Times*, August 9, 1990.

107. Arlie Hochschild, with Anne Machung, *The Second Shift* (New York: Avon, 1990); Lewis, *Becoming a Father*, p. 175.

108. Furstenberg, "Good Dads—Bad Dads," p. 207.

109. Furstenberg calls it "transient fatherhood"; ibid., pp. 204–5; on serial monogamy, see Lawrence Stone, *The Family, Sex, and Marriage in England, 1500–1800* (New York: Harper & Row, 1977), pp. 685–87.

110. Griswold, *Fatherhood in America*, p. 232.

111. David Popenoe, "The Family Condition of America: Cultural Change and Public Policy," in *Values and Public Policy*, eds. H. Aaron, T. Mann, T. Taylor (Washington, D.C.: Brookings Institution, 1994), p. 102; Blankenhorn, *Fatherless America*, chap. 1.

112. Arlie Hochschild, remarks as member of panel on "What's Behind the Debate on Family Values?" American Sociological Association Convention, Los Angeles, August 6, 1994; see also Robert Bellah, "The Invasion of the Money World," in Blankenhorn, Bayme, and Elshtain, *Rebuilding the Nest*, pp. 227–36.

113. Barbara Katz Rothman, *Recreating Motherhood: Ideology and Technology in a Patriarchical Society* (New York: W. W. Norton, 1989), pp. 114–16; see also Davis-Floyd, *Birth as an American Rite of Passage*, chap. 3.

114. Rothman, *Recreating Motherhood*, p. 36.

115. Ibid., pp. 42, 88.

116. Dion Sommer, "Fatherhood and Caring: Who Cares?" in Carlsen and Larsen, *The Equality Dilemma*, pp. 155–66.

CHAPTER TEN

1. W. Lloyd Warner, *The Family of God: A Symbolic Study of Christian Life in America* (New Haven, Conn.: Yale University Press, 1961), p. 167.

2. Michael Kearl, *Endings: A Sociology of Death* (New York: Oxford University Press, 1989), p. xi.

3. W. Lloyd Warner, *The Family of God*, p. 167; see also his *The Living and the Dead: A Study of the Symbolic Life of Americans* (New Haven, Conn.: Yale University Press, 1959).

4. Kearl, *Endings*, p. 476. People usually intend to bury or scatter the ashes but then find themselves unable to do so.

5. For American figures, see ibid., p. 239; on the English experience, see Gillian Bennett, *Traditions of Belief: Women, Folklore, and the Supernatural Today* (London: Penguin, 1987), pp. 27–29, and afterword.

6. Bennett, *Traditions of Belief*, p. 32.

7. Kearl, *Endings*, p. 474; ch. 2, n. 12.

8. Warner, *The Family of God*, pp. 171–79, 183–85. Tensions among survivors could also lead to reburials (pp. 173ff.).

9. Ibid., p. 168.

10. R. Porter and D. Porter, *In Sickness and in Health: The British Experience, 1650–1850* (Oxford: Basil Blackwell, 1988), pp. 263–4.

11. William Gladstone, *The Gladstone Diaries*, vol. 1, ed. M. R. D. Foot (Oxford: Clarendon Press, 1968), p. ixx; on the practice of daily dying, see Porter and

Porter, *In Sickness and in Health*, p. 247; Philippe Ariès, *The Hour of Our Death* (New York: Vintage, 1982), chap. 6.

12. Catrin Stevens, "The Funeral Wake in Wales," *Folk Life* 14 (1976): 40. Unchurched mothers were buried separately; Edward Shorter, *A History of Women's Bodies* (New York: Basic Books, 1982), pp. 293–95.

13. Irene Quenzler Brown, "Death, Friendship, and Female Identity during New England's Second Great Awakening," *Journal of Family History* 12, no. 4 (1987): 375. See Halttunen, *Confidence Men and Painted Women: A Study of Middle-Class Culture in America, 1830–1870* (New Haven, Conn.: Yale University Press, 1982), p. 126.

14. On play, see John Burnett, *Destiny Obscure: Autobiographies of Childhood, Education, and Family from the 1820s to the 1920s* (London: Allen Lane, 1982), p. 34; on contributions to burial clubs, see Thomas Laqueur, "Bodies, Death, and Pauper Funerals," *Representations* 1, no. 1 (February 1983): 109–12.

15. Clare Gittings, *Death, Burial, and the Individual in Early Modern England* (London: Croom Helm, 1984), p. 153; Bertram Puckle, *Funeral Customs: Their Origins and Development* (London: T. Werner Laurie, 1926), p. 75.

16. J. W. Frost, *The Quaker Family in Colonial America* (New York: St. Martin's Press, 1973), p. 42; Gittings, *Death, Burial, and the Individual*, p. 83.

17. Ruth Richardson, *Death, Dissection, and the Destitute* (Harmondsworth, Eng.: Penguin, 1988), p. 21; Brown, "Death, Friendship, and Female Identity," p. 368; Mary Chamberlain and Ruth Richardson, "Life and Death," *Oral History* 2, no. 1 (Spring 1983): 35–36. In France the mother-in-law gave the bride her "next day dress," which she wore to funerals and was buried in; Françoise Zonabend, *The Enduring Memory: Time and History in a French Village* (Manchester, Eng.: Manchester University Press, 1984), pp. 135–36.

18. Stevens, "The Funeral Wake in Wales," pp. 33–34.

19. Ibid., p. 28.

20. Richardson, *Death, Dissection, and the Destitute*, pp. 7, 23–24.

21. D. Parry-Jones, *Welsh Country Upbringing* (Sirral, Wales: Ffynnon, 1974), pp. 47–48.

22. Quoted in ibid., p. 48.

23. D. Parry-Jones, *My Own Folk* (Llandysul, Wales: Gomer, 1972), p. 154.

24. Edwin Grey, *Cottage Life in a Hertfordshire Village* (St. Albans, Eng.: Fischer, Knight and Co., n.d.), p. 158.

25. Quoted in Leonore Davidoff and Catherine Hall, *Family Fortunes: Men and Women of the English Middle Class, 1780–1850* (Chicago: University of Chicago Press, 1987), p. 109.

26. Quoted in David Stannard, *The Puritan Way of Death* (New York: Oxford University Press, 1977), p. 101; Steven R. Smith, "Death, Dying, and the Elderly in Seventeenth-Century England," in *Aging and the Elderly*, eds. S. Spicher, K. Woodward, D. van Tassell (Atlantic Highlands, N.J.: Humanities Press, 1978), pp. 210–11.

27. Petrus Spierenburg, *The Broken Spell: A Cultural and Anthropological History of Pre-Industrial Europe* (New Brunswick, N.J.: Rutgers University Press, 1991), pp. 151–54.

28. Quoted in Alan Macfarlane, *The Family Life of Ralph Josselin* (New York: W. W. Norton, 1970), p. 167.
29. Quoted in Stannard, *The Puritan Way of Death*, p. 108.
30. Smith, "Death, Dying, and the Elderly," pp. 210–11; for early nineteenth–century Quaker attitudes, see Thomas Clarkson, *A Portraiture of Quakerism*, vol. 2 (London: Longman, 1806), pp. 32–43.
31. Halttunen, *Confidence Men and Painted Women*, p. 129.
32. Richardson, *Death, Dissection, and the Destitute*, p. 29; Eileen Yeo, "Culture and Constraint in Working-Class Movements," in *Popular Culture and Class Conflict, 1590–1914*, ed. S. E. Yeo (Brighton, Eng.: Harvester 1981), pp. 169–70.
33. Clarkson, *A Portraiture of Quakerism*, pp. 32–4.
34. Stanley Burns, *Sleeping Beauty: Memorial Photography in America* (Altadena, Calif.: Twelvetrees Press, 1990), frontispiece.
35. Ariès, *The Hour of Our Death*, pp. 451–53; Halttunen, *Confidence Men and Painted Women*, pp. 125–26; Stannard, *The Puritan Way of Death*, pp. 154–56, 174.
36. Porter and Porter, *In Sickness and in Health*, p. 252.
37. Nehemiah Adams, *Agnes and the Little Key: Or, Bereaved Parents Instructed and Comforted* (1857), quoted in Halttunen, *Confidence Men and Painted Women*, p. 131.
38. Ariès, *The Hour of Our Death*, p. 609.
39. Ibid., p. 228.
40. Porter and Porter, *In Sickness and in Health*, p. 253.
41. William Chalmers Whitcomb, *The True Consoler, or, Balm for the Stricken, Original and Selected* (1861), quoted in Halttunen, *Confidence Men and Painted Women*, p. 25.
42. Ariès, *The Hour of Our Death*, p. 612.
43. Quoted in Stannard, *The Puritan Way of Death*, p. 138.
44. Thomas R. Cole, "The 'Enlightened' View of Aging: Victorian Morality in a New Key," in *What Does It Mean to Grow Old?* eds. Thomas R. Cole and Sally Gadow (Durham, N.C.: Duke University Press, 1986), pp. 125–26; Gerald J. Gruman, "Cultural Origins of Present-Day 'Age-ism': The Modernization of the Life Cycle," in Spicker, Woodward, and van Tassel, *Aging and the Elderly*, pp. 359–87.
45. Earlier, *finality* had meant "the goal of life." The meaning introduced in connection with the Reform Act of 1832 was "the final form which could not be altered"; see *The Shorter Oxford English Dictionary*.
46. Ariès, *The Hour of Our Death*, pp. 570–71; John Morley, *Death, Heaven, and the Victorians* (Pittsburgh: University of Pittsburgh Press, 1971), p. 72; John McManners, "Death and the French Historians," in *Mirrors of Mortality: Studies in the Social History of Death*, ed. Joachim Whaley (New York: St. Martin's Press, 1981), p. 120; Richardson, *Death, Dissection, and the Destitute*, p. 24.
47. Viviana Zelizer, *Pricing the Priceless Child: The Changing Social Value of Children* (New York: Basic Books, 1985), pp. 24–27.
48. Burns, *Sleeping Beauty*, captions 5, 6.
49. In earlier centuries, pregnant women had acted as pallbearers at maternal

funerals, a duty that was supposed to protect rather than endanger them; Gittings, *Death, Burial, and the Individual*, p. 111.

50. Spierenburg, *The Broken Spell*, p. 137.
51. Burns, *Sleeping Beauty*, captions 58, 69.
52. "Mummification" is Peter Marris's term; see his "Bereavement," in *Lost and Change* (London: Routledge and Kegan Paul, 1974), p. 28.
53. Quoted in Martha Pike, "Artifacts Relating to Mourning in Nineteenth-Century America," in her *Rituals and Ceremonies in Popular Culture* (Bowling Green, Ohio: Bowling Green University Press, 1980), p. 301. Stopping the clocks and covering the mirrors were modern middle-class "superstitions" with no antecedents; Richardson, *Death, Dissection, and the Destitute*, p. 27.
54. Thomas Baldwin Thayer, *Over the River; or, Pleasant Walks into the Valley of the Shadows, and Beyond* (Boston, 1864), quoted in Halttunen, *Confidence Men and Painted Women*, p. 133.
55. Alex Owen, *The Darkened Room: Women, Power, and Spiritualism in Late Nineteenth-Century England* (London: Virago, 1989).
56. Burns, *Sleeping Beauty*, caption 61.
57. Quoted in Richardson, *Death, Dissection, and the Destitute*, p. 24.
58. Burns, Afterword.
59. Orville Dewey, *On the Duties of Consolation, and the Rites and Customs Appropriate to Mourning* (New Bedford, Mass., 1825), quoted in Halttunen, *Confidence Men and Painted Women*, p. 139 (Dewey's emphasis); on British antiritualism, see Morley, *Death, Heaven, and the Victorians*, p. 24.
60. Morley, *Death, Heaven, and the Victorians*, chap. 2; Richardson, *Death, Dissection, and the Destitute*, pp. 27, 272–73; Halttunen, *Confidence Men and Painted Women*, pp. 146–50, 170–72.
61. Richardson, *Death, Dissection, and the Destitute*, p. 272.
62. Quoted in Puckle, *Funeral Customs*, p. 155.
63. Stannard, *The Puritan Way of Death*, p. 180; Richardson, *Death, Dissection, and the Destitute*, p. 273.
64. Ellen Marie Snyder, "At Rest: Victorian Death Furniture," in *Perspectives on American Furniture*, ed. Gerald W. R. Ward (New York: W. W. Norton, 1988), pp. 241–72.
65. Richardson, *Death, Dissection, and the Destitute*, pp. 2–4, 272–81; Thomas Laqueur, "Bodies, Death, and Pauper Funerals," *Representations* 1, no. 1 (February 1983): 109–26.
66. On the shift from graveyards to cemeteries, see Halttunen, *Confidence Men and Painted Women*, pp. 127–28; Stannard, *The Puritan Way of Death*, pp. 184–85; Ariès, *The Hour of Our Death*, chap. 11; Puckle, *Funeral Customs*, pp. 144–55; Richardson, *Death, Dissection, and the Destitute*, p. 274. In the American South, Decoration Day coincides with Mother's Day. Elsewhere it is a part of Memorial Day ceremonies, which have become less public and more private over the course of the century.
67. Ariès, *The Hour of Our Death*, p. 533.
68. Puckle, *Funeral Customs*, p. 86; Morley, *Death, Heaven, and the Victorians*, chap. 6; Halttunen, *Confidence Men and Painted Women*, chap. 5.
69. Morley, *Death, Heaven, and the Victorians*, p. 69.
70. Halttunen, *Confidence Men and Painted Women*, pp. 137–38; Burns, *Sleeping*

Beauty, caption 10; Puckle, *Funeral Customs*, pp. 87–90. The degree to which women are still expected to so mourn is discussed by Marris, *Lost and Change*, pp. 33–40.

71. Quoted in Morley, *Death, Heaven, and the Victorians*, pp. 63, 72–73.

72. Burns, *Sleeping Beauty*, captions 13, 25.

73. Puckle, *Funeral Customs*, p. 97 (Puckle's emphasis); on women's role in mourning generally, see Maurice Bloch, "Death, Women and Power," in *Death and the Regeneration of Life*, eds. M. Bloch and J. Perry (Cambridge: Cambridge University Press, 1982), pp. 211–30.

74. Grant McCracken, *Culture and Consumption: New Approaches to the Symbolic Character of Consumer Goods and Activities* (Bloomington: Indiana University Press, 1988), p. 106.

75. On the way past and present were used this way, see ibid., pp. 106–7.

76. Colleen McDannell and Bernhard Lang, *Heaven: A History* (New York: Vintage, 1988), p. 178; chap. 6.

77. Macfarlane, *The Family Life of Ralph Josselin*, p. 168.

78. McDannell and Lang, *Heaven*, pp. 179–80.

79. Quoted in ibid., p. 155.

80. Quoted in ibid., p. 173.

81. Quoted in ibid., p. 258.

82. Anthony Giddens, *Modernity and Self-Identity: Self and Society in the Late Modern Age* (Stanford, Calif.: Stanford University Press, 1991), p. 6.

83. McDannell and Lang, *Heaven*, p. 265.

84. Quoted in ibid., p. 274.

85. Quoted in ibid., p. 294.

86. Ibid., p. 293.

87. Ibid., p. 275.

88. Charles Taylor, *Sources of the Self: The Making of Modern Identity* (Cambridge, Mass.: Harvard University Press, 1989), pp. 226–27.

89. Quoted in ibid., p. 229.

90. Ariès, *The Hour of Our Death*, p. 471; see also Ann Douglas, *The Feminization of American Culture* (New York: Alfred A. Knopf, 1977), pp. 220–26; Morley, *Death, Heaven, and the Victorians*, chap. 9.

91. Quoted in McDannell and Lang, *Heaven*, pp. 273–74.

92. Douglas, *The Feminization of American Culture*, p. 226.

93. McDannell and Lang, *Heaven*, pp. 307, 309, 356.

94. Gwen Neville, *Kinship and Pilgrimage: Rituals of Reunion in American Protestant Culture* (New York: Oxford University Press, 1987), pp. 79–87.

95. Kearl, *Endings*, pp. 407–416.

96. Mary Douglas, "The Idea of a Home: A Kind of Space," in *Home: A Place in the World*, ed. Arien Mack (New York: New York University Press, 1993), p. 268.

97. Bennett, *Traditions of Belief*, p. 69.

98. Andrew Weigert and Ross Hastings, "Identity Loss, Family, and Social Change," *American Journal of Sociology* 82, no. 6 (May 1977): 1179.

99. Bennett, *Traditions of Belief*, p. 69.

100. Geoffrey Gorer, *Death, Grief, Mourning* (Garden City, N.Y.: Anchor Books, 1967), quoted in Richardson, *Death, Dissection, and the Destitute*, frontispiece.

101. On the hospice movement, see Kearl, *Endings*, pp. 440ff.

102. Janny Scott, "Another Legacy of Onassis: Facing Death on Own Terms," *New York Times*, June 4, 1994. It is interesting to note that middle-class people are more likely than working-class people to reject radical medical intervention. Those who have been deprived of medical services are the ones who want the fullest medical treatment.

CHAPTER ELEVEN

1. Marina Warner, *Six Myths of Our Times* (New York: Vintage, 1995), p. 19.

2. "Even in the Frenzy of the 90s, Dinner Time Is for the Family," *New York Times*, December 5, 1990; concern about family time had been noted earlier, "The Struggle to Keep Family Time Quality Time," *New York Times*, May 12, 1988.

3. "Family Rituals May Promote Better Emotional Adjustment," *New York Times*, March 11, 1992.

4. Dennis Orthner, "The Family in Transition," in *Rebuilding the Nest: A New Commitment to the American Family*, eds. David Blankenhorn, Steven Bayme, and Jean Bethke Elshtain (Milwaukee: Family Service America Press, 1990), p. 92.

5. Pepper Schwartz, "New Bonds: Para-Dads, Para Moms," *New York Times*, November 9, 1995; Judith Stacey, *Brave New Families: Stories of Domestic Upheaval in Late Twentieth–Century America* (New York: Basic Books, 1990).

6. Catherine Mangold, "These Days, You Make up Holidays as You Go Along," *New York Times*, December 24, 1992; Andre Brooks, "Finding Solace: Prayers Accepting Divorce," *New York Times*, August 31, 1987. For the full range of new rituals, see Evan Imber-Black and Janine Roberts, *Rituals for Our Times* (New York: HarperCollins, 1992); on lesbian rites, see Becky Butler, ed., *Ceremonies of the Heart: Celebrating Lesbian Unions* (Seattle: Seal Press, 1990).

7. Peter H. Lewis, "Strangers, Not Their Computers, Build a Network in Time of Grief," *New York Times*, March 8, 1994.

8. Ronald L. Grimes, *Marrying and Burying: Rites of Passage in a Man's Life* (Boulder, Colo.: Westview, 1995), p. 5.

9. Robert Fulghum, *From Beginning to End: The Rituals of Our Lives* (New York: Villard Books, 1995), p. x.

10. Juliet Schor, *The Overworked American: The Unexpected Decline of Leisure* (New York: Basic Books, 1991), p. 30.

11. Witold Rybczynski, *Waiting for the Weekend* (New York: Viking, 1991).

12. Pepper Schwartz, "The Silent Family: Together, but Apart," *New York Times*, February 16, 1995.

13. Ibid.

14. Schor, *The Overworked American*, pp. 11–13, 21; chap. 4.

15. Leonardo Paggi, "The Shaping of Post-Bourgeois Politics in Europe, 1945–1968" (paper delivered at Palmer House, Chicago, April 1, 1994), p. 4.

16. John Demos, *Past, Present, and Personal: The Family and the Life Course in America* (New York: Oxford University Press, 1986), p. 36.

17. On the Head Start program, see Joseph Kett, *Rites of Passage: Adolescence in America, 1790 to the Present* (New York: Basic Books, 1977), pp. 205–11.

18. Joshua Meyrowitz, "The Adultlike Child and the Childlike Adult: Socialization in an Electronic Age," *Daedalus* 113, no. 3 (Summer 1984): 19–48.

19. Rickie Solinger, *Wake up Little Susie: Single Pregnancy in the Pre*–Roe v. Wade *Era: A Cultural Study* (New York: Routledge, 1992), chaps. 1, 5, 6; Carin Rubinstein, "The American Family Is Adjusting to Teen-Agers' Work-Spend Ethic," *New York Times*, January 21, 1988.

20. Bernice L. Neugarten and Darl A. Neugarten, "Changing Meanings of Age in the Aging Society," in *Our Aging Society: Paradox and Promise*, eds. Alan Pifer and Lydia Bronte (New York: W. W. Norton, 1986), pp. 34–37; John Gillis, *Youth and History: Tradition and Change in Age Relations, 1750 to the Present* (New York: Academic Press, 1975), pp. 207–9.

21. Neugarten and Neugarten, "Changing Meanings of Age," p. 37.

22. On evidence of adolescent crises, see Kenneth Kenniston, "Youth: A 'New' Stage of Life," *American Scholar* 39, no. 4 (Autumn 1970): 631–54; on midlife crises, see Orville Brim Jr., "Theories of Male Mid-Life Crisis," *Counseling Psychologist* 6 (1976): 2–9; see also Stanley Brandes, *Forty: The Age and the Symbol* (Knoxville: University of Tennessee Press, 1985), pp. 17–18.

23. Matilda White Riley and John Riley, "Longevity and Social Structure: The Potential of the Added Years," in Pifer and Bronte, *Our Aging Society*, pp. 55–68; for a critical perspective on the crisis mentality, see Emily Martin, *The Flexible Body: Tracking Immunity in American Culture from the Days of Polio to the Age of AIDS* (Boston: Beacon Press, 1994).

24. Brandes, *Forty*, pp. 8, 15.

25. Grisela Labouvier-Vief, "Individual Time, Social Time, and Intellectual Aging," in *Aging and Life Course Transition*, ed. Tamara Hareven (New York: Guilford Press, 1982), pp. 151–82.

26. Brandes, *Forty*, chap. 2; Matilda White Riley, ed., *Aging from Birth to Death: Interdisciplinary Perspectives* (Boulder, Colo.: Westview, 1979); Neugarten and Neugarten, "Changing Meanings of Age," pp. 36–37.

27. Howard P. Chudacoff, *How Old Are You? Age Consciousness in American Culture* (Princeton, N.J.: Princeton University Press, 1989), chaps. 6–7; Elizabeth Colson, "The Least Common Denominator," in *Secular Ritual*, eds. Sally Moore and Barbara Myerhoff (Assen/Amsterdam: Van Gorcum, 1977), pp. 189–98; Barbara Myerhoff, *Number Our Days* (New York: Simon & Schuster, 1978), chap. 6.

28. Brandes, *Forty*, pp. 105–6.

29. Michael Murphy, "Measuring the Family Life Cycle: Concepts, Data, Methods," in *Rethinking the Life Cycle*, eds. Alan Bryan et al. (Basingstoke, Eng.: Macmillan, 1987), p. 37.

30. Neugarten and Neugarten, "Changing Meanings of Age," p. 37.

31. Martin Martel, "Age and Sex Roles in American Magazine Fiction (1890–1955)," in *Middle Age and Aging*, ed. Bernice Neugarten (Chicago: University of Chicago Press, 1958), p. 56.

32. Neugarten and Neugarten, "Changing Meanings of Age," p. 35; David Stannard, "Growing up and Growing Old: Dilemmas of Aging in Bureaucratic America," in *Aging and the Elderly*, eds. S. Spicher, K. Woodward, D. van Tassell (Atlantic Highlands, N.J.: Humanities Press, 1978), p. 18; see also Gail

Sheehy, *New Passages: Mapping Your Life across Time* (New York: Random House, 1995), p. 72.

33. "Conflict for Working Couples: When He Retires, Must She?" *New York Times*, November 9, 1993.

34. Peter Laslett, *A Fresh Map of Life: The Emergence of the Third Age* (Cambridge, Mass.: Harvard University Press, 1991), chap. 6.

35. Sheehy, *New Passages*, pp. 137–8.

36. Neugarten and Neugarten, "Changing Meanings of Age," p. 36.

37. Lebouvier-Vief, "Individual Time, Social Time," pp. 151–82.

38. Sheehy, *New Passages*, pp. 61–62; Neugarten and Neugarten, "Changing Meanings of Age," pp. 37–38; Marlis Buchmann, *The Script of Life in Modern Society: Entry into Adulthood in a Changing World* (Chicago: University of Chicago Press, 1989), chaps. 2, 8, and conclusion; Sharon Kaufmann, *The Ageless Self: Sources of Meaning in Late Life* (Madison: University of Wisconsin Press, 1985).

39. Neugarten and Neugarten, "Changing Meanings of Age," p. 40; Gerald J. Gruman, "Cultural Origins of Present-Day 'Age-ism': The Modernization of the Life-Cycle," in Spicker, Woodward, and van Tassel, *Aging and the Elderly*, pp. 359–87.

40. John Gillis, "Vanishing Youth: The Uncertain Place of the Young in a Global Age," *Young: Nordic Journal of Youth Research* 1, no. 1 (February 1993): 3–4.

41. David Harvey, *The Condition of Postmodernity* (Oxford: Basil Blackwell, 1989), pp. 202–10.

42. Gail Sheehy, *Pathfinders* (New York: Morrow, 1981), p. 294.

43. Sheehy, *New Passages*, p. 71 (Sheehy's emphasis).

44. Gruman, "Cultural Origins of Present-Day 'Age-ism,'" p. 364.

45. Colson, "The Least Common Denominator," p. 189.

46. Barbara Myerhoff, "Bobbes and Seydes: Old and New Roles for the Elderly Jews," in *Women in Ritual and Symbolic Roles*, eds. Judith Hoch-Smith and Anita Spring (New York: Plenum, 1978), pp. 207–41.

47. A useful summary of these trends is provided by Malcolm Waters, *Globalization* (New York: Routledge, 1995).

48. Quoted in Clifford Clark, *The American Family Home, 1800-1860* (Chapel Hill: University of North Carolina Press, 1986), p. 235.

49. Quoted in Orvar Löfgren, "Swedish Modern: Nationalizing Consumption and Aesthetics in the Welfare State" (unpublished paper, Rutgers Center for Historical Analysis, 1993).

50. Hermann Bausinger, "Auf dem Wege zu einem neuen, aktiven Heimatsverstandnis," in *Heimat heute*, ed. Hans-Georg Wehling (Stuttgart: Kohlhammer, 1984), p. 24; see also Dennis Wood and Robert Beck, *Home Rules* (Baltimore: Johns Hopkins University Press, 1994).

51. Harvey Levenstein, *Revolution at the Table: The Transformation of the American Diet* (New York: Oxford University Press, 1988), p. 164.

52. Herman Bausinger, *Folk Culture in a World of Technology* (Bloomington: Indiana University Press, 1990), pp. 54–60.

53. The family vacation is the fastest-growing part of Club Med's business; Carol Lawson, "Surviving Vacation (It's a Family Battle)," *New York Times*, August 1, 1991.

54. Bausinger, *Folk Culture*, p. 59; Bausinger, "Auf dem Wege," pp. 18–20; Michael Ann Williams, *Homeplace: The Social Use and Meaning of the Folk Dwelling in Southwestern North Carolina* (Athens: University of Georgia Press, 1990), p. 133.
55. Phil Paton, "Feeling at Home at the Office," *New York Times*, August 27, 1992.
56. Marian Burris, "Women: Out of the House but Not out of the Kitchen," *New York Times*, February 24, 1988; Susan Strasser, *Never Done: A History of American Housework* (New York: Pantheon, 1982); Jennifer Craik, "The Making of Mother: The Role of the Kitchen in the Home," in *Home and Family: Creating the Domestic Space*, eds. Graham Allen and Graham Crowe (Houndsmill, Eng.: Macmillan, 1989), pp. 48–63; Clark, *The American Home*, pp. 207, 234–35; Joan Kron, *Home-Psych: The Social Psychology of Home and Decoration* (New York: Crown, 1983), chap. 5: Orvar Löfgren, "Consuming Interests," *Culture and History* 7 (1990): 7–36; Dennis Chapman, *The Home and Social Status* (London: Kegan Paul, 1956), pp. 27–31.
57. Georgia Dullea, "Teen-Agers' Inner Sanctums, Where Many Worlds Collide," *New York Times*, January 10, 1992.
58. Enid Nemy notes that an increasing amount of living is now done in bedrooms; "The Living Room as Museum: Don't Touch," *New York Times*, August 6, 1992; on changing uses of the master bedroom, see Clark, *The American Home*, pp. 216, 243.
59. Robert Calem, "Working at Home, for Better or Worse," *New York Times*, April 18, 1993.
60. Löfgren, "Swedish Modern," p. 18; Arlie Hochschild, with Anne Machung, *Second Shift* (New York: Avon, 1990); for the English experience, see Fiona Devine, "Privatized Families and Their Homes," in Allen and Crowe, *Home and Family*, pp. 96–100.
61. "A House with a Picket Fence Still Fits the American Dream," *New York Times*, June 2, 1992; *East Bay Real Estate Weekly* 1, no. 20 (September 10, 1993).
62. Jane Gross, "More Young Single Men Hang on to Apron Strings," *New York Times*, June 16, 1991; see also Sheehy, *Passages*, p. 49.
63. Clare Cooper, "The House as Symbol," *Design and Environment* 3 (1972): 31–33; Clare Cooper Marcus, *House as Mirror of Self* (Berkeley: Conari Press, 1995).
64. See the contributions by Eric Hobsbawm, Breyten Brytenbach, and Simon Schama in *Home: A Place in the World*, ed. Arien Mack (New York: New York University Press, 1993).
65. Gina Kolata, "Family Aid to Elderly Is Very Strong, Study Finds," *New York Times*, May 1, 1993.
66. Tamar Lewin, "Aging Parents: Women's Burden Grows," *New York Times*, November 14, 1989; Kron, *Home-Psych*, pp. 159–60; John Higgins, "Homes and Institutions," in Allen and Crowe, *Home and Family*, pp. 161–73.
67. Williams, *Homeplace*, p. 117.
68. Rolf Meyersohn and Donal Malone, "Social Meanings of Second Homes for Urban Dwellers," in *The Apple Sliced: Sociological Studies of New York City*, eds. V. Boggs, G. Handel, and S. Fava (New York: Praeger, 1984), pp. 327–28.

The study was conducted in 1979; see also Rybczynski, *Waiting for the Weekend*, pp. 171–84. Americans still prefer to vacation with family; see Melinda Henneberger, "A New Poll Describes Vacation Preferences," *New York Times*, May 23, 1993 (travel sect.).

69. Amy Willard Cross, *The Summer House: A Tradition of Leisure* (Toronto: HarperCollins, 1992), p. xiii.

70. Orvar Löfgren, "Learning to Be a Tourist," *Ethnologia Scandinavica* 24 (1994): 124.

71. Jan Bernardes, "Do We Really Know What 'The Family' Is?" in *Family and Economy in Modern Society*, eds. P. Close and R. Collins (London: Macmillan, 1985), pp. 192–95.

72. Jan Bernardes, "'Family Ideology': Identification and Exploration," *Sociological Review* 33, no. 2 (May 1985): 275–79.

73. Arlene Skolnick, "Public Images, Private Realities: The American Family in Popular Culture and Social Science," in *Changing Images of the Family*, eds. Virginia Tufte and Barbara Myerhoff (New Haven, Conn.: Yale University Press, 1979), pp. 297–315.

74. Robert Bly, *Iron John: A Book about Men* (Reading, Mass.: Addison-Wesley, 1990); for a quite different view, see Michael Kimmel, *Manhood in America: A Cultural History* (New York: Free Press, 1995).

75. For a description of families doing just this, see Stacey, *Brave New Families*.

INDEX

Adam, Barbara, 42
Adoption, informal nineteenth-
century, 154
Adulthood, 230
Age
consciousness of numerical,
83–87
current perceptions of, 232
different understandings of,
47–52
of marriage, 8–9
as social force, 87. *See also*
Elderly, the; Middle age; Old
age; Retirement age
Age, numerical
of modern nation-state, 82–84
as predictor, 230–32
pre-nineteenth-century significance, 48–50
Protestant conception, 53–57
Aging
changes in conception of, 42–44
medicalization of, 210
modern family treatment of,
82
modern obsession with, 85
postmodern era of, 232–34
problem of, 87

rites and rituals, 233
Animals/pets, 76, 118
Antiques, 4, 75–76
Ariès, Philippe, 208–9, 214, 219
Arnold, Matthew, 66
Atkinson, Clarissa, 28, 30, 156,
158, 160
August Bank Holiday, 105
Augustine (saint), 47

Baptism
as family affair, 192
medieval rite of, 25
mid-nineteenth-century, 170
pre-nineteenth-century second-
birth, 163, 185–86
Barrow, Henry, 164
Bastardy, 34
Bauman, Zygmunt, 42
Beeton, Isabella, 92
Bell, Susan Groag, 109
Bender, John, 41
Berger, Peter, 62
Bernardes, Jan, 238
Best, Henry, 138
Birth
hospitalization for, 171–73

299

relation to paternity, 153
sanctification in Victorian era,
71–74
separation from idea of pater-
nity, 183–84
single, 197
Father Noyes, 68
Feminism, 171
Fertility rates
late-nineteenth-century, 70
pre-modern era, 153
Fishman, Robert, 110–11
Foley, Winifred, 49, 118
Foster, Stephen, 117
Foundling hospitals, 155
Froude, James Anthony, 5, 65–66,
103–4, 124
Fulghum, Robert, 227
Funeral parlor, commercial, 212
Funerals
as communal affairs, 205
displace the good death,
212–13
twentieth-century, 210
Victorian-style, 212–13
Furstenberg, Frank, 198

Gaskell, Elizabeth, 169
Gelis, Jacques, 159, 161
Genealogy
pre-nineteenth-century, 6
Victorian era, 75
Giddens, Anthony, 217
Gifford, Donald, 45
Gift exchange, Victorian, 79
Gladstone, William, 54, 168,
204
Glassie, Henry, 38, 47–48, 110,
116
Godparenthood, 26
Gouge, William, 34
Grandparenthood, 86, 155
Grief, 215
Grimes, Ronald, 227

Griswold, Robert, 189
Groaning party, 165

Hall, Joseph, 216
Handel, Gerald, 61
Hanukkah, 104
Hark, J. Max, 114
Harvey, David, 81–82, 87–88
Harvey, William, 184
Hausmutter culture, 33
Hausvater culture, 33, 122,
182–83, 187
Hazlitt, W. Carew, 98
Heaven, 215–19
Herlihy, David, 9, 22
Hesburgh, Theodore, 179
Hess, Robert, 61
Heterosexuality
modern era, 149
postmarriage Victorian affairs,
148
Holly, Henry Hudson, 120
Holy Family
centrality in Catholic devotions,
157
as feature of Christian worship,
28–29
symbolism of Reformation, 157
Home
Christian conception of, 25
conception of, 113–14
disappearance of fixed meaning
of, 234–35
early-nineteenth-century, 67
within the house, 235–36
kitchen as, 235
longing for, 236–37
mythic, 28
nineteenth-century sanctification, 126
pre-modern age definition,
15–16, 37
second homes, 228
as symbol of family unity, 113–14